the Entertaining Encyclopedia

Essential Tips and Recipes for Perfect Parties

Denise Vivaldo

Robert
ROSE

Disclaimer

The recipes in this book have been carefully tested by our kitchen and our tasters. To the best of our knowledge, they are safe and nutritious for ordinary use and users. For those people with food or other allergies, or who have special food requirements or health issues, please read the suggested contents of each recipe carefully and determine whether or not they may create a problem for you. All recipes are used at the risk of the consumer.

We cannot be responsible for any hazards, loss or damage that may occur as a result of any recipe use.

For those with special needs, allergies, requirements or health problems, in the event of any doubt, please contact your medical adviser prior to the use of any recipe.

Design and Production: Kevin Cockburn/PageWave Graphics Inc.

Recipe development: Denise Vivaldo and Cindie Flannigan of foodfanatics.net

Editor: Sue Sumeraj

Recipe Tester: Jennifer MacKenzie

Proofreader: Sheila Wawanash

Indexer: Gillian Watts

Illustrations: Kveta

Photography: Colin Erricson

Food Styling: Kathryn Robertson

Prop Styling: Charlene Erricson

Tableware for photography provided courtesy of Royal Doulton. For further information, please contact WWRD Canada, Inc. at 1-800-268-4040 or royaldoulton.com

We acknowledge the financial support of the Government of Canada through the Book Publishing Industry Development Program (BPIDP) for our publishing activities.

Published by Robert Rose Inc.

120 Eglinton Avenue East, Suite 800, Toronto, Ontario, Canada M4P 1E2

Tel: (416) 322-6552 Fax: (416) 322-6936

Printed and bound in Canada

1 2 3 4 5 6 7 8 9 CPL 17 16 15 14 13 12 11 10 09

To my sister Annie C.,
the best hostess I know

Contents

~~~~~~

Part 1
Essential Party Elements   15

Part 2
Recipes and Menus 201

Part 3
Quick Reference Guide
to Entertaining 435

Preface

I've spent much of my career as a professional caterer, handling everything from celebrity dinner parties to over-the-top weddings to the Academy Awards Governor's Ball (hey, I do live and work in Los Angeles). But when I'm not working, there's nothing I enjoy more than entertaining friends and family. My professional experiences developing recipes, creating innovative menus and styling food for print and television have been instructive, to say the least: over the years, I've discovered hundreds of ways to make parties delicious, beautiful and memorable — yet totally doable.

The Entertaining Encyclopedia gets back to basics for soirees you can host any time. In this book are all the ideas, menus and recipes you'll need to invite friends over for a cozy movie night or to host an exotic dinner party featuring the foods of Spain or Greece. The best part? These are impressive menus, but they won't require excessive time or unusual mail-order ingredients; you can pull off any one of them this weekend, if you choose.

In Part 1, I share the six essential elements of entertaining that will make planning your party easier, ensuring that before the party gets started, you will have thought of everything. In Part 2, you'll find a collection of essential entertaining recipes, as well as two dozen carefully crafted menus, ranging from casual to elegant, that are perfect for parties of six and are easily multiplied for larger parties. And in Part 3, you'll find a handy quick reference guide to entertaining. Turn to it when you want to know more about aperitifs, accommodating vegetarian guests or any of dozens of other entertaining-related issues. This guide encapsulates each topic for you and points back to earlier portions of the book that you are sure to find helpful.

Entertaining friends and family is one of the best gifts you can give them; parties are the stuff of memories, far more valuable than anything you can buy. And one of the best gifts you can give yourself is to learn how to enjoy your own parties, which makes them a lot more fun for everyone. With 200 of my carefully tested recipes and hundreds of time-proven party ideas and tips, this book can be your go-to resource guide for entertaining — and having a great time doing it.

— Denise Vivaldo

Acknowledgments

Publishing a book of this size, complete with more than 200 recipes, takes a lot of time, effort, faith and money. I am so grateful that I got to write *The Entertaining Encyclopedia*. But I didn't do it alone: many hands have helped to make this book possible. I will begin my thank yous with Bob Dees of Robert Rose Inc. Bob has a vision of the books he wants to publish: They are books crafted to give cookbook consumers their money's worth. His many authors are people who are experts in their field (and many of them are long-time friends of mine), people who are dedicated to sharing their years of experience with the reader. This is my first book with Bob Dees, and it's been an amazing experience. Bob, I truly thank you and your lovely wife, Judith, for helping me bring this big new book to life. I'd also like to thank everyone at PageWave Graphics and our editor, Sue Sumeraj — she deserves a medal!

I met Bob Dees through my agent, Lisa Ekus. Lisa is a legend in the cookbook and culinary world, and she's a tireless mentor to me. And she likes me even though I have never met a deadline in my life. (I'm always two weeks late.) I thank Lisa, Jane Falla, Sia Antunes, Sarah Baurle and all the talented people at The Lisa Ekus Group. Because of them, I get paid to cook and live my dream. Thank you all so much.

In my office, my thank yous begin with Cindie Flannigan. Cindie and I have worked side by side for the last 10 years; time flies when you are having fun and eating good meals. Thank you, Cindie, for your talent, common sense and endless support. Thank you for encouraging me, even when I know you are running on fumes and just want to go home and take a nap with Peanut. I also owe Jennifer Park a thank you for her help with and research for this book. Not only did Jen help test recipes, she also shopped, washed dishes and made us lunch. We live high on the hog here at Food Fanatics. You two pretty girls rock.

Almost last, but certainly not least, I thank Martha Hopkins of Terrace Partners. Martha was a client who became a friend and a colleague, and then I morphed into her client. When I have bitten off more than I can chew (which, by the way, is often), Martha's calming charm puts my energy and hysteria to work. Martha, I can never thank you enough for your friendship, help and talent. Of equal importance are Martha's colleagues, editors extraordinaire Laura Samuel Meyn and Kristen Green Wiewora. Without their exceptional writing and editorial talents, this book would not be the valuable, usable tool you hold in your hands. Thank you.

I owe much inspiration to my parents, who loved to entertain — it didn't matter if there were two guests or 20, entertaining was their way of sharing their happiness, prosperity and love. And to Ken Meyer, my second and last husband: on the days that I am not at all charming or fun, and when I'm too damn tired to cook, I thank you for your patience and love.

Introduction

Do you really need a reason to throw a party? The pleasure of getting together with great friends to enjoy good food and wine is reason enough for most of us, but life is full of fantastic excuses to celebrate, should you need one: birthdays, anniversaries, graduations, weddings, babies, promotions, homecomings, holidays and more.

While we all love *going* to parties, there's a lot to love about *throwing* parties, too — once you get past the intimidation factor of those dozens of details to consider, such as whether you're confident enough in your crème brûlée to prepare it for guests, or whether you can really invite your yoga buddies and fashionista friends to the same house at the same time. In fact, there's satisfaction to be found in bringing people together for little reasons as well as big ones. At smaller gatherings — which, after all, make up most of the entertaining that regular folks do in a lifetime — the conversation is more intimate, and you're more likely to have a chance to visit with each guest individually. But even with a smaller group, you still have to give plenty of thought to party details.

Relax: there are really only six basic elements to entertaining. Take it one step at a time, and you'll be on your way in no time, no sweat. Whether you're hosting an elegant dinner party in the seldom-used formal dining room, a big bash in your backyard or a game-day gathering in front of the television, the six elements are exactly the same:

1. Theme
2. Location
3. Decor
4. Guests
5. Food and Beverages
6. Entertainment

Any detail of your party planning will fall under one of those elements, so start with some overarching decisions and the smaller details will become a lot more obvious, and a lot easier to nail down. When the party's in full swing, with your favorite people gathered around, you'll feel the rewards of all the effort — and perhaps even the nirvana of entertaining: the realization that you're enjoying your own party. (Not to mention all those reciprocal invitations that will be crowding your social calendar in the coming months.)

Enjoying Your Own Party

~~~~~~

It might sound too simple to be true, but the best way to ensure that your guests are having a great time is to have one yourself. Take pleasure in the food you've prepared or purchased, take time to linger over an interesting conversation and have a swig of that wine you've been busy serving everyone else. With all the footwork of determining theme, location, decor, guest list, food and beverages, and entertainment, it's easy to lose sight of the fact that these things should lead to fun — for you *and* your guests.

Each chapter in this book contains tips for making the tasks involved in entertaining easier. If you're feeling short-handed or overwhelmed, incorporating them can mean the difference between enjoying your own party and not. To get you started, here are some general points of advice that will help you set yourself up for a good time:

- Hire a maid service to come the day before your party. This will free you up for the much more enjoyable tasks of attending to the food and decor, and will ensure that you aren't still vacuuming 10 minutes before the party starts.
- Err on the side of simplicity. Don't stress yourself out with an overly ambitious menu; instead, incorporate plenty of easily assembled or purchased items that will take some of the pressure off hosting. You'll enjoy your party more if you're not manning the stove the entire time.
- Allow yourself enough time to get ready for your party. Call it done at least 45 minutes before anyone will arrive, even if that means deciding to forgo an appetizer or side dish at the last minute. Take a shower, get dressed, put on the party music and light candles, and pour yourself a drink. You should feel energized and happy, not like you need a nap.
- Let your guests bring food. I don't usually let guests bring appetizers, because if they're late we'll have nothing to eat, but if they want to bring side dishes, salads or sweets, they're

encouraged to do so. Find out ahead of time what people are bringing so you can save yourself the trouble of preparing too much food. People who pitch in will also feel more included in the celebration and more invested in its success.

- Forget about networking for the night. Cross business chit-chat off your list and instead use this opportunity to get to know your guests better personally, asking about their hobbies and interests. Talking shop can make the evening more stressful for you, and dull for those guests who are in different fields.

- Take pleasure in your less-than-perfect house, place settings or linens. Don't apologize for anything that seems imperfect; try to embrace it as unique, quirky and fun. Who else has those wacky table linens from their crazy grandmother? Such imperfections will actually make your guests feel more at ease and make the gathering feel more personal and intimate.

- Learn to say thank you and smile when you get a compliment on the food. You know that you wanted to make baked Brie topped with homemade mango chutney, but your guests will be happy with the wedge of Brie and crackers that took a fraction of the time. Don't let on that you had to make last-minute shortcuts, or that a dish turned out less perfectly than you'd hoped, because your guests will never know or care.

- Let your guests help during the party. When someone asks what they can do, let them take charge of pouring the wine, refilling the tray of canapés or clearing the table. Enlisting such help makes you more available to socialize with your guests, and people feel good about pitching in, so it's a win-win.

- If you don't have help lined up, stick with family-style or buffet service, putting all food and beverages, including pitchers of water and other beverages, out on the buffet or dinner table. When people can help themselves, you'll have a lot less running around to do.

- Laugh it off. Accidents happen. Cakes stick to Bundt pans and custards curdle. When a dish is salvageable, such as a cake that can't be coaxed out of its pan, present it with a smile; it'll still taste great. If the item in question isn't salvageable, don't dwell on it. Dessert can be skipped or replaced with a box of chocolates, store-bought shortbread cookies or a simple dish of ice cream. Side dishes can fall by the wayside completely without anyone noticing. Even a burned-beyond-recognition main course can be replaced with takeout. If you're having fun, so will your guests.

Part 1

Essential Party Elements

Theme

Deciding on the theme is the most basic element of planning your party; in fact, it's the framework you'll design your party around. Your theme will guide all the entertaining decisions you make, from guest list to menu to decor. While the term "theme" can evoke not-so-sophisticated costume parties with gimmicky food, even the most understated, chic cocktail party has a theme, of sorts — a theme can be as simple as your reason for throwing the party, which naturally guides all your party-planning decisions.

While it's sometimes fun to go a little overboard with a theme (think Halloween for the kids), there are other times when a subtler theme is more appropriate (think grownups-only engagement party). In fact, most people won't care what your inspiration was, but they will definitely enjoy the ambiance and festivities your theme creates. Whether it's at the forefront or more in the background of the party, a theme tells the guests what you're celebrating and helps you focus your efforts. A theme will also build anticipation, from the invitations to the menu, by giving guests a taste of what's to come: they'll be on board with your well-defined purpose for partying, and they'll have time to look forward to the special day — and maybe even contemplate a carefully chosen bottle of wine or an extra appetizer that will complement what you're serving.

The inspiration for a party theme is sometimes as basic as a really good haul of fresh, seasonal produce from the farmers' market. Other times it's a long-anticipated anniversary. Keep in mind that inspiration is everywhere you look: the vibe of your favorite café, with its warm colors and funky mix of music (recreate a similar setting in your home for a cozy fireside dessert party or wine-tasting night); or a shawl that evokes the colors and textures of another place (let its colors and origin — perhaps India or Morocco — inspire the decor and menu for a dinner party).

For more ideas, peruse magazines that exemplify your ideal entertaining style (*Bon Appétit* and other cooking magazines often feature entire parties, with complete menus, decorating tips and sometimes even timelines); consider your own collections, such as a set of Fiesta Dinnerware in a rainbow of hues, which might make the perfect vehicle for a colorful diner-style supper with friends; and look around at what's on hand locally, such as springtime flowers that might inspire decor for the first warm-weather party of the season.

While some party themes might feel a little silly at first, as the details flesh themselves out you'll have a viable — and unique — party in the making (see "Decade Parties," page 34, or "Calendar of Lesser-Known Holidays," page 33, for a few examples). Even a slightly kooky theme can be carried off convincingly if you have the right group of guests. (Look for those who are serious about having fun!) Sandy Hill's entertaining book, *Fandango: Recipes, Parties, and License to Make Magic*, shows how one imaginative host pulls off unforgettable themed parties. Taking a bit of a risk can brand you as fearless and freethinking, and can elevate your parties from standard fare to the exotic.

As you narrow your decision on a theme, keep your location — likely your home or backyard — in mind, and consider a theme that will fit your location without too much fuss. If you're having trouble deciding, sketch out three potential themes and make lists of what you'd need to pull them off — and envision them unfolding in your chosen location. Some will be easier to accomplish than others. Once you've decided on a theme and begun shopping, stick with it! It's pricy and time-consuming to change themes, and your guests will be much more interested in the overall picture: having a good time.

Read on for some specific themes, and adapt or alter the details freely to make any of these ideas fit your occasion, personal style and resources.

Classic Party Themes

Sure, they've been done before — but for good reason. And remember that nobody's done these classic party themes exactly the way you can, so take a time-tested party theme and make it your own.

Around the Clock

Brunch

See the Garden Brunch menu (page 292).

Brunch is a great excuse to enjoy breakfast food — a universal favorite — a little later in the morning, and it's the perfect way to toast the guest of honor on Mother's Day or Father's Day, or to honor an out-of-town guest who would relish the chance to catch up with several local friends or family members at once. Planning an activity for after the meal, such as a hike, a swim or a visit to the local botanical gardens or a museum, keeps an early-in-the-day party moving along.

Afternoon Tea

See the Afternoon Tea menu (page 320).

Perfect for a baby or wedding shower, an afternoon tea typically includes diminutive savories (such as bite-size sandwiches) and sweets (such as mini scones and tartlets), and black tea with milk and sugar, of course. Make it interesting with Japanese- or Indian-style food, drink and decor instead of sticking with the traditional English take on tea.

Just Desserts

A desserts-only menu, paired with dessert wine or coffee, can be a great way to prolong the fun after dinner out with friends, or after an evening event such as a classical music concert or a play. Hosting a desserts-only party also allows you to extend your hospitality without planning and executing a full menu.

American Regional

Hawaiian Luau

For an easier island-style menu, centered on barbecued chicken and pork loin, see the Hawaiian Luau menu (page 380).

Have you always wanted to host a Hawaiian-style pig roast? This is your opportunity (see Kalua Pig Roast, page 383). Don't forget the sweet potatoes (or sweet potato chips), mai tais (with paper umbrellas) and mellow island tunes. End the meal with macadamia and white chocolate chip cookies.

New England Clambake

This late-summer party traditionally includes lobster, clams, corn and potatoes cooked in a carefully prepared sandpit on the beach. Adapt it to your locale with fresh, seasonal seafood. The version of this meal that's cooked in a pot — indoors or outside — is often called a clam boil.

Alaskan Salmon Bake

It doesn't have to be baked, of course — try grilling or poaching, if you like — but this theme centers on a main course of salmon and rustic decor that gives a nod to the 49th state.

See the Pacific Northwest Coast menu (page 374), for a party built around grilled salmon.

Mardi Gras

Beads, masks and party-time music: there's nothing like Mardi Gras to warm up winter. Keep the menu focused on Louisiana's party central, and end the evening with some chicory-laced café au lait and a plate of hot beignets dusted with confectioner's (icing) sugar (order the beignet mix online at www.cafedumonde.com if it's not available locally).

Western

Celebrate the American West with a casual barbecue (chicken, ribs, steaks — you name it) and some cold summer salads or, for cooler weather, spicy chili rounded out with cornbread and microbrews. Invite guests to wear their cowboy hats and boots, and ask any musically talented friends to bring their acoustic guitars and campfire songs so everyone can gather around the firepit or fireplace.

See the Western Hoedown menu (page 368).

Elegant
Black and White

Combine these two opposing colors for chic decor that's perfect for New Year's Eve or any other celebration that calls for festive elegance. Carry the theme through in cocktail napkins and serving pieces, too. For a real visual feast, invite your guests to dress in black and white.

Silver and Gold

All that glitters is silver and gold when you pair these two metallics for a stunning presentation. Use silver platters for serving and plenty of metallic taper candles. Try this theme for a special anniversary, for New Year's Eve or for an engagement party.

Shopping for Inspiration

Fresh out of ideas? Sometimes you just need a change of scenery to recharge your creativity — and shopping isn't called "retail therapy" for nothing. In fact, shopping (even if it's just browsing) is a great way to find inspiration for a party theme. You might happen upon a gorgeous table runner that sets the party's colors and feel, or you might discover magnificent blood oranges that inspire a menu (and conclude that they can, indeed, appear in the cocktails, the salad and the dessert). Here are some places to shop for inspiration — and maybe some tabletop items or ingredients, too.

- **Department stores** with large tabletop displays, such as Macy's (www.macys.com), Nordstrom (www.nordstrom.com), Saks (www.saksfifthavenue.com), Barneys New York (www.barneys.com), the Bay (www.thebay.com) — or the store that sets the bar in your locale. Even people on a budget can borrow ideas.

- **Home goods stores** (or catalogs), such as Pottery Barn (www.potterybarn.com); Crate & Barrel or its hip younger sister, CB2 (www.crateandbarrel.com or www.cb2.com); Design Within Reach (www.dwr.com); and IKEA (www.ikea.com). Photographs from catalogs can sometimes serve as inspiration for how to use tabletop items you already have.

- **Kitchen goods stores**, such as Williams-Sonoma (www.williams-sonoma.com), Sur La Table (www.surlatable.com), Kitchen Stuff Plus (www.kitchenstuffplus.com) and Bed, Bath, & Beyond (www.bedbathandbeyond.com). A new gadget alone can inspire a theme: for example, a kitchen torch might lead you to a French menu, where you can use it on French onion soup and crème brûlée.

- **Discount home goods stores**, such as Tuesday Morning (www.tuesdaymorning.com), T.J. Maxx (www.tjmaxx.com), Stein Mart (www.steinmart.com) and HomeSense (www.homesense.ca), sometimes have surprising tabletop offerings that you can build a theme around — not to mention cookware and small appliances that can ignite more menu ideas.

- **Craft stores**, such as Michaels (www.michaels.com), Hobby Lobby (www.hobbylobby.com) and Jo-Ann (www.joann.com), offer a variety of items that can inspire, from seasonal decor to fabrics to cake-decorating supplies to dried florals or river rocks that can be assembled to make custom centerpieces.

- **Flea markets**, **garage sales** and **estate sales** can yield retro china finds — plus linens, candelabra and other points of inspiration for the table and party. Check for sale announcements in your local newspaper or on craigslist (www.craigslist.org).

- **Restaurants** and **cafés**, with their decor, music and food, can work as examples for how to set the theme and mood for your party. Ethnic restaurants and hip or upscale spots can be especially rich in ideas.

- **Party stores**, local or online (such as Plum Party at www.plumparty.com and Oriental Trading Company at www.orientaltrading.com; see the Party Supplies listing on page 449 for more), are great places to browse for theme ideas, as they make a business of providing the elements for a variety of themes.

- **Magazines** — whether food, entertaining, craft or general — are rich with seasonal themes; even when you're not planning an event, pull out any pages you find especially inspiring and save them in a binder for future reference. Some of my favorite magazines include *Bon Appétit, Country Living, Martha Stewart Living, In Style, O, Real Simple* and *Vanity Fair.*

- **Food** is a great catalyst for party themes. Consider any local specialties your area has to offer as a jumping-off point. Farmers' markets, farm stands, pick-your-own orchards and even really good supermarket produce departments can all be inspiration for a seasonal theme that makes food the focus. Seasonal foods in some areas also include game and seafood; if you have any hunters or fishermen in your crowd, you can build a meal around their catch. (For more ideas on seasonal produce, see Crop Calendar, page 22.)

Winter Wonderland

Have fun this winter with a retro-cool dinner-dance that embraces the season. Be sure to plan for a dance floor (clear the furniture from a room with a hardwood or tile floor) and DJ (or premade mixes on your iPod), and don't forget a glittery mirror ball to set the mood (you can rent one from a party rental company).

Champagne and Caviar

Celebrate a new job, a promotion or an engagement with hors d'oeuvres that are elegant yet easy. This combination can kick off a dinner party or, for lazy hosts, can serve as an elegant toast to the guest or guests of honor before you head out on the town. For a complete cocktail party featuring this elegant duo, see the Champagne and Caviar Party menu (page 326).

Hearts

One shape says it all. You'll have fun collecting the elements, both food and decor, to pull together a hearts party. Use the shape in your decor, serving pieces — even the food! A hearts theme is appropriate for Valentine's Day, of course, but also for an anniversary, an engagement, a celebration of heart health (perhaps a year after surgery) or even a gathering of devoted card-players.

Crop Calendar

Every area has its own growing season, but there are certain types of produce we look forward to at certain times of the year no matter where we live in North America. Consult this crop calendar for seasonal produce you can base your party theme on, keeping your area's local specialties in mind. Remember that in-season produce tastes better (and it's usually less expensive, too, as it's abundant), making for a theme that's timely, budget-friendly and delicious. Also keep in mind that many items span seasons: tomatoes, for example, peak in late summer and last through September; truffles appear in fall and last all winter.

- **Winter:** avocados, broccoli, Brussels sprouts, cabbage, grapefruit, oranges, pears, spinach, truffles, wild mushrooms
- **Spring:** artichokes, asparagus, avocados, beets, cucumbers, lettuce, rhubarb, peas, peppers
- **Summer:** arugula, beets, berries, cherries, cucumbers, melons, peppers, plums, summer squash, tomatoes
- **Late summer:** beets, berries, corn, dates, figs, grapes, melons, peaches, peppers, plums, summer squash, tomatoes
- **Fall:** apples, beets, broccoli, Brussels sprouts, cabbage, cranberries, cucumbers, dates, grapes, lettuce, nuts, pears, persimmons, pomegranates, sweet potatoes, truffles, wild mushrooms, winter squash

Collectors' Themes

Consider using one of the collections you own as inspiration for a party theme. Doing so is earth-friendly and pocketbook-friendly, and it's the ultimate lazy man's solution because, of course, you already have the necessary elements. Do you collect salt and pepper shakers? Shot glasses? Milk glasses? Pull out your collection, size it up and see what you can do with it. What you have on hand might surprise you.

Cookie Jars

For a dessert party, or the desserts portion of a buffet, nothing beats a variety of cookies — universal favorites such as chocolate chip, sugar, oatmeal raisin, peanut butter and even brownies and blondies, piled high inside a variety of cookie jars. Be sure to have plenty of fresh organic milk on hand (in addition to coffee and hot tea); reaching into a cookie jar will send guests back to their childhoods, when a glass of milk was the only accompaniment.

Pitchers, Teapots, Vases or Tureens

Highlight any collection of containers by positioning the items on a table runner. Use the containers as serving vessels for small food items, such as pretzel rods or breadsticks, cookies or brownies, and mints or candies, when possible. You can also use them as vessels for flatware, napkins and, of course, flowers.

Seashells

A seashell collection sets just the right mood for an elegant but casual warm-weather gathering. Use a sandy-white tablecloth and top it with a raw silk runner of seafoam green or ocean blue. Arrange creamy white pillar candles in glass bowls filled with sand, and arrange the shells along the runner and around the candles.

Old Photographs

Perfect for a wedding anniversary (such as your parents' 50th), a significant birthday (such as your sister's 50th) or a high-school reunion (such as your — oh, never mind), old photographs of the honoree or honorees make for an unmistakably focused theme, and they also make great table decor that's unusually engaging. For a cohesive look, use frames with the same finish (whether black, natural wood, silver or gold) in various sizes and shapes. Present them to the honoree or divide them among honorees after the party as one-of-a-kind parting gifts.

Trophies, Artwork, Playbills or School Photos

Any such collection would make a great theme for a high-school graduation party. Honor the graduate by using his or her collection of sports' trophies, artwork or school play or band programs to highlight achievements of the last four years (or more). A framed photograph from each school year, arranged on a dessert buffet or by the drinks, will delight guests, if not the guest of honor.

Music Memorabilia

Do you have all the original Beatles' records on vinyl? Do you collect all things Elvis? Did you follow the Grateful Dead, gathering beads, tapes and tie-dyes along the way? Take a music or other fan collection that's uniquely yours and design a party theme around it, incorporating its elements into tabletop decor, music selections (consider renting a karaoke machine if you suspect some of your guests share your enthusiasm) and even dress. You can also give a nod to such a theme in the food; for example, serve Elvis's favorite: fried peanut butter and banana sandwiches.

International Party Themes

What is it about a foreign accent that makes things sound so much more profound? Who knows, but the same trick applies to party food: if you want to add a certain je ne sais quoi to your party, ponder some international themes that will lend their unique style to the soiree and bring out the excursionist in each of your guests.

Caribbean Cookout

In the Caribbean, it's all about the jerk seasoning — a dry rub that includes allspice, chile peppers, cloves, cinnamon and other spices and herbs. Use it to season pork or chicken for the grill and round the meal out with black beans simmered with spicy sausage, and a medley of cool tropical fruits. Put on island music (reggae is always great) and stir up some mojitos; this one is for friends who like to party.

Mexican Fiesta

For a grownups-only Mexican-themed party, see the Mexican Fiesta menu (page 386).

With lively cocktails and food that appeals to everyone, a Mexican theme lends itself well to a multigenerational party. If kids are on the guest list, consider setting up burro (or pony) rides and serving assemble-it-yourself burritos or tacos to head off picky eaters. Use a colorful serape as a table runner and draw inspiration from Mexico's vibrant colors for the rest of the decor. Make a variety of dips (salsa, guacamole, queso fundido) to serve with tortilla chips as an easy appetizer.

Brazilian Mardi Gras

If you think New Orleans has the corner on Fat Tuesday, then consider Carnival — the four days leading up to Ash Wednesday — in Rio de Janeiro. Inject some Latin flavor into your own celebration by spicing up the menu and putting on the samba music.

Irish Breakfast

Give breakfast or brunch an international flavor with a traditional Irish "fry-up": eggs, sausage, toast, boxty (an Irish take on the potato pancake) — and, if you dare, black pudding.

English Pub

Buy a variety of bottled Brit beers and cook some traditional fare, such as bangers and mash, to complement the brew. Purchase pub coasters from stores like World Market (www. worldmarket.com); extras can be used as party favors.

Spanish Tapas

Why not make a meal of appetizers? Buy some Marcona almonds, Spanish cheeses, olives, roasted peppers and anchovies; make tortilla Española and chorizo simmered in wine; and pour a Spanish wine, such as Tempranillo.

For a full Spanish meal, see the Barcelona Bash menu (page 392).

French Countryside

Add interest to any dinner party with a French country theme, which makes for such delicious possibilities as bouillabaisse and crusty baguettes. Carry the theme into the decor with bright linens and pottery characteristic of Provence; Williams-Sonoma (www.williams-sonoma.com) carries pretty examples of both.

German Beer Fest

You'll find no shortage of great German beers to choose from: Spaten, Beck's, Warsteiner, Bitburger . . . the list goes on. Ask your favorite retailer for additional suggestions that will represent a few different styles. To eat, be sure to include sausages with spicy mustard for dipping, pick up soft pretzels from a mall or street vendor, and choose an apple or plum dessert.

For another German-style meal, see the German Feast menu (page 404).

Viennese Desserts

In Vienna, desserts are king. Add that to the city's rich musical heritage, and you have the perfect theme for a post-symphony desserts party. Some items to consider: Sachertorte (a rich chocolate cake filled with apricot jam and glazed with chocolate), linzertorte (an almond- and lemon-crusted tart filled with raspberry jam), plum-topped cakes or tarts, and marzipan-filled candies, such as Mozartkugeln. To drink, hot chocolate or coffee, served in a glass mug, with freshly whipped cream.

Russian Cocktails

For a cocktail party with a Russian accent, set up a blini bar (toppings might include sour cream, caviar, smoked salmon, capers, chives and some less traditional foods, such as sautéed mushrooms or crumbled sausage) and serve chilled vodka. Look for a vodka set that includes an ice container in which individual shot glasses are nestled (try Crate & Barrel; www.crateandbarrel.com). If friends are sticking around for a full meal, make it a cozy fireside nod to Eastern Europe and pair borscht — the popular fresh beet soup — with polmeni (pierogi-like dough pockets stuffed with any combination of cheese, potato, cabbage, sauerkraut and meat).

Italian Pasta Party

For another Italian pasta-centered meal, see the Italian Pasta Party menu (page 398).

The easiest of dinner parties starts with pasta. Round it out with ciabatta, salad, Italian wines and gelato for dessert. You can serve this menu to picky eaters: everyone loves Italian. In fair weather, introduce your guests to the well-loved Italian game of bocce; it helps if you have a flat area in your front- or backyard.

Greek Lamb Roast

See the Grecian Get-Together menu (page 410).

Whether it's for Easter dinner or otherwise, roast lamb is a special-occasion meal that's just right for welcoming springtime. The Greek version has plenty of garlic and herbs.

Moroccan Dinner

Use a low table with cushions on the floor and serve the local specialties, such as kebabs, tagine (often chicken or lamb in a spicy stew) and couscous. For dessert, offer mint tea paired with purchased Middle Eastern pastries: honey, orange blossom water and almonds are popular flavors for sweets in Morocco. *The New Book of Middle Eastern Food* by Claudia Roden is a popular source for recipes from Morocco and beyond; it includes Turkey, Greece and Egypt, too.

Indian Dinner Party

Don't be intimidated: You can get takeout and just focus on decor and dessert. Or you can stock up your spice cabinet, get a copy of Madhur Jaffrey's *Quick & Easy Indian Cooking, Easy Indian Cooking* by Suneeta Vaswani or *Complete Curry Cookbook* by Byron Ayanoglu and Jennifer MacKenzie and try your hand at cooking delicious vegetable or chicken curries and naan. Set an oversize coffee table for dinner, with floor cushions for your guests. A steaming cup of masala chai, an Indian spiced tea, makes a fragrant accompaniment to dessert.

Thai Food Stalls

In Thailand, a variety of dishes is sold streetside, making for many different tastes. Capturing the flavors and feel of this vibrant scene can be as easy as dialing in takeout: order a variety of dishes, including spring rolls, soup, grilled meat skewers and, of course, a noodle dish such as pad Thai — and then focus your efforts on the decor and presentation. Those inspired to try it from scratch might peruse *Quick & Easy Thai* by Nancie McDermott or *Simply Thai Cooking* by Wandee Young and Byron Ayanoglu. Serve Thai coffee, made with spices and sweetened condensed milk, with dessert.

Chinese Banquet

With up to a dozen courses, including dessert, a Chinese banquet is traditionally held to honor a wedding, the new year or another special occasion. It can be held at a restaurant, for cooks who are daunted by the parade of food such a theme entails. You can also prepare some of the food at home and pick up takeout for the rest. Search online to read up on traditional recipes and their related symbolism, and check out Martin Yan's *China* or one of Yan's other titles, including his contribution to the super-accessible Dummies series, *Chinese Cooking for Dummies*.

For my five-course take on the tradition, see the Chinese Banquet menu (page 428).

Japanese Teppanyaki

Take the cooking to the table by preparing Kobe beef, shrimp, scallops or chicken and assorted vegetables on a grill in the center of the table (in a well-ventilated room). Round out the meal with fried rice. If you don't have a portable grill, try cooking the food in a grill pan set atop a portable burner, or in an electric wok.

Kids' Party Themes

Don't limit yourself to television cartoon characters to inspire children's parties: light their imaginations with out-of-the-ordinary themes. Enlist your child's help to ensure that everything from the food to the entertainment is right on target for age-appropriate fun, and encourage a budding host by including your child in preparation tasks he or she can handle, such as assembling the favors and putting out the snacks.

Chefs in Training

Invite your young guests into the kitchen with this thrifty party that includes make-your-own pizzas (prep the dough and ingredients ahead of time), an assemble-it-yourself salad bar (with crisp lettuce, baby carrots, cherry tomatoes, stringed sugar snap peas and ranch dressing) and decorate-your-own cupcakes. This is great for winning over picky eaters. Another option: set up a build-your-own-wraps sandwich buffet.

King of the Road

Whether it's a retro roadtrip down Route 66 or Nascar racing, take inspiration from the road to fete your future driver. Matchbox cars can be apt additions to a centerpiece and to the goody bags, and road signs or racing flags can work their way into the decor and invitations.

Jungle

Borrow your theme from *The Jungle Book*, *Tarzan* or Curious George stories for a party that features — in the decor and favors — such exotic (plush) animals as monkeys, zebras, lions and more. Decorate the table with bunches of bananas, binoculars and classic Barrel of Monkeys games that can also double as favors. Don't forget about animal prints, which are popular for grownup decor but are also a perfect fit for a kids' jungle theme. Look for animal-print placements, napkins, cups or balloons.

Circus

Recreate the spectacle of the circus at home: hang a striped "big top" tent from the ceiling over the party table. Serve popcorn and pretzels as snacks — from classic red-and-white popcorn tubs (www.worldmarket.com) — and keep the menu simple vendor-style: corn dogs, hamburgers or hot dogs. Consider such activities as face painting or making balloon animals, with the help of a hired clown, if you like.

Pirates

Invite children to dress the part for this swashbuckling party theme, and incorporate the pirate flag (also known as the Jolly Roger) into your decor. For young guests, plant buried "treasures" in the backyard sandbox for the finding; older children will enjoy a more elaborate scavenger hunt or goody-bag hunt. For the centerpiece, make a treasure chest by filling an antique container with chocolate coins and Mardi Gras beads, or top decorative fish nets, available at party stores, with toy fish and crabs.

Witches and Wizards

This party is perfect for school-age fans of the popular Harry Potter series. Invite guests to dress as witches or wizards. Serve food at your formal dining-room table, complete with candlelight, to mimic the great hall at Hogwarts. A magician can provide entertainment, or you can purchase magic tricks from a party supply store for each guest, inviting them to perform their trick for the party once they get the hang of it.

Backyard Campout

Pitch the tent, put fresh batteries in the flashlights and provide some snack mix (such as nuts, Craisins and M&Ms) in airtight containers, along with bottled water. Before nightfall, cook dinner on the grill or over the firepit and invite your campers to make their own s'mores. Provide constellation charts and a telescope to make stargazing more interesting, or get some age-appropriate ghost stories that they can read to each other by flashlight (just be ready for the party to move inside).

See the Backyard Campout menu (page 356).

Zoo

Does your local zoo allow on-site birthday parties? Many do, and some even give special tours and offer birthday party packages to make entertaining there a no-brainer (for other such options, see Kids on Location, page 52). Be sure to bring plenty of sunscreen and water, distributing take-home reusable sports bottles in a variety of colors so kids can keep track of theirs. For the preschool set, zoo-themed children's books, such as *Good Night, Gorilla* or *Dear Zoo*, make great favors.

See the Western
Hoedown menu
(page 368).

Cowboys and Cowgirls

In some parts of the United States and Canada (hello, Texas
and Alberta), nearly every kid has a set of Western wear.
Give them an opportunity to show it off with a Cowboys and
Cowgirls party theme that might include pony rides, campfire
stories and vittles, of course. If you don't live in the Wild
West, check out party supply stores such as Oriental Trading
Company (www.orientaltrading.com), which offers inexpensive
children's cowboy hats by the dozen.

Trains

Send out train "tickets" with the invitations and invite guests
to come aboard for a party that will please Thomas (the
Tank Engine) devotees. Set up your child's train as a fun
centerpiece that everyone can reach. Nordic Ware (www.
nordicware.com) makes train-car-shaped Bundt pans for a
cake that's right on track — and nine cars long. Wooden train
whistles make great favors.

Dance Party

Clear the furniture, dim the lights, hang a disco ball and
put on a music mix made especially for a kids' dance party
(consult your child for favorite songs). For fun at the party, and
to encourage those who'd rather be in the band than on the
dance floor, order a variety of inexpensive rhythm instruments
(www.orientaltrading.com), such as egg shakers and castanets,
which kids can use to play along with the music and then take
home as favors.

Not-Your-Typical-Celebration Party Themes

Unconventional situations call for unconventional gatherings. These are sometimes the most important occasions to honor, after all, because they might otherwise go unrecognized. If you have a friend who needs your support during a touchy time — or if you can't imagine letting a TV special go unheralded — these parties are for you.

Coming Out

Your friend is coming out: what better way to share the news than with a celebration that gives the honoree a strong show of love and support — not to mention getting that conversation out of the way with everyone at once? Treat this as you would any other cocktail party, asking the guest of honor ahead of time for input on the guest list and evening's activities. For an easy event, host cocktails and appetizers at home and then move the party to a favorite restaurant or club.

Soothing Day at the Spa

Complicated situations like a divorce, getting fired or an impending move can unsettle even the most stalwart friends, so it's a good time to reinforce your friendship and provide a welcome distraction. A relaxing spa day can do you and your friends a world of good. Book favorite treatments and lunch at a spa, or bring the party to your house; depending on your budget, you can either hire manicurists and masseuses to come to you (bigger cities often have local mobile spa services) or take turns pampering each other. Prepare a light lunch or supper to enjoy with white wine or tea.

For one appropriate menu, see the Girls' Night In party (page 336).

Going Green

Are you and your friends or neighbors trying to do your part to save the earth? Give your group a jumpstart by hosting a party that provides local resources for going green (recycling information, composting information, watering guidelines and locations of local farmers' markets or food cooperatives, for example). Lead by example by serving food prepared with local products, using recyclable containers and giving "green" party favors, such as attractive reusable shopping bags. This type of party works best with friends who have already expressed interest.

Hollywood

Do you count down the days to the Oscars? The Emmys? The Miss America Pageant? Indulge your fascination with Hollywood by bringing together a group of friends who feel the same way, and banish any naysayers from the TV room for the evening. Make food that's easy to eat from a plate in your lap, and take bets on winners ahead of time to keep the watching more interesting, awarding the winner with a related prize, such as a set of Best Picture–winning DVDs, at the end of the show. Copies of current gossip magazines can make great favors on their own or as part of a swag bag.

Any Excuse to Party Themes

Your guests won't mind if there's no special reason behind your party-giving efforts — they'll just be glad for an invitation. Here are some fun party themes that will give you an excuse to party any time.

Game Night

Whether it's bingo, Pictionary, Bunco, charades or one of the new DVD games, such as Scene It or Trivial Pursuit *Saturday Night Live* Edition, a game can provide the theme and entertainment for the evening, for girls or guys only, or a mixed group of friends.

Arts and Crafts

Knitters, quilters and scrapbookers are known for their love of socializing as they work. Take a craft that you and your friends enjoy and use it as an excuse to gather around the table together, letting that theme guide your invitations list, food, time and place.

Movie Night

Who doesn't have a list of movies they want to see? Select a title that you and your friends have been wanting to screen, and let the movie set the evening's theme. Or choose a classic that everyone has already seen (such as *Monty Python and the Holy Grail* or *The Graduate*), so that the inevitable commentary and conversation won't prevent guests from following the plot.

Calendar of Lesser-Known Holidays

There are hundreds of lesser-known holidays that can lend us unusual reasons to celebrate — and supply off-the-beaten-path party themes. While most of these aren't official holidays you'll find preprinted on your calendar, that's no reason to ignore them. Bear in mind that because so many of these are unofficial, some of the dates are debatable. Here are a few to consider:

Date	Holiday
January (first Saturday)	Fruitcake Toss Day
February (Shrove Tuesday)	International Pancake Day
February (last Saturday)	Open That Bottle Night
March 5	Learn What Your Name Means Day
April (first Saturday)	Tangible Karma Day
April 10	National Sibling Day
April 22	Earth Day
May 11	Eat What You Want Day
May 15	National Chocolate Chip Day
June 2	Leave the Office Early Day
June 28	Great American Backyard Campout
July 15	Cow Appreciation Day
July (third Sunday)	National Ice Cream Day
July (fourth Saturday)	National Cowboy Day
August 8	Sneak Some Zucchini onto Your Neighbor's Porch Night
August 10	National S'mores Day
September 13	International Chocolate Day
September 19	Talk Like a Pirate Day
September (fourth Sunday)	National Good Neighbor Day
October 6	Mad Hatter Day
October (second Saturday)	Universal Music Day
November (first Thursday)	National Men Make Dinner Day
December 4	National Dice Day
December 23	Festivus

Theme • Any Excuse to Party Themes

The Internet Movie Database (www.imdb.com) is a great source for finding titles by quote, character or actor.

Book Club

Starting a book club means you'll have a date on the calendar to get together with some favorite friends every month, not to mention a little healthy peer pressure to keep your mind engaged with some required reading. Book clubs are fun because the theme is built in with each month's book; many selections will inspire food, music and decor. (As an example, a friend's club read *Julie & Julia* by Julie Powell and enjoyed classic French appetizers from Julia Child's *Mastering the Art of French Cooking*, upon which it was based.)

Decade Parties

Decade parties are a fun way to revisit the iconic fashions, music and even food that defined an era — with a willing group of friends, of course. Think back to what was popular when you were in high school or college, and get creative in your efforts to summon the vibe of those days. Decade parties are a great fit for a major birthday, taking the honoree back to his or her youth. They're also fun for a big wedding anniversary (focus on the decade when the couple married) or a reunion of classmates.

The 80s

Draw your inspiration from *Miami Vice*, *Valley Girl* or *Flashdance*. Don't forget the dated pink-and-purple color combination for your decor — or leg warmers worn with pumps. Who wouldn't love the excuse to get down to the likes of Boy George, Duran Duran and early Madonna?

The 70s

It's disco time: bring out the bell-bottoms and hotpants, or stick to the earthier side of that decade's style with fringed vests and puka shell necklaces. For more reminders of 70s style, screen *Saturday Night Fever* (it's more sexist than you might remember), the hopelessly romantic *Love Story* or the retrospective sitcom *That 70s Show*. Spin some Elton John, Bee Gees, Earth Wind & Fire and KC and the Sunshine Band.

The 60s

It's the decade that culminated with Woodstock, so find your inner hippie with outer tie-dyes, peace signs and Birkenstocks. Consider serving a meatless meal, and play the Beatles, the Grateful Dead, Bob Dylan and Crosby, Stills, Nash & Young. Decorate the table with flower-child favorites like daisies or sunflowers, and add a drop of patchouli oil to a few light bulbs (those farther away from the food).

The 50s

Host your own sock hop with tunes from Elvis, Chuck Berry and Buddy Holly, for a celebration of rock 'n' roll's big beginning. Or focus on a different sort of 50s music with jazz greats Charlie Parker, Dizzy Gillespie and Miles Davis. Party stores love the 50s, so you'll find no shortage of accessories and decor to round out your guests' ensembles of poodle skirts and bobby socks or leather jackets and jeans.

> Serve your guests burgers and milkshakes for a 50s-themed party.

The 30s and 40s

While these decades saw more than their fair share of strife, they also saw the spread of swing dancing, which enjoyed another resurgence in the late 90s. Revisit the original era by hosting a swing dance party (perfect your moves ahead of time). Invite a dance instructor to give informal lessons for a couple of hours to help guests get the hang of it; such an instructor will also be able to recommend music you should have on hand. Be sure to include the classic Count Basie Orchestra, as well as some newer nods to swing like the Brian Setzer Orchestra.

The 20s

Celebrate the Jazz Age, when drinking was illegal (but more popular than ever), with a cocktail supper devoted to the decade's most enduring swill: the martini. Let guests who think of themselves as mixologists try mixing their best martini — you can even have a blind tasting and award the best martini-maker a new cocktail shaker (and bragging rights, of course). As an alternative, offer absinthe, a potent green liquor that was banned in the U.S. back in the early 20th century and only recently reintroduced. Don't forget the jazz music (Duke Ellington and others) or the flapper-inspired styles of the era.

Poached Pears

When I was a new chef and truly fearless, a very chic woman called me and wanted a 50th birthday party for her husband, to be held on his sailboat. She had already planned the menu. (It was after this party that I learned I have to plan all menus — and serve what I know people like and what I do best. In other words, I would learn to trust myself.)

My hostess was Hollywood-thin. That means she was a size zero. She ordered all the skinny food in fashion: steamed salmon with a no-cream sauce on the side; vegetables, but no carrots, because they have too much sugar; a huge salad for the first course; no pasta, no white flour and no birthday cake.

"Really?" I asked. "Doesn't everyone want chocolate cake for their birthday? With thick, sweet, gooey frosting and maybe some huge chocolate curls on top?"

No, her husband would like poached pears, she assured me. I didn't mention that I would bring whipped Chantilly cream to top the pears. I knew that would never be allowed in her world. I would hide the sweetened cream until dessert, and then place it as far away from her as I could, forgetting any thought of getting a tip. I like whipped cream, and I know other people do, too. Besides, they were *guests*, not hostages.

Eating seasonal food is in vogue now, but the more you cook and love the taste of food, the more you learn that this is simply the right thing to do. Now that a revolution has occurred, with farmers' markets popping up across North America, you can easily find beautiful, locally grown fruit and vegetables. I never plan a menu now without thinking of where I'll get my ingredients. But when I said yes to Madame Thin, I was not thinking about the time of year, or whether I would be able to find ripe pears in the markets. I just said yes.

Kitchens are small on yachts, sailboats, trains and planes. I learned that early in my career. It's best to prepare as much food as you can before arriving. I had my salmon filets ready in the roasting pan and the salad greens cleaned and dried. I'd made a delicious mustard dressing and had baked gluten-free crackers — they were kind of like birdseed when you ate them, but they looked appealing. I had chilled the white wine and packed my small French butter pears to poach aboard the boat. In fact, the produce man had packed them in straw for me so they would not get bruised in transit. I had never actually touched the pears.

After arriving at the marina with my assistant chef, we set the table, placed the candles and warmed up a ripe Brie in whole wheat phyllo pastry (I would tell my hostess the cheese was a gift — you can't turn down a gift).

The birthday boy was a big, charming man who obviously loved to eat. He did not look like he had been on a diet recently — or ever. He loved the warm, oozing Brie, he loved the walnut lemon pesto sauce I snuck onto the salmon, he devoured the wild and white rice pilaf, which had been cooked in butter. He was hungry, appreciative and delightful. Maybe I would get a tip after all.

After clearing most of the dinner plates, I joined my assistant in the galley, only to find her wild-eyed and sweating bullets, telling me the pears were as hard as rocks. *No, they can't be*, I told myself, but as I started to peel a pear, I knew she was right: they were like boulders. We continued peeling, and I was confident that after they were poached in the Zinfandel with cloves and cinnamon, they would be soft enough to eat. The simmering wine and spices smelled delicious. The pears went from pale yellow to deep pink in no time. I transferred them to a platter and continued to reduce my lovely syrup. I was sure the pears would be delicious once they cooled.

The pear platter was beautiful, with the Zinfandel syrup, the rosettes of Chantilly cream and the fresh mint garnish. As I placed the platter on the table, the birthday boy cried out, "What, no chocolate cake?" He said, "I'm full. And besides, I don't even like pears. My wife picked this dessert."

If only it could have ended there. But Madame Thin decided to serve herself a pear — no cream, just the pear. I helped her with the syrup. The beautiful pink pear, perched on the fine bone china, was placed in front of her. As she took her fork to taste the pear, which was still hard as a rock, it flew like a projectile off the plate and across the table, landing in the birthday boy's lap. Time stood still. I wanted to die. A bad dessert on your birthday and now, insult to injury, a dry-cleaning challenge. Wonder of wonders, the birthday boy laughed until he cried.

The rest of the guests never touched the pear platter, and as we docked, I heard Madame Thin saying that the yacht club was still open, and that ice cream sundaes would be perfect.

Removing the last of the wine glasses and coffee cups, I found an envelope with a huge tip, and a note on the back of the birthday boy's business card that said simply, "You owe me a chocolate cake."

I sure did.

Location

L ocation, location, location. Everyone knows how important it is in real estate, but it's crucial for successful entertaining, too. While the majority of smaller parties *could* be held at home, that doesn't necessarily answer the question of location. Maybe it would actually be easier or more fun to hold your celebration somewhere else, depending on what your theme calls for. If you do have it at home, deciding where in your home to center the party — whether in the formal dining room, in the basement rec room or, if you're really lucky, poolside — will change the backdrop of your party dramatically and, in turn, will have a significant impact on your decor needs. How does your proposed location lend itself to your final vision of the party?

Once you have your theme in mind, it's useful to contemplate what is necessary to execute that vision in a particular location. Be sure to take those needs into consideration when deciding where to have the party. Maybe the theme, say a midsummer's picnic, is a natural fit for your carefully landscaped yard, complete with a gurgling fountain and gorgeous gardens. But if your backyard is nonexistent, or if the grass has been ripped to shreds by your overzealous dogs, it might make a lot more sense to take your picnic to the picturesque local botanical gardens or city park rather than spend countless hours and dollars trying to overhaul and decorate your mud pit.

Some other basic considerations to ponder when deciding on a location include whether it offers the logistics necessary — enough room, enough electricity, enough plumbing — to comfortably accommodate the party you have in mind. The information in this chapter will help you choose the ideal location for your party and get a handle on the related details each location will require.

Your Home

How many people will comfortably fit in your home? For very small dinner parties, say, for six, you might have a dining-room table that seats that many, so you already know that you have enough room. But if you're thinking of hosting a larger party — or wondering if you can make it all happen in your studio apartment — you'll need to give some thought to how many people you can comfortably accommodate, and what sort of tables and chairs you might need to borrow or rent to do so.

For a seated dinner, you'll need tables that accommodate your guests, naturally, but you'll also need to allow an additional 2 to 3 feet (60 to 90 cm) beyond the diameter of each table to accommodate chairs, plus another 2 to 4 feet (60 to 120 cm) between the chair backs and the nearest obstruction — a wall or another chair back, for instance. See the chart and diagram on pages 40 and 41 for table sizes and shapes, and how many guests each option can comfortably seat.

When considering holding a larger party at home, think outside the dining room: a finished basement, a large sunroom or even a very clean garage can work. Whatever the space, make a to-scale drawing on graph paper to see how it would function logistically before committing to anything.

One way hosts for multigenerational gatherings such as Thanksgiving dinner have long accommodated dining-room overflow is to place a "kids' table" in an adjacent room, such as the kitchen or TV room. While young children might not mind this arrangement, it doesn't work well as a catchall for unmarried relatives (no matter what their emotional age). If you can't accommodate everyone who is an actual grownup (that's 18 and up) at the grownups' table, reconsider your arrangement rather than risk offending your guests.

If you decide that multiple tables in adjacent rooms are the best fit for your space and guest list, be sure to mix up the seating arrangements so that tables aren't coded by age, marital status or any other factor that places more importance on some guests than others. An exception would be elderly or handicapped guests, who, for physical reasons, should be given prime seating so that they can enjoy their meal and the party as much as those who are able to perch on a barstool and balance a plate and wineglass more adeptly.

Another way to host at home when you're tight on space is to abandon the idea of a seated dinner altogether and focus instead on a buffet or a cocktail party. Food for as many as 50 can be arranged on a 6- to 8-foot (180 to 240 cm) buffet table, and your dining table or kitchen counter can hold enough food for a buffet for smaller parties, say up to 24. Cocktail parties, with less food to serve (and bite-size snacks that don't require utensils, meaning people can eat while standing), take up even less room. Either way, your guests can help themselves and find a place to perch around the dining room, kitchen and living room, even on floor cushions or the hearth.

Still unsure whether you have enough space for the big night? The questionnaire on page 42 will help you figure it out. If you find you need to take the party elsewhere, the options range from outdoors at your own place (see page 44) to locations far beyond (see page 48).

Seating Diagrams and Guides

Round Tables		
Diameter	Guests	Maximum
24 inches (60 cm)	2	2
30 inches (75 cm)	2	2
36 inches (90 cm)	4	5
48 inches (120 cm)	6	8
54 inches (135 cm)	7	9
60 inches (150 cm)	8	10
72 inches (180 cm)	10	12

Square, Rectangular or Oblong Tables		
Length and Width	Guests	Maximum
36 inches (90 cm) square	4	4
48 inches (120 cm) square	6	8
60 inches (150 cm) square	8	10
60 x 30 inches (150 x 75 cm)	6	8
72 x 30 inches (180 x 75 cm)	6	8
96 x 30 inches (240 x 75 cm)	8	10

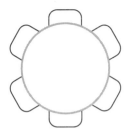

Seating for 6
(48-inch/120 cm table)

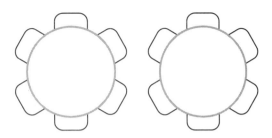

Seating for 12
(6 guests per 48-inch/120 cm table)

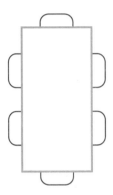

Seating for 6
(60- x 30-inch/150 x 75 cm table)

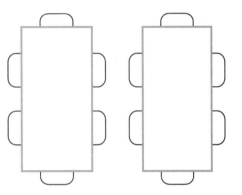

Seating for 12
(6 guests per 60- x 30-inch/150 x 75 cm table)

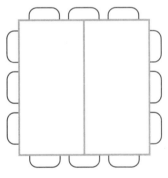

Seating for 12
(two 60- x 30-inch/150 x 75 cm table)

Seating for 30
(5 guests per 36-inch/90 cm table)

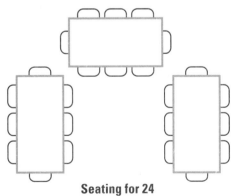

Seating for 24
(8 guests per 60- x 30-inch/150 x 75 cm table)

Seating for 20
(10 guests per 96- x 30-inch/240 x 75 cm table)

Kitchen and Home Floor Plan Questionnaire

Not sure whether your home can accommodate the celebration you have in mind? Here are some questions that will inspire you to use the space you have in creative ways.

1. Do you have enough clutter-free surfaces from which to serve food and drinks? Can you uncover more serving surfaces by putting away knick-knacks from tabletops in the living room or dining room, and putting away appliances that live on the kitchen counter? When looking for extra serving surfaces, think beyond the dining-room table and take into account console tables, coffee tables, sideboards and drink carts.

2. Do you have a few rooms you can devote to the party? Consider ways to encourage flow, such as positioning drinks in one room, a full buffet or just savory appetizers in another, and sweets in a third area. Use the kitchen, dining room and living room, if you have all three.

3. Can you make more space by rearranging furniture? Make sure there are clear, ample pathways to food, beverages, the coat closet and the bathroom. Pull dining-room chairs away from the table if you're using it for serving, and arrange the chairs in pairs or small groups to provide extra seating that doesn't interrupt the flow to and from the food.

4. Short on seating? Not having enough chairs actually encourages mingling among guests, and it's fine to expect some people to stand at a party, especially when you're not serving a fork-and-knife meal. To add casual seating, purchase large floor pillows that can be used in a variety of spots around the house. A garden bench, piano bench or sturdy toy box can also be repurposed as temporary extra seating.

5. Do you have a patio, balcony or deck that's adjacent to the party area? In fair weather, throw open the doors to give the party fresh air and a place for overflow; your patio or deck furniture can serve as extra seating for those in search of a spot. In cool weather, an outdoor firepit can provide another place for guests to congregate. To make it even more inviting, set up a backyard hot chocolate stand. Large coffee tureens are handy for dispensing hot water (let it "brew" without the coffee grounds). Set out single-serving instant hot chocolate packets, marshmallows, mugs and maybe even peppermint schnapps or amaretto, and let guests assemble their own fireside drinks.

Getting the House Party-Ready

If you've decided that your house is, indeed, the perfect location for the party you're planning, it's time to take stock of how you'll need to alter it to accommodate the crowd. Sure, you want it to be comfortable for your guests, but it's also a good idea to think about yourself and your home and head off potential disasters with a little forethought. (Nuts and bolts are included here; for ideas on decorating your space, turn to page 58.)

If you are thinking about borrowing a friend's home, all of these points still apply — in fact, you'll want to be especially careful to make sure that your friend's priceless items are secured and his or her privacy respected.

Privacy

Just because you're inviting people into your home doesn't mean they should have total access — it's okay to close a door and put a sign on it indicating PRIVATE AREA if you have some things you'd rather not share with the crowd. (It's your business whether those items are piles of dirty laundry or priceless pieces of art, furniture or rugs that you've removed from the house's common areas.) It works best if the closed area is as far away from the party as possible, like a bedroom. If you're having children over, or anyone else who doesn't take direction well, you might consider locking the door for the duration.

Pets

You know your pets, and you know your guests. Most cats would thank you for tucking them away for the evening, with plenty of food, water and fresh litter, in the designated private area — especially when children are involved. And while your dogs might prefer to join in the festivities, it might be better to exclude them, at least at the beginning of a party. Remember that some guests might be allergic to cats or dogs; other guests, perhaps unaccustomed to living with animals, might be overwhelmed by the attentions of a shameless sniffer. If the guests stay longer than four hours, it's okay to let Fido outside to relieve himself — and to let him resume his normal family life, even if that's free run of the house or backyard.

If your pet enjoys being part of the action, place small signs on any gates, so guests will know to keep them latched.

Breakables

If you're anticipating a lot of dancing or activity, remove breakables from the public spaces where the party will take place. Fragile items such as table lamps, picture frames, candleholders, potted plants, pottery and other tippy *objets d'art* are prime targets for over-enthused partygoers. If a little rearranging prevents your favorite vase from shattering — and circumvents the uncomfortable apologies that would ensue — then it's worth the effort.

Plumbing

For bigger parties, it's a good idea to have your toilet snaked ahead of time to prevent any backups or an expensive emergency plumbing call, but for smaller parties (and facilities in good working order), that's usually not an issue. Do make sure that at least one bathroom is spotlessly clean and available for guests; it's even better if you have two bathrooms available. A clear path to the facilities and a small nightlight left on are usually all that are needed to point the way.

Toiletries

Stock your powder room or bathroom better than you think you need to, so you won't be bothered during the party to attend to such tasks. Include plenty of extra toilet paper in an easy-to-find spot, tissues, fresh guest towels or pretty paper napkins for hand-drying, a full liquid soap dispenser (these are neater and cleaner than bar soap), a small but visible trash can and even a bowl of potpourri. While a votive candle is a nice touch, it's not advisable to leave a burning candle unattended; you can always have an unlit candle out, along with some matches, in case it's needed. Hand lotion is a nice extra.

Neighbors

If you expect more cars than can fit in your driveway, let your neighbors know ahead of time about your party, inviting them to stop by, if appropriate, or letting them know that your work friends or your child's playmates are coming over (in other words, a category that probably doesn't include neighbors, but also doesn't make them feel excluded). Neighbors in the know will feel more generous about forgiving the extra cars and extra noise a party can bring.

Garbage

Enlist a friend or slip $5 to your child to keep discarded disposables picked up.

A small space can take on a messy look pretty quickly when it's littered with a bunch of crumpled-up cocktail napkins and empty bottles. Keep your place looking great by setting up a bin in the kitchen for recyclables if you anticipate lots of them (such as for a beer and brats party), and set up an empty trash can in a visible spot in the kitchen, particularly if your party involves paper plates or plastic cups.

Your Backyard

If you have a large deck or a backyard that's company-ready, and you're anticipating fair weather, consider hosting the party at your home, but outside. The great outdoors can comfortably accommodate a crowd, you'll enjoy the weather and fresh air, and the setting can sometimes lend itself even better than the indoors to your party's theme. In fact, your backyard might be your first choice for warm-weather entertaining. While guests will still need to go inside to use the bathroom, you won't have to rearrange or decorate the rest of your house — or figure out how to squeeze everyone into a tiny dining room.

Outdoor parties are usually much more casual and come with fewer worries about putting away the breakables or preventing spills. Plus, the natural backdrop, especially in spring or fall (depending on where you live), might provide most of the decor necessary. Here are a few ideas for dressing up the great outdoors behind your house — the deck, yard and pool area.

Many front yards are great for parties, and driveways make excellent places to set up tables.

Plants

While we all wish for a lushly landscaped backyard, sometimes it's just not feasible to get it into great shape ahead of a party date. Some party rental companies or nurseries rent out trees or large shrubs, which can be used to conceal unsightly spots or create the effect of a mature, landscaped yard. If you were planning to devote some funds to landscaping anyway, you can purchase such trees and place them where you think you'll be planting them — after you're done pulling off the big party, that is. In addition to trees and shrubs, Boston ferns are inexpensive and can be hung on walls or placed on tables to add extra green where it's needed most.

Flowers

Decorate tables with small bud vases full of flowers, whether cut from your own garden or purchased locally. Or buy seasonal potted plants, such as pansies or mums, that you can decorate outdoor tables with now and plant in garden beds after the party. When choosing flowers for a buffet or dining table, be sure to select those without overwhelming scents, steering clear of paperwhites, for example. Depending on the season, irises, marigolds, poinsettias, daffodils or gerbera daisies make great choices. For a nice touch that lends welcome scents to the table, fill in vases of flowers with herbs that complement the food. Rosemary, thyme, basil, lemon verbena and bay laurels make especially pretty and fragrant additions. Bay laurels can also be made into pretty crowns to surround pillar candles.

Use garlands of faux leaves, decorated here and there with real flowers.

Lighting

When the sun sets, there's no prettier way to dress up your outdoor spaces than with white Christmas lights or candlelight. A big bonus of entertaining after sunset is that any less attractive reaches of the lawn won't be visible. Use twinkle lights in trees, on a wall or fence, under a market umbrella over tables, or along the lawn to create a path to the eating area (try plastic-hose twinkle lights on the ground). Luminarias, which are simply paper lunch bags with a couple of inches of sand and a votive candle, are inexpensive and festive. Flame-resistant bags are now widely available as a safer alternative; ask for them at your local crafts store. Votive candles placed in hurricane lamps (so they won't blow out) are also attractive on tabletops; floating candles, in a bowl of water or in the pool, create instant romance. Tiki torches are a great way to add island style to the yard for a tropical theme, and filling them with citronella oil can even help keep mosquitoes at bay.

Treating the Yard for Insects

Have a plan for dealing with these pesky party-crashers so your guests will be comfortable while enjoying the outdoors. If your area is especially plagued, consider treating it ahead of time. Commercially available yard foggers will take care of the problem, but the chemicals can be harmful to pets and people if ingested. Some garden centers with an organic bent offer natural alternatives, such as garlic concentrate that you can spray on your shrubs. And in areas that are especially hard hit — such as Florida and Texas — companies offer misting systems that can be installed to deliver a selected spray (some earth-friendlier than others) to your yard on a regular basis. Whatever you choose, be sure to apply it the morning of the party at the latest, so any scent will dissipate before it's time to serve the food.

More Bug Protection

Have insect repellent towelettes available for your guests' use.

Whether or not you treat your yard, it's probably a good idea to have some personal bug spray on hand that your guests can use if they like (choose varieties safe for children). It can also help to burn citronella candles or torches a half-hour ahead of time. If you have bees that are more interested in your potato salad than the flowers they should be pollinating, you can set up yellow jacket traps away from the buffet area, at the perimeter of the party site.

Firepit

Backyard firepits provide ambiance, warmth and a focal point for patio parties. If you have one, and the weather is right for using it, be sure to have plenty of firewood stacked and ready

Who's Responsible?

While most of the details are similar whether the party is held at home or elsewhere, there is one major difference: liability. When a party is at your house, it's your own things that could be broken, or your slippery steps a guest could fall on (ouch). What kind of homeowners' or renters' insurance coverage do you have to lean on if something unfortunate happens? And when you're entertaining at a restaurant, who pays for the broken wineglass — or worse, broken leg?

At your own home, your homeowners' or renters' insurance likely has provisions for your belongings and any on-site injuries, to a point. If you're inviting guests over, it's probably a good idea to familiarize yourself with your coverage; a quick call to your insurance agent should provide adequate explanation and upgrade options. It's also a good idea to do your best to prevent injuries ahead of time. Have your front porch and walkway well lit and clear of ice or snow; make sure that any stairs, whether interior or exterior, have sturdy handrails; secure all electrical and phone wires to avoid tripping hazards; put non-slip mats or double-sided tape under any area rugs and keep exposed floors dry; make sure you have enough lighting, using nightlights in dark hallways, stairwells and bathrooms; offer nonalcoholic drinks so people are encouraged to pace themselves (but be prepared for overnight guests); test your smoke detector; and post emergency numbers near your phone.

If you're renting a space, whether indoors or out, always insist on a rental agreement that specifies insurance coverage (not to mention fees, deposit and hours of rental, including adequate time for setup and cleanup). It's best to be clear from the beginning on such questions as this: If one of your guests accidentally breaks a sculpture in the gallery, who is responsible? Any additional insurance should be negotiated and included in the rental fee. You should also ask what they have done or can do to prevent such accidents or injuries.

to go, plus seating for everyone to gather around it. Inexpensive firepits can be purchased at Lowe's (www.lowes.com), Home Depot (www.homedepot.com) or Target (www.target.com). You can even make a homemade firepit using terracotta tiles as the base and three levels of bricks for the sides; as a safety precaution, be sure to set it up away from low-hanging branches, and generously water the ground underneath and around it before lighting the fire.

For a nostalgic and unusually easy dessert, have the makings for s'mores on hand: graham crackers, chocolate and marshmallows. If you want to create a more imaginative twist on the classic, purchase a variety of cookies and chocolates (try white or bittersweet chocolate).

Furniture

If your set of patio furniture doesn't include enough tables and chairs for your party, consider purchasing an additional set. Discounts on new patio furniture are often available at the end of a season, when the weather for entertaining outdoors is still quite agreeable. Used patio furniture is often sold at estate sales and garage sales. A mishmash of metal or wood sets can be painted to match each other.

If you're not ready to buy it — or don't anticipate needing it again any time soon — you can rent extra patio furniture. Some rental companies will waive their minimum order fee if you pick up and return the rentals yourself.

Picnic Blankets

If you don't have even close to enough seating, consider using picnic blankets on the grass instead. In fact, this arrangement can drum up nostalgia and break the ice for a backyard party (it's hard to be a wallflower when you're sprawled out with other partygoers on, well, bedding). Scatter the blankets with colorful throw pillows that coordinate with your theme for a sumptuous touch that makes the setup more comfortable.

Tablecloths

Topping outdoor tables with tablecloths is a quick way to give a mismatched collection a cohesive and festive look. To prevent tablecloths from billowing up in the breeze, tape or staple the ends of the cloth to the underside of your table. Or, for a casually elegant look, try tablecloth weights. These are available at party supply stores and barbecue stores, or you can make your own with wooden clothespins, holiday ornaments or metal clip rings (the ones sold for hanging curtains). Decorate these bases to coordinate with your theme, gluing on (or attaching with wire) felt flowers, shells or painted wooden stars, for example.

Other Indoor Locations

So you've given your pad fair consideration but have determined that it won't work for the party you have in mind. No need to panic or give up: there are plenty of other options. Do you have a friend with a great house? Does your neighborhood bistro have a back room for private parties? The following options will give you ideas that will help you tap into the resources around you.

A Friend's Home

A close friend has a fantastic dining room that will seat everyone, or a poolside setting that would be perfect for a sunset toast. The advantage is that it's free for the asking, but you'll need to take certain measures to ensure that your friend's generosity is received graciously. Make sure that any valuables are secure ahead of time (see Getting the House Party-Ready, page 42). It's also nice to offer to pay for a maid to come the day after the party, to restore the house to the condition you found it in. Another way to repay such generosity is with a thank-you gift: a shipment of fresh, seasonal fruit; an indulgent bottle of wine, presented after the party so it's off-limits to guests; a delivery of fresh flowers; or a gift certificate to a favorite store or spa. If you're on a tight budget, consider a homemade gift that your friend can enjoy the next morning, such as a pan of your famous cinnamon rolls or a bag of homemade granola.

Restaurants

While a service charge of up to 15% might apply and restaurant food will undoubtedly cost more than what you can make at home, entertaining at a restaurant can really take the stress out of a party — everything you need will be there already, so no scrambling for extra chairs or wineglasses. Plus, it makes for a nice change of venue for friends who don't get out as often as they'd like. To get the best deal, negotiate the price with the restaurant's special-events planner or catering manager before committing; they might offer less expensive menu options or allow you to bring your own wine. The day of the event, arrive in plenty of time to set up place cards, disposable cameras for documenting the evening and perhaps even small favors at each place setting — and to arrange for prepaid valet parking, if necessary.

Galleries

Many gallery owners are happy to rent their space out for events that might bring in future patrons; these spare, stylish settings also make the perfect venue for a cocktail party or any other meet-and-greet event that doesn't require a lot of seating. The size of the gallery, whether a tiny slice of a space or a cavernous loft, will dictate the size of the gathering you can pull off there. A cocktail hour held at a gallery is a great way to kick off an evening out on the town. You can privately toast the guest of honor before taking the party to a nearby concert, play, club or restaurant.

Coffee Houses

Does your town have a funky independent coffee house? These can be cozy settings, and can be made available for entertaining at the owner's discretion. For the best luck, try asking for a time that's after-hours, on an evening when the café is usually closed or on a night that's typically slow. Coffee houses are, naturally, great venues for a coffee and desserts party (hire one of the resident baristas). Consider this setting for a party celebrating your friend's new album or book, or first published poem. The evening's entertainment might include live music or poetry readings.

Country Clubs or Hotels

Country clubs allow members (and sometimes friends or family of members) to throw private parties in their facilities. Hotels, too, have a variety of settings that they make available for personal entertaining. While these options aren't cheap, they do offer a beautiful venue, often with picturesque grounds, elegant rooms and plenty of parking. Most will require the use of their on-site catering facilities and staff. While it will cost you, all that convenience can be very convincing.

Churches or Synagogues

Does your place of worship have a hall, complete with tables, chairs and a kitchen — not to mention plenty of free parking outside? Some churches even have a well-equipped activity center, game room or gym. Depending on the theme and scope of your event, it might be the perfect location for your party. Check with a worship hall administrator on the usual donation for such a rental, and run your party theme by him or her to make sure your intended use is okay. Common sense dictates that places of worship are fine for hosting the end-of-year Girl Scouts' potluck or a bridal tea, but not a bachelor party.

Other Outdoor Locations

Does your party theme call for the great outdoors but your backyard is less than great? When fair weather smiles on a host, there's no prettier setting for a casual gathering than a picture-perfect outdoor spot. Another advantage? Many outdoor locations are free, and taking the party there keeps the entertainment simple: When you're at a beautiful park with friends, what more do you need than a Frisbee? Consider the ideas below, as well as the one-of-a-kind offerings your area boasts.

Beaches

Public beaches are free for the taking and make a favorite location for their raw beauty and soothing ambiance. If you're heading there when the sun is high overhead, you'll need to plan for some shade for your guests — either set up a canopy ahead of time or ask your guests to bring any beach umbrellas they have. Be sure to scout out your spot a few hours ahead of time to secure a good location; for safety's sake, check with the lifeguard station for surf conditions and high-tide times. Bring plenty of sunscreen, bottled water and beach towels for your guests. For entertainment, pack Frisbees, kites, boogie boards and even a limbo setup. If you're hitting the sand near sunset, check with your local fire department ahead of time so you'll know the rules regarding alcohol and bonfires.

If a sink isn't readily available, keep Handi-Wipes or other towelettes handy so guests can keep their hands clean.

Parks

Not only are many parks free to the public, but many already have the basic necessities for an outside party: picnic tables and benches, bathrooms, trash cans, trees for shade and wide open spaces. Some even have barbecues for on-site cookouts. If your park doesn't operate on a reservations system, be sure to stake out your spot a couple of hours ahead of time. If children are included in the plans, try to choose a picnic area near playground equipment, which will offer young partygoers endless entertainment.

Rooftop

If your home address is a lot closer to the city center than it is to the wilderness, a rooftop party might be just the answer for taking your celebration outside. Some apartment buildings have rooftop garden areas for residents' use; check your building's rules and reservations requirements ahead of time, and familiarize yourself with any parameters regarding capacity and hours before you address those invitations.

Block Parties

Block parties are a great way to share the hosting responsibilities while celebrating warm-weather holidays (Memorial Day, the Fourth of July or Canada Day, for example) with the neighbors. The location (your neighborhood) is free, and it makes the

Kids on Location

Maybe the thought of a dozen five-year-olds partying at your place is just a little too daunting, or maybe a preschooler who spends a lot of time at home would be more excited to celebrate his birthday somewhere else. There are lots of compelling reasons to host a child's birthday party away from home, not the least of which is that many of these choices offer all-in-one deals where you pay one price for the location, food and entertainment (call your local outpost to check). If you have little ones to chase after, you'll appreciate the ease of such an option. Consider your child's age and interests first, then take inspiration from the following ideas for off-site party locations:

- Bowling alleys
- Zoos
- Children's museums or science museums
- Roller skating rinks
- Farms for pick-your-own seasonal fruit
- Kid-friendly restaurants (some also offer entertainment)
- Pottery or painting studios
- Kid-friendly spas or salons
- Movie theaters
- Inflatable bounce-house centers
- Miniature golf courses
- Parks or playgrounds (great for picnics)
- Kid-friendly gyms
- Kids' music class studios

logistics of setting up and taking down easy. A less tangible advantage is that such celebrations can bring communities closer together. Be sure to obtain any necessary permission (you might need a permit), and get together with the neighbors to divvy up responsibilities ahead of time. As block parties tend to be multigenerational events, you can also get older kids involved in planning games and other activities that the younger generation will enjoy. For name tags, shoot digital photos of each house on the street to go with each person's name, to help new or unacquainted neighbors put names, faces and houses together. Consider a combination of grilled and purchased food; for example, grill hamburgers and hot dogs and buy side dishes from a local deli or barbecue joint.

Botanical Gardens

Botanical gardens are gorgeous settings for anything from an impromptu picnic with friends to a painstakingly planned wedding. If your party leans more toward the formal, check well ahead of time for reservations and rules and to see what will be in bloom; off-season reservations are sometimes less expensive but still picturesque. Even if you're planning a casual picnic, it's good to know the ground rules. Call ahead to check on hours (many close at sunset) and to learn about any regulations regarding picnicking (such as whether alcohol is allowed).

Boats

Rent a boat to host a party on the water. If you live near the ocean, a major river or a large lake, chances are that a craft — whether a small yacht, a pontoon boat, a barge, a ferry or a riverboat — will be available for rent. Check with local marinas for information. Rentals range from permanently docked party boats to seagoing vessels. For the latter, there are some that you captain yourself and others that are rented out with a crew. If you plan to take your guests out on the water, be sure to check with them ahead of time to see if they're game, and have some motion sickness tablets or patches on hand.

Wineries

Consider entertaining at a winery if you're lucky enough to live near wine country. There are many, many wineries in the United States (in California, of course, but also from North Carolina to Washington, and from Ohio to Texas) and across Canada (especially in BC and Southern Ontario). A simple wine-tasting picnic on the grounds of a favorite local winery, with lush vines as the backdrop, can make for a super-easy and super-elegant afternoon party. If the winery has a tasting room, consider starting the party there, purchasing some of the group's favorite bottles. Then take the party outside for a picnic that includes plenty of cheeses, olives, breads and spreads to complement the vino.

Weather and Other Acts of God (Atheism Won't Help)

Imagine the following: Your party is in two days and your local meteorologist is breathless with breaking news about severe thunderstorms. Or the national park you love to picnic in is endangered by nearby forest fires. Or your town is under a flood warning as the usually mellow river swells to dangerous levels. Whatever the reason, things sometimes begin to look bad — very bad — for entertaining in that charming outdoor location you had in mind. That's why it's always a good idea to have a backup plan in place, just in case.

When You Need Security at a Private Party

For small gatherings at your home, say a dinner party for six, you shouldn't need any more security than you'd need on a daily basis. In many locations, that's none; in some, it might include the services of your building's doorman (or more likely, the services of your all-bark-and-no-bite retriever). But for larger parties with lots of coming and going, particularly in areas where all the activity at your house might invite unwanted interest, you may want to consider hiring a private security professional to work the door. He can check the guest list, keep an eye on the party's perimeter, make sure that departing guests get to their vehicles safely and discourage gate-crashers just by being there.

A simpler option is to enlist the help of a male friend or two to walk female guests to their cars as needed, particularly if they must park out of sight of your home.

For off-site events that have been announced in the local newspaper, such as weddings and funerals, it's a good idea to have someone, whether an acquaintance or a hired professional, stay behind at your home (with plenty of lights on and a car in the driveway) while you're hosting the event elsewhere. Unfortunately, criminals have been known to target a household after printed confirmation that the occupants will be away for several hours.

For parties that you hold off-site, whether at an art gallery, a restaurant or a hotel, the proprietor will be able to let you know what form of security is recommended. Discuss it ahead of time and make sure it's included in your contract.

Remember that a positive attitude is a must in these situations, so don't be a party pooper by complaining to guests about your luck. Instead, pique their interest by showing enthusiasm for any alternative plans you present. Here are a few ways you can be prepared, beyond praying for fair skies.

Bring in the Tents

You can buy or rent large tents to cover a portion of your backyard or another outdoor location. Tents can be expensive, but they can also be a lifesaver. They not only keep guests dry in case of rain, but also provide shade should the sun deign to appear. Have the number of a party supply rental company at the ready so you can call in the tents a day before if it's looking like you'll need them. Bear in mind that this option is great for protection against a light drizzle, but isn't recommended for major thunderstorms or blowing rains.

Designate a Backup Location

If the conditions for your outdoor party location are looking dubious, be sure that your home's public spaces are clean and ready to go. On short notice, for most smaller parties, your home will make the best backup plan. You can recreate a picnic theme inside with blankets and pillows on the floor, or you can drape the picnic blanket over your dining-room table and share the meal there. Have some alternative entertainment ideas in mind, such as board or card games instead of lawn games. Play up the coziness of your home, juxtaposed with the nasty weather outside, by lighting candles or starting a fire in your fireplace.

For other alternative locations, consider indoor spaces near your party's original spot. Many parks, for instance, have picnic shelters or club rooms that can be used in case of rain — reserve one ahead of time as insurance.

Set a Rain Date

If being outside is integral to your party, consider setting a rain date from the beginning and phoning guests (or sending an email or an e-vite notice) the day before to alert them if it's looking like the party will, indeed, need to be rescheduled. The downside is that by the time you make the call to postpone, you will likely have done all of the food and beverage shopping, and some of the food preparation. But if you're hosting a beach party for 20 and it doesn't make sense to move it to your studio apartment, then a rain date might be the best option. Seal any breads, cookies or meat for the party in airtight containers and freeze. Most cheeses, especially if unopened in their original packaging, will keep in the refrigerator for a couple of weeks.

Refocus Your Theme

Late-breaking current events can sometimes make a party that was planned earlier seem indulgent or out of touch. When a major natural or political disaster hits close to home, whether geographically or emotionally, consider shifting your gathering's theme from picnic in the park to up-to-the-minute concerned citizens. You can have partygoers bring canned goods or clothing to donate, or use the gathering as a time to organize: while you're drinking, eating and visiting, you can also write letters, make out lists of supplies that are needed or plot out some volunteer days that your group of friends can participate in together.

Layers of Wedding Cake

I'm not sure how actress Tracy Nelson found California Celebrations; I just remember that she was darling, tiny and so excited to be getting married. I had been the executive chef of the catering company for one year. She was marrying "Billy" from *Falcon Crest*. I can't remember if that was his character's name or his real name, and it doesn't matter — the union would be a fabulous, prime-time television–worthy special. And it was smack-dab in the 80s, when people still had money, shoulder pads and big hair.

After one meeting, I knew that Tracy had a very clear vision for her wedding. She had rented Catalina Island's Wrigley Mansion, a stately old manor with spectacular views of the harbor. It had become a fancy Victorian bed and breakfast, renamed The Inn on Mt. Ada. The mansion had been built around the turn of the century by the chewing gum tycoon.

Tracy had rented the entire mansion for the weekend, plus two big, plush yachts to take her guests back and forth from the mainland. Jacob Marse of Pasadena was the florist, I had rented antique silver, and Battenberg lace was everywhere. I got it: Tracy was to be a princess — no problem. Most days, sapphire blue water surrounds Catalina. It's as exotic as Capri. I was thrilled to have passed muster in the interview and to be her chef and caterer.

Innumerable lists were made, and weeks of preparation went into every detail. Ferrying the guests back and forth on the yachts, on time, became a military operation. Guests' shoes would have to be changed and carried from the yacht to the inn. Food and drinks were to be served the moment guests hit the decks, and then again as they arrived at the wedding. On the return trip, cookies and coffee would be served. All in all, guests would be in for about an 18-hour day. For the staff, it was twice that.

My true concern was the food. As it turned out, the local purveyors simply couldn't meet the demands of the ultra-gourmet menu. The shrimp, filet mignon, wild rice, caviar, handmade appetizers — all of it — would come from my commissary and be sent by barge to the island. The barge charged my kitchen by the pound. The thought of my expensive food for 150 guests bobbing in the hot sun and on the wild waves for an entire day was nerve-wracking, to say the least. Thank goodness for wine. I should also mention that there are almost no private cars on Catalina — just a few cabs and one patrol car. Once my 1,000 pounds of food landed, it had to be carted up the hill to the mansion. Eventually, I found a truck that belonged to the Department of the Interior, and the inn hired the ranger and his rig to transport the food. My sous-chef rode with the food the entire way from my kitchen to the back door of the inn, as its escort. She made sure the coolers stayed cool. She was armed with her knives in case of a holdup. I'm not kidding: I told her to guard the food with her life.

So, once I said bon voyage to my cases and cases of food, my coffin-sized coolers, my copper pots and pans, my sous-chef and my carefully packed silver trays, I assumed the worst was over. Ignorance is bliss.

The next morning, at 6:00 a.m., I arrived at the helicopter pad to take my 27-mile ride across the sea to Catalina. It was a glorious morning. I had nothing to fear. I had planned everything and it was perfect. As I approached the helicopter, the whirling blades drowned out everything. I didn't hear the baker call out to me. I will never know what made me turn and see the screaming, frantic wedding cake baker and the endless layers of wedding cake. I couldn't understand: the baker and the cake were supposed to ride that morning on a shuttle boat, but the baker hadn't booked a reservation and it was the middle of summer, when literally thousands of tourists visit Catalina on a daily basis. There wasn't a seat to be had.

I ran over to her. She apologized profusely, but wondered if I could carry the cake for her on the helicopter. I would have strangled her, but she had already shoved the bottom layer of the cake into my hands. I walked back to the helicopter, where the perplexed pilot and three other passengers, whom I had never met, were waiting. I handed off the big, heavy bottom layer to the older man in the back seat. And one by one I carried the layers from the baker to another of the passengers. I never said a word to anyone. I think my silence and the pale pink rose petals said it all. Though it's a quick ride, you'd be amazed how long it feels in utter silence.

A cab was waiting for me at the Catalina heliport. I took each layer of cake from each dear stranger's arms and smiled sweetly.

To this day — it doesn't matter whether I'm having a party for 6 or 60 — I never have the dessert delivered. I like to pick it up the day before my party and peek at it in my refrigerator every chance I get.

Decor

So you have a French country theme in mind for your party, and you'll be holding a seated dinner at your dining-room table. What's the difference between a dining room being used for homework and one being used to entertain your favorite francophiles? In a word, decor. That's how you give your location ambiance and elevate it from the everyday to the special-occasion.

The location you've chosen is itself a major factor in decor, as it provides the setting you'll need to work with. Your chosen theme can then help guide all of your decor-related decisions, including lighting; tabletop items such as linens, flatware and glassware; flowers and other centerpieces; and even party favors.

As you plot out how to execute your theme in your chosen location, assess the elements of the location that already work well for your party and play those up — it's a lot easier to work *with* your location than to completely overhaul it. Next, consider what you can add to the location to help set the mood for the party. The ambiance you create will give your guests a lasting impression. Use some of these design basics to get started.

Declutter

Removing extraneous items (textbooks, piles of mail) is the first step to decorating your space, as it eliminates unsightly distractions that would take away from the impact of your decor. Also rethink any collections that cover a surface such as a console table or a mantle. Interior designers suggest leaving out only a few items, storing the rest and changing out the items seasonally. The pieces that remain will have a better showcase, so they can be better admired. (Bonus: with clear surfaces, you'll also have more room for serving food and drinks.)

Determine the Focal Point

Every room needs a focal point, whether it's a fireplace, a picture window that offers a stunning view or a dining table and glittering chandelier that anchor the space. Rearrange furniture to make sure the focal point is clear (does the couch face the TV or the fireplace?), and your room will begin to come into focus. A large area rug can also do wonders for pulling together a space.

Form Follows Function

Don't lose sight of the point of your party: keep function in mind first, especially with smaller spaces. For instance, if you'll need the bulk of your table for place settings and platters of food, you'll want to choose a compact centerpiece that won't crowd things too much, such as several small vases of fresh flowers and herbs in lieu of a giant flower display, or small votives in diminutive candle holders spaced along the table runner in lieu of a large candelabrum.

Place side chairs in groupings of two or more to encourage conversation.

A Balanced Approach

A room can sometimes look a little out of whack: a grand piano on one end of the room and a blank wall on the other, for instance. This is where balance comes into play. Making sure that a room doesn't feel too heavy on one end can contribute to its overall ambiance, creating a well-proportioned, calm feel. To add balance to rooms, interior designers sometimes add pairs of items — whether sconces, lamps or chairs — to promote a pleasing symmetrical feel.

Color Your World

Pairing complementary colors (those that are opposite on a color wheel) is a surefire way to make a bold statement. Artists and graphic designers have long worked with such color combinations — red and green, blue and orange, yellow and purple. When choosing the colors for your party, make sure they will go with the colors already present in your location (the paint on the wall, the rug on the floor). You might choose one color that complements the location's existing scheme, or a single metallic, such as silver or gold, for an elegant accent.

First Impressions

Have you ever shown up for a party only to find the front porch dark and the morning newspaper still in the front yard? I have, and I always wonder if I have the right house and the right date. Just ringing the doorbell feels like a bit of a gamble. With all the attention you give to your party's exact location (the dining room, for instance), it's easy to forget that your guests won't be magically transported to the scene. Trust me: they will have to enter the old-fashioned way, through the front door. That's why it's important to give a little attention to your front walkway, front yard, porch and entryway in addition to making your dining room magazine-worthy. Here are some ways to make a great first impression:

- **Clear the path.** Sweep the front walkway, porch and any steps, and shake out the welcome mat. Mow and edge or rake the front lawn, if necessary. In case of rain or snow, provide an umbrella stand in a covered area. For safety, be sure to clean up any ice or snow blocking entry to your house and sprinkle the walk with de-icer or rock salt to prevent any moisture from freezing as temperatures drop throughout the evening.

- **Turn on exterior lighting.** If you have landscape lighting, use it. At the very least, make sure the light bulbs are working in any front porch fixtures, and keep them on for the duration of the party. You can also buy a plug-in exterior spotlight to illuminate a point of interest in your front yard, or simply the front door.

- **Add a splash of green.** Flowering plants or potted evergreen shrubs on both sides of the entrance can improve the look of your house dramatically, and for relatively little cost.

- **Decorate the front door.** An existing wreath can be accented with wired pine cones, baby rattles, team colors or any other theme-related decor. Coordinating front door decor with your party theme lets guests know immediately that they have the right place and date. At the very least, keep your front door decor up to date with the season.

- **Create a coat check area.** Once inside, people will need a place to put their coats (depending on the season) and other personal belongings, such as purses. For a small party, clear out a portion of your coat closet, leaving plenty of empty hangers for your guests. For larger parties, designate a bedroom as the coat area, making sure it is clean and tidy, with adequate lighting, so guests can find their things as they need them. Enlist the help of an older child: taking coats is a great task for budding hosts.

- **Lead guests in the right direction.** Once your guests are inside and their items stashed, it's time for them to join the party. If the party area isn't immediately inside your front door, create an attractive and well-lit pathway through your home to the celebration, with flowers, lit sconces or other festive touches along the way.

Ambiance

Some elements of setting the scene aren't highly visible, but they're critical, nonetheless. Guests distracted by too-bright lighting, grating music or warmer-than-comfortable temperatures won't be in the right state of mind to appreciate the unforgettable food and scintillating conversation that awaits them. For that reason, it's a good idea to think about the less visible elements of setting the scene as well as the more tangible ones — and ahead of time.

Lighting

The lighting you choose depends on your party theme, guests and any planned activities. There's nothing more flattering than candlelight; for an adults-only dinner party, dim the chandelier and light some candles on the table and in any wall sconces. Low, sexy lights make guests look (and more importantly, feel) more attractive — and as a result, such lighting can encourage conversation and flirtation, making the party more fun for everyone. Any harsh overhead lighting, such as the fluorescent lights some kitchens have, should be turned off in favor of under-counter lights and pendant lights.

Battery- and solar-powered lights come in all shapes and sizes, so you can have lanterns and candles without the danger of flames or a mess of wires and plugs.

For a child's birthday party, you'll generally want to keep the lights much higher in areas where there will be eating or games, as doing so can help prevent accidents.

Noise

You know how some industrial-chic, open-concept restaurants are *so* loud — whether with pulsing music or clattering dishes — that older folks (and even some younger ones) have a hard time hearing the conversation? Contrast that with old-school restaurants that have flowing curtains, light background music and cushy, upholstered seating: the conversations are lower and less challenging. Keep these models in mind when planning your own party. There's nothing louder than a space with all tile or hardwood flooring and no fabric, where sound bounces endlessly back and forth. Add some textiles, such as curtains, upholstered furniture, floor pillows or area rugs, and you'll notice how much more sound is absorbed. Design your party area with comfort and conversation in mind. Any music selections should follow the theme and guest list. If you hear guests repeating themselves or raising their voices, it's a good indication that you should adjust the volume of the music or close the door to a clattery kitchen.

Room Temperature

The thermostat is set to 75°F (24°C), which seems perfect — until you add 20 warm bodies to the room. One of my friends from the northeast was astounded the first year she held a Christmas party in her new home in Texas and had to turn the air conditioning on halfway through the festivities. At the beginning of the party, if you're expecting a crowd, you'll probably want to set the thermostat a few degrees cooler than you think necessary. Later on, you can make any necessary adjustments, no matter how unseasonable they seem. If you're getting hot under the collar, you can assume that your guests are too. Keep in mind that open windows can help pull hot air out and that a fire in the fireplace will affect room temperatures in different ways, warming up the room that the fireplace is in, but possibly tricking a nearby thermostat into thinking the entire house is warmer than it actually is. Think about your home's heating and cooling idiosyncrasies — and the party's location within your floor plan — and strategize accordingly. For outdoor parties, portable heaters or cooling misters can be rented to make guests more comfortable.

Linens

Linens can instantly give your tabletop a completely new look. It's typically much less expensive to buy a new tablecloth or a colorful set of napkins to fit your party theme than it is to purchase alternative sets of china or flatware, so linens are a great way to mix up the look for less.

While a white linen tablecloth and a set of coordinating napkins is customary for formal entertaining, for most parties, the quality of your linens doesn't matter quite as much as what you do with them. Every host should have a set of neutral table linens in white, cream or tan; those will serve as a great foundation for more festive additions, such as napkins or a colorful table runner that coordinate with the theme. Consider accents that will seem hand-picked for your party, such as bamboo mats for a Chinese-themed dinner party or a team flag for a game-day gathering's buffet table.

If you plan to purchase only one set of linens, choose a machine-washable 100% cotton fabric, and select a color that's less likely to fade with repeated washings, avoiding very dark colors like black or navy, which will fade the fastest. If you're looking to round out a collection of linens, adding more colors to the mix, shop for discounted linens toward the end of each season; red linens marketed for Christmas work just as well for Valentine's Day, and soft pastels sold at Easter can be used all spring and summer. Check the sale bins in your favorite kitchen goods stores and discount stores. You can also purchase used linens on eBay or craigslist, borrow them from a friend or relative, or rent them from a party supply rental company. See the chart on page 64 for help choosing the right size linens for your table.

No matter what you paid for your linens, the expertise with which they're ironed will determine how good they look. At least two days before the party (so you'll be ready to set the table a day ahead), use a spray bottle to liberally spritz your clean linens with water. Roll them up, place them in a plastic bag and refrigerate overnight. (A friend learned this trick from her mother, a Southerner; indeed, ironing damp, cool linens goes a lot faster, and with smoother results.) When it's time to iron, use spray starch for extra crispness and set your iron to whatever setting the linens' care label calls for. Iron light colors on the wrong side first, then on the right side; iron darker linens only on the wrong side. For a tablecloth, set up the ironing board near your dining table, so it can be directly transferred as you finish sections. Loosely fold ironed napkins until you're ready to finish setting the table.

To make entertaining easier the next time, it's best to wash and iron your linens immediately after the party, hanging them on a padded pants hanger inside a plastic bag for storage. When you need them, you'll only have to lightly press out any creases and they'll be party-ready.

One way to perk up table settings without spending a dime is to learn some neat napkin folds that elevate simple squares of cotton cloth to new heights — and new shapes. See the diagram on page 65 for six new folds you can teach yourself in no time.

Sizing Up Your Linens

The size of the tablecloth you'll need depends on your table, naturally, so have a few measurements in hand before you hit the stores. If you're using folding tables or other unsightly stand-ins that you want to drape completely, you'll need floor-length tablecloths. If you're setting the dining-room table or another table with pretty legs, you'll want a 10- to 14-inch (25 to 35 cm) drop around the table's perimeter, which means adding 20 to 28 inches (50 to 70 cm) to the diameter of a round tabletop or to the length and width of a square, rectangular or oval tablecloth.

Dinner napkins are (very roughly) about 18 inches (45 cm) square — larger than you might think, because they'll be folded. Cocktail or luncheon napkins can range from 6 inches (15 cm) square to nearly 12 inches (30 cm) square; the smallest ones act pretty much as coasters for cocktails, while luncheon napkins are simply smaller versions of dinner napkins.

Tablecloth Sizing

Round Tables		
Diameter of Table	**Guests**	**Tablecloth Size**
36 to 48 inches (90 to 120 cm)	4	60 inches (150 cm)
46 to 58 inches (115 to 145 cm)	6	70 inches (175 cm)
64 to 76 inches (160 to 190 cm)	8 to 10	90 inches (225 cm)
Rectangular Tables		
Length and Width of Table	**Guests**	**Tablecloth Size**
36 x 78 inches to 48 x 90 inches (90 x 195 cm to 120 x 225 cm)	6 to 10	60 x 102 inches (150 x 255 cm)
36 x 96 inches to 48 x 108 inches (90 x 240 cm to 120 x 270 cm)	8 to 12	60 x 120 inches (150 x 300 cm)
Square Tables		
Dimensions of Table	**Guests**	**Tablecloth Size**
28 x 28 inches to 40 x 40 inches (70 x 70 cm to 100 x 100 cm)	4	60 x 60 inches (150 x 150 cm)
Oval Tables		
Length and Width	**Guests**	**Tablecloth Size**
28 x 46 inches to 40 x 58 inches (70 x 115 cm to 100 x 145 cm)	4 to 6	52 x 70 inches (130 x 175 cm)
36 x 58 inches to 48 x 70 inches (90 x 145 cm to 120 x 175 cm)	6 to 8	60 x 84 inches (150 x 210 cm)
36 x 78 inches to 48 x 90 inches (90 x 195 cm to 120 x 225 cm)	8 to 10	60 x 102 inches (150 x 255 cm)
36 x 96 inches to 48 x 108 inches (90 x 240 cm to 120 x 270 cm)	12 to 14	60 x 120 inches (150 x 300 cm)

Six New Napkin Folds

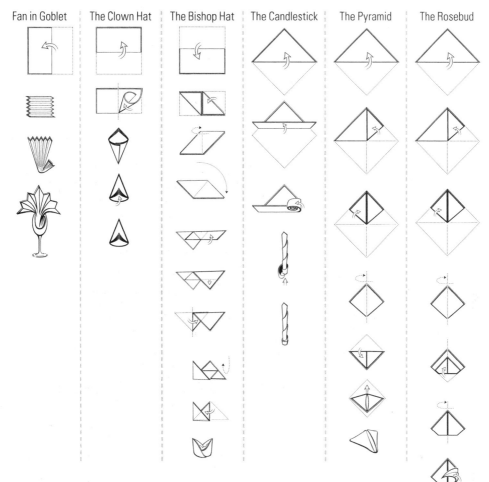

Fan in Goblet | The Clown Hat | The Bishop Hat | The Candlestick | The Pyramid | The Rosebud

China, Flatware and Glassware

Unless you're a bride-to-be planning a post-nuptial gathering, you'll probably have to work largely with what you have in terms of china, flatware and glassware. (If you *are* a bride-to-be, take this opportunity to register for 12 place settings in each of two china patterns that can be used together: one more neutral and one more decorative. That way, when you have larger dinner parties, you can put the two together for up to 24 place settings.)

Even if you have the budget for it (and most of us don't), buying china, flatware and glassware to match each party theme you dream up just wouldn't be practical — that's a lot to store and care for, after all. Fortunately, there are many ways you can perk up your existing place settings for a variety of uses.

Rental IQ

While renting party supplies costs a lot less than buying them, it can still take a bite out of your budget. If you have to rent tables, chairs, linens, china, flatware and glassware for your party, expect to pay at least $15 per person to do so. But don't take my word on the $15 figure: prices for party rentals vary dramatically depending on your area and needs, so do the research before deciding whether rentals make sense this time around. Look up "party rentals" in the Yellow Pages and get a few quotes. Also keep in mind that the price of oil has affected delivery fees, so be sure to include that cost if you need your rentals delivered. Nearby companies are the best places to start, because they should charge less for delivery than those farther away. Compare the final figure with what it would cost to host the party elsewhere — sometimes a "free" location isn't really free.

For planning purposes, you should also find out the company's hours of operation (some are closed on Sundays, meaning the goods for a Saturday night party might be parked at your house until Monday morning), contact information (will you be able to reach someone for after-hours emergencies, such as the need to add a tent for inclement weather?) and insurance coverage (who is responsible if there's damage to any of the rentals?). The pros will also lead you through other location-specific questions, such as whether you'll want to rent a dance floor.

Here are some ideas for keeping rental costs in check for your party:

- **Forgo delivery, setup and pickup.** Make sure you're clear on what the proposed rental fee includes; all details should be specified in your rental agreement. If the fee includes delivery, setup and pickup, you might be able to shave off some of the price by doing these things yourself — providing you have the right vehicle and a helper.

- **Streamline the details.** Look at the suggested rentals and see where you can cut costs. Maybe you can choose a plainer style of chairs or linens (plain white or cream can make an elegant backdrop that doesn't compete with fresh flowers or other colorful centerpieces). Maybe you can use a table or two of your own instead of renting all of them. Also, look for any extra items included in the pricing, such as trash bags, that you can purchase for less on your own.

- **Check out the competition.** Once you've trimmed your list down to the basic necessities for your party, get quotes from another rental company or two. You can ask your favorite business if they can match a competitor's price — most will.

- **Know company policies.** Make sure you know the company's payment, reservation and cancellation policies so you don't lose your deposit if you change your mind.

Purchase Chargers

Choose silver or gold metallic chargers (consider which one coordinates the best with your existing china) and use them in lieu of placemats, either atop the tablecloth or on a bare table. Silver or gold chargers add instant elegance to your china, they can be used in any season, they're inexpensive (look for them at stores like Target or Zellers) and they take up very little room on the table. I've seen hosts use chargers under everything from multicolored pottery to bone china, and they always elevate the look to special-occasion.

Get Creative with Crafting Supplies

Instead of traditional placemats or chargers, use a colorful 12-inch (30 cm) square sheet of scrapbooking paper (available in craft stores and at Target) underneath each place setting. With the wide variety of colors and designs available, many of them quite elegant, you'll be able to find something that complements your unique theme and color palette.

Buy, Borrow or Rent New Salad or Dessert Plates

If your china is neutral enough, you can successfully pair it with something new. Try sourcing some small plates that can serve as salad or dessert plates in a great new pattern that coordinates with what you already have, and you'll get a whole new look for less. Anthropologie (www.anthropologie.com) often has a selection of interesting and affordable salad and dessert plates that mix and match well. If the china you already have is ornate, choose plates in a solid color to coordinate with it; for a modern look, consider alternative shapes, such as square or oval.

Bring Out the Good Silver

It's easy to get into a rut with flatware. You probably use the same stainless set every day because it's in an easy-to-reach spot in the kitchen, it won't tarnish (so you don't have to polish it) and if a piece finds its way out the door with your spouse's lunch or into your child's sandbox, it's not the end of the world. But at party time, think about what you might have stashed deep in the reaches of your china cabinet. If you're lucky, you might have your own set of silver, or even your grandma's set. If you've got it, pull it out: it's elegant, sentimental and special.

If someone else was willed the family silver, now's a good time to borrow it.

Mix and Match Your Glassware

Heavy-duty plastic and acrylic glasses made for outdoor use are an inexpensive and attractive alternative to real glassware.

If you have a great set of crystal wineglasses, then by all means use them. You can dress them up with whimsical wine charms as simple as short lengths of ribbon that coordinate with your party theme and help guests keep track of which glass is theirs. But if you're looking for a change of place setting, consider this: I have a friend who refuses to pay more than $1 for a wineglass, because in her family they break too often. Follow her lead and look for interesting shapes of wineglasses at garage sales, estate sales and thrift stores — if the glass is not part of a large set, so much the better. If each guest has a one-of-a-kind wineglass, it's easy to remember whose is whose, and it's also a lot less upsetting if such a glass breaks: it wasn't expensive, and it wasn't part of a set. For a unified look, stick to clear glasses instead of those with hues.

Centerpieces

The centerpiece is probably the largest element of decor on your table — and it's the one that most says celebration. We use plates at every meal, but how many of us have a centerpiece on the table for a typical family dinner? Because of its placement and importance, the centerpiece should be given special consideration. It should be highly visible, of course, but not too large: guests should be able to see each other over it at a seated dinner, for instance. The centerpiece is critical in pulling together the party's overall look and theme, so it needs to coordinate with the rest of the decor, including any side arrangements.

Flowers make a traditional and attractive centerpiece (see page 69 for details on flowers for the party). Party favors can also double as centerpieces (for ideas, see page 75). Here are some other centerpiece ideas:

- Arrange fruits, vegetables or breads in an attractive basket. This edible display can be eaten in the week following the party, making it both economical and earth-friendly (use any stale bread left over from your display to make French toast, strata or bread pudding). For a lush look, combine a variety of shapes, textures and colors that complement your theme or menu. Depending on the season, consider pomegranates, pears, gourds, pumpkins, melons, heirloom tomatoes, asparagus, lemons, limes, tangerines, coconuts or bananas. Visit specialty or farmers' markets for unusual varieties that will add more interest to the table. A monochromatic look (all red or all green, for example) can also make a dramatic statement.

- Nothing beats candlelight for flattering lighting — it's no wonder that candles set a romantic, intimate mood for a gathering. Purchase floating candles to place in a bowl filled with water; use that antique candelabrum your grandma left you; set pillar candles of varying heights along a long, narrow tray lined with pressed fall leaves or parchment leaves from a kitchen supply or party store; or create three groupings of candlesticks of varying heights and fit them with long, lean taper candles in a coordinating color.

- Use coffee beans, river rocks or marbles to fill a shallow bowl, square vase or footed candy dish and nestle flower blossoms or tea light candles inside. Coffee beans give off a rich, appetizing aroma; river rocks lend a calm, cool, Zen-like feel to the table; and marbles have a luminescent look and come in a variety of colors to coordinate with any theme.

- Collect organics from the great outdoors. Your backyard might have all you need for an earthy (and free) centerpiece arrangement: cut branches, acorns, nuts, leaves, pine cones. The items can be arranged in bowls or vases, and can be left in their natural state or embellished. A brush of glitter gives earthy elements some holiday sparkle, while spray-painting them silver or gold lends elegance.

Place votive or small pillar candles in an assortment of stemmed glassware of different shapes and sizes. Group them together for a beautiful, sparkly centerpiece.

Flowers

Fresh flowers, whether cut or potted, add color, fragrance and beauty to your decor and make for an especially attractive centerpiece. Flowers, in fact, are very flexible: they can be selected and arranged to suit themes indoors or out, formal or casual, big-budget or thrifty, whimsical or traditional. In addition to using floral centerpieces, many hosts also use coordinating flower arrangements as accent pieces on side tables, in wall vases or even floating in the backyard pool.

Using flowers as the centerpiece doesn't have to mean sticking to the traditional large single arrangement. In fact, for some themes and some tables, it might make a lot more sense to go for a form that saves space or coordinates better with the party's look. Consider using several small flower arrangements, a garland that winds its way down the center of the table or single blossoms floating in clear bowls. Flowers can be combined with myriad other elements — fruit, twinkle lights, autumn leaves, greenery — to make a one-of-a-kind centerpiece that suits the season and theme of the party perfectly.

Pretty potted flowering plants, such as hyacinths, azaleas and chrysanthemums, make an attractive alternative to cut flowers. The advantages are that you can purchase them up to a week ahead, use them on your table for the party and then replant them in your yard after the event. For the party, place potted plants in an attractive container (a simple terracotta pot or a pretty piece of pottery) that's slightly larger than the plastic pot they came in.

Using a Florist

If you don't trust yourself with flower arranging (or sense that you already have your hands full with other party tasks) but *do* want a floral centerpiece or multiple arrangements, there are plenty of professionals who'd be happy to step in. If you decide to work with a florist, it makes sense to select someone whose sense of style meshes well with your own and who seems open to applying his or her expertise to the unique occasion you have in mind, for custom (rather than prefabricated) results. Be upfront and detailed about your ideas, naming specific flowers you have in mind and sharing pictures of arrangements you especially like. Use the flower seasonality guide (page 72) as a starting point, so that your choices will be in season — meaning they should be abundantly available and also (hopefully) less expensive.

Do-It-Yourself Flower Arranging

If you don't mind taking the time and summoning the creativity to design and put together your own floral arrangements, you'll save a bit of money and will have complete control over the outcome. Here are some tips for do-it-yourself flower arranging:

● Plan to arrange the flowers the day before the party and store them in a cool place overnight to keep them at their freshest.

- Incorporate flowers, herbs, leaves and other organic elements you have growing on your property — or visit a farmers' market for locally grown, freshly cut flowers.
- Remove any foliage that will be underwater and cut stems on an angle, trimming at least 1 inch (2.5 cm) from the bottom of the stem. To avoid crushing the stems, cut flowers one at a time, placing each stem in water immediately after cutting it.
- Use warm water and add fresh-cut flower food (from the florist) or a little bit of sugar to keep flowers fresher for longer.
- Place chicken wire across the mouth of the vase to hold stems in place. Conceal it with part of the arrangement or with decorative ribbon.
- Keep it low: short arrangements are easier to make than tall ones — and for seated dinners, they're also easier to see over, which makes for better conversation.
- If you're a beginner, go for a monochromatic look, choosing a single type of flower in one color, such as white roses or purple irises. Even inexpensive carnations are impressive when several are bunched together into a tightly bound puff.
- For an airy, open look, gently peel back the petals of tulips or roses (or try blowing on them to encourage them to open on their own).
- If you have only a few flowers to work with, use a clear vase or container with a narrow neck and a wide base, or fill a wider-mouthed glass vase with pebbles, marbles or fruit (cranberries or wedges of lemons or lime, for example) to help keep the flowers in place *and* add color and texture to the look.

> Dendrobium orchids are relatively inexpensive and come in white, lavender, purple and deep pink. They last for days and are beautiful all alone. Place five to six stems in a tall vase for a spectacular arrangement. If you need something bigger, place more stems in a bigger vase. But resist the urge to overdo it!

Pulling the Look Together

You've chosen your linens, china, tabletop accessories, centerpiece and flowers. Now it's time to pull the look together. Set the table or set up the buffet at least one day before the party, complete with linens, china, flatware and glassware. Consult the illustrations on page 74 for help with both casual and formal dinner settings. And remember this rule of thumb: place flatware in the order it will be used, starting from the outside and working your way in. If your centerpiece is not floral, you can place it on the table now too; if it is, you'll want to keep it cool until the day of the party. If you have a cat that's likely to walk on the table, hold off on the wineglasses and cover the rest of it with a clean bed sheet until party time.

Flower Seasonality Guide

Name of Flower	Colors
Spring	
Anemone	White, pink, red, purple
Baby's breath	White
Bachelor's button	White, pink, red, blue
Bells of Ireland	Green
Boronia	Pink
Calla lily	White, yellow
Calla lily, mini	Most colors
Carnations	Most colors
Casablanca lily	White
Daffodil	Yellow
Delphinium	White, blue
Gardenia	White
Gladiolus	Many colors
Heather	Pink
Hyacinth	White, pink, purple
Lilac	White, violet
Lily of the valley	White, pink
Narcissus	White
Orchid	Most colors
Peony	White, pink
Protea	Pink
Ranunculus	White, pink, orange, red, yellow
Rose	Most colors
Scabiosa	White, pink, purple
Stargazer lily	White, pink
Sweetpea	White, pink, red, peach, purple
Tulip	Most colors
Waxflower	White, pink
Summer	
Alstromeria	White, pink, yellow, orange
Aster	White, pink, purple
Baby's breath	White

Name of Flower	Colors
Summer	
Bachelor's button	White, pink, red, blue
Bells of Ireland	Green
Calla lily	White, yellow
Calla lily, mini	Most colors
Carnations	Most colors
Chrysanthemum	White, pink, yellow, orange
Cockscomb	Pink, yellow, red, green
Columbine	White, pink, yellow, orange, red, purple
Delphinium	White, purple, blue
Lavender	Purple
Forget-me-not	Blue
Freesia	White, pink, yellow, blue, purple
Gardenia	White
Gladiolus	Many colors
Gerbera daisy	White, pink, yellow, orange, red
Heather	Pink
Hydrangea	White, pink, purple, blue
Iris	White, purple, blue
Larkspur	White, pink, purple, blue
Liatris	Pink, purple
Lily	White, pink, yellow, orange
Lily of the valley	White, pink
Lisianthus	White, pink, purple
Orchid	Most colors
Protea	Pink
Queen Anne's lace	White
Rose	Most colors
Scabiosa	White, pink, purple
Snapdragons	White, pink, yellow, orange

Name of Flower	Colors
Summer	
Solidaster	Yellow
Statice	Purple, white
Stephanotis	White
Sunflower	Yellow, orange
Tuberose	White
Yarrow	White, pink, yellow
Zinnia	Pink, red, orange
Fall	
Aster	White, pink
Baby's breath	White
Bachelor's button	White, pink, red, blue
Cabbage, ornamental	White, pink, purple, green
Calla lily	White, yellow
Calla lily, mini	Most colors
Carnations	Most colors
Chrysanthemum	White, pink, yellow, orange
Dahlia	Most colors
Delphinium	White, purple, blue
Gardenia	White
Gladiolus	Many colors
Heather	Pink, lavendar
Lily of the valley	White, pink
Orchid	Most colors
Protea	Pink
Marigold	Yellow, red, orange
Rose	Most colors
Scabiosa	White, pink, purple
Statice	Purple, white
Zinnia	Pink, red, orange
Winter	
Amaryllis	White, pink, red
Anemone	White, pink, red, blue
Baby's breath	White

Name of Flower	Colors
Winter	
Bachelor's button	White, pink, red, blue
Bells of Ireland	Green
Calla lily	White, yellow
Calla lily, mini	Most colors
Camellia	White, pink
Carnations	Most colors
Casablanca lily	White
Cosmos	White, pink, yellow, orange
Daffodil	Yellow
Delphinium	White, purple, blue
Dogwood	White, yellow
Forget-me-not	Blue, pink
Gardenia	White
Gladiolus	Many colors
Heather	Pink
Holly	Green, red berries
Jasmine	White
Lily of the valley	White, pink
Narcissus	White, yellow
Nurine lily	White, pink, purple
Orchid	Most colors
Poinsettia	White, pink, red
Protea	Pink
Ranunculus	White, pink, red, orange, yellow
Rose	Most colors
Scabiosa	White, pink, purple
Stargazer lily	White, pink
Star of Bethlehem	White
Sweetpea	White, pink, red, purple
Tulip	Most colors
Waxflower	White, pink

Decor • Pulling the Look Together

Setting up a day ahead will prevent you from forgetting anything crucial that could add to last-minute mayhem, such as ironing table linens, polishing tarnished silver or rinsing out dusty wineglasses. During your last-minute preparations, you'll thank yourself for having a pristine table ready and waiting for the food, whether you're hosting a sit-down dinner or a more casual buffet meal.

While you're setting the table, take the opportunity to add a few details that give it a truly customized feel. I think of these as dressmaker details: the unexpected personal touches that can elevate a standard party to something truly memorable.

Formal Dinner Setting

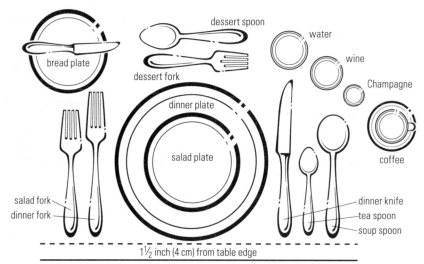

Casual Dinner Setting

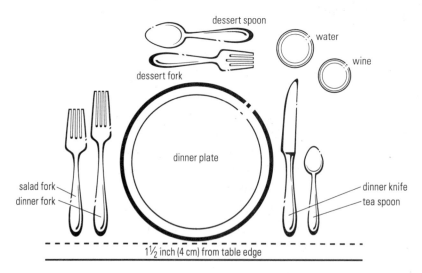

Here are some simple ways to set the scene:

- Use place cards. Creative hosts might like to make their own, but there are also many interesting place cards commercially available (visit www.crane.com or www.myownlabels.com). Find or create a pattern that complements the look you're going for, and use personalized place cards to dress up the table — and to make your guests feel special. Don't toss place cards at the end of the evening; you'll likely have the same folks gathered around your table again, so put the cards in the china cabinet so you'll have them for next time. Or create take-home place cards that double as favors: a small framed photo of each guest or a small potted herb with the guest's name written on the pot in chalk (for more ideas, see "Party Favors," below).

- Add charms to the wineglasses at each place setting. Not only is this practical (it eliminates confusion about which glass is whose once guests leave the table), but whimsical charms can add an element of entertainment as well, as guests realize which charm they were assigned — and why. Wineglass charms are available to coordinate with many a party theme, and they're also easy to make yourself: directions are available on a number of websites. Purchase charm rings (sometimes called hoop rings) at craft stores and attach to them any number of trinkets: large or small beads, jingle bells or pewter charms in a variety of shapes. The key is that they coordinate with each other but each one is different.

> For the most casual of parties, consider the low-cost alternative: plastic or paper cups and markers so guests can write their names on their cups.

Party Favors

Since the Renaissance, marrying couples of means (and generosity) have been giving their guests party favors, but any third-grader can tell you that party favors are always welcome at a party, from kids' birthdays to grownup dinners. Some fancy restaurants even send their guests home with a jar of house-made jam, a printed menu from the evening or a box of candies from the chef. The point? Such small gifts let guests know that their presence was anticipated and appreciated, and they also serve as a memento of the occasion — it makes the fun last just a little longer. Party favors aren't a requirement, but who doesn't love a present?

Party favors become part of the decor, so it's important to match them to the overall theme of your event. Especially attractive favors can even do double duty as your centerpiece. While looks are important, it's also thoughtful to choose something that your guests can actually use. (It's anyone's guess how many children's birthday party "goody bags" wind up in the trash.) Consider gifts that can be used up, such as candles or candies, or gifts that your guests will continue to enjoy, such as potted herbs or recipes.

The easiest way to present favors is to arrange them at each place setting, but if your party doesn't involve place settings, you can set a large basket of parting gifts, with name tags on them, in a visible location near the door and enlist the help of a friend to make sure departing friends know to take one. For larger parties, ask a friend to serve as "exit hostess" to pass out favors as guests leave or, if you have valet service, ask the valet to hand them out as guests get into their cars.

Choose from any of the following ideas, or use them as inspiration for creating your own unique party favors.

Music

You've spent time thinking about the music for your party, so make the most of your efforts by burning a CD of your party mix for each guest or couple. Creative types can purchase stick-on CD labels at office supply stores and create a custom design, but plenty of companies are willing to do the work for you if you'd rather outsource.

Gifts from the Kitchen

Chinese-style takeout boxes, available in a wide array of sizes and colors, are a creative way to pack up edible favors.

Fill pretty takeout boxes with cookies, candies, spiced nuts or other small gifts from your kitchen. When packaged nicely, even a slice of cake from the party is a great little gift. Your guests will be reminded of the special evening they spent with you — and they'll have something to share with the children (or spouse) who might have been left out this time.

Edible Place Cards

Decorate a cookie with cake decorating gel or dip fortune cookies in chocolate and insert a small strip of paper with each guest's name on it to serve as tasteful take-home place cards. Handmade truffles can also hold name cards for cool-weather celebrations.

Mulling Spices

Pretty sachets of mulling spices are perfect for fall and winter parties. To make each one, cut out a 10- by 5-inch (25 by

12.5 cm) rectangle of cotton cheesecloth and fold it in half to create a 5-inch (12.5 cm) square. Place a small bay leaf, a cinnamon stick broken into small pieces, four whole cloves, three whole allspice berries, a strip of dried lemon peel and two strips of dried orange peel in the center of the square. Gather the corners together and tie with cotton twine. Attach a handmade tag with the guest's name and directions for using the spices: they're great steeped with apple cider or a bottle of red wine — add sugar to taste to the latter for a delicious mulled wine.

Hot Chocolate Mix

It's as easy as unsweetened cocoa powder, granulated sugar, powdered milk and a pinch of salt — and you'll find plenty of recipes online for this favorite wintertime mix. Package your favorite version in glass jars or plastic treat bags from the craft or dollar store, and add a ribbon and instructions.

Cookie Cutters

Cookie cutters can be found in all sorts of whimsical shapes. Choose shapes that fit your party's theme, print out a rolled sugar or gingerbread cookie recipe (look on www.epicurious. com for recipes that have been reviewed and rated) on heavy card stock, and tie the recipe to the cookie cutter with a ribbon or a length of artsy yarn.

Jelly Beans

Buy small tins, glass jars or plastic treat bags and fill them with jelly beans in appropriate colors (for example, for a football party, choose jelly beans in your team's colors). World Market (www.worldmarket.com) and Super Target locations (www.target.com) now carry a variety of Jelly Belly candies (www.jellybelly.com) that can be purchased by individual color.

Gifts Just for Kids

For kids, choose gifts that will hold their attention (without resorting to candy). Try stickers, lacing cards, modeling clay or crayons paired with small coloring books. Or make jars of cookie mix (recipes are available online; check www. verybestbaking.com) so your young guests can make cookies at home the next time they need a rainy-day activity: layer the ingredients in a clear mason jar and tie it with a pretty ribbon and a card with baking instructions. Your own kids will enjoy helping to assemble these.

> Silly novelties make great favors. OrientalTrading.com carries inexpensive and fun items like stretchable flying frogs, insect finger puppets, balloon-powered racecars, jacks, dominos, paddleball sets, yoyos and magic tricks.

It's Easy Being Green: Tips for Earth-Friendly Party Planning

Want to keep your social consciousness firmly intact while you're planning and setting up a party? No problem. Keep the following tips in mind for a party that's as green as it is fun:

- For casual gatherings, issue e-vites instead of paper invitations. Using email, text messaging or even the old-fashioned phone will save both paper and money. If you want to send invitations for a more formal gathering, choose 100% recycled paper.

- Forgo paper plates and napkins and plastic flatware and cups in favor of their earth-friendly counterparts: cloth napkins and real china, flatware and glassware. If you use what you already own, you'll save money, too.

- Make a centerpiece from items you can repurpose after the party. Construct a gorgeous arrangement of seasonal fruits or vegetables that you can use up in your kitchen in the week following the party, or arrange potted plants, herbs or flowers (instead of cut varieties) that can be planted in your garden after the celebration is over.

- Compost the cuttings. Chances are that your party preparations will yield a sizable amount of waste. Coffee grounds, tea bags, egg shells and fruit and vegetable peelings can easily be mixed with lawn clippings and leaves and composted in a small pile in the far reaches of your yard or in a sealed urban composter. Such kitchen waste will yield rich compost that will add nutrients to your garden, and it's an easy habit to incorporate into your daily routine, helping you reduce your footprint. To learn more about composting, visit www.howtocompost.org.

Ladies' Night Favors

Having girlfriends over? Make sachets by cutting 6- to 12-inch (15 to 30 cm) pieces of tulle, filling them with potpourri, then gathering the edges together and tying them with a pretty ribbon. Or look for organza gift bags (inexpensive sheer fabric bags) at craft and gift stores. Fill them with bath salts or favorite candies, or make them into mini manicure kits with small bottles of nail polish and pretty nail files.

Fun-in-the-Sun Gifts

If you are having a beach party or luau — or just hosting a cookout in your sunny backyard — send your guests home with a fun-in-the-sun gift. Roll a travel-size tube of sunscreen, protective lip balm and a small bottle of water in a small towel.

Or give each of your guests a Frisbee: they are inexpensive and universally appealing, even to the canine set. Younger guests will enjoy bubbles or sidewalk chalk.

Candles

Purchase small votives or pairs of elegant tapers, wrap them in tulle or linen and tie them with a ribbon. These are especially nice parting gifts for romantic occasions, such as an anniversary dinner.

Garden-to-Go

Garden-themed favors double as great centerpieces. Use one bud vase per guest and place a single-stemmed flower in each. Or plant herbs in small, individual flowerpots, tie a satin, organza or gingham ribbon around each pot and arrange them in a circular pattern in the center of the table, with the centermost slightly elevated on an inverted saucer. For garden-themed place cards, write each guest's name on a 4-inch (10 cm) terracotta pot and fill it with seed packets or flower bulbs that your guests can take home to plant.

Green Thumb Gifts

Do you grow adorable mini pumpkins? The best cherry tomatoes on the block? The sweetest-smelling roses? Sending guests home with a gift from your garden is personal, earth-friendly and economical.

Chic Corsages

Place an orchid with a corsage pin at each place setting. The flowers will make delicate corsages and boutonnieres for your guests. These are especially nice for Mothers' Day brunches or bridal teas.

Tie a couple of colorful feathers together with a pretty ribbon, for a corsage that will tickle your guests!

Book Club Favors

The book sets the theme each month, so you can have a lot of fun with favors for these parties. Consider magnetic poetry, take-home wineglasses with personalized charms or packs of pretty note cards.

Swimming in Mink

For years, I've sworn to write my memoirs, recounting 20 years spent cooking in Hollywood, and those who might appear in it have been warned to behave themselves. Well, not everyone listens. This is one of my favorite stories, and I know there is a lesson in this tale for you.

Cooking on yachts was my first training ground for catering parties. I was hired as a chef's assistant, and the very first event I worked was a birthday party for Miles Davis. Herbie Hancock was the piano player, Dionne Warwick sang for her supper, Rosey Greer was handsome, Tom Bradley was the mayor of Los Angeles and Eddie Murphy arrived with his entourage. I was dazzled. The party went off without a hitch, and I thought all my parties would be star-studded successes. This was definitely not the case!

What I learned about entertaining on yachts was to make lengthy lists, and a bunch of them, because forgetting something important at sea and having to do without can become your worst nightmare. Visualize, if you can, serving rice pilaf with a teaspoon to 100 people in a line. See? I know I'm always going to make mistakes, but I try not to repeat them. Large serving spoons for the buffet went right into my party toolbox after that night.

I also learned that people drinking on a yacht aren't up and about, testing their motor skills. They might choose a seat and stay there the entire length of the cruise. Here's a tip: get your guests involved — dancing, games, charades — have them do anything but just sit and drink.

One cold and windy night aboard a yacht, a well-groomed couple was hosting their company party. No coins were spared: dinner was served, there were flowers and fine linens, and a harpist played like an angel — yet it was as dull as a mortuary on a Monday night. (Statistically, very few people die on Monday in L.A. I don't know why; maybe for the same reason the freeways are less crowded.)

When bored at a party, most guests will either leave or drink more, trying to make themselves or the other guests more interesting. Because we were on a yacht, they couldn't very well leave. And so they drank. That included our hostess, who, like many hostesses, did not take time to eat at her own party. Anxious to ensure that her guests were having a great time, but also worrying about the amount of money she was spending, she drank her dinner. I believe the six olives were considered her entrée. When the boat finally docked, after hours of martinis, her husband realized she was a wee bit tipsy. He was not amused. He made his way off the boat in a huff, saying goodbye to his guests from the parking lot. His wife, our hostess, was furious. And staggering. Disembarking a yacht wearing a $100,000 mink coat without using the handrail can make for a party surprise. In fact, it became the much-needed entertainment of the night.

I saw this beautiful woman slide between the boat and the gangway, timed perfectly with the swell of the water. With horror, the captain, crew and most of the party guests heard the splash. Her mink coat not only doubled in size in the water, it also doubled in weight. Yes, we were witnessing a potential drowning in just four feet of water. The first mate removed his shoes and jumped in after her. Our hostess was not about to remove her mink coat, and a struggle ensued. After several more crew members went in after her, she was lifted, coat and all, onto the pier. Guests were clapping. Now they were having some fun!

I often think of that lovely hostess when I'm entertaining: she reminds me to take time to eat at my own party, to remember that some things can't float and to take my wet, smelly dogs to be bathed.

Your Guests

You have decided on the party theme, location and decor, but who exactly will be coming to the event? Your guests are one of the six essential elements of entertaining for good reason: the opportunity to socialize is at the heart of our motivation to entertain, and the chemistry of the group you invite can make or break the party. Even when you've gone to great lengths with your theme, location and decor, undoubtedly setting up the potential for a special and successful gathering, it's usually the company (and sometimes the food) that people talk about, enjoy and remember the most.

Attending to the element of guests begins, of course, with creating the guest list. But it doesn't end there: once you've settled on the perfect mix of people, you must decide how to invite them (by phone, email or the old-fashioned way — a written invitation); how to guide guests in their own party preparations, answering questions about what to wear and what they can bring; how to determine who is actually planning to attend; and how to facilitate your guests' enjoyment of the celebration by making introductions and keeping in mind any special needs.

The element of guests, because it's comprised of human beings instead of flatware or food, is much less predictable than some of the other elements in party planning. While I can tell you without any reservations how to set the table or make canapés, it's not possible to anticipate every single situation that guests might thrust upon a party host: the neighbor who fails to respond to an invitation, the colleague who brings along an uninvited date, the relative who insists on talking politics, the friend who stays too late. People are, relatively speaking, unpredictable; while that's a good thing that can make for exciting conversation, that same unpredictability can also present some unique challenges for the host.

Read on for guidance on many guest-related topics, from issuing the first invitation to saying goodbye to the last guest at the end of the night.

How Many?

A guiding factor to consider when determining the guest list is its length. How many people can you really accommodate, both space-wise and money-wise? You'll only be able to invite as many people as you can entertain, so before you get too far with the guest list, you'll want to have a head count in mind. Remember that you'll need less space for a cocktail party or even a buffet dinner than you will for a sit-down dinner. (See page 39 for help in determining what size party you can pull off in your chosen location.)

Also keep in mind that, with smaller dinner parties, it's more critical to carefully consider and balance the guest list. Smaller parties work well with folks who share some interests and common social skills, while larger parties can better absorb the eccentricities of an opinionated relative or the antics of energetic children.

Make an actual list of guests to use as your guide when sending out invitations, planning the menu, making seating arrangements and sending out any necessary thank yous afterwards. You'll also want to make note of any special dietary needs or physical limitations your guests might have so you can bear these in mind as you create the menu and determine seating.

Who to Invite

You can't invite everyone you know to every party you have — and nobody could expect you to. That said, the process of determining a guest list, which will naturally exclude some people and include others, can be an uncomfortable task for many hosts. Those of us who enjoy entertaining are, after all, the gregarious sort: we don't want to leave out anyone we think would enjoy our party. Most of all, we don't want anyone we care about to *feel* left out.

Simplify the process of making your guest list by considering, first, your motivation to entertain. The reason for the party will guide your guest list. (And really, isn't that a better guide than guilt?) When you focus on your party's purpose or theme, you will be sure to include the appropriate people; next time, your motivation to entertain will be centered on something else, and you'll be inviting a different group of guests.

Will you be celebrating your spouse's 40th birthday with a formal dinner party? Then your guest list should include the dozen or fewer friends or relatives your spouse would most like to celebrate with (he or she is, after all, the guest of honor) — and that probably means not including your own work friends. When you stick to your theme, you take yourself out of the equation, making it a lot easier to answer any questions that might come up later. If uncomfortable questions ensue, you'll have a ready-made reason that's tough to argue with: "We're having Bob's golf group over tonight. We're looking forward to entertaining family again soon — hope you'll be able to make it."

It's also useful to remember that, as much as someone might love you and your parties, most guests don't want to be included every single time. There's a reason we call them "guests" and not "hostages." Try to consider each guest's personality and preferences when determining whether to invite him or her. While your club-hopping friend from college never forgets *your* birthday, she might or might not want to spend her Saturday afternoon chasing preschoolers when your son turns four, or listening to long-winded relatives at a family gathering. Have you ever been invited to the wedding of people you barely know? Wouldn't it have been a relief to pass on the opportunity to drop $100 on a gift? Even smaller parties come with some obligations for guests, so if you're unsure, it's helpful to consider whether they'd want to be in on the festivities this time.

Most parties will be dominated by one group, as determined by the purpose of the gathering. Here are some categories of guests and things to keep in mind when you're focusing on entertaining their ilk — or attempting to mix and match.

> For larger parties, consider enlisting a co-host to share party-day responsibilities, easing your stress and helping to make sure everything goes smoothly.

Family

Thanksgiving, Mother's Day, your father's birthday: there are occasions when you'll be inviting mostly, or all, family. Only you will know if it's wise to mix in a few friends with your own unique bunch, or if you even have the room to do so. I have a friend who is one of six adult children in her family; they all live within an hour's drive of each other and are all now married with children of their own. This friend throws a fantastic Christmas party every December, and everyone wants to come. She has begun hosting a family party one evening and a friends party the next. She has manageable numbers of people, is able to enjoy each party and only has to shop once. (It helps that she has an extra fridge in her garage.) Speaking of keeping the peace with family, I have another friend whose house rule is this: Leave your shoes and your politics at the door. Not a bad motto, especially with mixed groups.

Neighbors

If you have neighbors who are similar to you and your friends in age and stage, or who share special interests with you and your friends, it can be fun to include them. Unless you know the neighbors well already, it's easier to invite them to a larger party, where they're more likely to find someone they can relate to, than to an intimate dinner party of old friends, where they might feel left out of the group's collective history. Including the neighbors once in a while can create goodwill on the street and smooth out future discussions about who mows the strip of grass between their driveway and yours.

Whenever you have new people over, it helps to make introductions early in the event, purposefully linking up guests you think would enjoy one another. With larger mixed groups, name tags are also helpful in breaking the ice, as are some party games (see page 191 for ideas).

Business Associates

Entertaining work friends and clients is a great way to get to know them better; socializing outside business hours can create friendships or, at the very least, improve everyday relations. But the disastrous holiday office party isn't part of our society's lore for nothing. It's important to offer nonalcoholic beverages as well as wine, beer or cocktails, if you choose. It's also a good idea to steer clear of certain divisive topics: politics, religion and gossip about other work associates, to name a few. Entertaining can show colleagues that you have a fun-loving side — but while you're letting your hair down, do keep the gloves on.

Children

Keep kids busy by setting up three or four activity or game areas (check out AmazingMoms. com). Award prizes for the best, but be sure that every child goes home with a prize.

For children's birthday parties, be sure that you're clear about your expectations as to whether parents will stay or drop off their kids. If they'll stay, which is usually the case with the younger set, it's nice to include any siblings on the invitation. Most parents aren't enthused about paying for a babysitter for one of their children while attending a party with another.

If you want to include children in a gathering where entertaining the grownups is your real focus, such as a seated dinner party, consider hiring a babysitter or nanny and providing the kids with arts and crafts supplies, board games or an age-appropriate movie.

Older Teens and Young Adults

Even at seated adult dinner parties, older teens or young adults can be a charming addition to the mix, especially those who have good party manners and have crossed the great divide to begin realizing that adults aren't here only to serve as buzz-kills. You'll need to make an effort to include them in conversation, asking about their school year or future plans and special interests. Enlisting their help (with passing appetizers, for instance) can sometimes make them feel like part of the festivities and, as a result, help them feel less self-conscious. Depending on their age and how many are in attendance, it's nice to have an "out" available for younger guests later in the evening: a few newly released DVDs or board games to choose from, books of crossword puzzles or sudoku, or other activities they can take refuge with should they tire of chatting up the, um, old folks.

Adults Only

Sometimes adults just want to be with other adults. If one of your friends is a stay-at-home parent, for example, her idea of a relaxing evening probably doesn't include dealing with other people's kids — particularly when her own kids are at home with a sitter. If a grownups-only party is on tap, be sure that *all* parents in attendance are on the same page. Mention that

Bob and Cindy got a sitter, for instance, or that your own kids will be at their grandma's. If your kids will be home, make sure they have plenty to occupy them (including a sitter or nanny if they're very young) and that they stick to their normal bedtime, meaning they'll likely be asleep for a portion of the evening. Another option is to hire a sitter or two to keep your children and a guest's children entertained at the guest's house, if nearby.

Seniors

Family parties, neighborhood gatherings and even parties with friends are often multigenerational, so they're likely include some seniors as well as children. Everyone has his or her own needs, but in general it's a good idea to plan on eating at a decently early hour (probably by 7:00 p.m.) and to have a setup that keeps any physical limitations in mind: wheelchair accessibility, if necessary, plus comfortable seating and an appropriate menu that accommodates sensitivities. Be considerate of a guest's limited sight or hearing by printing menus or place cards in a large font and limiting the level of music and other noise that might otherwise impair the guests' ability to follow the conversation.

Extending the Invitation

There's nothing like a party invitation to perk up a mailbox full of junk mail and bills — it can make the recipient's day. Something about the color and shape, handwritten address and stamp, and the promise of a coming social event to liven up the calendar, makes mailed invitations exciting. Who doesn't love to open one? Of course, the same can be said of email invitations found among virtual junk mail, or a phoned invitation that comes amid telemarketing calls. A party promises your guests a little something different, a little something to look forward to.

The invitation itself — how you announce the happening — is your opportunity to make a great first impression. By using an invitation appropriate to your theme, you'll be letting your guests know whether the party is going to be elegant, silly, casual, fun, formal or irreverent. You can also use the invitation as a chance to give your guests an idea of what you'll be serving, what they should wear and what you'll be doing. It's their first taste of what's to come.

While the invitation's design is integral to conveying your theme, the information you include is critical. Think of yourself as a reporter who needs to fit a few important bits of information into a small number of words. Here's what you really should include, and a few extras you can decide on:

The only guests that are invited to a party are the guests the invitation is addressed to. Clearly specify if people can bring others with them.

- **Who** is throwing the party? Be sure to put your name and contact information on the actual invitation somewhere; people usually throw away the envelope, so a return address isn't enough. Include "RSVP" and a phone number and/or email address if you want to hear from guests ahead of time — and that's highly recommended (see page 94 for more on figuring out who's coming). It's also nice to give invitees an idea (in general terms) of who's coming to the party: "a gathering of friends and family" or "a family celebration," for instance.

- **What** is the party's theme, and **why** are you having it? If it's a game-day gathering, guests might want to wear a team jersey; if it's a backyard luau, they might want to wear that fantastic Hawaiian shirt. Share the party's theme from the beginning to create anticipation and excitement among your guests, and to give them insight as to what they should expect and what they should wear (see Letting Guests Know What to Wear, on page 95, for more on how to suggest a dress code). The reason for the party ties into the theme, but also makes clear who the guest of honor is (if there is one) and what you're celebrating. Guests will be on board with your purpose to party if they know it's your wife's 50th birthday or the launch of your long-anticipated girls-only book club.

- **When** is the party? Be specific about the start time. For dinner parties, have appetizers ready at the beginning and plan to serve dinner 45 to 60 minutes later, allowing guests to have a drink and latecomers to arrive. For open houses, it's fine to put an end time, too, so guests know, for instance, that they can drop by any time between 6 and 9 p.m. Children's birthday parties can also include an end time, particularly for kids who will be dropped off (and picked up promptly, you hope) or for very young children who might need an afternoon nap after the festivities.

- **Where** will the party be held? If it's at your house, give the complete address and consider including a small map if it's difficult to find (most people are happy to use the address to find an online map, but you'll save them a step if you include one). If you live in an urban area or on a street that doesn't allow parking, include instructions, perhaps printed separately, for finding nearby parking. The same goes for holding a party at another site: guests need to know how to find it and where to park their cars; if you've prearranged for valet parking, let them know in advance.

- **How** will you be celebrating? Guests like to know ahead of time if they'll be playing games, dancing or just eating and drinking. If it's a dinner party, say so — that way they'll know to arrive on time. If it's a cocktail party, they'll know it's fine to show up a little late. If you're planning a karaoke hour after dinner, include that information so guests will come prepared to join in.

- **Extras.** In addition to specifying the nuts and bolts of the party, you can get creative and add some poetry or song lyrics (come up with something original, or be sure to give credit to the author) to the front or the facing inside of the card. Other ideas include artwork, a copy of a wine label or the party's menu. For a formal dinner party, use restaurant-style wording to tempt the palate: Red and Green Garden Salad with Creamy Vinaigrette and Sourdough Croutons is a lot more exciting than plain old Salad. Anything you choose to add to your invitation should help create anticipation and convey the ambiance of the upcoming celebration.

Make-Your-Own Invitations

Let brides-to-be worry about whether to spend their money on engraving or thermography for their invitations. When you're hosting a smaller party, the invitations can be much less formal and much more personalized. You can make your own, either by hand or with the help of your computer and printer, by purchasing plain note cards and envelopes at an office supply or paper store and decorating them according to the theme of your party.

If you'll have time to hand-deliver invitations, you can think outside the note-card-and-envelope formula to develop an invitation that is rolled and tied with a pretty ribbon or attached to a small potted herb or bottle of wine. And if you're trying to keep the party budget in check, consider sending postcards instead of sealed invitations — they'll cost less to make *and* less to send.

Wording Your Invitations

Here are some examples of wording for party invitations.

**Susan and Jeff
are back from Germany!**

Please drop by for an autumn wine and cheese tasting in celebration of their homecoming.

Friday, September 26, 6 to 9 p.m.

Dot and Leslie Samuelson

3720 Washburn Avenue

RSVP 330-555-1212 or dsamuelson@home.com

Please join us at the

Fort Worth Botanic Gardens

for a boxed picnic lunch (and a few rounds of Frisbee) in celebration of Gus's high-school graduation.

Saturday, June 14, at noon

Hanna & Thomas Paget

RSVP 817-555-1212 or hpaget@home.com

Please bring a picnic blanket.

It's Oscars time!

Please come for a casual cocktail supper, some friendly betting and the show we've all been waiting for.

Sunday, February 24, at 5 p.m.

Katherine and Richard Browning

502 Rodney Drive, Apartment 109

RSVP 323-555-1212 or kbrowning@home.com

Extra parking is available at the church on Rodney and First.

To make your invitations one of a kind, peruse the offerings at your local paper, craft or scrapbook supplier. Large chains such as Michaels (www.michaels.com) and Target (www.target.com) have good selections of craft supplies. Here are some items to look for.

Rubber Stamps

Use inkpads to stamp designs onto your invitations. Choose inks in theme-related hues, or metallics for an elegant touch, and rubber stamps that coordinate to your theme: the monogram of the birthday girl, a sun for an outdoor picnic or a pumpkin for a fall party. You can begin a collection of inks and rubber stamps that can be used in new ways for future parties and other projects.

Embossers

Have your monogram — or one of any number of designs, holiday and otherwise — made into a custom embosser, which you can use to emboss your symbol onto card or envelope stock for an upscale look (visit www.finestationery.com for some options). For practicality, choose something you can use for many occasions in the future; embossers are an investment at around $60, but because they don't require ink, you can use them forever.

Paper Punchers

Like a large hole-punch, paper punchers cut a decorative shape in paper, along its edge or around its corners. They look especially pretty with a second paper color inside, peeking through from behind. Paper punchers come in many, many designs to coordinate perfectly with holidays and other occasions.

Decorative Scissors

Pinking shears and other decorative scissors can make a pretty edge that looks custom-made for your invitations.

Cutouts

If you think you're not crafty enough to make your own cutouts, there are plenty available to coordinate with almost any theme; just browse in the scrapbook section of craft stores. Glue cutouts to the front of your cards for unique invitations that convey your theme from the start.

Ribbon

High-end baby announcements often include a blue or pink ribbon at the top. Borrow the idea for any theme by choosing a ribbon that coordinates with your decor for the event and tying it to the front of your cards (use a small hole punch to create two holes to lace it through) or around the fold of the invitation.

Ordering Custom Invitations

There are plenty of reasons to outsource your invitations, including time and creativity constraints or the desire for more formal-looking results. But even when you outsource the design and printing, you'll still be in charge of the wording (see page 90 for some suggestions). If you have a good local stationer, that's a great place to start: most can work with you to create custom invitations quickly. Some of my favorite places to turn for the design and printing of invitations include

Invitation Timing

It's a good idea to send party invitations at least two weeks ahead of time for smaller dinner or cocktail gatherings at your home. For parties that will be held around the holidays or at other especially busy times, even more advance notice — up to a month — is recommended. For more formal occasions, such as weddings, a six-week lead is standard, giving guests plenty of time to find attire and a gift.

Save-the-date cards, which give guests who might need to travel a heads-up, can be sent up to a year in advance for destination weddings, but with in-town events, a few months is usually plenty of time. While save-the-date reminders have become customary for weddings, they can be practical for any special occasion that you want guests to prioritize, as they allow guests to keep that chosen night open. On the other hand, sending save-the-dates can be seen as being too demanding of others' time: it's hard to gracefully decline attendance at an event you've known about for a year. That said, they're always appropriate in instances when some guests will need to travel.

Save-the-date notices can take many forms: postcards, magnets or even pens and other novelty items (search online for "promotional products" for a host of unexpected items). Whether you're using custom-printed save-the-date cards or making your own, be sure to include your name and the date and location of the party, as well as a note that an invitation will follow.

French Blue Papers (www.frenchblueonline.com), Dauphine Press (www.dauphinepress.com) and InvitationBox.com (www.invitationbox.com).

Ready-Made Invitations and Fill-Ins

For almost any entertaining occasion (save for the most formal) — and for the host who would rather devote his or her creativity to the menu and decor — predesigned invitations that you customize at home using your computer and printer are a great choice. In addition, many companies offer fill-in invitations that require you only to write in the occasion, date, time, place and RSVP information; these are particularly nice for children's birthday parties (and busy parents).

These days, there are more invitation designs available to purchase and print yourself than ever before, and many are very chic. Look for ready-made invitations, from very inexpensive to very upscale, wherever you buy stationary. Target and InvitationBox.com have many to choose from; for more suggestions, see the Invitations listing in the reference guide, page 446.

Invitations by Phone or Internet

The charm of paper invitations aside, inviting guests by phone or Internet sometimes just makes the most sense: maybe the gathering is so small or so last-minute that printed invitations aren't a viable option, or maybe you're trying to set an earth-friendly example by using less paper. Whatever your reason, making the invitation at all is what's important.

If you choose to extend your hospitality by phone, and particularly if you have a long list of people to call, you might want to jot down all of the information you'll need to share, so that you'll remember to tell each guest at least the bare essentials: who, what, why, when, where and how — including anything out of the ordinary, like the fact that it's a costume party or that they should bring bathing suits for the hot tub. If you get an answering machine or voice mail, be sure to also leave your phone number and request a return call so you'll have an idea of who can make it to the party.

Because there is some important information to disseminate with an invitation, the Internet can be preferable to the phone, as it allows you to send the same details to everyone at once, with no call-waiting or voice-mail systems to contend with. While it's certainly fine to simply email the details to your guests or send a mass invitation on Facebook or MySpace, you can show a little more flair — as well as tempting guests with a hint of the party theme and the fun to come — by taking advantage of one of the many sites that offer free virtual invitations. Evite (www.evite.com) is one of my favorites.

RSVP

If you do include an RSVP request on your invitation, don't bury it in small type! Make sure it is clearly marked.

In an ideal world, we would all be up on basic etiquette, which certainly includes responding in a timely manner when you're issued an invitation. Instead, we're living in a world where wedding hosts, seemingly the most desperate to know a head count for the caterer, have largely resorted to the practice of sending a response card with a box to check and a prepaid envelope. (Will you attend? Check yes or no.) And yet many people *still* can't manage to RSVP.

Rather than fight a losing battle, I have dropped "RSVP" from my invitations for larger parties, assuming that about 50% of the invitees will show up. This saves some frustration and works fine for cocktail parties. I have a friend who tried the "Regrets Only" method — once. Nobody called. She found herself wondering if that meant that everyone was coming (and just following directions not to call unless they couldn't make it) or that nobody was coming. It turned out to be the former, but it's easy to second-guess such a response, and she has sworn off "Regrets Only" ever since.

Larger, looser gatherings are one thing, but when you're hosting a seated dinner party, with place cards and perhaps even party favors, it's not good for your sanity to wonder whether you're feeding 6 or 12. That's why you should always include "RSVP" on invitations for smaller parties — and follow up by phone or email with any invitees you haven't heard from, before you do the bulk of your party shopping. You can always say you are calling to make sure they got the invitation. That way, you'll have enough food — but not way too much — and you'll feel calmer, knowing how many guests will be there. It also helps to include an email address that guests can use to respond to an invitation; some people have a hard time finding their way to the phone during the day, but will drop you an email when they think of it, whether that's at 6 a.m. or 11 p.m.

Letting Guests Know What to Wear

Many of your guests will ask what they should wear to the party, and even those who don't ask will wonder. It's a good idea to give guests some guidance from the start, especially if you're planning a costume party or a very formal or very casual gathering. Comfortable, confident guests are happy guests, and you don't want anybody feeling like they missed the memo that this was a pool party or a black-tie event. Your guidance can be as subtle as letting them know, in the invitation, that you'll be playing outdoor games (so they can choose cool, breezy clothing and comfortable shoes) or that you're having a New Year's Eve dinner-dance (so they'll know it's a more formal occasion).

When the guests' dress will be part of the theme and decor — black and white, for instance — it's important to indicate that on the invitation: "Please dress in black and white" says it all. For parties with an overt theme, say a Beatlemania birthday bash or a Halloween-night chili supper, the invitation should include explicit instructions about the suggested dress: "Come as your favorite Beatle" or "Costumes encouraged."

With phone invitations, it can be as easy as letting your guests know what you (and any co-host) will be wearing: "We're planning to dress up as John and Yoko" or "We'll be wearing comfortable shoes, since we plan to play bocce in the backyard."

If you're trying to decide on the proper wording for indicating dress on a written invitation, visit the Emily Post Institute online at www.emilypost.com and click on "Etiquette Everyday," which has an entertaining section that breaks down every sort of attire, from "Beach Casual" to "White Tie."

Letting Guests Know What to Bring

Eager guests, especially those who are close to you, will probably ask what they can bring to the party. If you'd like to outsource a dish or two, and you know that your guests are serious in their offer, go ahead and make assignments that fit with your menu, keeping in mind each guest's limitations on time, money or,

When is a Thank-You Note Necessary?

Sure, you'd love it if, a couple of days after the party, you received some thank-you notes saying how great your gathering was. (When you've been a guest at a dinner party, it's always thoughtful to express your thanks — at the very least by email and, better yet, with a handwritten note.) But should you be writing any notes as the host, for the wine or cookies your friend brought, the tablecloths you borrowed or the dishes your sister stayed behind to do? The bottom line is, it's never wrong to express your appreciation. People enjoy doing nice things for those who show gratitude; it's just more satisfying to help those who appreciate it.

But if you opened the wine in front of the giver and were able to express your thanks verbally (and warmly), then you're off the hook. The same goes for any other small contribution to the party, such as the chocolate truffles someone brought for dessert or the mashed potatoes a guest contributed. Give credit where credit is due, and thank them verbally for anything they contributed to the table.

When a friend goes above and beyond making a small contribution to the meal they'll share with you, perhaps loaning you some nice linens or glassware or providing tireless assistance with setup and cleanup, it's important to write a note of thanks — and promptly. A thank-you note is also required for any presents, wrapped or otherwise, that you weren't able to acknowledge during the party. Send a note as soon as possible that lets the guest know how much you appreciate the gift, and how much fun it was to see him or her at the party.

let's be honest, kitchen skills. For instance, if you're asking an overworked, under-domesticated friend to bring dessert, you might mention that it's fine if she picks something up from the bakery instead of making it from scratch.

That said, it's smart to avoid outsourcing appetizers, champagne or anything else that needs to be ready to serve at the evening's start, because if the contributing guest is running a few minutes late, or forgets to bring the promised dish or bottle, the party will be left without food or drink temporarily.

If you really prefer to do it all yourself, it's fine to let guests know that you have everything under control, but do let them in on your plans. Many people genuinely enjoy bringing something to the party, so if they know you're cooking Italian food, that gives them the opportunity to select a great Italian wine to go with it, or bring a special box of amaretti cookies or Baci candies to complement what you have planned.

Many hosts wonder if they should open that bottle of wine a guest brings to the party. A bottle of wine is a gift, so whether or not to serve it at the party is completely up to you. If you think it will go well with the food on your menu, you might ask the guest, "Would you like me to open this now, so we can both enjoy a glass?" If you suspect it won't complement what you've prepared, or if you've already opened more than enough vino, thank them warmly and let them know you're going to save it for the next special occasion. The same goes for cookies, candies and any other packaged goodies that will keep.

Seating Arrangements

You only need seating arrangements if you're having a seated dinner party of six people or more; fewer guests, and it's really fine to let them sit where they like. When you're deciding where people should sit, it's worth taking a look back at what the old-school etiquette books have to say: the host and hostess should occupy the heads of the table, at opposite ends; a male guest of honor should be seated at the hostess's right and a female guest of honor at the host's right; couples should be seated separately; and all guests should be seated to alternate between male and female, if possible.

When entertaining guests who know each other only slightly, if at all, seat people who have similar interests together.

It might sound a little stuffy, but there's a compelling rationale behind all that protocol: such seating encourages conversation among people who might not know each other well, it discourages the compulsion of established couples to talk only to each other (about their kids) all night, and it gives everyone more to catch up on after the party is over. In short, it keeps things interesting and encourages participation in the conversation from everyone.

Of course, you don't want things to get *too* interesting. Your cousin who just went hunting seated beside your PETA activist sister-in-law does not a happy pairing make. At a large table, guests will be best able to talk to those on either side of them, so seat people who you think might enjoy each other's company within arm's reach of each other and separate any potentially troublesome pairings by a few places, if possible. Other tactics to consider: seat someone who's shy by someone who's a great conversationalist, and seat buddies apart so they'll have a chance to meet new people. Think about your guests' personalities ahead of time and try to devise a seating plan that brings out their best, ensuring the most fun for everyone.

When Guests Won't Leave

Try this obvious but gentle hint: flick the lights on and off to grab your guests' attention, then thank everyone for coming and making the night such a special one.

Depending on your guests — your friends, family, colleagues and neighbors, in other words — your party might wrap up neatly after a few hours, with everyone saying their goodbyes at the same moment and driving away in unison, or you might have a few hangers-on waving goodbye to everyone else along with you and staying on for another couple of hours. My friend used to entertain a colleague known for his love of partying late into the night. He would come for dinner at 6 and stay until dawn. And that was a lot of fun for everyone — until my friend had a baby. She stopped issuing him invitations not because her fondness for him subsided at all, but because her sleep became a lot more important; she knew she would be getting up at the same early hour the next morning whether she entertained until 10 p.m. or 2 a.m.

While I love it when a close friend lingers a little later than the rest of the crowd to sit down and chat one on one after the hubbub is over, sharing another cup of coffee and some uninterrupted conversation, there are times when you just need to move people along. If you're tired and ready to turn in, and you feel that the party has run its course, here are some tips for handling your favorite night owls.

An Ounce of Prevention

If turning up the lights, turning off the music and picking up the debris doesn't encourage those last guests to go, take them by the hand and walk them to the door, saying, "It's been wonderful seeing you! But I am beat and it's time for you to go."

I sometimes let people know on the invitation that the party will end by 11 p.m., for example. You can simply list the ending time with the starting time (8 to 11 p.m., for instance), or you can use wording such as "Since it's Sunday night and we all have to work the next morning, we won't keep you past 11." Party ending times are routinely given for children's birthday party invitations and open houses, but it's fine to be upfront about your limits on any invitation. Honesty works.

The Guest Who's Still Having Fun

This is a compliment, really. If you have a guest who doesn't want the party to end, you can pat yourself on the back for having thrown a successful fete. If you begin putting away the food, doing the dishes, yawning and letting your pets out of captivity, most guests will realize that you're heading back to your household routines and that the party has come to a close. (Bars often turn off the music, turn up the lights and stop serving drinks, which kills ambiance and clears out a place pretty quickly.) While some of these tactics seem passive-aggressive, they're really meant to maintain everyone's pride: a hint issued and a hint taken means there's no need to get more overt about booting out partygoers. I have a dear friend who only leaves after I stop serving wine and open the front door.

The Hard-Partying Guest

Perhaps your lingerer is hanging around because he's not quite up to driving; people often drink too much at parties, and it's possible that a hanger-on is trying to wait out a buzz and sober up. If you're ready to call it a night, you have a few choices: offer him your sofa bed or guest room to spend the night in; offer to call a cab; or offer to walk or drive him home — but don't send him to his car prematurely. It's important to play it safe in these situations. *Insist* that a wobbly guest stay over, or be walked or driven home by yourself or a trusted friend or relative.

When you serve alcohol to your guests, you are legally liable if they get involved in a car accident while driving home.

The Fastidious Guest

This is often a well-meaning mother, mother-in-law or best friend — someone you don't want to risk offending, in other words. But if you're not on board with her mission to wash and dry all 12 place settings before leaving, you can usually get the message across by saying, "I'm so tired, I think I'd rather turn in and deal with the dishes in the morning" or "Let's sit and catch up for a few minutes. I can only stay up for another half-hour, and I'd rather visit with you than do the dishes." She can always come back in the morning if she really wants to do those dishes, right? Please?

The Couch Potato

He's been sitting on your couch all night, and now it seems that he's grown actual roots. I have a friend whose husband used to, in such situations, matter-of-factly announce that he was going to bed, leaving her to deal with the late-night couch potato. For late-staying guests who are unfazed by one of their hosts going to bed, you're going to have to be overt — something along the lines of "I've had so much fun visiting with you, but now I'm ready for sleep. May I pack up some leftovers you can take with you?" Sandwiching requests in such a fashion (nice/to-the-point/nice) is a polite way to get what you want, and it usually works.

Blowing Out the Candles

You can sometimes learn as much by attending others' parties as you do by hosting your own. You aren't under any stress: your only responsibilities are to dress up, show up, mingle with friends and taste delightful new treats. The first moments of every party are magical to me. Preparation and atmosphere collide, and you can feel the excitement in the air.

After many years of entertaining, personally and professionally, my first impressions are always trustworthy. My most memorable one is from a Christmas party years ago. I remember thinking, as I walked into the room, how bright and glittery the votive candles were. It occurred to me that those candles, lining the floor along every wall, spelled trouble, but as it was not my event, I told myself I was just being a worrier.

The party was hosted by one of my celebrity clients, who throws a très chic, très expensive Christmas party every year. As a nice gesture, she generously invites everyone who works on her team. Her family is in attendance, as are her accountants, assistants, agents, publicists, makeup artists, hair weavers, designers, decorators — you name a position, and those who fill it are invited. It's a company party, and we all support the brand. The guests wear handmade name tags so that names and faces finally connect (often you just do business with a name and never see the face), making for instant camaraderie.

On this particular occasion, the party was held at Granita, Wolfgang Puck's Malibu restaurant. My client had rented the entire place for the night, and a hundred people arrived right on time. There were cocktails and pizza on the patio, and then we moved into the dining room, where flower arrangements, party favors and the guests' gifts were stacked high on every table. It was a lovely sight: starched white linens, white roses, buffed wineglasses and thousands of votive candles shedding flickering light everywhere.

One of the publicists — "The Legend," as she is called in Los Angeles (bigger than Pat Kingsley, in case you hazarded a guess) — who is almost as famous as her clients, arrived late but had requested that I save a seat for her. I did. Larger than life, a cellphone to each ear and constantly talking, she slid into her chair, draped in her Armani cashmere shawl. Immediately ordering champagne and requesting more pizza, The Legend settled in to get the lay of the land. We sat with our backs to the wall, a trick you quickly learn in L.A. when you don't wish to be surprised or have people sneaking glances behind your ears, checking for tiny facelift scars.

The Legend was carrying a beautifully wrapped and very expensive box: the French label spoke volumes. Obviously a present for our hostess and too fragile to send ahead, it was tucked carefully under her seat as she waited to present it.

Our hostess made a point of getting to every table to say her hellos and thank yous, so we knew there would be private time with her later.

The dinner was part buffet and part sit-down. Space in the room was tight with tables, chairs, guests, a five-piece band and 20 waiters passing tray upon tray of taste sensations and many, many bottles of wine. Wines had been carefully selected: great California bottles made to be easily drunk, and drunk with pleasure. Having worked in the Napa Valley several times as a chef, I knew them all and I drank them all. It was no problem, as The Legend and I had a designated driver. The windy highway up to Malibu is trying enough without oodles of champagne and wine. And who can forget that infamous mug shot of Nick Nolte? The grand bash was under way.

It was the smell of the burning Armani that first signaled trouble. You'd think cashmere would smell better than, say, newspaper, but no: pricey smoke smells just as bad. The ribbons on the expensive package tucked under The Legend's seat were the next victims of the floorboard votive candles. It was quite the blaze.

The party was in full swing: noisy and crowded. Unfortunately, the few of us who noticed the burning package were absolutely frozen with fear and seemed to have lost the good sense to scream. Instead, we wildly waved our arms, pointing at the flaming package. And then, from across the room strode a tall, beautifully dressed assistant. He scooped up the box, carried it to the patio and jumped on it with his expensive Prada loafers, stomping the fire into submission. He now had everyone's attention.

The Legend put down one of her phones. "Oh my God!" she yelled. "Be careful, there are Limoges glasses in that box!"

Well, I thought, not anymore.

Food and Beverages

That food and beverages are an essential element of entertaining really goes without explanation. You just can't have a party — any party — without offering some form of sustenance, even if it's just beer and pretzels. But how to decide on the menu, enlist the help, shop, prepare some of it ahead of time and have it all at its ideal temperature, on the table and gorgeously presented at exactly the right moment? Now *that* takes some explanation. While the prospect of coming up with food and beverages for a party leaves some would-be hosts shaking in their boots, it doesn't have to. There are many ways to plan and host a great party, and for most of us, knowing how to delegate is just as important as knowing how to do it all yourself.

Once you've decided on the theme, location, decor and number of guests for your party, it's time to develop a game plan for the food and drink that will fuel the celebration. Can you really feed all these people yourself? Should you even try?

This chapter guides you through answering these questions. Once you've decided on your approach, it's time to spring into action. The following pages lead you through catering your own party if you've decided to do so. Just as important, they contain helpful hints for outsourcing some or all of the food-and-beverage-related tasks. Perhaps cooking five courses, each paired with its own wine, is an invigorating challenge that you look forward to. Or maybe you feel that the non-food tasks, such as issuing invitations, setting the table and decorating your location, will keep you plenty busy. Either way, we've got you covered.

Can I Make All This Food Myself?

I'm never one to turn down a painstakingly prepared meal, but it's useful to keep things in perspective when you're planning a party. Is the most important thing that the food you serve be awe-inspiring? Not at the expense of your sanity or your budget. Parties are about people getting together to enjoy each other's company; it's great if the food is exceptional, but it helps to remember that "exceptional" doesn't have to mean overly complicated. An heirloom tomato from your summer garden, sliced, drizzled with olive oil and sprinkled with a little kosher salt, is exceptional. And so are miniature goat cheese and ratatouille tartlets in homemade crusts. If your menu threatens to make you hyperventilate, go easy on yourself and exchange a few high-maintenance or high-ticket items for alternatives that are more reasonable, and no less appealing for their ease.

Begin by sketching out your ideal menu, reading through the following sections for help in developing and balancing it. If the menu you come up with is something you can pull off easily, then congratulations. If it's not, you have some options: simplify it to the point where you're comfortable with it, incorporating some do-ahead dishes and some purchased items; enlist the help of a friend or two for some side dishes or desserts to reduce your work load (and grocery bill); or outsource some or all of the menu to the professionals.

If the party you want to throw far exceeds your culinary skills or available time, you can't get better peace of mind than that which comes with hiring a good caterer. In fact, caterers do a lot more than cook: many are also event planners and have contacts with other industry professionals, so they can handle food, beverages, rented items, wait staff and even flowers. Plus, they can sometimes work out discounts for you when you allow them to pull it all together. As an alternative, many caterers will provide drop-off food service, meaning that all of the food arrives fully or partially cooked, with reheating instructions. That way, you can present it on your own platters if you like and host your party as if you'd prepared the food yourself.

> Keep in mind that you are throwing a party, not an Iron Chef competition. No one is going to have fun if you are completely stressed out.

When considering ways to outsource the food for your party, don't count out local restaurants, as many have catering services. Even super-casual food, such as barbecue or burritos, can make festive party fare. And arranging for it ahead of time can be a tremendous relief, allowing you to focus on appetizers and dessert, if you choose, or just the drinks and decor.

Another popular and practical option is to create a menu that incorporates one or two made-from-scratch dishes, then round them out with purchased items. For instance, you can make a trip to a well-stocked market and gather the fixings for an antipasto platter (marinated artichoke hearts, olives, peppers, cheeses, cured meats and more) to serve with crusty bread as a start to the meal, and you can order an Italian cream cake from the bakery for dessert. Consider ice cream from that favorite neighborhood scoop shop, a locally made goat cheese, roasted salted nuts from a nearby grower, baba ghanoush from a Middle Eastern deli or olive bread from the bakery. Outsourcing a few items brings new flavors to the table without adding to your workload; it's also fun to introduce your guests to some local specialties they might not have tried yet. If you've ever lived in a neighborhood without a good bakery or cheese shop, then you already know the importance of supporting local specialty food purveyors: their continued presence guarantees you a higher quality and better selection of foods.

Hiring a Caterer

Outsourcing is a great relief — if you're outsourcing to somebody you can count on, without a doubt, for fabulous food and service. To better prepare yourself for checking out potential caterers, think through the following questions and bear these prompts in mind as you decide on the ideal caterer to make your party a delicious success:

1. Do you have friends or colleagues who have hosted catered affairs successfully in your area? Word-of-mouth recommendations are a great place to start.
2. Is the caterer licensed and insured in your city?
3. Does the caterer have experience executing the kind of party you're planning? Ask to see photos of previous parties they've done, for an idea of how it will all look.
4. Can the caterer provide a list of previous clients or references? Check them out to make sure the caterer was on time, billed

the amount agreed upon and provided food and service as wonderful as promised. Ask if the client would hire the caterer again.

5. Will the caterer provide a tasting? Even if there's a fee, this is money well spent, as it will give you a preview of the sort of food you can expect for your party.

6. Is the caterer amenable to any special requests that are important to you, such as customizing a package to fit your needs, providing drop-off food service without hired wait staff or allowing you to prepare some of the food yourself to save on costs?

7. Does the caterer have a standard contract that spells out the services that will be provided and the fees? Remember, some caterers specify that a guest count can go up but not down, so if you have fewer guests than expected, you'll still be paying for the count you gave the caterer.

Hiring Individual Help

If you opt not to hire a caterer, but are pretty sure you will need some extra helping hands, you can hire individuals to assist with any of a number of party-related tasks, ensuring that you can pull off the party you want and still enjoy your celebration. An extra pair of trained hands can take the pressure off you where you need it most — whether that's with dishes, cooking, mixing drinks or serving guests.

If budget is a concern and perfection isn't high on your priority list, you can always hire a teenager to help pass trays of appetizers or enlist a good friend or co-host to man the bar for the evening. But if you want everyone to have a chance to enjoy the party, and you want to be sure that each task is professionally executed, you'll do well to go through a staffing agency; check in the Yellow Pages under Bartending Services or Party Staffing, or contact cooking schools or colleges with hospitality programs. Hiring through an agency means that the agency should provide insurance and legal documentation, whereas if you hire privately, you could be held responsible for any accidents or injuries that person has while in your employ.

Some people feel uncomfortable letting a stranger into their home. If you're seriously considering hiring help but have some lingering concerns, then arrange to meet with potential employees well ahead of time to get references,

Contact a local culinary school or gourmet store for recommendations on someone you can hire to help you, either before or during your party.

discuss the expected dress code, conduct and job description and lay out the specific timeline and tasks. Doing so will let them and you know what to expect, so on party day there shouldn't be any surprises.

Consider hiring one or more of the following helpers to help make your party perfect.

Waiter

You'll want to seriously consider hiring a waiter if you plan to have passed appetizers, if you're hosting a formal dinner or if you're hosting an informal dinner for 20 or more guests. Have the waiter come at least an hour before the party so he or she can help with last-minute jobs, giving you a chance to get ready for your party. Before the party starts, a waiter can heat up appetizers, light candles, fill the ice bucket or open the red wine. You can also go over any last-minute details during this time so that everything goes smoothly. After the party starts, a waiter is there primarily to help serve food and drinks, of course.

Bartender

If you are hosting a medium to large party (say, 20 or more) that will involve made-to-order cocktails, it's a good idea to hire a bartender. Otherwise, you or a friend will be stuck making drinks all night, and that can get in the way of visiting with your guests and enjoying the festivities. Professional bartenders are also better than most of us at cutting off wobbly guests as needed; you can strategize with a bartender ahead of time about such issues.

Kitchen Helper or Chef

For dinner parties that require any last-minute cooking, a kitchen helper can be indispensable. Whether it's chopping vegetables, frying chicken or even just doing the dishes, that extra pair of skilled hands will free you up to act as host. Depending on the scope of their duties, you might want to have a kitchen helper or chef arrive earlier in the day, or you might just want them to be there shortly before the party starts, so they'll be ready to handle the meal's finishing touches while you're visiting with your guests. Discuss specifics ahead of time, and be sure you're hiring the right person, with the skills for the job: a chef won't want to wash dishes all night, and a kitchen helper might not be comfortable executing fussy desserts.

Creating a Balanced Menu

I love spaghetti and I love mashed potatoes, but never at the same meal. Creating a balanced menu is, well, a balancing act. You'll need to keep in mind the various flavors, textures, colors and even basic nutritional content of each dish to determine if it will meld perfectly with the other components of the menu or if it's an ill-advised carb overload or a cross-cultural mishmash that wouldn't qualify as the good kind of fusion.

If you're using a menu from this book (see Part 2, page 288, for more than two dozen party menus), then we've already done the balancing work for you. The birthday party menu (page 314), for example, is composed of a Shaved Artichoke and Bibb Lettuce Salad, Chicken Eggplant Rollups, Asiago Asparagus, Orzo Salad with Fresh Herbs, and Ice Cream Terrine with Raspberry Sauce. You'll notice that the food includes many traditional Mediterranean flavors, so its various components work well together. But there's a lot of variety in color, texture, flavor and even temperature, meaning that by the time guests lift a fork for a bite of that delicious terrine, they aren't already overloaded on berries or cream.

The first step in balancing your menu is to write it down and read it aloud. Does it make you hungry? If so, you're on the right track. Here are some other factors to keep in mind as you fine-tune it.

Temperature

You don't need to serve all foods hot; in fact, many flavors benefit from cooling at room temperature for a bit. A rice pilaf can be served at room temperature alongside warm roast meat, for instance. And a cool, crisp salad provides the counterpoint to a hot pot of cheese fondue better than a warm vegetable dish would. It is also a lot easier on the cook if the meal includes room-temperature or refrigerated components, because that means you can prepare them well ahead of time and have fewer things to finish on the stovetop or in the oven at the last minute.

Flavors

The various flavors in the menu should complement each other and flow from appetizer to entrée to dessert, but they should also provide contrast from one dish to the next. The Wine and Cheese Tasting menu (page 332), for instance, includes Spiced Nuts with Dried Fruit, a Cheese Board, a Fresh Fruit Assortment, a Bread and Cracker Assortment and a Baby

Greens Salad. It wouldn't make sense to add meatloaf to that menu, because it would conflict with the theme; a big, messy diner-style meatloaf with ketchup just wouldn't work with the chic look, texture and flavors of this menu. But you could easily add a platter of prosciutto or even smoked sausages, sliced on the diagonal, if you felt like your crowd would appreciate some meat in the mix or if you're serving it at an hour that requires heavier food.

Visual Appeal

Appealing to the eyes is a surefire way to appeal to the appetite, so a balanced menu always represents a variety of colors. Pork served with mashed potatoes and homemade applesauce might be balanced in flavor, but it's going to be awfully beige. Think about how the finished plate will look; if the food is all one color, consider swapping out one dish for something more visually appealing, adding a colorful sauce or getting creative with your garnishes (for more on garnishing, see page 150). For added visual interest, it's a good idea to use a variety of shapes, too. For instance, you can cut bell peppers into strips or triangles, slice zucchini on a deep diagonal or thinly slice pork and fan it out on plate.

Texture

Variety in texture also makes for a more interesting and satisfying meal. A creamy pasta dish goes better with tender-crisp asparagus than it would with creamed spinach, for instance. You can add texture to dishes with simple touches: top a creamy puréed soup with crispy croutons, or sprinkle chopped toasted nuts over cooked vegetables.

Variety

Keep things interesting by avoiding the repetition of an ingredient, flavor or cooking procedure throughout the meal. For example, a grilled main course is nicely rounded out with a cool side dish such as potato salad or coleslaw. And an appetizer that's heavy on garlic is best followed by a meal that's not. Even when your theme means that you're featuring the season's best tomatoes or blood oranges, you can still alternate cooking techniques and accompanying flavors to highlight a repeated ingredient in new ways.

Accommodating Special Diets

If you're inviting someone new to the party, it's a good idea to ask about any food allergies or preferences they might have. Inquire as soon as you know that they're coming, such as when you receive an RSVP by phone or email. An increasing number of people are following vegetarian diets these days, and some are even going vegan, which means nothing that comes from an animal, including meat, dairy, eggs and even honey. Those who follow kosher diets have their own set of dietary constraints and, as with vegetarians, some are stricter than others.

You'll need to find out ahead of time what these guests can eat and make sure to have a few dishes available that keep their preferences in mind. You don't have to prepare an entirely vegetarian meal if your other guests are the meat-and-potatoes type, but having prior knowledge will allow you to leave the bacon out of the vegetables, use vegetable stock instead of chicken stock in the risotto and pass the Parmesan cheese separately instead of tossing it in with a salad. Such minor changes can mean the difference between a guest enjoying a full meal or having nothing to eat. It's also fine to request that they bring a dish to the party: they'll get a chance to share their favorite food with friends, and you'll have your bases better covered.

For guests with food allergies and other health concerns, sticking to their prescribed diet can be a very serious matter. It's best to avoid the problem area (peanuts or shellfish, for example) for the entire menu, because of the possibility of cross-contamination. If you're having a larger buffet and aren't sure about each guest's dietary limitations, it's wise to point out any highly allergenic ingredients with a card or verbally, especially if they could go unnoticed, as in sauces or purées. If you feel uncertain about cooking for a special diet, ask the guest for some suggestions ahead of time; they'll likely be grateful for your interest and happy to help.

Nutritional Value

Think about the four major food groups when you're planning a menu. While party menus are often more indulgent than what we eat on a typical day, and party food *should* be special, overkill is still possible. If you're serving a very rich main course, consider a dessert that's fruit-based rather than cream- or chocolate-based. Acidic ingredients can help cut through the richness of creamier ones. And avoid going too carb-heavy by making sure a pasta dinner is balanced by some protein and vegetables instead of, or in addition to, that fresh loaf of bread.

Do-Ahead Food

Any portion of the menu that you can completely or partially prepare ahead of time will make the day of the party that much easier on you, so it makes sense to incorporate some menu items that offer such flexibility. Read through the following ideas for do-ahead items, and consider replacing that soufflé on your menu with something a little easier on the cook. You'll thank yourself later!

Appetizers

Bread for crostini or bruschetta can be toasted the morning of the party and then stored in airtight packaging. Prepare toppings, such as a tomato, garlic and basil mixture, a day ahead of time, leaving just the assembly to do before the party. Dips, including hummus, can almost always be made well ahead, covered and refrigerated until serving time. Cut up crudités a day ahead and store them in resealable bags in the refrigerator. Favorite nibbles such as spiced nuts (store in an airtight container at room temperature and recrisp in the oven if necessary), marinated olives (store in an airtight container in the refrigerator) and cheese straws (store in an airtight container at room temperature for up to two days or freeze them) can all be prepared a few days ahead.

> To keep cut-up veggies for crudités from drying out, wrap them in damp paper towels before storing them in resealable plastic bags in the refrigerator. They'll keep overnight this way.

Cocktails

If you're planning to serve a special cocktail and nobody wants to spend the entire evening working the bar, consider making it a pitcher drink. Margaritas, sangria, mojitos, spiked lemonade, Bloody Marys, fruity rum punches and more can all be mixed up in big batches well ahead of time and refrigerated until the party gets started. If your recipe involves something fizzy like ginger ale or club soda, mix everything else ahead of time, then top each beverage with freshly opened club soda at serving time. For smaller parties, I buy the small bottles of club soda, tonic water and ginger ale so I always have fizzy components on hand; they're more expensive, but there's less waste because only small portions go flat.

First Courses

Soups and salads are ideal candidates for the do-ahead cook who wants to serve a sit-down first course. Soups, particularly the puréed ones that are so elegant as first courses, can be made well ahead of time and frozen; heat them up on the stovetop when needed, saving the addition of cream for finishing time. Salads can be washed and mostly assembled, then refrigerated a day ahead. Toast any nuts for such salads ahead of time and store airtight at room temperature for up to a few days. Prepare the vinaigrette a day ahead and refrigerate. At serving time, whisk the dressing again and toss together all components for a fast first course.

Main Courses

One-dish meals such as lasagnas and enchiladas can be fully prepared a day ahead of time, refrigerated overnight and then simply popped in the oven in time for the party. Some recipes can be made weeks ahead and frozen until the day before the party. Your guests will enjoy the aroma of freshly cooking food as they arrive, and you'll enjoy no last-minute fuss. Quiche, which can be served warm, at room temperature or chilled, is another easy do-ahead main course, especially for brunches or lunches.

Side Dishes

Sides that are served cold or at room temperature are the easiest to do ahead of time, because they won't require any last-minute heating. Consider refrigerated pasta, orzo or couscous salads; potato salads or coleslaw; sliced fresh melon or fruit salads; or chilled steamed asparagus, to name a few. Potato gratins and other cool-weather casseroles can be fully assembled ahead of time and baked in time for the party.

Desserts

This is probably the easiest category to take care of ahead of time. Ice creams, cakes, pies, tarts, cookies and brownies are easy to make ahead (or even purchase) and are fine to serve cold or at room temperature. For a special touch, make (or purchase) a chocolate or caramel sauce in advance and zap it in the microwave briefly just before serving. Pie with cold ice cream and warm caramel sauce, for example, makes a fantastic dessert; with its various textures, flavors and temperatures, it'll seem custom-finished, not made-ahead. The same goes for brownies or cookies à la mode.

Getting Ready to Cook

Long before you can get down to the actual business of cooking, you'll need to take care of some other requirements. Is your kitchen stocked with all the equipment you'll need? Is it clean and ready for action? Are you? Then there's shopping for food, beverages and supplies. Only when your kitchen is completely party-ready is it time to lift the whisk.

Equipment Basics

Every cook's kitchen needs some essential knives, pots and pans and other basic equipment. While specialty items like a wok, an ice cream maker or a waffle iron might be important to you, depending on your cooking habits and personal taste, the following are basics that no home cook should be without. Because these are items you'll use over and over again for many years to come, I recommend splurging on the highest-quality kitchen equipment you can manage — or at least splurging on a subscription to *Cook's Illustrated* (www.cooksillustrated. com), which provides numerous unbiased reviews of cookware. You can sometimes find great deals on quality equipment at discount stores like TJ Maxx (www.tjmaxx.com), Tuesday Morning (www.tuesdaymorning.com) or HomeSense (www. homesense.ca). Also take advantage of sales at department stores and kitchen retailers. Another bonus of purchasing quality items is that the manufacturer will usually stand behind them: one of my friends burned up her pricey Chantal tea kettle by leaving it on the stove unattended, and the company replaced it free of charge.

Knives

These are real workhorses in the kitchen. A good 8- to 10-inch (20 to 25 cm) chef's knife will be your most important piece of equipment, but you'll also benefit from having a good paring knife. Some cooks also like serrated knives for slicing bread without crushing it.

High-carbon stainless steel is the best choice for cutting most foods; it's expensive, but worth it. A blade that is riveted through the handle is a sign of quality. Make sure to choose knives that are comfortable to grip. Your chef's knife should have a wide, heavy blade that can crush garlic without bending and easily cut through tough ingredients like butternut squash or chicken bones.

Essential Equipment and Supplies List

The following are some essential tools of the trade that you should have in your kitchen. For more details, including shopping and care tips, see the additional sections on equipment, beginning on page 112.

Equipment

- Baking dishes: 8-inch (20 cm) square and 13- by 9-inch (33 by 23 cm)
- Baking sheets: the heavy-duty rimmed aluminumized steel kind (without nonstick coating) with 1-inch (2.5 cm) deep sides are much more useful than the flat type
- Colander
- Cooling rack
- Cutting board: I prefer the plastic kind because they are dishwasher-safe
- Electric mixer (hand mixer or stand mixer)
- Food processor
- Grill pan: cast iron is best
- Mixing bowls in various sizes (glass is best, as they are microwave-safe)
- Muffin pan
- Roasting pan
- Saucepans: large (4-quart/4 L); medium (2-quart/2 L); small (1quart/1 L)
- Skillets or sauté pans: large (12- to 14-inch/30 to 35 cm); medium (8- to 9-inch/20 to 23 cm)
- Springform pan: 8- to 9-inch (20 to 23 cm)
- Stockpot or soup pot: 10- to 12-quart (10 to 12 L)

Utensils

- Box grater
- Can opener
- Chef's or santoku knife (8-inch/20 cm)
- Citrus reamer
- Corkscrew
- Ice cream scoop
- Instant-read thermometer
- Ladle
- Measuring cups, dry, and measuring spoons
- Measuring cups, liquid (in 1 and 2-cup/250 and 500 mL sizes, and larger)
- Melon baller
- Paring knife
- Pepper grinder
- Rolling pin
- Scissors
- Serrated knife (best for slicing cakes and bread)
- Sharpening steel
- Slotted spoon
- Spatula, heat-proof silicone
- Spatula, metal (for spreading)
- Tongs
- Vegetable peeler
- Wire whisk
- Wooden spoon
- Zester

Supplies

- Aluminum foil
- Bamboo or wooden skewers
- Kitchen twine
- Paper towels
- Plastic wrap
- Resealable plastic bags (1quart/1 L and 1gallon/4 L size)

Take care of your investment. Wash knives by hand — never put them in the dishwasher. Dry them with a soft cloth and store them separately in a wooden knife block. These days, there are compact, horizontal knife blocks that fit neatly into kitchen drawers; look for them at well-stocked kitchen supply shops and department stores. Fans of the industrial look will like those wall-mounted magnetic knife holders that keep the most-used blades within arm's reach at all times, and protected from the dulling influences of a drawer or knife block.

Keep your knives sharp. It might seem counterintuitive, but working with sharp knives is actually *safer* than working with dull ones; dull knives tend to slip and cause accidents, while sharp knives are more efficient and make much neater slices. Avoid purchasing knives that say they don't need sharpening; in my experience, that's never true. Straighten the blade with a steel before each use — as you use a knife, it tends to get tiny nicks and bends in the metal. Home cooks should sharpen their knives at least every six months, either with a sharpener or a stone. If you'd rather outsource the task, take your knives to the professionals at your favorite meat counter, butcher shop, knife store or hunting store. Asian knives, such as Global and Shun, have a different angle to their blade than the heartier German knives. Be sure to match the original angle of the blade when sharpening.

> Other good knives to have on hand are a paring knife, a utility knife (similar to a chef's knife but shorter), a serrated bread slicer and a meat carver.

Pots and Pans

Look for high-quality pots and pans that will suit your cooking style the best. Heavy-bottomed pots and pans are a sign of quality and will do a better job of evenly distributing heat and preventing scorching than their thinner counterparts. To acquaint yourself with brands and prices, check out reviews by *Cook's Illustrated* (www.cooksillustrated.com) and Epicurious (www.epicurious.com).

There are several types of pots and pans, and you'll likely want to purchase a few different types to suit a variety of cooking tasks, so consider purchasing each piece individually instead of buying a set. While the idea of having a matching set of gleaming stainless steel or copper cookware is appealing, I find that I use cast iron for searing steaks, stainless steel for a big pot of chili and nonstick pans for omelets. Be sure to take note of the handles; some cooks will want a skillet that has an oven-safe handle, for finishing frittatas or tarte Tatins in the oven. You might also want an oven-safe covered Dutch oven. You should also keep in mind the size of your oven; some large roasting or baking pans might not fit in smaller ovens, so take your oven measurements with you when you shop.

Here are some of the most common cookware types.

Stainless Steel

This material is easy to care for, durable and good-looking. Shop for $1^8/_{10}$ stainless steel with a copper core in the bottom to better conduct heat evenly; a heavy bottom will also keep food from burning. To help prevent sticking, preheat a stainless steel skillet before using it, add oil or butter to the hot pan, then add the food. Stainless steel is great for browning food. An all-purpose stockpot with steaming and pasta inserts and a lid is a practical piece to start with.

Half-sheet pans, which are 18- by 12-inch (45 by 30 cm) stainless steel baking pans, are useful for a number of tasks, from baking to roasting to freezing. Choose lighter-colored baking sheets over their darker-metal counterparts, and go for heavier rather than lighter. Look for them in restaurant supply and cookware stores.

Nonstick

Nonstick skillets are one item for which quality might not matter as much; the nonstick coating will get scratched or wear off a pan eventually, requiring you to replace the pan, so feel free to pick up your nonstick skillets on the cheap. Store them with a paper towel atop the nonstick surface to protect it from scratches.

Add oil or butter to the pan before heating these up — while there's some debate about the fumes nonstick pans can emit, it's generally agreed that not heating them to extremely high temperatures and not heating them empty are safer practices. When cooking with nonstick pans, use wooden or heat-resistant silicone utensils to avoid damaging the coating.

Nonstick cooking oil spray can ruin the surface of nonstick pans. Instead, use just a little oil and wipe off the excess with a paper towel before cooking.

Cast Iron

Cast-iron cookware is relatively inexpensive, and it holds heat and withstands high temperatures really well, so it's ideal for long-simmering stews and for searing meat. However, cast iron shouldn't be used to cook acidic ingredients, such as tomatoes, because they can cause iron to leach into the food (enameled cast iron, like the colorful lines made by Le Creuset and Staub, and the new, inexpensive line from Lodge, gets around the problem of leaching).

Regular cast-iron cookware should be seasoned before its first use. To season it, brush the pan generously with vegetable oil and place it over low heat for about an hour. Let cool, then wipe excess oil away with a paper towel. To prevent rust, always wipe the pan with a little oil before storing it. Cast-iron pans should become more and more nonstick as you use them. If a cast-iron pan does rust, rub it with a solution of 2 teaspoons (5 mL) lemon juice or vinegar mixed with 1 cup (250 mL) water, or a mixture of salt and oil.

Copper

Copper is the classic material for cookware — it's a superb heat conductor, but it's very expensive and requires more maintenance than other materials. Copper comes lined in tin or stainless steel; uncoated copper is for decorative purposes only and not for cooking. You'll have to polish copper cookware regularly to keep its original luster, and tin-lined copper cookware must be retinned eventually. Stainless steel–lined copper is sturdier than tin-lined, but some argue that a stainless steel lining detracts from copper's usually superior ability to conduct heat.

> Here's an old-fashioned copper-cleaning solution: Mix together $\frac{1}{4}$ cup (50 mL) vinegar or lemon juice, 2 egg whites and $\frac{1}{2}$ cup (125 mL) salt. Use a sponge or dishcloth to rub the mixture onto the copper surface. Rinse well before drying.

If you feel you absolutely need a piece of copperware to complete your kitchen, go for a large mixing bowl. Whipped cream mixed in a cold copper bowl whips up higher and fluffier than you'll get in anything else.

To polish copper, rub it with the cut side of half a lemon dipped in salt. Alternatively, dissolve 3 tablespoons (45 mL) salt in 1 cup (250 mL) vinegar, pour into a spray bottle and spray onto tarnished copper. Let it sit a few minutes before rubbing it clean.

Glass

Heatproof glass is the material of choice for casserole and baking dishes; it's inexpensive, practical and sturdy, and is safe to use in the microwave, oven, refrigerator, freezer and dishwasher. For safety, though, be careful not to transfer a cold dish to a hot oven, or place a hot dish under cold water. Extreme temperature changes can cause the glass to shatter. Every cook will need at least one or two basic 13- by 9- by 2-inch (33 by 23 by 5 cm) baking dishes for lasagna, potato gratins and other casseroles. Baking enthusiasts will also want to have a few glass pie dishes on hand.

Other Essentials

Besides knives, pots and pans, you'll need a bevy of other items to fully equip your kitchen. A quality stand mixer, a food processor and a blender will save you time and effort on numerous tasks, making cooking for company — not to mention your own family — easier. Here's a list of smaller basics you'll find essential for entertaining.

Citrus Reamer

Wood, glass, metal and plastic citrus reamers are available to help you make the most of lemons, limes, oranges and grapefruits, extracting much more juice than you could by hand.

Cooling Racks

Cooling racks aren't just for bakers; any home cook will find it useful to have a few. Anyone who's ever had their cooktop crowded by a cooling casserole or roast will appreciate the utility of a cooling rack that frees up their burners. Look for metal racks: larger, oven-safe commercial versions are the most useful, as you can also roast meats on them for a crust that's crispy on all sides (place them over a pan to catch the drippings). You'll find better-quality, yet still inexpensive, options at restaurant supply stores.

Grater and Zester

A large-hole grater makes short work of shredding cheeses for lasagna or fondue, potatoes for latkes and cabbage for slaw; small-hole graters are used to grate hard cheeses, spices and citrus zest. Microplane is an extremely reputable manufacturer to consider. If you have a lot of grating to do, a food processor fitted with a grating attachment proves very efficient. A small hand-held zester is the best tool for removing zest from citrus fruits, for a variety of sweet and savory uses.

Kitchen Scale

A kitchen scale will help you execute recipes accurately and consistently. I like scales that have a digital display, for an exact read. If you plan to do a lot of quantity cooking, look for scales that measure weight up to at least 5 pounds (2.5 kg).

Long-Handled Metal Utensils

Long-handled metal utensils are sometimes sold as a set, but whether you purchase them individually or all together, make sure you have a ladle, a slotted spoon and a pasta fork. A ladle is essential for large pots of soup, chili or stew. A slotted spoon has a number of uses, some as simple as scooping up a piece of macaroni to check for doneness. You'll need a pasta fork for tossing and serving long pastas, such as spaghetti or linguine.

Measuring Spoons and Cups

Buy heavy-duty sets of stainless steel dry measuring cups and spoons from a quality manufacturer (you'll find such sets in kitchen goods stores and sometimes in discount home goods stores). They cost more, but they last a lot longer than lighter versions. You should also have a variety of glass measuring cups to use as liquid measures. I like the classic Pyrex ones, as they're microwave- and dishwasher-safe. While almost everybody has the 2-cup (500 mL) version (it's essential to have at least one or two of those), you'll be surprised how often you'll use the 4-cup (1 L) and even 8-cup (2 L) versions once you have them.

Mixing Bowls

Stainless steel bowls are durable and inexpensive, while glass ones are usually microwave-safe. And they're not just for mixing: purchase several sizes and use them for everything from mise-en-place bowls to mashing potatoes to tossing salad. Some mixing bowls come in sets of various sizes, which is a good way to start.

Pastry Brushes

Pastry brushes are great for pastry, of course, but they're also useful for basting on marinades, brushing sauté pans evenly with butter or oil and brushing egg whites onto breads. The newer heat-resistant silicone basting and pastry brushes work well for everything from barbecue basting to baking, and they're dishwasher-safe (in the top rack). Be aware that old-fashioned, natural-bristle pastry brushes sometimes leave behind a hair or two, so watch for that and remove any such strays from your food before serving.

Rubber Spatulas

More likely made of heat-resistant silicone than of rubber, these spatulas come in a variety of sizes, shapes and colors, including a very handy spoon-shaped spatula that's proven essential in my kitchen. You'll reach for these often for a variety of kitchen tasks great and small, from removing the last bit of sour cream from its container to folding beaten egg whites into a cake recipe. Make sure the spatulas you choose for flipping pancakes and other items are rated for the level of heat you'll be subjecting them to; I've seen cheaper ones melt on the front edge.

Thermometers

Thermometers are inexpensive but incredibly important. An oven thermometer will help you gauge whether your oven is correctly calibrated, and until you can have the oven adjusted, an oven thermometer can help you make temperature adjustments so your recipes come out perfectly every time. A meat thermometer is a great way to test for doneness without cutting into the meat, and it will help you ensure that the food you're serving has reached safe temperatures (for a chart of such temperatures, see page 136). An instant-read thermometer can have a digital readout or a dial. It displays the temperature very quickly, so you don't have to interrupt the cooking time to get the temperature. Candy thermometers are useful not only for making candy, but in some cases also for testing the temperature of oil for frying; check the packaging before using it for oil. There are also laser thermometers that read the surface temperature without touching; you point the laser at the surface of something (hot coals, simmering liquid, a skillet), and it will tell you the temperature. How fancy is that?

Tongs

Tongs are useful kitchen tools for a number of tasks, from grilling to frying to tossing salads. They're great for turning and plating foods that require a delicate touch. You'll find yourself reaching for them often, so have a few sizes on hand. I even have a pair with coated ends for use in my nonstick skillets.

Vegetable Brushes and Peelers

It's good to have a couple of each; peeling enough potatoes for Thanksgiving, for instance, is a time-consuming task, so when someone asks what they can do to help, it's nice if you have an extra vegetable brush and peeler to hand them. Both are also essential for everyday cooking. Peelers come in horizontal (Y-shaped) and vertical formats; both work well, so go with what feels best in your hand.

Whisks

For everything from making vinaigrette to mixing up pancake batter, whisks are basics you won't want to be without. Purchase several sizes: balloon whisks are great at incorporating extra air; narrower versions work just fine for mixing up scrambled eggs.

Wooden Spoons

They're cheap, they're natural and they don't scratch up your cookware — it's imperative for home cooks to have a good stash of wooden spoons in a variety of lengths. Longer ones are perfect for stirring big pots of soup, and shorter ones are good for sautéing veggies. It's recommended that you hand-wash them, although I'll admit that I put mine in the dishwasher and still get many years out of them.

Prepping Your Kitchen

Having a clean kitchen in which to begin your party preparations isn't only inspiring, it's crucial. You'll be able to better find your tools and ingredients if they're orderly, and you'll be ready to safely handle meat, poultry, seafood, eggs and dairy. Here are some tips for getting your kitchen party-ready — several days ahead of time, if possible.

Clean Out Your Refrigerator and Freezer

If you have limited space in your kitchen's largest appliance, be sure to toss out spoiled food and rearrange or use up excess stores of fresh or frozen foods in advance of shopping for the party. You'll need the space not only for the ingredients, but for any dishes you make ahead of time, as well. It's nice to know there will be room in the fridge to store your Black Bean and Roasted Corn Salad and Salsa Fresca for your Mexican Fiesta (see page 386). By the time you've begun cooking, you won't want to slow down to clear out much-needed space.

Uncover More Counter Space

Do you have a tangle of small appliances and cookbooks on your kitchen counters? Store anything you won't need for this particular party so you can maximize your counter space for all that food preparation.

Disinfect Surfaces

Food poisoning can cause one or more of the following symptoms: nausea, vomiting, diarrhea, headache, fever, stomachache and fatigue.

Wash your countertops with hot, soapy water and an antibacterial cleanser or diluted bleach, depending on the surface. Wash cutting boards thoroughly with hot, soapy water after each use to avoid cross-contamination. While wooden cutting boards are, somewhat surprisingly, considered safer than plastic ones to use for meat and poultry, using *separate* cutting boards is probably the safest option of all. Many companies now sell color-coded cutting board sets so you'll never slice your veggies where you once cut chicken parts.

Keep Sponges Safe

Bacteria thrive on kitchen sponges, rags and dishtowels, meaning that when you think you're cleaning, you could actually be spreading bacteria around your kitchen. To avoid doing so, wash sponges frequently, preferably in a bleach solution. To quickly disinfect a sponge or rag, dampen it and then microwave it on High for at least 1 minute. Or put it in the dishwasher basket and select Heat Dry or Sanitize for higher temperatures. When in doubt, toss out old, smelly sponges and replace them with new ones. Rags and dishtowels can be sanitized by washing them in hot water in your clothes washer.

Wash Your Dishes

Wash and set aside the place settings and serving dishes you'll be using. Have you ever gotten to party time only to find that a couple of the dinner plates you'll need are dirty? Or that the "good" wineglasses you thought were clean have collected some dust since you last entertained? That's why it's important to get the place settings and serving dishes ready at least a day ahead. Many people like to set their tables a day in advance, and doing so does help you visualize any missing components that require your attention. For serving dishes, place a slip of paper with the food name written on it atop each, so you and any helpers will know where each prepared course should go.

Empty Your Dishwasher

Empty your dishwasher before you begin preparing food. That way, you'll be able to load it with dirty items as you're working. Get in the habit of washing pots, pans and dishes as you go, to keep things running smoothly and prevent a huge pileup that nobody wants to deal with later. Remember that people tend to congregate in the kitchen during parties. Take it from me: it's easier to keep your kitchen company-worthy than it is to keep company out of the kitchen.

Personal Hygiene

As a food professional, I feel it necessary to remind home cooks that there's good reason to follow some personal hygiene protocol in advance of food preparation. At the least, these tips will serve as reminders of what you already know, but they can also help prevent some very embarrassing food flubs.

Clean Your Hands

Everyone knows they should wash their hands before preparing food, but you should also wash them during and after food preparation, using soap, a nail brush and hot water, to prevent cross-contamination. Don't cook with lotion on your hands, and always wash your hands after using the restroom, smoking, coughing, sneezing or scratching. I'm a fan of what I'll call the preschool sneeze, where young children are taught

Equipment-Cleaning Tips and Tricks

- **Burned pots and pans:** It's best to prevent burns by using heavy cookware and not leaving food unattended, but when you are faced with burned pots and pans, try this trick: Fill the pot with water and dishwasher detergent and let it stand for a few hours. Place it on your cooktop, bring it to a boil and then use a wooden spoon to scrape up any stubborn burned bits.

- **Coffee grinder or spice grinder:** If you don't want the flavor of what you ground last in what you'll grind next, you'll need to clean the hard-to-navigate chamber of these small countertop appliances. Try grinding white rice or torn-up pieces of white bread; they should absorb odors and clean the blades of the machine. Toss out the rice or bread, then wipe out the inside of the appliance with a soft, dry cloth.

- **Coffee makers:** For coffee makers in need of freshening up, try this trick: Fill the water chamber of the pot with white vinegar and turn the machine on, as if you're making coffee. After that, fill the chamber with water and allow the pot to "brew" that. Run water through it twice for added assurance that all vinegar has been flushed through.

- **Kitchen equipment with small crevices:** Graters, garlic presses, strainers, citrus zesters and pastry bag tips can be difficult to clean. Keep a toothbrush on hand in the kitchen for scrubbing such small nooks and crannies.

- **Silver:** Silver flatware and serving pieces require regular polishing to erase the tarnish that develops, particularly after they come into contact with salt, egg yolks, broccoli or fish. Salt, in particular, has a reputation for pitting silver, so don't leave the two in contact long-term. To polish silver, put strips of aluminum foil in a large bowl or in the bottom of a plugged kitchen sink. Place the silver on top of the foil. Pour in enough boiling water to cover, then add $\frac{1}{4}$ cup (50 mL) baking soda. Let soak for 10 minutes. Rinse the silver well and dry with a soft cloth. Commercial silver polishes are also available, though they are more time-consuming.

- **Wax drips:** Candles are great at setting the mood for a party, but they're infamous for the mess they can leave behind. If wax drips on a bare tabletop, use a hairdryer on its low setting to soften the wax, then scrape it up with a credit card. For linens, peel off as much wax as you can by hand, then place the cloth wax side down over the sink, pour a kettle of boiling water over the wax, then scrape the fabric with a credit card. For glass votive holders, freeze them overnight, then hold them upside down and tap on the bottom until the wax pops out.

to sneeze into the crook of their elbow instead of into their hands. Ingenious, isn't it? I also advise cooks to leave their nails unpolished — nobody wants shiny red flakes in their food unless they're crushed red pepper.

Avoid Jewelry

Jewelry can get caught in appliances or fall into dishes, so it's safest to remove it before you cook. If you do wear jewelry, use common sense and discretion when cooking. A scone recipe that needs a few turns of kneading also requires you to remove your rings; we all know that we don't keep our jewelry as clean as we should, and bits of dough can work their way in and out of the settings.

Secure Your Hair

You don't have to get a cafeteria-lady hairnet (although that's not a bad idea), but do tie your hair back if it's long. Finding a hair in the food is really off-putting, and unfortunately it's fairly common. If you have shorter hair, wear a hat while cooking.

Cover Wounds

If your hands have any cuts or open wounds, dress them properly and wear disposable plastic gloves to keep any infection from spreading. To avoid cross-contamination, remember to change gloves between working with meats and unwashed produce and handling cooked foods.

Food poisoning is especially harmful to young children, pregnant women, the elderly and anyone with a weak immune system.

Avoid Eating While You're Cooking

If you are hungry, stop and take a snack break. Chewing food or gum while cooking can lead to unwanted surprises in the food. Of course, you'll have to taste a sauce to determine how to season it, or try a green bean to see if it's cooked to perfect tender-crispness. But be careful how you taste: use a spoon or fork, not your finger. After tasting, wash the spoon before using it again.

Food Shopping

Before you even think about heading to the store, you'll need to figure out how much food you'll need, what can be purchased well ahead of time and what needs to wait until the last minute, and how to get it all collected and back into your kitchen while it's still at its peak. The following sections will lead you through smart ways to make your lists and gather your ingredients.

Estimating Food Amounts

You've settled on the menu, but before you go shopping, you'll need to decide how much food you'll need. Consult the per-person serving quantities charts on pages 125 and 126 for help determining how much food you'll need to prepare for the number of guests you'll host. Always take a calculator to the market when shopping for parties: it will make it easier to convert ounces to pounds (or to grams or milliliters), which you might need to know, depending on how packages are labeled at the store. Also keep in mind the following factors, which affect how much people eat.

Party Length

Will you be serving appetizers before a seated dinner? For a cocktail hour that will last an hour and a half, you can count on needing seven canapés or hors d'oeuvres per person — fewer if the cocktail hour will be shorter, as it usually is for home dinner parties, and probably more if the reception time is early and people will come straight from work.

Time of Day

Speaking of timing, even if you've only invited people for snacks and cocktails, guests will eat more at a dinnertime cocktail party than they would at a later-evening cocktail party. In fact, a dinnertime cocktail party is usually a cocktail supper, with heavier hors d'oeuvres that can stand in for a meal. Count on 12 to 14 canapés or hors d'oeuvres per guest when dinner won't be served, and choose recipes that will be more filling.

Style of Service

People usually eat fewer hors d'oeuvres when they're served butler-style, from passed trays, than when they're served buffet style and can help themselves.

Age of Guests

Older people tend to eat less than younger people, and certainly less than hungry teenagers. If you've ever hosted college students during the school year, or recent graduates who are out on their own for the first time and hurting for some home-cooked meals, you've seen this point made.

Type of Food

Lighter foods tend to go more quickly than rich ones, so take your menu into account when calculating how much you'll need to make.

Meat, Poultry and Seafood Serving Quantities

Meat and Poultry	Quantity per Person (uncooked)
Beef, lamb or pork (boneless)	4 to 6 oz (125 to 175 g)
Steak or leg of lamb	6 to 8 oz (175 to 250 g)
Pork chops (bone in)	1 large
Pork or beef ribs or shanks (bone in)	1 lb (500 g)
Beef, pork or lamb roasts	8 to 11 oz (250 to 325 g)
Beef, pork or lamb roasts (boneless)	4 to 6 oz (125 to 175 g)
Chicken thighs, legs or wings (bone in)	Two 3- to 4-oz (90 to 125 g) pieces
Chicken breast (boneless and skinless)	One 6- to 8-ounce (175 to 250 g) breast
Chicken or turkey (whole)	12 oz to 1 pound (375 to 500 g)
Seafood	**Quantity per Person (uncooked)**
Crab meat, lobster meat, octopus, shrimp, scallops, squid	4 to 5 oz (125 to 150 g)
Lobster (in shell)	$1\frac{1}{2}$ to 2 lbs (750 g to 1 kg)
Crab (in shell)	$1\frac{1}{2}$ to 2 lbs (750 g to 1 kg)
Mussels	12 each
Oyster and clams	4 to 6 each
Whole fish (not cleaned, guts intact)	12 oz to 1 pound (375 to 500 g)
Whole fish (cleaned and guts removed)	8 to 12 oz (250 to 375 g)
Fish fillets and steaks	5 to 8 oz (150 to 250 g)

Troubleshooting Tips

For peace of mind, consider having some extra food on hand to meet any unexpected demands. Choose items that require very little preparation and that can be frozen or will keep well if you don't need them immediately. Frozen appetizers are great in a pinch; they can be quickly heated if needed. Extra baguettes (have the bakery run them through the slicer as a time-saver) and a jar of tapenade, marinated olives and artichoke hearts, roasted salted nuts and even sliced deli meats can be life-savers when the crowd threatens to pick the buffet clean.

Organizing the Shopping List

Write or print out one master shopping list for the party, even if you anticipate that some things will come from different stores. It helps to divide a sheet of paper into columns that correspond to seven areas: produce, dairy, cheese and deli,

Hors d'Oeuvres and Side Dishes Serving Quantities

Other Foods	Quantity per Person (cooked or prepared)
Potatoes	3 to 4 oz (90 to 125 g)
Salad	3 to 4 oz (90 to 125 g) or 1 heaped cup (250 mL)
Vegetables	3 to 4 oz (90 to 125 g)
Desserts	4 oz (125 g)
Hors d'oeuvres	4 to 5 oz (125 to 150 g)
Rice	2 oz (60 g)
Pasta	3 oz (90 g)

meat and seafood, pantry items, beverages and miscellaneous. That way, you don't have to search the entire list when you're standing in the produce section.

Using a master list also allows you the flexibility to buy various items in unexpected places, depending on sales, availability and freshness. For instance, if you couldn't find the ripe avocados you wanted at the farmers' market, but you did buy the tomatoes you'll need there, you can take the same list with you to the grocery store and fill it in appropriately. I always take a pen with me to cross off items as I add them to the cart; in my mind, that makes the list progressively less overwhelming, and I don't have to wonder if I bought lemons at the first stop when I get to my second one.

Don't forget paper goods such as cocktail napkins or items like cleaning products or cooking fuel for the fondue pot. You can use the same list to buy non-perishables well ahead of time, and save it for when you'll purchase meats and produce a couple of days before the party.

Shopping Safely

Food safety really begins with your shopping trip. Perishables should be unrefrigerated for the shortest amount of time possible, so if you're doing your shopping in very warm weather or have several stops to make, consider placing a cooler packed with ice in the trunk of your car to transport such groceries safely.

Always check the "use by" or "best before" dates when you're purchasing food, to make sure it won't be past its prime by the time you're cooking for the party. This is particularly important with meats, poultry, seafood, eggs, milk and other dairy products and tofu (for more help selecting meat, turn to page 133). When selecting milk and eggs, I often look behind the front containers to find those marked with later dates. I also stick with reputable dealers; while you might, depending on your locale, see roadside trucks selling seafood on the cheap, it's not worth the risk. When in doubt, don't buy it.

While shopping, I always place meat, poultry and seafood on the lowest rack of the shopping cart, where their juices won't drip on the other ingredients. Even meat that's sealed in a plastic wrapper can drip; you can grab a couple of extra bags in the produce section to enclose meat or poultry for added protection. Remember that cross-contamination, which happens when bacteria are transferred between foods, is responsible for many outbreaks of food poisoning.

Safe Food Storage

The following are tips for the safe storage of a variety of foods. Remember that proper refrigeration will preserve freshness and prevent food-borne illness; bacteria thrive between 40°F (4°C) and 140°F (60°C), which is called the "danger zone" by pros. Foods should not be kept in that range for more than four hours, so keep that rule of thumb in mind when grocery shopping, serving a buffet and storing leftovers.

Berries

Most fruits keep well in the refrigerator, but delicate berries require special handling if they'll be stored for more than a day or so. Spread them in a single layer on a baking sheet lined with paper towels, and throw away any moldy ones. Cover them lightly with additional paper towels, then refrigerate. You can freeze cranberries in their original packaging. To freeze blackberries, blueberries, cherries, raspberries or hulled strawberries, wash and dry them, then spread them in a single layer on a baking sheet and freeze them. Once they're frozen, transfer the berries to resealable freezer bags, remove any excess air from the bags, seal and freeze them.

Breads

If you're planning to store fresh bakery breads for more than half a day, keep them in top form by sealing them in airtight plastic. If I'm planning to make crostini, I ask the bakery to run the loaves I purchase through the slicer, saving valuable preparation time. Sliced baguettes can be transferred to freezer bags, sealed (to prevent freezer burn, always remove excess air from freezer bags before sealing) and frozen until the morning of the party. It's amazing how much better breads are when

Don't throw out stale bread. Instead, cut or tear it into small pieces and pulse it in a food processor until it's chopped into crumbs. Place the crumbs in resealable plastic bags and freeze until ready to use.

they're enjoyed the day they're baked — or frozen on the day they're baked and thawed just in time for the party. Whole baguettes can be sealed in plastic wrap, then overwrapped in foil before freezing. Avoid refrigerating breads.

Butter

Butter picks up flavors from other foods, so always refrigerate it in a covered butter dish or wrap it well. If you have more butter than you'll need over the next few months, remember that it can be frozen in its original packaging and then thawed in the refrigerator when needed. To keep butter soft and spreadable, try a butter bell (visit www.butterbell.com for a few examples). This small French crock keeps spoilage at bay with its design: softened butter is packed into the crock's lid and then stored upside down over a water-filled base, limiting the oxygen that makes contact with the butter and making refrigeration unnecessary for a couple of weeks or longer.

Cakes

If you're making cake for dessert, go ahead and make it well ahead of time so you can focus on other tasks at the last minute. Once they're cool, wrap cake layers individually in waxed paper, seal in airtight storage bags or containers and freeze until the morning of the party. Defrost them at room temperature, then frost and assemble the cake. As an alternative, you can freeze frosted cakes uncovered until they're frozen solid, then wrap them well and return them to the freezer.

Canned Goods

If you're using a partial can of food, it's fine to cover the remaining portion in the can with plastic wrap and store it in the refrigerator for up to one day, unless the canned food is acidic, such as fruits, tomatoes or sauerkraut. Once opened, acidic canned foods should be transferred to a plastic or glass container, covered and refrigerated for up to three days.

Cheeses

Harder cheeses, such as Parmesan or aged Cheddar, will keep for up to a month in the refrigerator after they're opened; soft cheeses, such as Brie, generally need to be used within a week of opening. After opening, wrap cheese in plastic to prevent it from drying out or developing mold. If you've had soft cheese out at a party for more than four hours, discard any that remains. You can safely cut off small amounts of mold on hard cheeses that have been refrigerated, removing and discarding at least 1 inch (2.5 cm) around and below the spot, and use the remaining cheese (except when serving pregnant women or people with weakened immune systems). With soft, sliced, crumbled or shredded cheeses, discard all cheese if a portion of it develops mold.

Chocolate

Chocolate, including baking chips and bars, should not be refrigerated but should be stored in a cool, dry place. (Chocolate can develop a white bloom, or coating, when refrigerated. It doesn't affect taste, but it certainly affects its appearance.) Wrap chocolate well, such as in a layer of parchment paper and then foil, to keep it from absorbing the odors of other foods. Because chocolate should be kept from excess humidity, it's also a good idea to seal it in an airtight container. When properly stored, baking chocolate is good for up to a year unless otherwise noted by a best-before date on the label.

Cooked Foods

Refrigerate cooked food as soon as possible. Letting the food cool at room temperature in the pot or dish it was cooked in allows it to spend longer in the danger zone of 40°F to 140°F (4°C to 60°C). At the same time, adding hot foods to the refrigerator can increase the temperature of the refrigerator to the danger zone. So it's best to help speed along the cooling process by pouring warm foods into cool wide pans so that the food is no more than 2 inches (5 cm) deep, stirring large pans occasionally while they cool or setting a hot pan in an ice bath to cool the food faster. If you live in a cold climate, you can take advantage of a snowy day or freezing outdoor temperatures for help in quickly cooling a pot of chili or soup.

Dry Goods

Dry goods, or any of those center-of-store items that don't require refrigeration, are best stored in a cool, dry place. While the ideal storage temperature for dry goods is 50°F (10°C), most of us don't have a place that cool in our homes (modern houses don't seem to come with root cellars), other than the refrigerator. Store all-purpose flour airtight at room temperature for up to six months; refrigerate it if you want to extend its life. Store whole wheat flour, which is more prone to going rancid, in an airtight container in the refrigerator. Use airtight containers (such as Tupperware or sealed freezer bags) for any open pantry items, both to discourage pests and to keep them from absorbing other flavors.

Eggs

Fresh raw eggs will keep in the refrigerator for up to five weeks. Always check the best-before date when you're purchasing eggs, as freshness varies, and discard any eggs that are cracked. Store eggs on an interior shelf, not in the door — frequent opening and closing of the door can make it the warmest part of the refrigerator. If you're unsure about the freshness of eggs, fill a pot with water and place the eggs in it. Fresh eggs will sink, while rotten eggs will float. Eggs that should be used up soonest will stand on one end. Hard-cooked eggs can be stored in the shell for up to a week.

Fruits

Most fruits will continue to ripen at room temperature, so store them in a basket if they need to ripen, or if you plan to eat them in the next couple of days. Bananas, peaches and tomatoes (technically a fruit) are best unrefrigerated to preserve their flavor, texture and good looks, but most other fruits, like apples, pears, melons and citrus fruits, may be refrigerated if ripe to lengthen their lives. Some fruits can be successfully frozen: try freezing grapes, cherries, berries and chopped peeled melon, peaches, apples or nectarines. I've even frozen overripe bananas to use in banana nut bread a few days later; the skin will shrivel and darken, but the fruit will be fine for use in baking. All fruits that are refrigerated or at room temperature should be checked daily; remove and use up overripe or bruised fruits right away, and discard any fruit that's moldy, slimy or smelly.

Herbs

Herbs from your garden that will be used the day you pick them can be put in a fresh glass of water on the countertop to await use. For longer storage, stand fresh herbs upright in small glasses or plastic cups with an inch (2.5 cm) of water in the bottom, place a plastic bag loosely over them and refrigerate. Alternatively, rinse fresh herbs and pat dry, then wrap in damp paper towels and put in resealable plastic storage bags before refrigerating. Dried herbs should be kept in a dark, dry place and used within six months.

Meat, Poultry, Fish and Seafood

Store meat, poultry and fish in containers with sides, to prevent dripping. Always store raw protein in the lowest section of the refrigerator, away from cooked food, to prevent contamination from any stray drips. For added safety, use disposable aluminum trays or pans underneath wrapped meats. Store fish, liver and ground meats loosely wrapped in the coldest part of the refrigerator, and use them within one day. Remove the giblets and rinse fresh chicken before storing; rewrap the chicken well and use it within two days. When freezing, separate pieces of meat with waxed paper first to prevent them from sticking together. Seafood should be put on ice for anything but very brief transportation; store it in the refrigerator for up to two days, or wrap it tightly in freezer paper or foil and freeze it.

Milk

Milk should be stored below 40°F (4°C) to prevent bacterial growth, and used within a week of opening. Moving a gallon container of milk in and out of the refrigerator many times will shorten its life and increase the chance of bacterial growth. Don't pour milk that has been left out back into the container, as it can contaminate the whole container.

Nuts

Raw nuts go rancid quickly because of their high fat content, so unless you plan to use the entire container immediately, seal them airtight and freeze them. Raw nuts may be frozen for up to a year; roasted salted nuts may be frozen for up to six months.

Spices

Purchase spices in small amounts and store them in a cool, dark place. Bright lights and warm temperatures shorten an already short shelf life. Most spices need to be replaced every six months, although whole spices retain their pungency longer than ground ones.

Vegetables

Remove any dead leaves from vegetables before storage. Use a salad spinner to dry greens as much as possible. Store the cleaned greens in a resealable plastic storage bag, layering the greens with paper towels. Potatoes and onions are best stored in a dark place at room temperature, but don't store them together, because doing so makes each spoil faster. Individual vegetables vary: while winter squash can be stored at a cool room temperature for a few months, asparagus should be refrigerated and used within a few days. When working with vegetables you're not familiar with, ask for advice where you purchase them; farmers' markets and upscale markets with exceptional produce sections tend to be more knowledgeable than other sources.

Thawing Food Safely

After you've frozen food for safe storage, it's just as important to thaw it safely. While there's no trick to thawing nuts, fruits and vegetables, you do need to be more careful with meat, poultry, fish and prepared foods such as stews or soups. Keep the following in mind:

- For safety, thaw frozen foods in the refrigerator. Avoid the temptation to thaw food on the kitchen counter at room temperature, or to run hot water over it, as these methods invite bacterial growth.
- You can run cold water over smaller pieces of food that are tightly wrapped in plastic or use the microwave's defrost setting.
- Cook thawed food immediately and thoroughly.

Safe Food Handling

See page 120 for cutting board tips to avoid cross-contamination during preparation. And see the chart below for the ideal temperatures, for everything from your refrigerator to your kitchen to your oven, for help keeping food safe from storage to handling to cooking. See the chart on page 136 for proper cooking temperatures, and check food package labels for additional guidance. For more information, as well as timely updates on any areas of current concern, visit the U.S. government's food safety website at www.foodsafety.gov or the Canadian Partnership for Consumer Food Safety Education site at www.canfightbac.org.

Ideal Temperatures

Location	Temperature
Freezer	0°F (−18°C)
Refrigerator	8°F to 40°F (−13°C to 4°C)
Cool room temperature	65°F (18°C)
Warm room temperature	70°F to 75°F (21°C to 24°C)
Lukewarm or tepid liquid	95°F (35°C)
Warm liquid	105°F to 115°F (40°C to 46°C)
Hot liquid	120°F (50°C)
Boiling water	212°F (100°C)
Rising bread	80°F (27°C)

Location	Temperature
Low/slow oven	180°F to 225°F (80°C to 110°C)
Warm oven	300°F to 325°F (150°C to 160°C)
Moderate oven	350°F to 375°F (180°C to 190°C)
Hot oven	400°F to 450°F (200°C to 230°C)
Very hot oven	475°F to 500°F (240°C to 260°C)

Shopping for and Preparing Meat, Poultry and Seafood

Always purchase meat, poultry and seafood from a reputable vendor and follow the food-safety tips on pages 126 to 132 to make sure you transport, store and handle it safely. And remember this rule of thumb: If it doesn't look, feel or smell right, pass it over. Don't purchase anything in damaged packaging that might have been torn or crushed, and avoid packages that are above what's called the "frost line" — the top of the freezer case — where it might be warmer than ideal.

There are many ways to cook meat, poultry and seafood, and you'll find recipes in Part 2 (page 201) with specific instructions for a number of preparations. Here, I'll suggest some of the classic best methods for each cut, but remember that there are always other ways, and always new recipes. Lately, for instance, high-temperature roasting has been used to great advantage for many cuts of meat and poultry, helping it to develop a crisp crust and be done in less time, but lower-temperature roasting is still the better choice for tougher cuts that benefit from a longer time in the oven. Don't be afraid to try new methods of cooking; as long as the internal temperature gets high enough (see Proper Temperatures, page 136), what you cook should be safe.

Meat

When selecting meat, opt for cuts that have white external fat, not yellow. Beef or lamb should be red to brownish red, with marbling throughout. Pork and veal should be fine-grained and pale pink. Cuts of meat should be used within a few days or frozen for up to a few months; liver and ground meats should be used within one day or frozen.

Before cooking, meats should be seasoned with salt and pepper and any additional seasonings, such as a dry rub or marinade; doing so ahead of time allows the flavors to mingle and mellow. (When the meat is done, you can add additional salt and pepper to taste.)

Dry rubs are mixtures of spices and herbs that are rubbed onto the meat just before cooking or a day or two ahead of time; the longer it's refrigerated with the dry rub on, the more flavor the rub will impart.

Wet marinades are used for flavoring, and in some cases for their tenderizing effect; they're recommended for sirloin, chuck, top round (London broil), flank steak and chops. Depending on the meat, you can marinate it in the refrigerator for anywhere from 30 minutes to several hours, but don't marinate tender, thin or small cuts for more than a few hours, because the acidity in the marinade can break down the meat, making it mushy.

Tough cuts of meat, like brisket, can be made tender by braising or stewing. First brown the meat on all sides in a little oil over high heat, then remove it from the pan and deglaze the pan by adding broth or wine and bringing it to a boil, using a wooden spoon to scrape up any brown bits. Next, return the meat to the pan and add additional cooking liquid. Cover and simmer over low heat for several hours, or until the meat is tender.

Wondering what the difference is between a flank steak and a rump roast? Here's a rundown on cuts of meat, and how to best use them. See the chart at right for a visual guide.

- **Top back:** The ribs, short loin and sirloin are in this section, and steaks and roasts are cut from it. These tender cuts, with their fine-grained texture, benefit from dry-heat cooking, such as grilling, broiling, roasting and sautéing. Filet mignon and tenderloin are the most tender and expensive of these cuts. New York strip, or top loin, Porterhouse, T-bone and rib-eye steaks, also from this section, are slightly less tender, but more flavorful and less expensive.
- **Shoulder and side:** You'll find the chuck (or shoulder, cross-rib and blade), flank, plate and brisket (or foreshank) in this section. These tougher cuts are more coarse-grained than others, with tougher connective tissue. Try moist, low-heat cooking to help soften such cuts; braising and stewing are recommended.
- **Leg:** In the middle of the tough/tender scale you'll find the leg, or the round. Cuts such as top round marinate really well, and doing so will have a tenderizing effect. Rump roasts, also in this category, are great flavored with a dry rub and slow-roasted. Tougher bottom round and round steaks are best braised.

Major Cuts of Meat

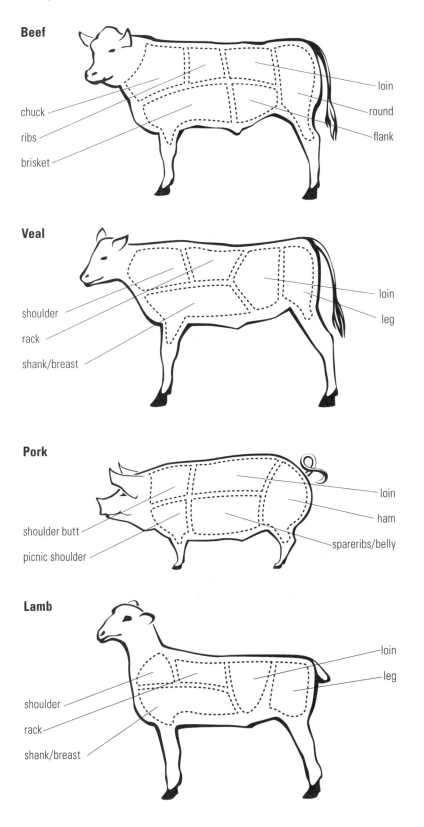

Beef

chuck
ribs
brisket
loin
round
flank

Veal

shoulder
rack
shank/breast
loin
leg

Pork

shoulder butt
picnic shoulder
loin
ham
spareribs/belly

Lamb

shoulder
rack
shank/breast
loin
leg

Poultry

When selecting poultry, look for plump, moist whole chicken or chicken parts, and check to make sure it's been cleaned well and has no feathers remaining. Fresher chicken will have bones that are still pink at the end. The meat on younger birds will be more tender; feel it to see if it yields easily. Many people are opting for organic poultry these days, though it's a matter of personal preference. Avoid ground turkey or chicken that's grayish in color, as that can indicate it's been sitting a bit too long.

When purchasing a turkey for Thanksgiving, purchase a fresh one if your budget allows. If you opt for a frozen bird, remember that it will require a few days' defrosting time in the refrigerator, so begin the process in plenty of time.

Poultry can be cooked successfully with almost any technique. While roasting a stuffed turkey has long been the standard for holiday cooks, these days brining the turkey before roasting, and cooking the stuffing separately, has become very popular. And increasing numbers of people in warmer climates are skipping the roasting altogether and opting to grill their Thanksgiving turkey; others are even deep-frying them. Chicken can be roasted, fried, sautéed, grilled or stewed. See the chart on internal temperatures below to avoid overcooking (and drying out) poultry, which is one of the most common mistakes.

Proper Temperatures

Meat	Temperature (F°/C°)
Chicken and turkey (all cuts)	165°F (74°C)
Beef and lamb	
Rare	130°F (54°C)
Medium-rare	140°F (60°C)
Medium	150°F (65°C)
Medium-well	165°F (74°C)
Ground beef and lamb	160°F (71°C)
Veal	
Medium	150°F (65°C)
Medium-well	165°F (74°C)
Ground veal	160°F (71°C)
Pork	
Loin and tenderloin	160°F (71°C)
Tougher braised cuts	170°F (77°C)
Ground pork	160°F (71°C)

Seafood

When selecting fresh fish, you might want to be flexible about the type you purchase, asking the seller what's best and freshest and opting for that rather than sticking with your list above all else. Improperly stored fish can develop toxins that can make you sick, so it's important to be vigilant about selection and storage.

If purchasing whole fish, look for those with a fresh, mild ocean smell. The eyes should be clear, shiny and bulging a bit, rather than cloudy or sunken. Look for a red or pink color around the gills and shiny, bright scales that are tight on the skin. Pass on any whole fish that is slimy or soft to the touch; when pressed, the fish should be firm and elastic, not easily dented.

With fish fillets or steaks, rely on your sense of smell to judge freshness; fish shouldn't smell overly fishy or like ammonia. When in doubt, skip it in favor of frozen fish. Fish is frequently frozen on the boat immediately after being caught, so going with frozen can actually give you the freshest-tasting fish possible. Fish fillets shouldn't have any discoloration, or any drying around the edges.

For shellfish, discard any broken or cracked clams, mussels or oysters. Do a "tap test" to determine if they're alive: they should close when tapped. Crabs and lobsters should be sold live; check for leg movement. (If you live in the U.S., the FDA requires a tag or label on containers of shellfish that states the processor's certification number, meaning the shellfish should have been processed safely. If in doubt, ask to see the tag or label.)

Most seafood should be cooked until its interior reaches 145°F (63°C), but with seafood it's also possible to rely on visual clues: fish flesh will be opaque and separate easily; shrimp and lobster flesh will be pearly opaque, scallop flesh will be firm and milky white or opaque; and clams, mussels and oysters should open when they're done (discard any that do not open).

Preparing the Food

Measuring

If you want to cook and bake successfully, it helps to have a good set of measuring cups and a kitchen scale (see the equipment section on page 112), and it's also important to know how to do some conversions. When a quiche recipe calls for 1 cup (250 mL) of crumbled cooked bacon, how much raw bacon do you need to purchase? And if you want to serve each guest 6 ounces (175 g) of pork, how many pounds (or kg) do you need? Consult the following charts for help bridging the gap between recipes and shopping lists, and from shopping lists to package sizes, so you'll get exactly what you need, every time.

Useful Ingredient Equivalents

Dry Goods	Quantity	Equivalent
Brown sugar	1 lb (500 g)	$3\frac{1}{2}$ cups (875 mL)
Brown sugar	1 lb (500 g)	$2\frac{1}{4}$ cups (550 mL) packed
Granulated sugar	1 lb (500 g)	$2\frac{1}{4}$ cups (550 mL)
Confectioner's (icing) sugar	1 lb (500 g)	$3\frac{3}{4}$ cups (925 mL)
Superfine sugar	1 lb (500 g)	$2\frac{1}{4}$ cups (550 mL)
All-purpose flour	1 lb (500 g)	$3\frac{3}{4}$ cups (925 mL)
Whole wheat flour	1 lb (500 g)	$3\frac{1}{3}$ cups (825 mL)
Cake flour	1 lb (500 g)	$4\frac{1}{2}$ cups (1.125 L)
Chocolate chips	1 cup (250 mL)	about 5 oz (150 g)
Chocolate chips	12 oz (375 g)	about $2\frac{1}{2}$ cups (625 mL)
Unsweetened cocoa powder	2 tbsp (25 mL)	1 square unsweetened chocolate
Unsweetened cocoa powder	1 cup (250 mL)	3 oz (90 g)
Unsweetened chocolate	1 oz (30 g)	3 to 4 tbsp (45 to 60 mL) cocoa powder + $1\frac{1}{2}$ tsp (7 mL) butter
Rolled oats	1 lb (500 g)	$5\frac{1}{3}$ cups (1.325 L)
Shredded coconut	14 oz (400 g)	$5\frac{1}{3}$ cups (1.325 L)
Shortening	1 lb (500 g)	2 cups (500 g)
Meat and Poultry	**Quantity (Uncooked)**	**Equivalent (Cooked)**
Chicken	3 lbs (1.5 kg)	4 cups (1 L) shredded
Chicken breasts	$1\frac{1}{2}$ lbs (750 g)	2 cups (500 mL) diced
Bacon	1 lb (500 g)	3 cups (750 mL) crumbled

Pasta, Rice and Legumes	Quantity (Uncooked)	Equivalent (Cooked)
Pasta	1 cup (250 mL)	2 cups (500 mL)
Spaghetti	7 oz (210 g)	4 cups (1 L)
Macaroni	1 cup (250 mL)	$2\frac{2}{3}$ cups (650 mL)
Rice	1 cup (250 mL) or 7 oz (210 g)	3 cups (750 mL)
Rice	1 lb (500 g)	6 cups (1.5 L)
Lentils	1 lb (500 g)	7 cups (1.75 L)
Split peas	1 lb (500 g)	6 cups (1.5 L)
Other dry beans	1 lb (500 g)	6 cups (1.5 L)

Vegetables and Herbs	Quantity (Uncooked Produce)	Equivalent
Beets	1 lb (500 g)	2 cups (500 g) diced
Bell pepper	1 large	1 cup (250 mL) chopped
Broccoli bunch	1 medium (9 oz/270 g)	$3\frac{1}{2}$ cups (875 mL)
Broccoli florets	1 lb (500 g)	6 cups (1.5 L)
Cabbage	½ small head	3–4 cups (750 mL–1 L) shredded
Carrots	1 lb (500 g), 6–8 medium	3 cups (750 mL) shredded
Celery	2 medium stalks	1 cup (250 mL) diced
Eggplant	1 medium (12–14 oz/375–420 g)	5 cups (1.25 L) cubed
Green onion	1 stalk	2 tbsp (25 mL) sliced
Lettuce, pre-washed	6 oz (175 g)	about 3 cups (750 mL)
Mushrooms	8 oz (250 g)	2 cups (500 mL) sliced
Onion	1 large (5–6 oz/150–170 g)	1 cup (250 mL) chopped
Onion	1 lb (500 g)	4 cups (1 L) chopped or 3 cups (750 mL) diced
Potato, mashed	1 medium potato	½ cup (125 mL) cooked
Pumpkin	1 lb (500 g)	1 generous cup (250 mL)
Spinach, cooked	1 lb (500 g)	$1\frac{1}{2}$ cups (375 mL)
Spinach, raw	1 lb (500 g)	8 cups (2 L)
Sweet potato	1 lb (500 g)	$1\frac{1}{2}$ cups (375 mL) cooked
Tomato	1 lb (500 g)	$1\frac{1}{2}$ cups (375 mL) peeled, seeded, and diced
Zucchini	1 lb (500 g)	$3\frac{1}{2}$ cups (875 mL) sliced or 2 cups (500 mL) grated

Food and Beverages · Preparing the Food

Nuts	Quantity	Equivalent
Almonds, shelled	1 lb (500 g)	3 cups (750 mL)
Peanuts, shelled	1 lb (500 g)	3 cups (750 mL)
Pecans, shelled	1 lb (500 g)	4 cups (1 L) chopped
Pecans, in shell	1 lb (500 g)	2 cups (500 mL) shelled
Walnuts, shelled	1 lb (500 g)	4 cups (1 L) chopped
Walnuts, in shell	1 lb (500 g)	2 cups (500 mL) shelled

Dairy	Quantity	Equivalent
Butter	1 lb (500 g)	2 cups (500 mL)
Cream cheese	3 oz (90 g)	6 tbsp (90 mL)
Cheese, Parmesan	3 oz (90 g)	1 cup (250 mL) grated
Cheese, shredded	1 lb (500 g)	$4\frac{1}{2}$ cups (1.125 L)
Heavy or whipping (35%) cream	1 cup (250 mL)	2 cups (500 mL) whipped

Fruit	Quantity	Equivalent
Apple	1 medium (5–6 oz/150–175 g)	1 cup (250 g) diced
Apples	1 lb (500 g), 3 medium	$1\frac{1}{4}$ cups (300 mL) purée
Bananas	3 medium	1 cup (500 mL) mashed
Berries, other than cranberries	2 pints (1 L)	$3\frac{1}{2}$ cups (875 mL)
Cherries	1 lb (500 g)	$2\frac{1}{2}$ cups (625 mL) pitted
Cranberries	1 lb (500 g)	3 cups (750 mL) sauce
Cranberries	12-oz (375 g) bag	$2\frac{1}{2}$ cups (625 mL) sauce
Lemon	1 medium	2–4 tsp (10–20 mL) juice, 1 tsp (5 mL) grated zest
Lime	1 medium	1–3 tsp (5–15 mL) juice, $\frac{3}{4}$ tsp (3 mL) grated zest
Orange	1 medium	4–5 tbsp (60–75 mL) juice, 3–4 tsp (15–20 mL) grated zest

Dried fruit	Quantity	Equivalent
Raisins	1 lb (500 g)	3 cups (750 mL) seeded
Dates	1 lb (500 g)	$3\frac{1}{2}$ cups (875 mL) unpitted
Dates	1 lb (500 g)	$2\frac{2}{3}$ cups (650 mL) pitted
Candied fruit or peel	8 oz (250 g)	$1\frac{1}{2}$ cups (375 mL)

Miscellaneous	Quantity	Equivalent
Egg whites	1 large egg	3 tbsp (45 mL)
Egg yolks	1 large egg	1 tbsp (15 mL)
Fresh herbs	$\frac{1}{2}$ oz (15 g)	$\frac{1}{4}$ cup (50 mL) loose, or 2 tbsp (25 mL) chopped

Miscellaneous	Quantity	Equivalent
Fresh herbs	1 tbsp (15 mL)	1 tsp (5 mL) dried herbs
Garlic	1 clove	$\frac{1}{8}$ tsp (0.5 mL) garlic powder
Bread	4 slices	1 cup (250 mL) crumbs
Graham crackers	14	1 cup (250 mL) crumbs
Vanilla wafers	20	1 cup (250 mL) crumbs
Coffee	1 lb (500 g)	5 cups (1.25 L) ground
Marshmallows	12 oz (375 g)	40 large
Popcorn	$\frac{1}{4}$ cup (50 mL) raw	5 cups (1.25 L) popped
Mustard	1 tsp (5 mL) dry	1 tbsp (15 mL) prepared

Common U.S. Measurement Equivalents

Teaspoons	Tablespoon	Fluid Ounces	Cups	Pints	Quarts	Gallons
1 teaspoon	$\frac{1}{3}$ teaspoon					
1$\frac{1}{2}$ teaspoons	$\frac{1}{2}$ teaspoon					
2 teaspoons	$\frac{2}{3}$ teaspoon					
3 teaspoons	1 tablespoon	$\frac{1}{2}$ ounce				
	2 tablespoons	1 ounce	$\frac{1}{8}$ cup			
	3 tablespoons	1$\frac{1}{2}$ ounces				
	4 tablespoons	2 ounces	$\frac{1}{4}$ cup			
	5$\frac{1}{3}$ tablespoons		$\frac{1}{3}$ cup			
	6 tablespoons	3 ounces				
	8 tablespoons	4 ounces	$\frac{1}{2}$ cup			
	10 tablespoons	5 ounces				
	10$\frac{2}{3}$ tablespoons		$\frac{2}{3}$ cup			
	12 tablespoons	6 ounces	$\frac{3}{4}$ cup			
	16 tablespoons	8 ounces	1 cup	$\frac{1}{2}$ pint		
		16 ounces	2 cups	1 pint		
		32 ounces	4 cups	2 pints	1 quart	
		128 ounces	16 cups	8 pints	4 quarts	1 gallon

Quick U.S. Weight Conversions

Ounces	Pounds
4 ounces	$\frac{1}{4}$ pound
8 ounces	$\frac{1}{2}$ pound
12 ounces	$\frac{3}{4}$ pound

Ounces	Pounds
16 ounces	1 pound
24 ounces	1½ pounds
32 ounces	2 pounds
40 ounces	2½ pounds
48 ounces	3 pounds
56 ounces	3½ pounds
64 ounces	4 pounds
72 ounces	4½ pounds
80 ounces	5 pounds
160 ounces	10 pounds

Metric Conversion Tables

U.S. Measurements	Metric
Dry measurements	
$\frac{1}{16}$ ounce	1 gram
$\frac{1}{3}$ ounce	10 grams
$\frac{1}{2}$ ounce	15 grams
1 ounce	30 grams
3½ ounces	100 grams
4 ounces (¼ pound)	125 grams
5 ounces	150 grams
8 ounces (½ pound)	250 grams
10 ounces	300 grams
12 ounces	375 grams
16 ounces (1 pound)	500 grams
32 ounces (2 pounds)	1 kilogram
3 pounds	1.5 kilograms
4 pounds	2 kilograms
Liquid measurements	
1 teaspoon	5 milliliters
1 tablespoon	15 milliliters
1 fluid ounce (2 tbsp)	25 milliliters
2 fluid ounces (¼ cup)	50 milliliters
8 fluid ounces (1 cup)	250 milliliters
16 fluid ounces (2 cups/1 pint)	500 milliliters
32 fluid ounces (2 pints/1 quart)	1 liter
128 fluid ounces (4 quarts/1 gallon)	4 liters

Seasoning Your Food

If I could only have two seasonings in my kitchen, they would be salt and pepper — nothing goes as far in making flavors pop. Salt heightens and brightens the natural flavors in food; it's hard to imagine potatoes without it. Pepper brings pungent, aromatic flavors that add interest and bite to almost any dish. But things aren't as simple as table salt and ground black pepper any more. Try some of their other guises; you'll be glad you did. Here's a rundown on what you'll see at the market.

Salt

- **Table salt:** This finely ground salt, from mined rock salt deposits, contains chemical additives to keep it pouring smoothly. It's used for general cooking and baking.
- **Kosher salt:** A purified, coarse-grained salt mined from rock salt. I love it because it has a pure salt taste, it dissolves more quickly than table salt, and you seem to need less of it to make dishes pop. It's also inexpensive and widely available. This is what you'd use on the rim of margarita glasses.
- **Sea salt:** Sea salt, collected by evaporating sea water, comes in coarse to fine grains. It has no additives and a pure salt taste; many people prefer it for cooking. You'll see versions of it from various parts of the world, including France and Italy.
- **Fleur de sel:** This coarse-grained, unprocessed French salt is harvested by hand from the skin that forms on saline pools during summer months when weather conditions are just right. It has a delicate flavor and earthy aroma that make it perfect for finishing cooked foods or adding to salad or dips.
- **Other specialty salts:** Gourmet stores and higher-end groceries are carrying a vast array of other specialty salts as well. You'll see smoked salts, pink salts, gray salts, blended salts and more. Most are best used as a final garnish on a special dish, so that you can appreciate their subtle nuances. They make an interesting addition to a dinner table and a conversation-starter at parties.

Pepper

- **Black pepper:** Familiar ground black pepper comes from unripe peppercorns that have been dried at a moderate temperature. Black pepper can be used in almost any savory recipe, and sometimes in sweet ones, too, such as black pepper biscotti.

Make your own flavored salt. Place 1/4 cup (50 mL) dried herbs or spices or 1/2 cup (125 mL) dried mushrooms (porcini works especially well) in a food processor and pulse four to five times. Add an equal amount of kosher or coarse-grained salt and process until well ground.

- **White pepper:** White pepper comes from fully ripened pepper fruit, with its outer hull removed. This is used in sauces where black pepper would spoil the color, and where pungency is preferred to the peppery taste and aroma of black pepper.

Seasoning with Herbs and Spices

Have you ever wondered what, exactly, tarragon should be used on? What about nutmeg? Knowing how to use herbs and

Vegetable Seasoning Guide

Food	Seasoning
Beans (dried)	Bay leaf, black pepper, cumin, garlic, parsley, thyme
Beets	Basil, dill, ginger, mint, mustard, parsley
Carrots	Cinnamon, cloves, dill, mint, nutmeg, parsley, savory, tarragon, thyme
Cauliflower	Chives, curry powder, nutmeg, parsley
Corn	Basil, chives, chile powder, dill, mint, parsley
Eggplant	Basil, cilantro, cumin, garlic, parsley, thyme
Green beans	Basil, black pepper, garlic, marjoram, savory, thyme
Peas	Basil, marjoram, mint, parsley, savory, tarragon
Potatoes	Chives, dill, garlic, rosemary, parsley, thyme
Spinach	Curry, garlic, nutmeg
Summer squash	Basil, chives, garlic, marjoram, oregano, parsley, savory
Winter squash	Allspice, cinnamon, cloves, mace, nutmeg
Tomatoes	Basil, chives, garlic, marjoram, oregano, parsley, savory, tarragon, thyme

Meat, Fish and Poultry Seasoning Guide

Food	Seasoning
Beef	Bay leaf, black pepper, chile powder, cumin, garlic, ginger, thyme
Chicken	Basil, bay leaf, chives, cilantro, cinnamon, cloves, cumin, curry powder, garlic, ginger, marjoram, mustard, rosemary, sage, tarragon, thyme
Duck	Parsley, sage, thyme
Fish	Basil, bay leaf, chervil, chives, cilantro, cumin, curry, dill, marjoram, mint, mustard, oregano, paprika, parsley, saffron, savory, tarragon, thyme
Lamb	Cumin, curry, garlic, mint, oregano, rosemary
Pork	Allspice, bay leaf, cumin, fennel, garlic, ginger, marjoram, mustard, rosemary, sage, thyme
Turkey	Bay leaf, rosemary, sage, savory
Veal	Basil, bay leaf, lemon, parsley, savory, tarragon, thyme

spices is integral to adding interest to your cooking: the right herbs, for example, can elevate boring roast chicken to French country cuisine.

I prefer fresh herbs for most uses, but a stash of carefully selected dried herbs can be convenient, and wonderful for certain uses. Dried thyme and bay leaves do really well in stews, but dried basil doesn't resemble, in color or flavor, its fresh counterpart. Always use fresh basil, cilantro and rosemary when possible. They are easy to grow, whether in a simple pot on the patio or balcony, or as part of a larger garden.

Spice Mixtures

Using a blend of different spices in the same dish gives it a depth of flavor and interest that you can't get by using one spice alone. Fortunately, there are several commercially prepared spice mixtures on the market, so we don't have to mix up our own at home. Here are some of my favorites, and how to best use them. In addition, look for herbes de Provence, poultry seasoning and Greek seasoning herb mixtures, among others.

- **Curry powder:** Curry is a term for any number of different spice mixtures. In India, for example, each cook might have his or her own unique mixture, with regional variations. Here in North America, what we call "curry powder" is pretty uniform: it usually includes ground coriander, fenugreek, turmeric, cumin, nutmeg, cloves and ginger, among other ingredients. It can be used in a variety of ethnic dishes, as well as to add interest to North American recipes such as chicken salad or carrot soup.

- **Pumpkin pie spice:** This blend of cinnamon, ginger, nutmeg and allspice is already balanced for the home cook and ready to use — only one bottle of ground spices to purchase instead of four. Try it in pumpkin pie and cheesecake, of course, but also to flavor pumpkin bread, puréed squash soups, mashed sweet potatoes and other seasonal specialties.

- **Garam masala:** Like curry powder, garam masala is a blend of spices that varies wildly in its native India. In North America, this blend strikes a bold balance of sweet, spicy and savory notes with its combination of coriander, black pepper, cumin, cardamom and cinnamon. It's recommended for use in Indian dishes and lamb stew. One of my friends makes amazing spiced pecans with it.

- **Cajun or Creole seasoning:** Use these spicy mixes of garlic, pepper, cayenne, oregano, sea salt and onions in jambalaya, chicken dishes, chili, fish or pork chops — anywhere you want a little spice along with your salt and pepper. There are several brands, each with a different recipe. I like Tony Cachere's Original Creole Seasoning, and use it in vegetable soup to give it an extra kick of heat.

And even if you don't grow them yourself, fresh herbs are available year-round in almost all supermarkets these days. When you do purchase dried herbs, buy small containers so you'll use them up quickly, and replace any that you haven't been able to use within six months (mark containers with the purchase date when you get home from the market).

Spices, on the other hand, are nearly always purchased bottled. Purists will enjoy grating their own nutmeg (it does make a difference!), but to me that's not as important as using fresh basil. To bring out the flavor of dried spices or seeds, toast them in a heavy skillet on the stovetop until fragrant and slightly darker, taking care not to burn them.

The charts on page 144 are classic seasoning guides, to give you some background and to spark your creativity, allowing you to use herbs and spices more freely in your cooking.

Oops: Tips for Rescuing Food Bloopers

It's the day of the party and there's no turning back. You've burned the food or overcooked the veggies, and you're thinking of throwing in the towel and ordering out. Not so fast: with many common food flubs, there are some quick-fix solutions that mean less wasted food and no takeout necessary — all in time for the party.

Soup or Stew Burned on the Stovetop

If you're just beginning a stew, soup or other recipe with onions and/or garlic, and you burn them, throw them out and start over. But if your soup or stew is bubbling along beautifully when you notice that it's burning on the bottom, you can save it. Remove the pot from the heat immediately, carefully ladle the soup or stew into another pot, avoiding scraping or disturbing the burned portion and, if need be, add a little sugar to negate any burned flavor. Using heavy-bottomed cookware and reducing the temperature to a simmer will help prevent this next time.

Crystallized Honey

It's usually fine to use crystallized honey; as a frame of reference, honey is said to keep for up to two years when stored airtight at room temperature. Crystallization is a naturally occurring process (refrigerating honey speeds up crystallization), and many people will just spread it on their toast that way. However, if getting honey back to its liquid state

How to Mise en Place

It sounds fancy because it's French, but the concept of mise-en-place is designed to make your cooking life less complicated. It simply means having everything in place and ready to go. If you've ever watched a cooking show where bowls of already-prepped ingredients are used to make short work of putting together the final dish, you have seen mise-en-place in action. It also helps if you've read through the recipe carefully to make sure you understand the procedures before you fire up the oven. If you'll still be doing some measuring during preparation (olive oil or wine, for example, are easy enough to pour on the fly), have your measuring cups washed and within arm's reach as well. Devotees of mise-en-place cooking will enjoy having a set of prep bowls in various sizes. Some prep bowl sets even come with plastic lids, making it easy to grate cheese a day or so ahead, cover and refrigerate it, and take it out when it's go time.

better suits your plans, place the jar in warm water and stir until smooth. Or place it in a microwave-safe container and zap in 30-second intervals, stirring between each, until smooth.

Dry Pasta

You've made the pasta and you've made the sauce, but there's not quite enough of the latter. Add vegetable, chicken or mushroom broth or white wine, depending on the recipe, by ¼ cupfuls (50 mL), until the pasta is moist. Sometimes just a tablespoon or two (15 or 25 mL) of olive oil will solve the problem. Next time, reserve some of the pasta cooking water as you drain it, and add the cooking water back to the pasta by ¼ cupfuls (50 mL) to make the sauce go further and to lend it a creamy texture from the starch in the water.

Lumpy Gravy

Pour lumpy gravy into the blender and blend until smooth, then return it to the saucepan and simmer until the raw-flour taste cooks out. To avoid lumpy gravy in the future, make a roux in the pan with equal amounts of flour and butter or pan drippings, stirring frequently until the mixture is pale brown. Whisk constantly as you gradually pour in the hot liquid.

Overbaked Cake

If the cake you baked is too dry to serve but not burned, you have some options. One is to make a simple syrup by boiling 1 cup (250 mL) of sugar with 2 cups (500 mL) of water or fruit juice; cook for two minutes, then cool the syrup to room temperature. Once cool, extracts or alcohol can be added to the syrup to flavor it. Use a skewer to make holes in the cake, then pour the syrup over it and let it stand for a few hours before serving it with freshly whipped cream or ice cream. An alternative solution is to use cubed pieces of overbaked cake in a bread pudding or a trifle. To make a trifle, layer the cake cubes with custard and chopped fresh fruit, such as strawberries or peaches, in a large clear bowl or serving dish. Top with whipped cream and garnish with toasted chopped nuts.

Overbeaten Egg Whites

Add an extra egg white or a teaspoon (5 mL) of sugar to egg whites that have been beaten too long and are difficult to fold.

Overcooked Vegetables

If you've overcooked potatoes, consider serving mashed potatoes instead of a gratin or potato salad. Mash the potatoes by hand, adding a bit of butter or cream and salt and pepper, and grated Parmesan cheese, if you like. With other vegetables, such as carrots or broccoli, use the blender or food processor to make a purée to serve with the meal, or turn them into an elegant first course by puréeing them and adding some broth and cream to create vegetable bisque. Garnish it with a crusty crouton, and it will seem like it was always part of the plan.

Oversalted Food

If you've oversalted a dish, try adding an acid to counteract it; vinegar or citrus juice might do the trick. With soups or stews, cut up a raw potato, add it to the dish and simmer for 20 minutes (remove the potato pieces before serving). The potato will absorb some of the salt. To prevent the problem in the future, be sure to under-season rather than over-season while cooking. Salt and pepper are usually passed at the table, and it's always easier to add than to take away.

Overly Spicy Food

It's tough to get the spiciness quotient right every time; in fact, fresh hot peppers vary in their heat level from crop to crop, so even the same ingredients might yield different results from one attempt to the next. Tame your fiery dishes by adding sour cream or yogurt, and serve the dish with bread, potatoes or rice to offer a bland counterbalance. Guests will appreciate a dish of sour cream or yogurt passed at the table as well, so they can doctor their portion as they see fit.

Seized Chocolate

Add 1 teaspoon (5 mL) of solid vegetable shortening to each ounce (30 g) of seized (hardened) chocolate and stir until smooth. Chocolate can be fussy to work with; for best results, keep water away from chocolate when melting it (water causes chocolate to seize) — your pot and whisk should be clean and dry before you begin. Chocolate also scorches easily, so melt it in a heavy-bottomed pot over very low heat, or use the microwave in very short time increments.

Stale Bread

Dinner rolls can quickly go stale if placed on the table too early. To give them new life, mist them lightly with water and wrap in foil. Place in a 250°F (120°C) oven for 10 to 15 minutes to lightly steam them. If a long loaf of bread is stale, consider making crostini instead of simply serving it sliced. A little extra crunch doesn't hurt a slice of bread when it's holding a generous helping of chopped marinated artichoke hearts or roasted red peppers — nobody will even notice.

Uneven Baking

If your cake comes out lopsided, your oven is probably not heating evenly. You'll want to have it looked at, but in the meantime, here's a quick fix: Spray the underside of a nonstick baking sheet with vegetable oil spray and place it on top of the cake as it's cooling; its weight should even out the top of the cake. For next time, be sure to rotate cakes and other dishes halfway through the cooking time to promote even baking or cooking.

Plating and Serving

For smaller dinner parties you'll be hosting at home, for which you'll likely be preparing much of the food yourself, restaurant-style plating of individual portions might not be part of your plans. Many home dinner parties are held family-style, meaning that platters of food are put on the table and guests help themselves. But even with family-style dinners, you'll need to arrange each dish on its own platter or in its own serving bowl. Presentation still counts, and garnishes are still relevant. However you plan to serve your food, consult the following tips for help with presenting it.

For buffets, use plates that are 10 inches (25 cm) or less in diameter; they are easier for guests to carry.

Plate or Serving Dish Size

Use correctly sized dinner plates or serving dishes. Plates or platters that are too small will look crowded and will have the potential to promote spills, making them unwieldy for passing. Plates or platters that are too large will look sparse, making it seem like you didn't have enough food for the party.

Taking Food to New Heights

If you're plating each guest's meal, follow the lead of restaurants and caterers by building the plate high. Place the vegetable and starch either next to each other or one on top of the other, then place the meat atop them or lean it up against them. For platters or bowls, mound salads, vegetables, fruits and other side dishes highest in the center. Prop steaks, pork chops or other cuts of meat one against the other on a platter, so that one side is raised.

Deconstructing the Plate

If stacked food is not your style, you might try the trendy deconstructed look. This presentation works best on long, rectangular plates, where you can place each component in a line. Instead of tossing together all the ingredients for a Caesar salad, for instance, you might toss only the lettuce and dressing to coat the leaves. You'd plate the lettuce, then arrange the other ingredients separately: large shards of Parmigiano-Reggiano, a fresh anchovy coiled into a small circle, grilled baguette cubes for croutons and a wedge of lemon for extra zing and a splash of color on the plate.

Food Stylist Tricks

Among the many tricks food stylists use to make food look even better is to reserve some of the ingredients as a garnish, to call out a dish's flavors visually. For instance, you'll probably toss a salad of greens and raspberries before bringing it to the table, but keep out a few raspberries to nestle atop it. If a steak has a creamy blue cheese sauce, save a few blue cheese crumbles for the top to bring that flavor to diners' attention. For more on garnishing, see below.

Garnishing

Garnishing is how you accentuate your food to give it the most appealing presentation, so it makes sense to garnish whether you're plating individual portions or serving family-style. Here are some tips for coming up with creative garnishes that bring out the best in your party food.

- Garnishes should be edible, above all. Make sure they're safe to eat and organic, if possible.
- Keep it simple. Garnishes are meant to enhance food visually, not compete with it. You don't want to make the plate busy or use garnishes that detract from the food's natural appeal.
- Choose relevant ingredients for your garnishes. A dish with chopped chives can be garnished with whole chives, arranged in an X. Lemon bars might be topped with a curl of lemon zest, whether candied or fresh.
- Consider using edible flowers. Pansies, lavender, nasturtiums, squash blossoms and chive blossoms all make pretty garnishes that add color and whimsy to a number of dishes, and guests can choose to eat them or not. Use flowers from your own garden or from the herb section of your grocery store; avoid flowers from the florist, because most have been sprayed.
- Don't forget classic garnishes. Italian (flat-leaf) parsley and curly parsley are timeless garnishes that look good with almost any savory dish. Use parsley in large sprigs or finely chop and dry it before sprinkling it over dishes. Cilantro, which looks a lot like Italian parsley (but tastes very different, of course), makes a pretty and piquant garnish for Mexican and Asian fare.
- Fruit garnishes are pretty and edible. Whether it's a twisted slice of orange, clusters of grapes, a few berries or thin slices of melon, fruit always lends fresh flavors and colors to the mix.

> Make pretty carrot flowers by peeling a medium-size carrot, then cutting shallow wedges down the length. Make five or six cuts, evenly spaced around the carrot, then thinly slice the carrot. Small cucumbers, with the peel on, and radishes also make pretty flowers.

Presenting the Food: Three Party Styles

Buffets

If you're short on seated dining space, there's no more efficient way to serve a full meal than with a buffet. Buffets also keep things a little more casual, and they encourage mixing and mingling at a party — particularly if you allow people to eat with plates in their laps in the family room, dining room and living room, rather than having formal seating with place cards. If you think all or part of your particular crowd would do better with tables and chairs, you can always set that up in another room (see page 39 for ideas on extra seating).

A 6- to 8-foot (180 to 240 cm) dining-room table will hold all the food, plates, napkins and flatware you'll need for as many as 50 guests; for smaller parties, smaller tables will work just fine. The placement of the buffet will impact the flow of the party, so keep a few things in mind: place the buffet table reasonably close to the kitchen so it's easier to replenish; keep it away from other busy areas (such as the bar or a frequently used door) to prevent the flow of the party from becoming backed up; and if you have the space, arrange the buffet table away from the wall, so guests can access food from all sides. For help with tablecloth selection, centerpieces and other tabletop decor, turn to page 62. The following sections offer more specifics to consider.

How to Build a Buffet Menu

Foods that taste great at room temperature are ideal for buffets. Frittatas and quiches, pasta and grain salads, sandwiches and cheeses are all buffet-friendly, as are most desserts.

A buffet is traditionally a full meal; as such, the menu might include a salad or soup (use mugs or deep bowls), an entrée or two, two side dishes, bread and condiments such as butter, salt and pepper. Keep in mind the party's logistics: all guests will be filling their plates and carrying them to another location, so it makes sense to avoid dishes that are very messy or labor-intensive for the diner, such as cracked crab or lobster, especially if guests will be perched around your house. You'll also want to keep in mind how well the items in your proposed menu will hold when sitting out. A soufflé wouldn't make sense for a buffet, nor would sorbet. Round items like peas, which have a tendency to roll off the plate, should probably be left out. Buffet foods should be in manageable-size pieces that will fit on plates and be easy to transport; you can slice meats and cut vegetables into bite-size pieces to make it easier on your guests.

Setting Out a Beautiful Display

Fruit and veggie trays are colorful, easy and inexpensive to make, and are must-have additions to any buffet.

Besides the tabletop decor (which you can read about on pages 62 to 79), the food itself will be a major part of your buffet table's appeal — in fact, it will be the most alluring part. Use risers or pedestals (even bricks or small crates can be used and then covered with tablecloths) to elevate your food to different heights, adding interest to the table. Leave hot foods at table level for safety.

Platters, cake stands and bowls will become mainstays for entertaining, so purchase a set that complements the food (white is always safe), and one that will give your buffet a cohesive look to show off the food to its best advantage. Clear bowls present colorful salads beautifully, and baskets are an inexpensive mainstay for entertaining. Baskets can be dressed up with a fresh coat of spray paint (metallics are elegant on wicker) or ribbons or flowers. Line baskets with linen napkins, pretty dishtowels or aromatic herbs.

Here are additional tips for presenting food buffet-style.

Designing Buffets for Best Flow and Guest Ease

The location of the buffet table itself is of prime importance, but so is the placement of each item *on* the table. Thinking through placement ahead of time makes for a buffet that's easier on guests and therefore flows more efficiently from plates to food to flatware. See the diagrams below and on page 154 for examples of user-friendly buffet configurations that you can use for your party.

Fill empty spots on buffet tables with bowls of marinated olives, spiced nuts, pretty crackers, baguette slices or breadsticks.

Arranging the Buffet Table

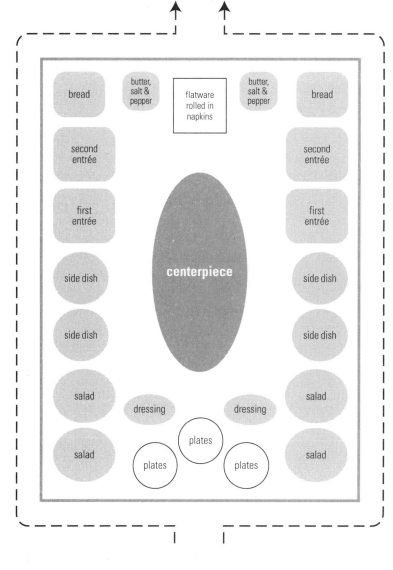

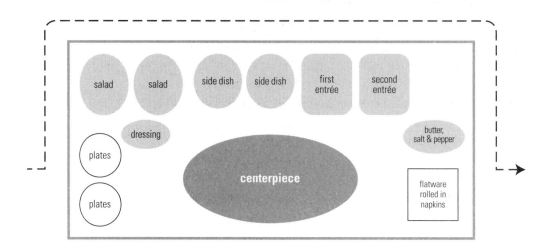

Successful Serving

Keep things moving along by putting out the correct serving utensils for each dish ahead of time. Tongs are user-friendly for a variety of items. Spoons of the correct length are important, and spoon rests for the table will keep things neat. For casseroles such as lasagna, provide a 3-inch (7.5 cm) wide offset spatula for guests to use; scoring casseroles into portions ahead of time makes quick work of serving them.

You'll need to monitor the table to make sure you're not running out of anything. Place a cooler under the table to keep hot food warm or cold food cool for short periods (about 20 minutes), making for a quick change-out when the time comes. Or keep items in your warming drawer in the kitchen or in the refrigerator. If you completely run out of an item, simply remove the tray and add an extra bread basket or bowl of salad, or shift the remaining offerings a bit to fill in the gaps.

Creating a Cheese and Fruit Display

Cheeses, crackers and fruit work well for any buffet, from brunch to late-night, adding to the spread of food significantly without giving you something else to cook. Use chunks of marble or mirror tiles, which will stay relatively cool, as a surface for a fruit and cheese display — you can even chill them ahead of time, if you like. Or line platters with parchment paper leaves, available in many kitchen supply stores, or nontoxic leaves such as lemon leaves or banana leaves. Even a rustic wooden cutting board can make an attractive display piece.

Choose a selection of cheeses that represent a variety of colors, shapes and textures, such as one semi-hard cheese, one blue cheese and one soft cheese (see the Cheese Glossary on page 164 for help). Complement the richness and saltiness of the cheeses with a variety of fruits: grapes (look for globe or Champagne varieties for interesting sizes), apple and pear slices (spritzed with lemon juice to maintain their color) and slim pieces of melon, fresh pineapple or mango make sweet accompaniments. Dried fruits are also a great counterpart to a cheese display, especially in cooler weather; look for dried apricots, figs, dates and cranberries. Fill in the gaps with whole almonds, walnuts or pecans. If you have room, arrange crackers and fruit around the cheese display; otherwise, arrange them more compactly nearby. You'll need roughly 6 to 10 crackers per guest, depending on the extent of the menu and the length of the party.

Creating a Crudités Display

Another way to make your buffet menu go further without adding much to your to-do list is to create a crudités display. "Crudités," for the uninitiated, is simply a fancy word for a plate of crisp raw or barely blanched vegetables (blanch them for half a minute in boiling water). You can build your own display with a variety of veggies, such as carrots, celery, jicama, broccoli, bell peppers, snow peas and cauliflower. Try to incorporate something unique to the season, such as asparagus or bite-size tomatoes. Set a bowl of a simple homemade or purchased dip in the center of a tray or platter, with the vegetables arranged around it. Keep in mind that you'll want a variety of colors represented, and alternate between colors when setting up your display. In a pinch, look for prepared crudités trays, available at most supermarkets and even at warehouse stores like Costco. Transfer them to your own platters for serving.

Keeping Food at the Right Temperature

Keeping hot food hot and cold food cold can be a challenge for buffet-style parties, where the food is sitting out on a table for a couple of hours or longer. Keeping food at the right temperature isn't just a matter of appeal — it can also be a matter of food safety. See the Ideal Temperatures chart on page 132 for safe storage temperatures, and remember the danger zone of 40°F to 140°F (4°C to 60°C), in which bacteria have a tendency to breed. Room temperature always falls within that range, so it makes sense to take measures to keep hot food hot and cold food cold when it will be sitting out.

Put any cold items that are highly likely to spoil — sushi, for instance — on a bed of crushed ice. If you're serving hot food, you will likely need a chafing dish; if your menu plans dictate that you'll need more than one, consider purchasing, borrowing or renting different shapes or sizes to avoid that food-service look. For smaller parties, you can also use a fondue pot, a slow cooker or a covered soup tureen to keep things warm. I've used my fondue pot for everything from meatballs to queso fundido.

Sit-Down Meals

Sit-down meals can be formal or casual, special-occasion or any night of the week. What they all share is that food is served at the table, not from a buffet. This gives you the flexibility to serve anything you dare, from testy first-course cheese soufflés to messy peel-and-eat shrimp. You have two main choices when serving sit-down meals: family-style, in which large platters of food are passed around the table for guests to help themselves, and plated, in which each plate is prepared and garnished in the kitchen and presented to each guest individually.

Family-Style

It's better to divide food among several serving dishes than to make a dish that's too heavy to lift easily. Keep the additional dishes covered and in the kitchen until the one at the table is nearly empty.

The advantage of family-style meals is that everyone can help themselves to what they like — and pass over anything they don't — without special arrangements. Of course, if guests aren't careful, certain diners can be short-changed on popular items. But eating meals family-style also promotes an intimate feel as guests pass each other platters of food to share, and it's practical, too: most of us don't run our households with a staff, and family-style service means you can usually get by without an extra set of helping hands behind the scenes. Rather than garnishing individual plates, you can garnish the platters for pretty presentations (see page 150 for specific ideas). With family-style service, you might find that the table gets quite full with serving dishes, but you can always remove items as you work your way through the courses, or consolidate similar items.

Plated

The formality of a plated dinner, served course by course, really makes a dinner party seem special. You'll want to have an extra set of hands at the ready, whether that's hired help (see page 105 for more on hiring wait staff) or a designated guest, to help you get each course plated and out from the kitchen in a timely manner. Plated dinners give you the opportunity to incorporate cool, artsy garnishes, like a swirl or heart of cream atop a puréed soup. They also help you control portions among the plates.

When executing such a dinner, it's a good idea to have everything planned out exactly. Assign your helper to specific tasks ahead of time, and see the plating chart below for help in planning and carrying it out. Follow the lead of caterers and designate a plating area between your kitchen and dining room. Keep plates warm in your warming drawer or a low oven (150°F to 200°F/70°C to 100°C). Chill dessert and salad plates in the refrigerator or a cooler.

Plating Chart

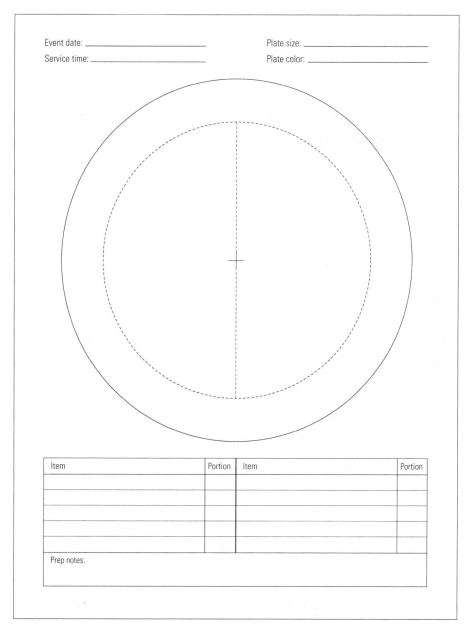

Event date: _____   Plate size: _____

Service time: _____   Plate color: _____

Item	Portion	Item	Portion

Prep notes:

Cocktail Parties

Dust off your old TV trays — they're perfect for cocktail parties! Place them against walls, where they won't be knocked over, and cover the surface with placemats.

Cocktail parties are a great way to entertain while maximizing your time to mix and mingle and minimizing your responsibility — you won't be expected to prepare a full meal for each of your guests when you haven't promised dinner. And because you won't need seating for every guest (though it doesn't hurt to have a few tall cocktail tables to add to the serving space and to give people a place to gather), cocktail parties mean you can include more people.

That said, it *can* be just as much work to pull off a cocktail party as it is to host a seated dinner; it all depends on how ambitious your menu is and the time of the party. A cocktail party held at suppertime will quickly morph into a cocktail *supper*, meaning you'll need some pretty hearty fare in the mix or you'll be cleaned out quickly. I have often been talked into having a few people over for drinks and snacks, only to find myself planning dinner for eight because of the hour. For ideas on how to bolster your offerings with minimum effort, check out the cheese and fruit display suggestions on page 154, the crudités display suggestions on page 155 and the easy hors d'oeuvres on page 160. To help you get started on planning your menu for a cocktail party, here are two popular approaches.

Wine and Cheese Parties

As a general rule, soft cheeses and strongly flavored cheeses go best with whites; hard cheeses with a mild flavor go best with reds.

This is one of my favorite types of cocktail parties: it's clear that you're only serving wine and cheese, so it's easier to stay on track; it can be held before or after the dinner hour; and it's a great excuse to try new cheeses and wines — and who doesn't love those? For those who can't help but add a bit more to the offerings, fruits and cured meats are natural accompaniments and are easy to pull together. See the menu on page 332 for a great way to host such a party, or develop your own menu based on your motivation to entertain or any new offerings at your favorite cheese shop.

The fat in soft cheeses coats the inside of the mouth, somewhat masking the flavor of a wine.

As mentioned earlier, any offering of cheeses should represent a variety of flavors and textures, so offer something from each of the following categories: soft or semi-soft, blue and firm. See the chart at right for some surefire pairings, and read through the Cheese Glossary on page 164 for more ideas.

Cheese, Wine and Fruit Pairings

Cheese	Wine	Fruit
Blue cheese, Roquefort	Strong reds	Apples, grapes, pears
Brie, Camembert	Cabernet Sauvignon, Merlot, Pinot Noir, dry port	Plums, berries, apples
Colby	Port, sherry, Madeira, Burgundy	Melons, peaches, pears
Edam, Gouda, Cheddar	Cabernet Sauvignon, Merlot, Pinot Noir, Burgundy	Apples, grapes, pears
Goat cheese, chèvre, feta	Chenin Blanc, Sancerre, Pouilly Fumé	Apples, pears, peaches
Gorgonzola	Sauternes, Champagne	Pears
Gruyère, provolone	Chardonnay, Sauvignon Blanc, Beaujolais	Melons, peaches, pineapple
Monterey Jack	Chardonnay, cream sherry	Plums, strawberries, apples
Mozzarella	Pinot Blanc, Pinot Grigio	Melons, peaches, pineapple
Muenster	Beaujolais, Zinfandel, cream sherry	Melons, peaches, pineapple
Neufchâtel, cream cheese	Champagne	Apples, grapes, pears
Parmigiano-Reggiano	Chianti, Burgundy	Figs, grapes, apples
Stilton	Port	Pears
Swiss, Emmentaler	Riesling, Gewürztraminer	Apples, grapes, pears

Hors d'Oeuvres Parties

These gatherings have a more work-intensive menu than just wine and cheese, but they also have more flexibility; if the hors d'oeuvres are heavy enough, you can hold this type of party during the dinner hour as a cocktail supper. As with all cocktail parties, you will need to serve finger foods, forgoing anything that requires a knife and fork. Most foods should be consumable in one or two bites, and it's even better to serve foods that can be eaten without a plate, such as skewered meat or cubes of cheese. It's also nice to avoid anything drippy or messy, to save all those silk neckties and pretty tops.

Easy Hors d'Oeuvres

Your cocktail party menu can be as easy as you want it to be. Try replacing a few high-maintenance items with these in-a-flash appetizers, to lighten your kitchen load and leave you more time to enjoy the party.

Grilled Baguette Slices with Boursin and Caramelized Onions

Thinly slice 1 medium onion and sauté in 1 tablespoon (15 mL) olive oil over medium heat until golden, about 15 minutes. Set aside. Slice a baguette diagonally into 1-inch (2.5 cm) thick slices. Brush one side with a little olive oil. Heat a grill pan over high heat and grill baguette slices, oiled side down, for about 30 seconds. Spread Boursin cheese over the grilled side of each slice and top with onions.

Stuffed Mushrooms

Buy a package of frozen precooked meatballs. Thaw them and cut them in half. Place inside upside-down mushroom caps and sprinkle a little mozzarella cheese on top. Place on a baking sheet and bake in a 350°F (180°C) oven until cheese melts and meatballs are heated through, about 15 minutes.

Cheesy Artichokes

Start with a drained 14-ounce (398 mL) can of artichoke bottoms. Combine 4 ounces (125 g) goat cheese with 2 tablespoons (25 mL) heavy or whipping (35%) cream, 1 teaspoon (5 mL) fresh dill and salt and pepper to taste. Spread thickly on top of artichokes, place on a baking sheet and bake in a 350°F (180°C) oven until cheese is golden brown on top, about 12 minutes.

Shrimp Skewers

Thaw a 1pound (500 g) bag of frozen cooked jumbo shrimp. Place each shrimp on a small skewer, along with a cherry tomato. Cook over high heat in a grill pan until shrimp are heated through. Add salt and pepper to taste.

Fresh Figs

Cut a dozen fresh figs in half and place cut side up on a serving dish. Spoon 1 teaspoon (5 mL) ricotta cheese atop each fig. Drizzle with a little honey and sprinkle with cracked black pepper.

Sausage Bundles

Cut 8 ounces (250 g) of cooked sausage into 1-inch (2.5 cm) thick slices. Roll out 1 lb (500 g) prepared pizza dough to $1/8$ inch (3 mm) thick and cut into 3-inch (7.5 cm) squares. Place a piece of sausage in the center of each square of dough. Top with a little Monterey Jack cheese. Fold ends of dough up and over to cover, pinching to seal. Place on a baking sheet and bake in a 375°F (190°C) oven until golden brown and heated through, about 10 minutes.

Garden Brunch
Chilled Melon Soup (page 292) and Potato Onion Torte with Sausage (page 293)

Picnic Boxed Lunch
Roasted Chicken Chopped Salad with Blue Cheese Vinaigrette (page 298)
and Herbed Parmesan Cheese Straws (page 301)

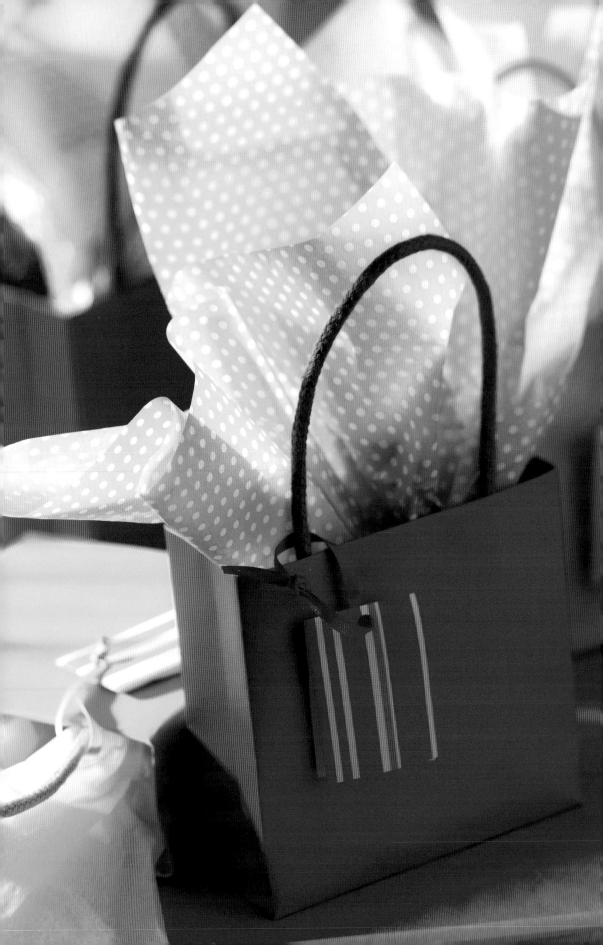

Kids' Treasure Hunt
Confetti Fruit Salad (page 305) and Chocolate Cupcakes with Whipped Cream Filling (page 306)

Birthday for a Special Mom
Chicken Eggplant Rollups (page 316), Asiago Asparagus (page 317) and Orzo Salad with Fresh Herbs (page 318)

Champagne and Caviar Party
Prosciutto-Wrapped Mango (page 326), Bay Shrimp Crostini (page 330) and Death by Chocolate Cookies (page 331)

Mushroom and Onion Bundles

Finely chop 8 ounces (250 g) of mushrooms and sauté in 1 tablespoon (15 mL) olive oil until they release their liquid. Continue cooking until liquid evaporates, then remove to a bowl. Finely chop 1 medium onion and sauté in 1 tablespoon (15 mL) olive oil until light golden; combine with mushrooms. Stir in 2 ounces (60 g) of cream cheese and season with salt and pepper. Roll out 1 lb (500 g) prepared pizza dough to $\frac{1}{8}$ inch (3 mm) thick and cut into 3-inch (7.5 cm) squares. Place 1 tablespoon (15 mL) mushroom mixture in the center of each square of dough. Fold ends of dough up and over to cover, pinching to seal. Place on a baking sheet and bake in a 375°F (190°C) oven until golden brown and heated through, about 10 minutes.

Creamy Olive Spread

Place 1 cup (250 mL) pitted black olives, 1 cup (250 mL) pitted green olives, an 8-ounce (250 g) package of cream cheese and $\frac{1}{4}$ teaspoon (1 mL) dried thyme in a food processor and blend until olives are chopped into small bits. Season with salt and pepper.

Mac 'n' Cheese Bites

Line a 12-cup muffin tin with paper liners. Cook 8 ounces (250 g) of small elbow pasta according to package directions. Mix $1\frac{1}{2}$ cups (375 mL) shredded Cheddar cheese with cooked pasta and press into prepared muffin cups. Combine $\frac{1}{2}$ cup (125 mL) panko crumbs and 2 tablespoons (25 mL) melted butter; sprinkle on top of pasta. Bake in a 400°F (200°C) oven until cheese is bubbly and starting to brown, about 12 minutes.

Biscuit Sandwiches

Use a biscuit mix to make 12 small biscuits (about 2 inches/ 5 cm across). Bake according to package directions. Split open and fill with sliced ham and Dijon mustard, or cooked and crumbled sausage. Sprinkle with a little shredded Cheddar cheese. Broil until cheese browns, about 1 minute.

Tortilla Cones

Cut 3 flour tortillas into 4 wedges each and brush both sides with canola or corn oil. Roll each into a small cone and fill with one of the following mixtures: $\frac{1}{2}$ cup (125 mL) finely chopped cooked chicken, $\frac{1}{3}$ cup (75 mL) shredded Cheddar cheese and 1 tablespoon (15 mL) diced green chiles; $\frac{1}{2}$ cup (125 mL) refried beans and $1/3$ cup shredded Cheddar or Monterey Jack cheese; or $1/2$ cup (125 mL) chopped cooked shrimp, $1/3$ cup (75 mL) shredded Monterey Jack cheese and 3 tablespoons (45 mL) salsa verde. Place filled tortillas seam side down on a baking sheet and bake in a 350°F (180°C) oven until toasted and crispy, about 10 minutes.

Crackers for Any Occasion

Cut flour tortillas (use spinach, sun-dried tomato or whole wheat for color) or pitas (for sturdier crackers) into desired shapes with cookie cutters suited to your occasion. Place in a single layer on a baking sheet and spray lightly with olive oil cooking spray. Turn and spray the other side. Sprinkle with salt. Bake in a 375°F (190°C) oven until crispy, about 8 minutes.

Customized Potato Chips

Spread a large bag of potato chips (salted only, no other flavors) on two baking sheets and sprinkle with a little ground cumin, paprika, cayenne pepper, ground black pepper, seasoned salt, lemon pepper, garlic powder or onion powder, or any of your favorite seasonings. Bake in a 300°F (150°C) oven for 5 minutes. Serve warm.

Even Easier Appetizers: Just Buy Them

These appetizers won't require much doing: purchase them, heat if necessary, plate them and you're done. Don't forget to check Costco or Sam's Club — quantity purchasing can be very cost-effective for entertaining, and they often have prepared trays that you can make your own by rearranging the food on your own platters and garnishing. If you have an upscale gourmet food market nearby, check out its prepared food offerings. Many have house-made items that would be difficult to distinguish from homemade.

- Cheese, fruit and crackers display (see page 154 for selection and presentation tips).
- Vegetable crudités and dip display (see page 155 for selection and presentation tips).
- Edamame: Purchase in-the-shell frozen edamame, cook and sprinkle with sea salt. Serve warm or cold.
- Caviar and toast points.
- Freshly prepared salsas (purchase a variety if available), such as tomato, corn or tomatillo, and a mixture of yellow and blue corn chips.

- Prepared spreads (purchase a variety if available), such as pimiento cheese, tapenade, hummus, pesto and flavored cream cheeses, to serve with a variety of crackers, flatbread and crostini.
- Prepared salads (purchase a variety if available), such as marinated fresh mozzarella salad, roasted marinated vegetables, egg salad or chicken salad. Serve with a variety of crackers, flatbread and crostini.
- Hummus, baba ghanoush, stuffed grape leaves, marinated olives and fresh pitas or flatbread from a Middle Eastern market or deli.
- Roasted and salted mixed nuts or candied nuts.
- Appetizers from the frozen foods section, such as egg rolls, savory pastries, meatballs and gourmet pizzas that you can slice into small squares. Look for unusual flavors (such as pear and blue cheese pizzas) from quality labels, and dress up the offerings with a garnish of fresh herbs.

Handling Leftovers

Leftover party food is one of the best arguments for entertaining: what's better than a few days during which you can enjoy your best cooking without having to do any cooking? You get to put your feet up after a big party when you have leftovers. But handling them safely is paramount.

Cool any leftovers that you deem salvageable after the party, then place them in airtight containers and refrigerate them as soon as possible. Skip saving any dips that you think might have fallen victim to double-dipping, and any perishables that sat at room temperature for four hours or longer. Eat any refrigerated leftovers within three days, and reheat cooked foods to at least 170°F (77°C) before consuming them.

Cheese Glossary

Whether you're hosting a dedicated cheese and wine reception, bolstering your buffet or cocktail party offerings with a cheese display or just cooking with cheese, consult this glossary for help making selections. When putting together an assortment, remember that having at least three different types of cheeses represented will give any spread added interest in texture, flavor and perhaps even color. See the chart on page 159 for help pairing specific cheeses with wines and fruits.

Fresh or Unripened Cheeses

These uncooked cheeses have a mild, creamy texture and a slightly tart flavor. This category includes cottage cheese, a favorite of dieters but one I don't use for entertaining. Here are some of my favorite fresh cheeses for parties.

- **Cream cheese:** This soft, spreadable cow's milk cheese is a popular ingredient in baking and for topping bagels, but it also has a special role for parties. Cream cheese can be served on crackers, simply topped with chutney or preserves, or it can be the basis for a variety of dips. Neufchâtel is similar to cream cheese, but is lower in calories and fat.

- **Feta:** A Greek semi-soft cheese made from sheep's, goat's or cow's milk, feta is white and crumbly, and is usually packed in brine. Feta is a staple of Greek salads and is perfect for crumbling over pastas, too. This cheese also shows up in some sauces and fillings.

- **Mascarpone:** This soft, rich cow's milk cheese from Italy has a flavor that makes it a popular addition to sweet and savory dishes. While mascarpone is probably best known and loved for its role in tiramisu, it can also be served simply with fresh berries.

- **Fresh goat cheese:** Sometimes called chèvre (which is French for "goat," so the term can be applied to a variety of cheeses made from goat's milk, from soft to hard), fresh goat cheese is soft and crumbly, with a tart flavor and creamy texture. It's delicious in a number of dishes, from simple crostini to vegetable tarts and pizzas to salads, and it pairs well with figs. Aged goat cheese has a harder texture and a nuttier, richer flavor.

- **Fresh mozzarella:** This softer version of the shredded mozzarella we're all used to using on pizza is sold packed in water. It was traditionally made with water buffalo's milk, but is now sometimes made with cow's milk or a combination. Fresh mozzarella can be used on pizza like its aged counterpart; it's integral to insalata Caprese, a layered salad of fresh mozzarella, tomatoes and basil; and it's great on sandwiches. Marinated bite-size fresh mozzarella balls (also called bocconcini, and available at higher-end grocers and specialty markets) make an easy hors d'oeuvre, served with crostini.

- **Ricotta:** A soft, fluffy, moist cheese with small grains and a sweet flavor, ricotta is important in many pasta dishes (lasagna, for instance) and desserts (such as the tart on page 402). It also makes a great spread for crostini when topped or combined with additional ingredients. One of its alter-egos, ricotta salata, has been enjoying popularity lately; this version is pressed, salted and dried to form a hard white cheese that's grated or shaved for use.

Blue Cheeses

Blue cheeses are usually streaked or pocked with bluish or greenish mold, the result of mold introduced during the aging process. There are a variety of blue cheeses from a variety of locales, but they all lean toward the assertive end of the cheese spectrum: these are classic stinky cheeses, a great addition to the cheese board to play off pairings with fruit, and delicious crumbled atop salads, pastas or even steaks.

- **Gorgonzola:** A cow's milk cheese from Italy with bluish-green veins, Gorgonzola is creamier than Stilton or Roquefort, with a more pungent, spicy, earthy flavor.

- **Roquefort:** A blue-veined sheep's milk cheese from France that's intensely pungent, with a rich, salty flavor and a strong aroma, Roquefort is great served before or after dinner, and it's a popular addition to creamy salad dressings and spreads.

- **Stilton:** This cow's milk cheese with blue-green veins hails from England. It's pungent, rich and tangy, combining the best of the Cheddars and blues. Stilton is great for a cheese board, as it's best served with plain crackers and paired with port.

Soft Cheeses

Soft cheeses are characterized by their creamy centers. The ones on this list are party favorites because they need little, if any, embellishment — simply set them out with crackers.

- **Brie:** This French rind-ripened cow's milk cheese is rich, creamy and oozy when ripe. While Brie makes a great showing on a cheese display or served after dinner, it's also occasionally used in cooking and can be baked whole as a favorite appetizer, in the rind (which is edible) and encased in pastry, if you like.

- **Boursin:** A triple-cream cow's milk cheese usually flavored with peppers, herbs or garlic, Boursin is smooth, creamy and spreadable. It makes an excellent hors d'oeuvre cheese or filling for baked chicken or stuffed mushrooms.

- **Camembert:** A rind-ripened, creamy-smooth cow's milk cheese, Camembert is similar in taste to Brie, but milder. Serve it with fruit before or after dinner.

Semi-Soft Cheeses

These cheeses have a mild, buttery taste and a smooth, sliceable texture.

- **Bel Paese:** Made from cow's milk, this Italian cheese has a mild and creamy texture and a fruity flavor. It makes an excellent snack, paired with fruity wine.

- **Fontina:** This cow's milk cheese from Italy has a dark gold, crusty rind and a pale gold dense interior with a nutty, rich flavor. It melts easily and can be used on pizzas and in hot sandwiches, among other uses.

- **Gouda:** This mild, buttery cheese from Holland is very popular for snacking and for use in fondues. It's similar in texture and flavor to Edam, also from Holland. Both are sold in wax-coated wheels. You'll sometimes see smoked Gouda, which has an earthier flavor.

- **Havarti:** A cow's milk cheese that's very similar to the Danish Tilsit, Havarti is pale yellow with many small, irregular holes, and it has a mild, tangy flavor and creamy texture. It's often flavored: dill-flavored Havarti makes an especially appealing addition to a cheese display.

- **Monterey Jack:** Unaged Jack cheese is a sandwich standby like Cheddar or Muenster; it has a mild flavor and a rich texture that's softer than Cheddar and easiest to slice if well chilled. Aged Jack is firm, with a nutty, sharp flavor, and it's dry enough for grating.

- **Pain de Pyrenees:** This pale yellow cow's milk cheese has irregular holes and a sweet, mellow, nutty flavor.

- **Port Salut:** A French cow's milk cheese that is smooth, rich and savory, Port Salut is great for snacking or for serving with fruit.

Firm Cheeses

Firm cheeses aren't hard or brittle; this category encompasses a variety of textures, from flaky cheddars to holey Swiss.

- **Cheddar:** An (originally) English cow's milk cheese, Cheddar has a dense, crumbly texture. The best Cheddars are made from raw milk and are aged for several months. For cheese displays, I prefer white Cheddars to those that have been dyed orange with annatto, though orange Cheddar is more appealing in some cooked dishes, such as homemade macaroni and cheese. Cheddar's flavor ranges from mild to very sharp, depending on the age; sharpness is indicated on the packaging. Colby and longhorn are two well-known mild, soft-textured Cheddars.

- **Gruyère:** A cow's milk cheese that is moist and highly flavored, with a sweet nuttiness similar to Swiss, Gruyère melts easily and is often used in fondues, with meats and in sauces. It's also frequently served after dinner.

- **Jarlsberg:** This Swiss-type cow's milk cheese from Norway has a mild, delicate, sweet flavor and large holes. It's popular for sandwiches and snacks, and for cooking.

- **Manchego:** This golden sheep's milk cheese from Spain is great for melting or snacking on. Manchego comes in curado and viejo varieties: the former, aged a few months, is softer and milder; the latter, aged longer, is firmer and more assertive.

- **Provolone:** A mild, smooth cow's milk cheese from Italy, provolone works well in sandwiches and for cooking. It is often melted on pizza and pasta dishes. Aged provolone can be grated.

- **Swiss** or **Emmental:** A cow's milk cheese with mellow, rich and nutty flavors, a natural rind and a light yellow interior full of large holes, this is the classic fondue cheese, though it's often used in combination with other cheeses. It's also used in sandwiches and snacks, and can be served after dinner with fruit and nuts.

Hard Cheeses

Hard cheeses are carefully aged for extended periods, and their texture is the most conducive to grating. All that time spent aging it also yields rich, deep flavors.

- **Asiago:** This sharp, nutty cow's milk cheese has a Cheddar-like texture; if aged for more than a year, it's suitable for grating. Milder than Parmesan, it melts easily and is often shaved onto salads and used in cooking and baking.

- **Parmigiano-Reggiano** or **Parmesan:** Parmigiano-Reggiano is characterized by its addictive granular texture — it's Italy's best take on Parmesan cheese, which is now made in many countries. Parmesan is a hard cow's milk cheese used for grating and cooking. It is rich, spicy and sharp, and is excellent served with nuts and fruit. The rind can be used to add flavor to rich sauces.

- **Pecorino Romano:** This sheep's milk cheese is brittle and sharp, with a sheepy tang, and is excellent with olives, sausages and red wine. Although it has a sharper flavor, Pecorino Romano can be used interchangeably with Parmesan in some recipes.

Beverages

Every party needs beverages, no question about it. But will you be serving only nonalcoholic drinks or will you also offer alcoholic ones? If there's alcohol, will it be limited to beer or wine, or will you set up a full bar? And what constitutes a full bar, anyway? This section will serve as a primer on the drinks end of entertaining, answering all of your questions about getting your bar ready for the big day.

Safety First

Since consuming alcohol is known to impair judgment, and impaired judgment can lead to all kinds of fiascos, it's a good idea to consider who's coming to the party before you make a final call on which beverages to offer. For most smaller parties, you'll know your guests, their beverage preferences and their drinking habits well enough to know what you and they can handle. But for larger parties, or when you're inviting new people into the mix, serving alcohol can feel like a big responsibility — and it is. Here are a few ways to make serving alcohol to a crowd a little safer and more manageable for the host.

Taking away a guest's car keys is a last resort, but is sometimes necessary. Be firm. The alternative is too gruesome to consider.

Enlist the Help of a Designated Driver

Have a good friend on hand who's willing to play designated driver for the evening. You pay for the gas, and he or she remains available to transport anyone home who needs the help. Also keep the number of a cab company by your phone so you can easily dial one up as needed.

Hire a Bartender or Waiter

Professionals are used to looking for red flags, and they're used to cutting people off. For potentially rowdy gatherings, an off-duty police officer or security professional can help keep an eye on the crowd, and even drive revelers home as needed.

Limit the Offerings

If your guest list includes some hard-partying types and you don't want to deal with the fallout, you can keep things somewhat in check by offering only one type of alcoholic beverage — beer or wine, for example — keeping hard liquor out of the equation. You can also hold the party earlier in the day, when people tend to drink less. A good friend who married soon after college purposely planned her wedding for the early afternoon, with a Champagne-only reception at the local botanical gardens, because she was concerned that rowdy college pals would turn the reception into something out of *Animal House*. Given the setting, bar offerings and time of day, they weren't able to.

How Much to Buy?

Determining the amount and type of wine or alcohol to purchase has left many a host stumped. It's impossible to always predict accurately whether people will drink more red wine or more white wine, or whether they'll take you up on your offer for a margarita to go with that Mexican fiesta you're hosting.

As far as quantity, you know your guests best. Some barely drink, while others make their way through your stash at a dizzying rate. As a rule of thumb, you can count on needing two drinks per person for the first hour of the party, and one drink per person for each hour thereafter. So, if you're having eight guests for a cocktail supper that you imagine will last no longer than four hours, you'll need 40 servings of alcohol (16 for the first hour, plus 24 for the remaining three hours). Check the bottle yields chart opposite to determine how much you'll need to purchase.

Bottle Yields

Bottle Size	Beverage Type	Yield	Serving Size
750 milliliters	Champagne	6 servings	4 oz (125 mL)
750 milliliters	Wine	5 servings	5 oz (150 mL)
1 liter	Spirits	16 cocktails	$1\frac{1}{2}$ oz (45 mL)
1.5 liters	Spirits	33 cocktails	$1\frac{1}{2}$ oz (45 mL)
1 liter	Mineral water	4 servings	1 cup (250 mL)
2 liter	Soda	8 servings	1 cup (250 mL)
12 ounces (341 mL)	Beer	1 serving	12 oz (341 mL)

Partial Bar Guide

Ingredients	6 guests	12 guests	25 guests	50 guests	75 guests
White wine	4 750-mL bottles	7 750-mL bottles	15 750- mL bottles	30 750-mL bottles	45 750-mL bottles
Red wine	2 750-mL bottles	4 750-mL bottles	8 750-mL bottles	16 750-mL bottles	24 750-mL bottles
Beer	9 12-oz (341 mL) bottles	18 12-oz (341 mL) bottles	32 12-oz (341 mL) bottles	64 12-oz (341 mL) bottles	96 12-oz (341 mL) bottles
Mineral water	2 1liter bottles	3 1liter bottles	5 1liter bottles	10 1liter bottles	15 1liter bottles
7-Up or Sprite	1 1liter bottle	1 1liter bottles	3 1liter bottles	6 1liter bottles	9 1liter bottles
Cola	1 2-liter bottle	2 2-liter bottles	4 2-liter bottles	8 2-liter bottles	12 2-liter bottles
Diet cola	1 2-liter bottle	2 2-liter bottles	4 2-liter bottles	8 2-liter bottles	12 2-liter bottles
Glasses	16 10-oz (300 mL) glasses	30 10-oz (300 mL) glasses	75 10-oz (300 mL) glasses	150 10-oz (300 mL) glasses	225 10-oz (300 mL) glasses
Ice	10 lbs (4.5 kg)	18 lbs (8 kg)	38 lbs (17 kg)	75 lbs (34 kg)	115 lbs (52 kg)

Food and Beverages • Beverages

Full Bar Guide

Ingredients	6 guests	12 guests	25 guests	50 guests	75 guests
White wine	2 750-mL bottles	4 750-mL bottles	9 750-mL bottles	18 750-mL bottles	27 750-mL bottles
Red wine	2 750-mL bottles	3 750-mL bottles	7 750-mL bottles	14 750-mL bottles	21 750-mL bottles
Beer	3 12-oz (341 mL) bottles	5 12-oz (341 mL) bottles	12 12-oz (341 mL) bottles	24 12-oz (341 mL) bottles	36 12-oz (341 mL) bottles
Gin	1 375-mL bottle	1 750-mL bottle	2 750-mL bottles	4 750-mL bottles	6 750-mL bottles
Rum	1 375-mL bottle	1 750-mL bottle	2 750-mL bottles	4 750-mL bottles	6 750-mL bottles
Vodka	1 375-mL bottle	1 750-mL bottle	3 750-mL bottles	6 750-mL bottles	9 750-mL bottles
Scotch	1 375-mL bottle	1 750-mL bottle	1 750-mL bottle	2 750-mL bottles	3 750-mL bottles
Bourbon	1 375-mL bottle	1 750-mL bottle	1 750-mL bottle	2 750-mL bottles	3 750-mL bottles
Mineral water	2 1-liter bottles	4 1-liter bottles	6 1-liter bottles	12 1-liter bottles	18 1-liter bottles
7-Up or Sprite	1 1-liter bottle	1 1-liter bottle	2 1-liter bottles	4 1-liter bottles	6 1-liter bottles
Cola	1 2-liter bottle	2 2-liter bottles	3 2-liter bottles	6 2-liter bottles	9 2-liter bottles
Diet cola	1 2-liter bottle	2 2-liter bottles	3 2-liter bottles	6 2-liter bottles	9 2-liter bottles
Tonic	1 liter bottle	2 1-liter bottles	3 1-liter bottles	6 1-liter bottles	9 1-liter bottles
Glasses	16 10-oz (300 mL) glasses	30 10-oz (300 mL) glasses	75 10-oz (300 mL) glasses	150 10-oz (300 mL) glasses	225 10-oz (300 mL) glasses
Ice	10 lbs (4.5 kg)	24 lbs (11 kg)	50 lbs (23 kg)	100 lbs (45 kg)	150 lbs (68 kg)

Barware and Glasses

Real glassware, whenever possible, is preferable for serving drinks. Something about paper or Styrofoam cups can really kill the ambiance of an otherwise sophisticated gathering, although clear plastic cups are okay for casual outdoor events. For those who regularly entertain on a large scale, a collection of inexpensive wineglasses can be a great investment, saving you each time on disposables or rentals. You can store them in a crate in the basement, garage or attic when not entertaining so you don't take up precious cabinet space. Wine snobs will probably want separate glasses for red wines and white wines. Others may find that an in-between all-purpose wineglass makes an efficient choice. Renting wine or beverage glasses is another way to go. Most rental companies simply request that glasses be rinsed and retuned in the original boxes — you won't have to thoroughly wash them.

Planning to serve beer or mixed drinks too? A complete bar should include Pilsner or pint glasses, old-fashioned glasses, highball glasses, martini glasses and more. See the illustrations at right and on page 172 for examples of the glassware you'll want to consider outfitting your bar with, depending on your party plans and personal preferences.

Stocking the Bar: Beyond Liquor

If you plan to offer a full bar, you'll want to make sure to have the liquor recommended in the chart on page 170. But you'll need a few additional items beyond the alcohol. What about the olives for that classic martini, or the squeeze of lime for that gin and tonic? Even if you'll only offer beer and wine, you'll still need the tools for opening and serving them. Here's a list of items that can help make a bar truly well stocked and ready for anything:

- **Cocktail napkins:** Because guests will probably get a fresh one with each drink, have on hand at least five napkins per guest. Any extras can be saved for the next party. Look for great deals at discount stores.
- **Corkscrews:** It's a good idea to have a few corkscrews on hand. While the latest artificial corks do a pretty good job of sealing wine, they can do a real number on your corkscrew, so you might need a backup. For traditional corks, I love the smooth-operating corkscrew pulls. These used to be

Glassware

water

red wine

white wine

Burgundy

Champagne flute

Pilsner

old-fashioned

highball

martini

brandy snifter

available only in expensive designer versions, but most home goods stores now carry cheaper versions that do a great job.

- **Bottle openers:** When it comes to bottled beer, I don't think of any as truly screw-top: an opener works on either way, and it hurts my hands a lot less. Party hosts should have a few hand-held bottle openers for popping open bottled beer and sodas. Serious beer enthusiasts will enjoy having one of those old-fashioned wall-mounted bottle openers — which come in dozens of designs, mostly cast iron or brass — for easy opening. Just be sure to screw it into a stud or other woodwork.

- **Ice buckets:** If you plan to serve anything on the rocks (or shake up anything icy in that cocktail shaker), you'll want to have a clean, full ice bucket in your bar area. Insulated, covered versions do a good job of keeping the ice cold, and you can restock from your freezer as necessary. For gatherings where a larger capacity will be more practical, wash out a cooler to use for ice. Want a permanent solution? Installed below-counter ice makers are a luxury that some frequent hosts make good use of, whether in the bar area or in the kitchen.

- **Ice tongs or scoop:** You'll need a way to get the ice from its storage place into cups. For small jobs, ice tongs are a good way to keep your paws out of the mix. If you're scooping cups full of ice for sodas all night, a scoop will make short work of the job. It's best to have both options on hand.

- **Cocktail shaker:** For martinis and other swank cocktails, there's nothing as cool as a cocktail shaker to make the mixture ice-cold without getting any of that pesky, diluting ice into the glass. There are many versions, from very simple to very complicated. Start with a couple of basic stainless steel shakers; you'll probably find that they work very well. Alternatively, you can stir your cocktails and use a hand-held strainer (often sold as part of a bar set) to pour it into the glass.

- **Cocktail spoon or swizzle sticks:** These are used when somebody wants that drink stirred rather than shaken. You can use any spoon, of course, but a well-stocked bar has its own utensils at the ready. Swizzle sticks can also be used to stir coffee.

- **Jigger:** These small, cone-shaped measures come with most bar sets and are used to dole out shots. The double jigger has two cone-shaped measures, one on each side, with one side measuring a full shot and the other a smaller shot. Experiment ahead of time so you're familiar with the size of shots your jigger produces, as they come in a few different sizes. A clear shot glass with measures on the side can stand in for a jigger.

- **Stoppers and pour spouts:** Stoppers are good for recorking wines and other bottles. I am particularly fond of the tight-sealing Champagne stoppers that help a bottle retain its bubbly. For wine enthusiasts who purchase good bottles but don't finish them in one sitting, a vacuum pump set can help save those precious last drops, better preserving the wine's aroma and flavor than a simple stopper alone. If you plan to do a lot of bottle-slinging, you can outfit liquor bottles with pour spouts, which will help keep things neat; bar-style measured pour spouts will keep drinks consistent.
- **Blender:** If blended drinks, such as daiquiris, are on the menu, you'll want a powerful blender. It's worth it to invest in quality — for blending drinks, you'll want a machine sturdy and strong enough to make short work of pulverizing ice without overheating.
- **Garnishes and more:** Depending on the types of drinks you plan to serve, you'll need to have certain fruit or vegetable accoutrements prepped and at your fingertips, including fresh lemon and lime wedges or twists, maraschino cherries, cocktail onions, pimiento-stuffed green olives and celery sticks. You'll also need kosher salt and sanding sugar (a coarse-grained sugar available in many colors) for rimming glasses. If you don't precut the lemon wedges and other garnishes, you'll want to have a bar knife and a small cutting board on hand too.

Ice

We all seem to underestimate our ice needs during a party. It's inexpensive, and it's difficult to serve drinks without it, so I recommend that party hosts count on $1\frac{1}{2}$ to 2 pounds (750 g to 1 kg) per guest. It may seem like a bit too much at first, but if it later saves you or a friend a mid-party trip to the market, then it's worth it.

To save room in the refrigerator, and to keep it from being constantly opened and closed, I purchase chilling tubs — large, heavy-duty plastic containers to chill drinks in. Fill them with ice and a little water and add bottles of white wine and other drinks that are best served cold. Begin chilling them about 30 minutes ahead of time, and count on 40 to 50 pounds (18 to 23 kg) of ice to fill each tub.

What's on Tap

Be careful what you offer: asking someone if they want a drink should be preceded with "We have wine, beer or soda" if that's what you're really offering. If you want to treat guests to a partial or full bar, see pages 169 and 170 for guides on stocking these for the party. Because I don't like to take time away from my other guests by looking up an obscure cocktail recipe for the guest who requests a Sex on the Beach when everyone else is drinking Chardonnay, I let guests help themselves. Mixing up pitchers of specialty cocktails ahead of time — if you want to offer sangria or margaritas, for example — can keep the drinks flowing without chaining anyone to bar duty.

All About Wine

When shopping for a party, it's a good idea to purchase a wine you've had before, so you'll know what to expect. A trusted wine-seller or the wine manager at your favorite market can make recommendations that will go well with the meal you have planned. Specialty wine shops often host tastings — many of them free — for their customers. Attending is a great way to try a number of new wines ahead of when you'll need them; be sure to take notes or save labels so you can find what you want again.

While most people feel a little less strict these days about following protocol for wine-pairing, opting to go simply with what they like and what tastes good, many people gravitate toward light, refreshing white wines, rosés and lighter reds in the summertime, preferring robust reds and heavier fortified wines during the cooler months.

No matter what the weather, it's important to serve wine at its optimal temperature to enjoy its best qualities. In general, Champagne should be served between 45°F and 50°F (7°C and 10°C), white wine between 50°F and 55°F (10°C and 13°C) and red wine between 55°F and 65°F (13°C and 18°C). If you want to preserve the label of a wine you're chilling in an ice-filled bucket, slip the bottle into a clear plastic bag (like the one your newspaper comes in) to protect the label. When serving wine, pour the glass only one-third to one-half full, to allow the wine to aerate.

A good dessert wine is a scrumptious thing. Look for wines labeled "late harvest," "Muscat" or "ice wine." Some Rieslings are sweet enough to serve as dessert wines.

Fortified wines have alcohol added, usually in the form of brandy. Sherry, Madeira, Marsala, port and vermouth are all fortified. Serve them as aperitifs or for dessert.

Sauterne is made from grapes affected by the fungus *Botrytis cinerea*, which causes them to shrivel on the vine, concentrating their sweetness (this process is known as "noble rot"). It is excellent served with foie gras or blue cheeses.

Wine Glossary

Here's a rundown of some common varieties of wine:

- **Barbera:** This Italian grape produces a light and fruity red wine; it's also used for blends.

- **Cabernet Sauvignon:** This one's popular for good reason — a rich, full-bodied red wine, Cabernet Sauvignon often tastes of black currants and sometimes of mint and eucalyptus. It improves with age and is at its best when served with red meat.

- **Chardonnay:** This is probably the most popular white wine. Depending on how it's made, it is either dry and light or full-bodied and buttery. It's excellent served with creamy sauces.

- **Chenin Blanc:** This French white wine grape can produce wine that ranges from dry to sweet. Sweet Chenin Blanc generally tastes of honey, while dry Chenin Blanc is fresh and fruity. Dry versions are excellent with shellfish.

- **Gamay:** This French red wine grape makes up the vast majority of vines in the Beaujolais region. Most of the resulting wines are light, fruity reds that are meant to be consumed while the wine is young. The taste of pears, bananas and raspberries can often be detected in Gamays. They are great for summer picnics.

- **Gewürztraminer:** This spicy, full-bodied white wine can be dry or sweet. With its rose perfume and litchi flavor, Gewürztraminer is one of the few wines that goes well with spicy food.

- **Merlot:** Merlot grapes make a rich, smooth red wine, and are also used in blends. While this varietal suffered a setback with its wimpy characterization in the movie *Sideways*, its softer flavors make it a popular choice for parties.

- **Muscat:** This musky white wine is often very sweet, and sometimes sparkling. Sweet Muscats make excellent dessert wines, with their flavors of peaches and apricots, and sometimes pineapple. They're also excellent with fresh fruit.

- **Pinot Grigio:** This white wine tends to be aromatic, light and smooth — it's excellent served with fish dishes. The French version is known as Pinot Gris.

- **Pinot Noir:** A light- to medium-bodied red wine, Pinot Noir often has a strawberry aroma and hints of red currants and cherries. Pinot Noir is the main grape grown in France's Burgundy region, and is one of three grapes allowed in real Champagne.

- **Riesling:** This white wine grape native to Germany produces wine that can vary from bone-dry to extremely sweet; it's light in body, yet strongly flavored. The high acidity balances the richness of this wine. Riesling is wonderful paired with spicy foods, and late-harvest Riesling, served as a dessert wine, is often paired with dessert or after-dinner cheeses.

- **Sangiovese:** This Italian grape is the main one used to make Chianti (usually at least 10% of the grapes come from other varietals). As a wine, Sangiovese is typically acidic and earthy.

- **Sauvignon Blanc:** Also known as Pouilly Fumé or Fumé Blanc, this very dry, fresh white wine has notes of green grass and gooseberries. It's good with fish and with salads dressed with vinaigrettes.

- **Sémillon:** This grape is widely grown and is usually blended with other white wine varietals, such as Sauvignon Blanc, to produce wines that range from dry to very sweet. On the sweet end is France's Sauternes, some of the best sweet dessert wines; serve it with fruit.

- **Syrah/Shiraz:** The grapes known as Syrah in France are called Shiraz in Australia. They make dark, full-bodied red wines that are less tannic when aged and have aromas of black currant, raspberry, cedar, black pepper and spice.

- **Viognier:** This white wine grape is relatively rare but sought-after, making these wines more expensive than some other varietals. Viognier is a perfumed, intense and full-bodied white wine.

- **Zinfandel:** Widely planted in California, Zinfandel grapes can produce a number of wines, from the light white or rosé wines called "white Zinfandel" to the massive and tannic red wine simply known as Zinfandel. Whatever its guise, Zinfandel has berry notes.

All About Beer

Beer, some argue lately, has become as nuanced and interesting as wines. Whether or not you believe that, there's no disputing that the wide range of craft brews available today has given beer drinkers a lot more to enjoy. The incredible variety makes it possible to host an upscale party centered on tasting such beers (not unlike a wine-tasting), or simply to complement the menu with something more exciting than your average domestic brew. Beer is a natural for game-day gatherings, pizza and movie nights, a fireside chili supper, spicy ethnic menus and Oktoberfest.

If beer will be on tap at your party, you have several options. Many well-stocked stores offer dozens of kinds of beer in 6- and 12-packs so you can mix and match. Some markets even sell single beers, for the ultimate mix-and-match collection — no two beers alike. Have some large tubs of ice on hand to keep all that beer cold and save your refrigerator the stress of constant traffic.

For larger parties, or when you want to pair a particular beer with your menu, you might choose to purchase a larger volume of one kind of beer. A keg is 15.5 gallons (58.67 L) and serves 124 16-ounce (454 mL) glasses of beer; a half-keg, or pony keg, holds 7.75 gallons (29.34 L) and serves 62 16-ounce (454 mL) glasses (and it's perfectly acceptable to serve beer in smaller 12-ounce/341 mL glasses or cups). Several brands, such as Heineken, offer mini kegs at beer retailers; these kegs serve closer to 10 16-ounce (454 mL) glasses. Once tapped, a keg should be used within a couple of days, so you'll want to estimate your needs as closely as possible to avoid waste. Remember, you'll need a way to keep that keg cold; while devoted beer enthusiasts might have a keg fridge in the garage, most of us don't. Ask when you're renting; many companies offer the necessary tap, tub and ice along with their keg rentals.

Beer Glossary

What kind of beer to serve? It's fun to try something new, but it helps to know how to decipher the lingo on the labels first. Start with the category of beer that appeals to you, or suits your menu the best, and then narrow it down from there. Here are some popular styles of beer to try:

- **Ale** is a large category. These beers are made with top-fermenting yeast; the resulting beer is generally dark amber in color, with hops providing a sweetness balance, though there are several that deviate. The category also encompasses pale ale and India pale ale, brown ale and red ale.

- **Bock** (also called bockbier) is a strong, dark lager (see below). These days, bocks can also be amber or pale in color. Double bock (or doppelbock) has a higher alcohol content and is characterized by its rich, malty, even sweet flavor.

- **Lager** is another large category that encompasses many different styles. In general, these are bottom-fermented beers that are light and crisp, though there are styles that are darker in color. Pilsner and bock are both types of lager.

- **Stout** is the darkest of beers, top-fermented and made with dark-roasted barley that contributes to its deep color, rich flavor and full body.

- **Porter**, though lighter in body than stout, is also strong and dark.

- **Wheat beers** are top-fermented beers made with a significant portion of wheat. They tend to be light in color, with a light, sweet, even fruity flavor. Depending on their origin and style, wheat beers are also called weizen, weissbier, weisse or witbieren. Hefeweizen is a popular unfiltered cloudy wheat beer, while dunkleweizen is a dark version of the same beer; these are sometimes served with a lemon slice in North America.

How to Make an Ice Ring

For a stunning and easy way to keep beverages in a punch bowl chilled, make an ice ring with fruit or edible flowers frozen inside. The key is using distilled water, because it freezes clearer than tap or filtered water, which tends to freeze cloudy.

You will need:

1. A ring mold, Bundt pan, angel food cake pan, gelatin ring mold or other ring-shaped mold. You want a mold with a hole in the center so that the ice will float upright. Solid shapes can be too easily flipped upside down.
2. Two quarts (2 L) of distilled water.
3. Whatever decorations complement your punch or beverage, such as small to medium-sized edible flowers, petals from larger edible flowers, citrus leaves, fresh herb sprigs, kumquats, sliced lemons, limes or oranges, pineapple or mango chunks, melon balls, whole berries, cherries, sliced peeled kiwifruit, short cinnamon sticks or star anise pods.
4. Flat space in your freezer large enough for the ring mold to fit.

Instructions:

1. Add decorations to sides and bottom of the ring mold. Pour in distilled water to a depth of $1\frac{1}{2}$ inches (4 cm).
2. Place in freezer until almost frozen, about 40 minutes.
3. Add more decorations. Fill with more distilled water to a depth of 3 inches (7.5 cm).
4. Return to freezer until frozen solid, at least 2 hours. Some items may float to the surface of the water as it freezes; check every 15 minutes or so and push the floaters back into the water.

Nonalcoholic Beverages

When teetotalers or kids are invited to the party, you'll need something for them to drink. Even if you imagine that most of your guests will be imbibing, it's a good move to have some nonalcoholic beverages on hand. You never know who's newly pregnant, dealing with health problems or recovering from an addiction. Besides, the presence of nonalcoholic options helps all partygoers pace themselves, and that in itself is reason enough to offer them. There's a lot beyond soda, and these days many people are switching to more healthful alternatives. Choose two or three nonalcoholic options to have on hand, and purchase them in individual sizes so that any that go unused can be saved for the next party. Here are some options.

Iced Teas

Look for fruit-flavored bottled iced teas, or even iced green teas. Be sure to note whether they contain sugar or artificial sweeteners, so you can keep your guests' preferences in mind.

Juice Boxes

For kids, nothing seems to be more popular than a stash of juice boxes on ice. Look for those that are 100% juice (parents will thank you) and for flavors that are less likely to stain — apple juice instead of fruit punch, for example (you'll thank yourself).

Mocktails

"Nonalcoholic" doesn't have to mean "boring." Have club soda and some flavored syrups on hand at the bar so guests can make their own Italian sodas. Or make a spritzer with half club soda and half pomegranate-cherry juice or cranberry-raspberry juice. Garnish mocktails with a lemon or lime wedge or a cherry from your bar.

Nonalcoholic Beer

For those who are trying to limit their intake of alcohol, nonalcoholic beers such as O'Doul's and St. Pauli N.A. can be welcome stand-ins (serve them super-cold). Keep in mind that even nonalcoholic beers may have very small amounts of alcohol in them, so they might not be the best choice for certain guests.

Punches or Lemonade

An old-fashioned bowl of punch or lemonade is a festive way to encourage nonalcoholic drinking. It can also make quite a show on the table, especially if you make a pretty ice ring with fresh fruit and water to float in it (see "How to Make an Ice Ring," opposite). Plus, individual portions can be dressed up with a splash or rum or vodka, if desired.

Sodas and Juices

Think beyond the typical soda pop and look for natural alternatives that combine carbonated water with fruit juices. Orangina is a classic fizzy citrus drink that everyone loves, and sparkling apple juice is nearly as festive as Champagne (and comes in a Champagne-like bottle). Hansen's natural sodas are terrific too. More brands crop up all the time — look for interesting flavors that will complement your party's menu or theme.

Water

At most parties, especially those that involve the outdoors, most guests will want water at some point. You can set up a few pitchers of ice water from which guests can help themselves, adding lemon, lime or orange slices for color and flavor. If you purchase bottled water, be sure to set up a bin to collect the bottles for recycling. Another option for outdoor entertaining is to purchase reusable water bottles, fill them with ice water and distribute them to guests as a party favor — one that they can use during the party and then take home.

Coffee

There are four types of coffee roasts: light, medium, medium-dark and dark. Light roasts are the mildest in color and flavor. Medium roasts have a mild, slightly deeper flavor and color. Medium-dark roasts are darker in color and richer in taste, and have a slightly bitter aftertaste. Dark roasts are the most bitter, but because of their longer roasting time, they have the least amount of acid.

I almost always offer coffee after a dinner party; it goes well with dessert, and it's a nice excuse to get up from the table and head to an adjoining room to continue the conversation in a more comfortable setting. It's ideal to have two coffee pots so you can brew regular and decaf simultaneously. If you only have one, stick with decaf. Most coffee drinkers will be okay with forgoing caffeine at night, and some people have health reasons for skipping it.

Speaking of health issues and coffee, while I'm a purist and don't personally like artificial sweeteners, I always keep packets of sugar substitute on hand for guests, and those on strict diets are always grateful. You'll also want to stock up on half-and-half (10%) cream, fill the sugar bowl and consider purchasing a liqueur that pairs well with coffee: Irish cream, Kahlúa and even whiskey are a few options. If you want to get really fancy, look for fun stirrers, such as chocolate mint sticks or small wooden stir sticks coated in sugar crystals.

Consult the chart opposite as a guide for how much coffee to make, keeping in mind that it was designed for standard 5-ounce (150 mL) mugs; if you have oversize mugs or expect your guests to drink more than one cup, plan accordingly. And if you regularly entertain on a large scale, you'll enjoy having a party-size coffee pot: 40-cup and larger versions are available at stores like Target and Walmart.

Coffee Service

Ingredients	6 cups (5 oz/150 mL)	12 cups (5 oz/150 mL)	25 cups (5 oz/150 mL)	50 cups (5 oz/150 mL)	75 cups (5 oz/150 mL)
Ground coffee	⅔ cup (150 mL)	1¼ cups (300 mL)	2½ cups (625 mL)	5 cups (1.25 L)	7½ cups (1.875 L)
Bottled or filtered water	4½ cups (1.125 L)	2 quarts plus 1 cup (2.25 L)	1 gallon plus 1 pint (4.5 L)	2 gallons plus 1 quart (9 L)	3½ gallons (14 L)
Half-and-half or cream	¼ cup (50 mL)	½ cup (125 mL)	1 cup (250 mL)	2 cups (500 mL)	3 cups (750 mL)
Sugar	¼ cup (50 mL)	½ cup (125 mL)	1 cup (250 mL)	2 cups (500 mL)	3 cups (750 mL)
Sugar substitute	9 packets	18 packets	36 packets	72 packets	108 packets

Good Manners Never Go Out of Style

Elizabeth Taylor has been a movie star my entire life. I've followed her story through her movies, marriages, illnesses, weight gain and loss, you name it. I love her the most because, when my gay friends were dropping like flies in the 1980s and no one seemed to care, she threw her fame, money and power into the public arena and said, "Let's help these people." I worship her honesty, candor and spirit. She's one hell of a women.

I had been catering for many years by the time Macy's asked me to work on their big AIDS fundraiser. The event, named Passport, was billed as the biggest fashion show in the world. It was held in San Francisco and Los Angeles every year. One year, I was hired to make the green-room food for the celebrity talent. (The green room is where the talent waits until they are brought onto the stage.) Our green rooms were actually fancy trailers, or "honey wagons," pulled up outside of Barker Hanger at the Santa Monica Airport.

The celebrity talent that year was Elizabeth Taylor, Magic Johnson and, if memory serves, Sharon Stone.

I hope you are not shocked to hear this, but the celebrity talent gets better food than everybody else. The models, the vendors, the underwriters and sponsors, the volunteers, the weatherman from a local TV channel — they all get celery sticks and Costco pinwheel sandwiches. The budget in fundraising is everything. As it should be.

There was a sit-down dinner served to those who bought the high-end tickets to the show, but even this food was produced by an underpaid caterer who was trying to feed a lot of people on a very thin dime.

When you are feeding celebrities, or working with them, you almost never speak to them directly. You speak to their people. And when it's a big, big star, their people have people. A handler (another Hollywood term for someone responsible for the handling of the star, the parrot or the dog, depending), in this case a VP from Macy's, was supposed to tell me what food to prepare, but he was too busy worrying about other matters. So I got no direction.

I decided on several trays of fancy finger food. I've fed a lot of stars and, when they are all dressed up in formal wear, very seldom do they want a big old plate of ribs. My feeling was that several small, delicious items would work.

I made a freshly poached Maine lobster salad — big chunks of diced lobster in a homemade Dijon mustard sauce — served on crispy endive leaves with chopped chives as a garnish; miniature beef Wellingtons served with a creamy horseradish dipping sauce; and, to finish off, huge strawberries dipped in dark chocolate, then in crushed walnuts. I assigned a waiter to each green room to serve the food and bus the room for glasses and napkins.

When Miss Taylor arrived, she was traveling with an entourage of eleven friends, and her trailer was full of partying people. Never expecting to speak to her, I walked into her trailer to check on things, carrying a tray of strawberries. There she sat, with a sweet little dog on her lap. She looked like a queen.

I heard a breathy little voice say, "Are you the chef?" That would be me. She was speaking to me! As sweet as she was pretty, she praised the food and told me she loved really good food. She thanked me and said how nice I was to make all this.

I was speechless. Elizabeth Taylor's good manners and kind words made me speechless. I thought of my mother, who always said good manners never go out of style. I stood there dumbstruck — or, rather, star-struck. She went on to tell me that she had never been able to go to the grocery store because she had always been famous. Finally, I was able to speak. I told her she hadn't missed much. Then one of the many handlers appeared to escort her to the stage.

But not before she smiled and said, "Goodbye, Chef, and thanks again."

Entertainment

~~~~~~

Isn't a party — complete with that carefully chosen theme, location, decor, guest list and food and beverages — entertainment enough for partygoers? When we host a party, most of us do call that "entertaining," after all, and we don't mean that we're tap-dancing for our guests, although that certainly would be entertaining with the right friends. For many groups, the party itself is, indeed, entertainment enough. The right mix of people will provide nonstop conversation, with relatively equal, back-and-forth, good-natured banter. They'll be grateful for the chance to catch up with friends, appreciative of your efforts to arrange such a gathering and impressed and satiated by the fabulous food and drink. Let's hope that, on the way home, they'll be discussing how they can reciprocate the invitation by entertaining *you* soon.

But there are times, even with smaller gatherings, when a party needs a little boost. Even with a group of old friends, it's helpful to have a bag of tricks at the ready to ensure a successful party when it might otherwise threaten to sag a bit. And when you're gathering a group of people who don't know each other well, or a group that includes some people who aren't quite as gregarious as you are, having some ideas for entertainment in the mental queue is downright vital. This chapter includes a number of ways to make sure your guests are having a great time. Read on for ideas that will suit your group and occasion.

Introductions and Name Tags

The subtlest and easiest way to boost your party is to follow one of etiquette's most basic dictums and introduce people who don't already know each another. This is like leading a horse to water: you can't *make* great conversation happen between guests, but you can help it along by introducing them, offering a little context and pointing out any common interests before dashing off to answer the door or finish up in the kitchen. Here's the sort of thing I usually go with: "Arlen, this is my friend Amy; we work together. Amy, this is my friend Arlen; she's in my yoga class. I think your toddlers are right around the same age . . ."

Most reasonably social people can easily take it from there. You've already spared them the slightly uncomfortable task of introducing themselves, and you've even given them a few tidbits to go on, conversation-wise. For small groups of 12 or fewer, such simple verbal introductions are usually sufficient. It also doesn't hurt to reintroduce guests who might have met only once or twice before; they'll be grateful to hear a new acquaintance's name again, because chances are good that they've forgotten it.

For larger groups with some new faces, you can help people along by providing name tags. After all, it's difficult for most of us to learn more than a few new names at a time, and name tags take the pressure off by serving as a friendly reminder. I myself have been guilty of having long conversations, even fairly intimate chats, with new acquaintances, only to realize I've forgotten their names. Name tags can be a real life-saver.

As a conversation-boosting icebreaker, some creative hosts have their guests write a little something extra on their name tags: a year when something important happened to them; an adjective that describes their personality and begins with the same letter as their name; or something related to the party theme, such as how long they've known the guest of honor.

Unfortunately, most of the name tags you'll find at office supply stores look awfully corporate. But there are some other options:

* Do you have a great stationery store in your area? Check to see if they carry any unusual name tags, or if they can custom design and print some to match your party theme.

- If you made your own party invitations with a special card stock, stamp, ribbon or cutout, you can easily use the same materials to make coordinating name tags. If you use card stock or another non-sticky material for name tags, provide safety pins for people to attach them with. Guests who don't want to attach such a tag to their shirt can always put it on their wineglass (provide rubber bands to loop through a hole in the top of the tag).
- Design your own name tags on the computer and print them out on plain sticky labels from the office supply store. You can incorporate a photo of the guest of honor or any other graphic elements that fit your theme. For those without the time or interest to play graphic designer, there are some free printable name tags to be found online, though most are designed for children's parties.
- If you're hosting a more formal party where sticky name tags might not go with the attire or setting, consider using wineglass name tags instead. The round paper kind that you can write on won't look dorky or pose any threat to guests' formal duds, but they still do the job. Ask for them where you buy wine, visit www.winetag.com or make them yourself.

Tabletop Diversions

Check out www. partydirectory. com/games/ for ideas for games of all kinds: quizzes, outdoor games, ice breakers and shower games.

For seated dinners, where guests will be relatively stuck in place for a good while, it can be fun to include an at-the-table diversion to break the ice and inspire conversation. Here are some ideas.

Christmas Crackers
A holiday tradition from England, these gift-filled cardboard tubes encased in festive paper are roughly the shape of a Tootsie Roll, though much larger. Christmas crackers make for a pretty presentation for holiday tables, and are especially fitting from Thanksgiving through New Year's. It doesn't seem to matter that the typical contents are a tissue paper crown, a cheap trinket like a toy measuring tape and silly jokes that nobody would otherwise find funny — these are terrific icebreakers. Who can take themselves seriously when wearing a pretend crown?

Fortune Cookies

When you're serving Asian fare, there's no better icebreaker than fortune cookies. While they're usually broken open at the end of a meal, you can have guests open theirs at the beginning instead. I sometimes use fortune cookies as place cards, inserting a sheet of paper with a guest's name into each. Having each guest read the fortune aloud is common practice, and can make for ongoing conversation and jokes throughout the evening. For adults-only parties among good friends, try adding the words "in bed" after each saying for slightly risqué, and silly, results.

Angel Cards

If your circle's tastes lean toward the esoteric, consider passing a cup of Angel Cards (available in New Age bookstores or at www.innerlinks.com) at the table and inviting guests to select one without looking. These small cards each contain one inspirational word (such as "Freedom," "Creativity" or "Abundance"). You're supposed to focus on a particular life situation while drawing one, taking guidance from the angel you select. If you draw something as dull as "Efficiency," you can, as one of my favorite people often does, explain that you weren't focusing correctly and select another card.

Tavern Puzzles

These cast-iron puzzles (www.tavernpuzzle.com), some based on historic designs and others original designs, usually require the player to remove a ring from an intricate iron puzzle. They are great entertainment for those who like puzzles, although some people won't be able to put them down until they're solved (in a pinch, you can find the solutions online). Because of their history as a diversion for tavern patrons, they make particularly apt entertainment for parties that feature craft beers.

Music

Music contributes significantly to the ambiance you create for a party; it can simply be in the background or it can constitute the evening's main entertainment. Unless the party's theme dictates that you're watching something on television, such as a movie, football game or awards show, it's always a good idea to select some sort of music to play. Such party music, depending on the gathering's theme, size and scope, can range from a few carefully chosen CDs or an MP3 compilation to a live band.

Recorded Music

The least expensive option is to use recorded music, and for many smaller gatherings, where the music will be in the background, recorded music makes the most sense. In most cases, such as for a dinner party, you don't want music to compete with the conversation, so soft jazz or classical music, depending on the party theme, make a good selection. I've found that music without lyrics does the best job of setting the mood without threatening to come to the forefront. Soft music sung in another language can similarly fade into the background, yet offer a lot of ambiance.

While a CD changer set to "random" with a few reliable selections can stand in as DJ for the evening, it's also easy to put together a custom mix that goes with the party's theme — with no annoying or oddball tracks to skip over. I often use my iPod to create custom mixes that can be played through an iPod docking station with speakers; you can also use MP3 files to burn a CD or set of CDs to play custom mixes. Visit websites like www.itunes.com and www.mp3.com for downloadable music to create one-of-a-kind playlists for your party. To make it even easier, iTunes 8 offers a new aptly named "Genius" feature: you select a single song that you have in mind for a party, and Genius creates a playlist from songs in your library that go well with the initial tune. Genius can even introduce you to new music for your party playlist by displaying songs in the iTunes store that go well with your song choice.

Try an online radio site such as www.pandora.com, which allows you to enter an artist or song you like and then creates your own radio station, featuring music similar to it.

DJs

If people will be dancing at your party, music won't just be part of the ambiance, it'll be the main entertainment for the evening. Hiring a DJ is a great way to outsource the musical entertainment duties without the risk or expense of hiring live musicians. DJs are not just experienced mix-masters, they are also great at setting the scene and keeping guests engaged. In addition to spinning the tunes, many also provide lighting and lead games, and some even host karaoke.

While word-of-mouth referrals are a great place to start, you can also find a local DJ through the American Disk Jockey

Association (www.adja.org) or the Disk Jockey in Canada Network (www.djin10.tripod.com). Any DJ you hire should be insured and experienced, should carry backup equipment and should be versatile and punctual. Be sure to discuss specific types of music that you definitely do and do not want to hear; agree on the level of chit-chat and DJ–guest interaction ahead of time; and discuss the timeline and dress code.

Live Music

Hiring a live band or musician is a step above all other options — providing that the band or musician in question can offer just the right sort of music and ambiance for your party. Don't rely on word-of-mouth alone when choosing a band or musician; be sure to at least listen to a demo CD or, better yet, go and see them live in advance of booking them. Beyond their musical skills, it's also important that performers interact well with the audience. You'll want to agree on the time needed for setup and takedown of equipment; set lengths and what you'll play between sets; desired playlists; and even the musicians' presentation, including dress. Keep in mind that it is customary to feed and tip the band.

For more formal affairs that might not involve dancing, a single performer such as a classical guitarist, a pianist (providing there's a piano on site) or a harpist can make a great choice, adding unexpected elegance to a cocktail party or reception. Chamber groups, such as a string quartet, are another option. To locate a classical solo musician or group, check in with the nearest symphony to see if any of its members freelance for such events. If a local university has a good music program, you can call its office to see if any of the professors or advanced students perform as soloists or have performing groups. As always, ask for a demo recording and list of repertoire before committing.

Other Entertainers

If you've settled on recorded background music rather than a DJ or live band but want to hire in another type of entertainment for your party, there are several ways to go. Here are some professionals you can hire to entertain your guests.

Food or Wine Expert

If you and your friends are into learning new things, consider hiring a wine, cheese, tea or other food-related expert, or even a cooking instructor. Such experts can introduce your friends to some exciting new tastes, sharing a bit of background or technique. You can, for example, build a party around tasting and learning about French wines, or making Christmastime tamales. Be sure to discuss ahead of time how in-depth you want the expert to get, including a time frame. You might also discuss the level of guest participation, as audience involvement always makes learning more fun. Remember that experts can range from delightfully enlightening to boringly verbose, so choose carefully.

Spa Professionals

If a gathering of girlfriends is in the cards, it can be fun to hire spa professionals to make girls-only pampering the party's main event. Manicures, pedicures or massages are all treats that will make your guests feel indulged. For safety, be sure to hire licensed professionals, preferably ones you've personally used before, and make sure that any equipment will be sanitized between clients. Many spa professionals are moving toward using disposable tools as much as possible.

Children's Entertainers

Not sure what to do with a dozen six-year-olds at your son's upcoming birthday party? Plenty of parents outsource the entertainment to a professional. Many clowns do balloon-twisting and face-painting in addition to their usual act. You can also look for a magician, a storyteller or another age-appropriate act. Children's birthday parties are often held off-site for the purpose of entertainment: look into such options as Kindermusik, bounce houses, zoos and other destinations that offer all the entertainment you'll need. See Kids on Location (page 52) for more ideas.

Dance Instructor

If you want to host a salsa or swing dance party, you'll do well to hire a dance instructor (or a couple who teach together) who can come to the party to share some moves with guests. A little knowledge can go a long way toward inspiring enthusiasm for dancing among guests. If you will have a band or DJ for the event, they might have some appropriate connections. Or check with local dance studios and area bars that feature certain styles of dancing. While salsa and swing dancing are a lot of fun for couples, an all-female party of good friends might enjoy learning some moves from a belly-dance instructor.

Games

There's nothing like a game to break the ice. People have to talk, team up and compete when there's a game in the works, bringing their spirited sides up front and center and banishing any shyness to the background. Games can be played at a party's beginning to get it rolling, or can provide a welcome change of scenery and conversation after dinner. To make it more interesting, be sure to have small prizes for winners or winning teams.

Remember that for parties, with the distractions of socializing, eating and drinking, it's a good idea to stick to games with a few simple rules, or games that everyone already knows how to play. You and your guests will likely find it tiresome if explaining the rules takes much longer than a few minutes. Here are some types of games to consider, depending on your event, location and guest list.

Lawn, Beach or Park Games

When the party's happening outdoors, you'll have plenty of options for more physical game play. Inexpensive equipment for such games is usually available at sporting goods or discount stores. Some guests will want to play the games, while others will prefer to be spectators or scorekeepers. It doesn't really matter who does what — watching a game has entertainment value too.

Badminton

This racquet sport for four involves the use of a feathered projectile called a shuttlecock (or shuttle) and a portable net. While it's an Olympic sport, it's also easy enough to pitch your net in the sand or grass for a low-key game.

Bocce

This Italian game is traditionally played on a clay court, but it's fun to draw out a court on the sand if your party is set at the beach. Perhaps the most common and easiest option is to simply find a flat stretch of lawn to play on (or even an irregular surface for added challenge, though this breaks with tradition). A bocce set includes eight heavy, colorful bocce balls, plus a smaller ball called a *pallino*, or jack. Pair this game with an Italy-inspired picnic or cookout and you've got a well-focused theme and all the entertainment you'll need.

Croquet

A croquet set should come with nine wickets, six mallets, six balls and two stakes that you can set up in your backyard or at the park. Casual play is sometimes called guerilla croquet, and that's the freewheeling sort we recommend for a party.

Frisbee

Some people take their Frisbee seriously, with such games as Ultimate Frisbee. If everyone knows how to play, go for it; otherwise, a few brightly colored Frisbees tossed between friends makes a great, unstructured diversion for those who are too restless to hang out on a picnic or beach blanket. A big bonus is that it's easy to enter and drop out of the game at will.

Horseshoes

I like this classic lawn game because you don't have to toss the horseshoes perfectly to score. You'll need a horseshoe set, which includes four horseshoes and two stakes, and you can set up the game in any grassy or sandy area. If it suits your theme, you can play up the horseshoe as a symbol of good luck, or even award winners with metal horseshoes worthy of hanging.

Volleyball

Volleyball is another Olympic sport that doubles surprisingly well as a casual party game, and it's flexible enough to accommodate anywhere from four to a dozen or more players. You can play it on the sand or on the grass — all you need is a net and a ball.

Indoor Party Games

Sometimes an indoor party game, such as poker or Bunco, is the theme for the night. Your guests are coming over for a specific game that they (hopefully) already know how to play, so the entertainment's in the bag. At other times, the game is simply a post-dinner diversion. In this case, I often keep the option of playing in mind as a possibility, rather than a definite. If the party is roaring, there's no need to interrupt it, corral guests and insist that they do what you had in mind. But if the conversation could use a change, or if people are looking sleepy or bored, a game can refocus the direction of the party and engage those who might have been checking out. Even with groups of old friends, a game can relieve the pressure to make interesting conversation. Some games call for a specific number of people, but remember that, with many of these, guests can work in teams.

Card Games

Perhaps you and a group of friends gather regularly to play poker, Bunco or bridge, or maybe the idea of playing card games with friends is a new one to you. Many card games are for a limited number of players, so you'll need to consider your guest list when suggesting these. Some popular card games for small gatherings include hearts, spades, crazy eights and euchre.

Board Games

Board games aren't just for kids; in fact, there are dozens of popular board games that are appropriate for grownup parties or even mixed ages. Some of my favorites for after-dinner entertainment include Pictionary, Catch Phrase or one of the many, many versions of that classic, Trivial Pursuit.

DVD Games

A relative newcomer to the games category is board games with the multimedia element of a DVD added to the mix. They make for fun, interactive party games to enjoy in front of the television. Some of the most popular DVD games include Scene It, Are You Smarter Than a 5th Grader? and Trivial Pursuit's *Saturday Night Live* Edition.

Dominoes Games

Like a deck of cards, a set of dominoes is a simple game-closet staple that can be used to play any number of games. I'm partial to Mexican train dominoes for small gatherings, but there are several other games to choose from, including Texas 42 and matador.

Parlor Games

These games have been around long enough that they don't require a game set; pencils and paper are usually enough. Everyone knows charades, the enduring guessing game in which guests take turns acting out a word or phrase silently, but don't forget about Twenty Questions or Truth or Consequences (rules can be found online).

Children's Party Games

Games are an especially popular diversion for young children's parties. Such structured entertainment can focus the attentions of those who might otherwise misbehave or bore easily, making the typical two-hour celebration fly by. Have a few games in mind; many children's party games are brief and most kids will want to move on to the next game as soon as the first one ends. Some of these are appropriate only for very young children, while others are better for the middle-school set. Think about what your group can handle and plan accordingly. Here are some classics worth remembering.

Musical Chairs

Have a CD player and a CD of fun party music ready in the area where the party will be held, plus enough chairs to accommodate all but one guest.

Bean Bag Toss

Set up a board with one or more holes cut out of it (it's even more fun if the board is painted or decorated with something related to the party theme) and provide bean bags for tossing. You can award prizes for each toss that goes through. The Midwest has a similar game, called Cornhole (www.playcornhole.org), with "bean bags" made from corn kernels. This is a favorite outdoors pastime for grownups, too.

Pin the Tail on the Donkey

You can purchase a game set for Pin the Tail on the Donkey or make your own; you'll also need a blindfold or scarf. This game can be adapted for many themes, such as Pin the Tail on the Monkey or Pin the Hat on the Cowboy. I've even seen it adapted for a bachelorette party.

Duck Duck Goose

No equipment required — just energetic kids. Adapt this to a party theme by changing its name to something related, such as "monkey monkey giraffe" or "engine engine caboose."

Scavenger Hunt or Treasure Hunt

Keep it in the backyard for younger kids: treasures buried in the sandbox or planted around the yard can make for fun hunting. An indoor "alphabet hunt" can be made up of objects beginning with different letters of the alphabet; set a time limit and have participants write down the item's name and location rather than collecting it, awarding the team that finds the most letters.

Piñata

These festively decorated hollow containers are often in the shape of an animal but can be found to coordinate with almost any theme. If you don't want to give more sugar to the already revved-up crowd, fill the piñata with dollar-store goodies instead, such as boxes of crayons, kid-sized sunglasses and small toys. To prevent accidents (you are, after all, blindfolding a child and giving them a bat or stick to swing), have kids stand behind a line while they wait their turn. Check out www.pinatas.com for ready-made piñatas; creative types can construct one at home. Adults enjoy whacking piñatas as well, and you'll be surprised at how quickly they dive for the goodies once they fall.

Chocolate Bar Game

Wrap a large chocolate bar in several layers of wrapping paper and place it in the center of a circle, with a knife and fork. Children take turns rolling a die; if they get a six, they run to the chocolate bar and attempt to cut through the wrappings and cut off a piece to eat, while the other players pass the die and continue rolling until the next six makes it somebody else's turn. Some versions of the game include a set of clothes or accessories that must be put on after rolling a six but before getting to work on the chocolate, making the game more challenging.

Backyard Games

If you have a fenced-in backyard, even the youngest of guests can be set loose for most of the above games, and more. Other backyard games that kids of varying ages will enjoy are hide and seek, tag (or Super Soaker tag or, at night, flashlight tag), capture the flag, kickball and red rover.

Crafts, Clubs and Work Nights

Sometimes the party's theme and the party's entertainment are one and the same. Do you have a knitting circle? A book club? Two hundred invitations to address in calligraphy? These participatory gatherings come with all the entertainment you'll need, built right in. If you don't have a regular group, consider starting one; such clubs can inspire you to learn a new skill or keep up with non-required reading, or can simply serve as a periodic prompt for the super-busy to do some much-needed socializing.

Book Clubs

Discussing the book serves as the main entertainment for book club parties, providing a fresh topic for each meeting and often inspiring background music, decor and food and drink as well. When members take turns hosting, you'll find yourself reading beyond what you'd normally pick up, which can be a good thing. Look at online book reviews (try www.goodreads.com or www.amazon.com) for points to ponder.

Craft Groups

Do you and your friends like to knit, crochet, quilt or scrapbook? Or do you want to learn how? Forming a crafting group means that hands-on activity is always at the center of the party's entertainment. You'll learn new skills from other members, share ideas and get help with a project when you need it. Plus, you'll have something to show for the time you spent socializing.

Supper Clubs

A supper club can be a great way to try new recipes. While the cooking is usually done individually in advance, food is still the central purpose of the gathering. Some clubs have the host assign a dish to each guest, inspiring the sharing of recipes and techniques ahead of time, which builds anticipation for the gathering. Parties might focus on the fare of a particular country or region, vegetarian cooking or low-fat fare — whatever your group is interested in exploring.

Group-Effort Cooking

If your group of friends loves to cook and your kitchen can accommodate them, join forces for an evening that will make short work of an otherwise sizable task: canning the summer's bumper crop of tomatoes, making or decorating holiday cookies or assembling casseroles to freeze for the busy weeks ahead, for instance. Make sure to divide the results so each guest enjoys the fruits of their efforts in the coming days or weeks.

Big Event Prep Nights

Are you or is someone in your circle getting married soon? Hosting a large anniversary party? Getting ready for the family reunion to come to town? You can host smaller parties leading up to a big event to help yourself or a friend with addressing and stuffing invitation envelopes, making party favors, compiling music play lists and other tasks that a group can knock out in no time. You'll all have your hands full with the evening's task, but you'll enjoy the chance to catch up and reminisce in a more relaxed way than the big day will offer.

Screen Time

A low-key gathering with friends can sometimes be inspired by an upcoming television special, like the *Academy Awards*, that's more fun to watch with a group than by yourself. Even the DVD release of a favorite movie can be a good enough reason to invite people over. Such nights spent in front of the small screen are easy to pull off from a social perspective: they encompass the evening's theme and entertainment all in one. Be sure to offer snacky fare that's easy to eat away from a table and, better yet, without utensils. Here are some catalysts for gathering friends in front of your television.

Sporting Events

From the Super Bowl to the Olympics, from college basketball to the Kentucky Derby, there are many sporting events that are fun to watch with sports-loving friends. Be sure ahead of time that your television plan, whether cable or satellite, includes any specialty channel you'll need, or arrange for pay-per-view as necessary.

Awards Shows

Can't get enough of your favorite celebrities? Awards shows are fantastic for Hollywood stargazers, as well as for fashion buffs and music, movie and television enthusiasts. Invite friends over who share such interests for an evening of people-watching and reminiscing over the year's best in entertainment.

Pageants

Whether or not you think they should be a thing of the past, there's no disputing the campy appeal of pageants and the human-interest stories they offer. If you like to watch pageants, gather friends who feel the same way and make a night of it.

Movies

Maybe you've always dreamed of watching the entire *Star Wars* saga in consecutive weekend sessions, or maybe you've finally gotten your hands on a hotly anticipated DVD release. Movies are natural entertainment for hosting friends informally, and their length makes them particularly well suited to parties. Be sure to start the flick early enough to allow for some time afterward to banter over a film's strong points and weaknesses.

Television Series

A dramatic season opener or finale can be a great way to visit with friends and connect briefly, even on a weeknight. Depending on the timing, you might have them over for snacks and wine or sweets and coffee. Watching the same season of an interesting show, even on the weeks when you do so apart, can inspire plenty of conversation and musings as you follow story lines together.

He Called Me Dolly

I met Frank Sinatra not once, but twice in my life. I was eleven the first time. My family vacationed at Lake Tahoe in August every summer, and he had a restaurant and casino there named Cal Neva. It sat right on the California–Nevada state line, hence the name. It was posh in 1961. Very posh. I had cream of mushroom soup there for the first time — not out of a can, but freshly made. I loved it. I think of it every time I make a cream soup: it set the bar for my palate.

Tahoe in August is hotter than a firecracker. My two sisters and I loved it and would get as brown as berries. The 60s were great: nobody knew about skin cancer, and sunblock was unheard of.

My young and beautiful Aunt Lois would come with us on these trips, along with some of her girlfriends. They wore makeup and drove fast cars, and they'd go gambling at the casinos. Oh, how I longed to be thirty and glamorous, like my aunt.

On the weekends, when my father arrived, we'd vie for his time and attention. We water-skied, went out for burgers and got dressed up for Saturday night dinners.

That year, I forgot to pack my fancy dress. Here was our big dinner at Cal Neva, and me with nothing but shorts. Luckily, there was a clothing store not too far away, and my mother and I went shopping that morning. The dress we found was a deep raspberry color and had a "sexy" back. My mother said, "Maybe too sexy for eleven." Like I knew what "sexy" meant. It was slightly scooped, and I could see my shoulder blades. I'd never known they were there before. What I did I know was that I looked a little bit like my Aunt Lois, and that was good enough for me. My sister Ann put my hair up into a French twist. I felt so grownup. I felt glamorous.

There were keno tickets on the tables in the dining room. My dad played, and his numbers won something. So between the mushroom soup and the steaks, my father and I walked to the cashier's cage in the casino, just outside the restaurant.

And there he was, Frank Sinatra, leaning against a roulette table. I didn't know who he was, though my parents had told me about him. I heard someone say, "Who's this dolly?" before I realized he was talking to me. My father and I stopped, and Mr. Sinatra held out his hand and said, "Hi, I'm Frank." I fell in love.

Jump ahead 25 years. I'd been an executive chef in Los Angeles for about three years when I met Frank Sinatra again. I was 36, cooking for a charity event in Palm Springs. I was not as brown as a berry, was not wearing a dress with a scooped back, did not have my hair up in a French twist. Rather, I was wearing chef's pants.

When Mr. Sinatra walked into the kitchen, he came right up to me and said, "What're you cooking?" It was a red sauce for a lasagna that would be made later that day and served the next day. "Smells good, can I have a taste?" he said.

He tasted the sauce off the wooden spoon I was stirring with and said, "Great gravy, Dolly. Tastes a lot like my mother's."

I told him we had met before, and he told me how much he'd loved having that "joint." He promised to remember me the next time we met.

I believed him, but we never did meet again.

Part 2

Recipes and Menus

Essential Recipes

Appetizers

Salads and Dressings

Soups

Entrées

Sides

Sauces

Desserts and Dessert Sauces

Beverages

Phyllo Bundles

*These delightfully
crisp bundles are the
ultimate buttery, one-
bite cocktail appetizer.
Though working with
the phyllo dough may
seem time-consuming, it
will be worth the effort.*

Tip

If increasing the
recipe, butter phyllo
in batches, keeping
remaining phyllo
covered with waxed
paper to keep it from
drying out.

Make Ahead

Phyllo pouches can
be frozen for up to
2 weeks. Assemble
through the end of
step 3 and place baking
sheet in the freezer
until pouches are
frozen, about 2 hours.
Transfer pouches
to a sealable plastic
bag and keep frozen
until ready to use. To
cook, place frozen
pouches on a baking
sheet and cook in a
350°F (180°C) oven
for 25 to 30 minutes
or until golden brown
and crispy.

- Preheat oven to 375°F (190°C)
- Baking sheet, sprayed with nonstick cooking spray

2	eggs, lightly beaten	2
1	package (10 oz/300 g) frozen spinach, thawed and excess moisture squeezed out	1
2/3 cup	crumbled feta cheese	150 mL
1/4 tsp	salt	1 mL
1/4 tsp	freshly ground black pepper	1 mL
16	sheets phyllo dough (about 1/2 package, or 1/2 lb/250 g)	1
1/2 cup	butter, melted	125 mL

1. In a bowl, combine eggs, spinach, feta, salt and pepper. Set aside.

2. Place 1 sheet of phyllo dough on a clean work surface and brush with melted butter. Add another sheet and brush with butter. Repeat twice more, until you have a stack of 4 buttered sheets. Cut stacks in half lengthwise, then into thirds widthwise, cutting each stack into 6 squares.

3. Place 1 tbsp (15 mL) filling in the center of each square. Pull corners up to cover the filling. Twist and pinch to seal in filling, leaving the edges gathered in a twist. Place on prepared baking sheet. Repeat with the remaining phyllo and filling. You should have 24 phyllo pouches in all.

4. Bake in preheated oven for about 20 minutes or until golden brown and crispy.

Easy Extra

▸ Add 1/2 cup (125 mL) crumbled cooked bacon or sausage to the filling mixture.

Variations

▸ Hot Crab Dip (page 211), prepared through step 2, also works great as a filling for this recipe.

▸ Replace the feta cheese with 1/2 cup (125 mL) finely chopped cooked chicken and 1/2 cup (125 mL) shredded mozzarella cheese.

▸ For a pierogi-like filling, replace this filling with 1 cup (250 mL) mashed potatoes, 1/2 cup (125 mL) peas and 1 tsp (5 mL) curry powder.

Pupusas

MAKES 8 TO 12 PUPUSAS
or can be multiplied up to 4 times

Pupusas are a common street food in Latin America, often served with shredded cabbage dressed with a little cider vinegar.

Tip

If multiplying the recipe, you may need to cook the pupusas in batches — just be sure to adjust the heat as necessary and add more oil to the skillet between batches.

Make Ahead

Pupusas can be made up to 2 days ahead if refrigerated in an airtight container. To reheat, place in a single layer on an oiled baking sheet in a 350°F (180°C) oven until heated through, about 12 minutes.

2 cups	masa harina (approx.)	500 mL
1 1/2 cups	warm water (approx.)	375 mL
1/2 tsp	salt	2 mL
1/3 cup	shredded Cheddar cheese	75 mL
1/3 cup	canned refried beans	75 mL
2 tbsp	vegetable oil	25 mL

1. In a large bowl, combine masa harina, water and salt, stirring with a fork to blend, until dough is soft enough to form into balls, but not sticky. Add a little more masa harina if dough seems too sticky, or a little water if it crumbles.

2. Roll dough into golf ball–size balls and press a deep well in the center of each ball with your thumb. Place about 1 tsp (5 mL) cheese and about 1 tsp (5 mL) beans in the well. Stretch sides of dough up and over to completely encase the filling. Flatten each ball to about 1/4 inch (0.5 cm) thick.

3. In a medium skillet, heat oil over medium-high heat. Add pupusas and cook for 2 to 3 minutes per side or until golden brown. Serve warm.

Variations

▸ Replace the Cheddar cheese and refried beans with 1/4 cup (50 mL) each diced green chile peppers, Monterey Jack cheese and corn kernels.

▸ Replace the cheese and refried beans with 1/2 cup (125 mL) finely chopped Carnitas (page 235) or cooked ground beef mixed with 1/4 cup (50 mL) tomato sauce and use about 1 tsp (5 mL) per pupusa.

▸ Use a filling of 1/3 cup (75 mL) each finely shredded cooked beef and shredded pepper Jack cheese.

Herb-Stuffed Shrimp

SERVES 6
or can be multiplied
up to 4 times

Serve these shrimp with Easy Roasted Garlic Aïoli (page 252) as a dipping sauce.

Tip
The shrimp can also be cooked in a skillet with a little olive oil over medium-high heat. Sauté for about 3 minutes per side or until shrimp are pink and opaque.

- **Preheat oven to 375°F (190°C)**
- **Baking sheet, sprayed with nonstick cooking spray**

½ cup	cottage cheese	125 mL
2 tbsp	chopped fresh tarragon	25 mL
1 tbsp	chopped fresh chervil	15 mL
1 tbsp	chopped fresh chives	15 mL
	Salt and freshly ground black pepper	
1 lb	jumbo shrimp, peeled and deveined	500 g
4 oz	thinly sliced pancetta, cut into 1-inch (2.5 cm) strips	125 g

1. In a food processor, process cottage cheese until smooth, about 40 seconds. Add tarragon, chervil and chives; pulse until herbs are incorporated. Season lightly with salt and pepper.

2. Cut deeply along the back side of the shrimp, making sure not to cut all the way through. Fill shrimp with 1 to 2 tsp (5 to 10 mL) cheese mixture. Wrap a strip of pancetta around each shrimp, securing with a toothpick. Place in a single layer on prepared baking sheet.

3. Bake in preheated oven for about 15 minutes or until shrimp are pink and opaque. Remove toothpicks before serving.

Petite Lobster Pot Pies

These are a huge improvement over frozen mini quiches, and are worth the trouble to make at home.

Tip

If you're multiplying the recipe more than 2 times, use a large, heavy saucepan instead of a skillet.

Make Ahead

These pot pies can be made ahead up to 2 weeks if kept frozen. Let filling cool to room temperature before filling. Place muffin tin in the freezer until pies are frozen through, about 3 hours. Transfer pot pies to sealable plastic bags and freeze until the day of your party. Place frozen pies back in muffin tin and bake in a 350°F (180°C) oven until filling is hot and crust is golden brown, about 35 minutes.

- Preheat oven to 375°F (190°C)
- 24-cup mini muffin tin

$1/4$ cup	unsalted butter	50 mL
$1/4$ cup	very finely diced carrots	50 mL
$1/4$ cup	minced onion	50 mL
$1/4$ cup	very finely diced peeled russet potato	50 mL
$1/4$ cup	all-purpose flour	50 mL
$1^3/4$ cups	Quick Chicken Stock (page 223) or reduced-sodium chicken or fish broth, heated	425 mL
1 lb	shelled lobster meat, cooked and chopped	500 g
	Salt and freshly ground black pepper	
2	recipes Basic Pie Crust dough (page 261)	2

1. In a large skillet, melt butter over medium-high heat. Sauté carrots, onion and potato for about 4 minutes or until light golden. Sprinkle with flour and cook, stirring frequently, for 4 minutes. Gradually stir in stock. Reduce heat and simmer for about 5 minutes or until thickened. Stir in lobster and cook just until heated through. Season to taste with salt and pepper. Set aside.

2. On a floured surface, roll out pie dough to $1/8$ inch (3 mm) thick and cut into twenty-four 3-inch (7.5 cm) rounds and twenty-four 2-inch (5 cm) rounds. Press each of the larger rounds into the bottom and up the sides of a muffin cup. Fill each with 1 scant tbsp (15 mL) lobster mixture and cover with smaller dough rounds, pinching edges to seal.

3. Bake in preheated oven for about 20 minutes or until crusts are golden brown.

Essential Recipes · Appetizers

Chicken Satay

SERVES 6
or can be multiplied
up to 4 times

These are the perfect stand-up appetizer, and are much more sophisticated than cocktail wieners. You can add chopped vegetables or chunks of pineapple to the skewers if you wish.

Tips

Satay can be served hot or warm.

You can also cook satay in a grill pan over high heat or under a broiler.

• **Twelve to eighteen 6½-inch (16 cm) bamboo skewers**

2	garlic cloves	2
½ cup	coarsely chopped onion	125 mL
2 tbsp	coarsely chopped lemongrass (or 1 tbsp/ 15 mL freshly squeezed lemon juice)	25 mL
1 tbsp	chopped gingerroot	15 mL
1½ tsp	ground cumin	7 mL
1½ tsp	ground coriander	7 mL
¼ tsp	ground turmeric	1 mL
¼ cup	coconut milk	50 mL
3 tbsp	soy sauce	45 mL
3 tbsp	chunky peanut butter	45 mL
1 lb	boneless skinless chicken breasts, cut into ¼-inch (0.5 cm) thick slices	500 g
	Peanut Sauce (page 260)	

1. In a food processor, combine garlic, onion, lemongrass, gingerroot, cumin, coriander, turmeric, coconut milk, soy sauce and peanut butter; process until nearly smooth.

2. Place chicken in a large sealable plastic bag and pour in marinade. Seal and refrigerate for at least 1 hour or overnight.

3. Meanwhile, soak skewers in water for 30 minutes and preheat barbecue grill to high. Remove chicken from marinade, discarding marinade. Thread chicken onto skewers and grill for about 2 minutes per side or until no longer pink inside.

Variation

▶ You can substitute beef or pork for the chicken. For a vegetarian version, use baked tofu or tempeh.

Cheese Fondue

SERVES 6
or can be multiplied
up to 4 times

Popular in the 60s, fondue is making a comeback. Kirsch (cherry brandy) is a traditional addition, but you can substitute any type of brandy or liqueur you like.

• **Fondue pot**

8 oz	Swiss or Emmental cheese, shredded	250 g
8 oz	Gruyère cheese, shredded	250 g
1 tbsp	cornstarch	15 mL
1/4 tsp	ground nutmeg	1 mL
1 1/3 cups	dry white wine	325 mL
1 tbsp	kirsch	15 mL
1	loaf crusty sourdough bread, cut into 2-inch (5 cm) cubes	1

1. In a bowl, combine Swiss, Gruyère, cornstarch and nutmeg; toss to coat.

2. In a medium saucepan, bring wine and kirsch to a simmer over very low heat. Add cheese mixture, 1/2 cup (125 mL) at a time, stirring between additions until mixture is smooth.

3. Transfer cheese sauce to a fondue pot and keep warm. Serve with bread cubes to dip in the sauce.

Easy Extras

▷ As the wine comes to a simmer, add 1 tbsp (15 mL) mashed roasted garlic before adding the cheese.

▷ Add 1 tsp (5 mL) coarsely ground black pepper to the shredded cheese.

Variations

▷ Replace the wine and kirsch with dark beer or stout, and replace the Gruyère with Cheddar.

▷ For a Southwestern flair, replace the wine and kirsch with a light-colored or amber beer, replace the Gruyère with Cheddar and substitute 1 to 2 tsp (5 to 10 mL) ancho chili powder for the nutmeg.

Essential Recipes • Appetizers

Zesty Chipotle Dip

SERVES 6
or can be multiplied
up to 4 times

This is an easy topping for tacos or nachos, or makes a casual chip dip.

Tip
Serve with tortilla chips, jicama sticks or corn chips.

Make Ahead
Can be made up to 1 day in advance if refrigerated in an airtight container.

4	canned chipotle peppers in adobo sauce, or to taste	4
1	package (1¼ oz/35 g) taco seasoning	1
⅔ cup	mayonnaise	150 mL
⅔ cup	sour cream	150 mL
1 tbsp	freshly squeezed lime juice	15 mL
	Salt and freshly ground black pepper	

1. In a food processor, combine chipotles, taco seasoning, mayonnaise, sour cream and lime juice; blend until smooth. Transfer to a bowl and season to taste with salt and pepper.

Variation
▸ Add a 14- to 19-oz (398 to 540 mL) can of rinsed drained canned black, white or pinto beans for a great-tasting bean dip.

Hot Crab Dip

SERVES 6 TO 8
or can be multiplied
up to 4 times

*A little fresh crab goes a
long way in this creamy
dip, which is elegant
and easy to serve at the
same time.*

Tips

Look for premixed
seasonings specially
created for seafood,
such as Old Bay
seasoning. If you don't
have it, the dip will
still taste delicious.

This is great with
vegetable crudités,
crackers or baguette
slices.

Make Ahead

Can be assembled
through step 2 up
to 1 day ahead if
kept covered and
refrigerated, or can be
frozen for up to 1 week.
If cooking from frozen,
add up to 15 minutes to
the baking time.

- **Preheat oven to 350°F (180°C)**
- **8-inch (20 cm) square glass baking dish, greased**

½ cup	panko bread crumbs	125 mL
1 tbsp	unsalted butter, melted	15 mL
1 tsp	salt	5 mL
⅓ cup	minced onion	75 mL
¼ cup	finely sliced green onions	50 mL
10 oz	lump crabmeat	300 g
8 oz	cream cheese, softened	250 g
½ cup	mayonnaise	125 mL
½ cup	sour cream	125 mL
2 tbsp	freshly squeezed lemon juice	25 mL
1 tsp	hot pepper sauce (optional)	5 mL
½ tsp	garlic powder	2 mL
1 tsp	seafood seasoning (optional)	5 mL

1. In a small bowl, combine bread crumbs, butter and salt until crumbly. Set aside.

2. In another bowl, combine onion, green onions, crabmeat, cream cheese, mayonnaise, sour cream, lemon juice, hot pepper sauce, garlic powder and seafood seasoning (if using). Spoon into prepared baking dish and sprinkle with bread crumb mixture.

3. Bake in preheated oven for about 20 minutes or until top is golden.

Variation

▶ Make this with chopped cooked shrimp or drained white tuna instead of the crab.

Essential Recipes • Appetizers

Pâté de Foie de Volaille (Chicken Liver Pâté)

SERVES 16
or can be multiplied
up to 4 times

Some things just sound better in French! This rich pâté is divine smeared on fresh, crusty baguette slices.

Tip

If you need to multiply the recipe, it's best to only make a double batch at a time. While the first batch is baking, you can prepare the next double batch (there's no need to wash all the equipment between batches that way).

Make Ahead

The pâté can be frozen for up to 1 month. To protect it from freezer burn, coat the top with a layer of softened butter about $\frac{1}{8}$ inch (3 mm) thick before wrapping it.

- Preheat oven to 325°F (160°C)
- 8- by 4-inch (20 by 10 cm) loaf pan, oiled
- Large baking dish or roasting pan

$1\frac{1}{2}$ lbs	chicken livers, trimmed	750 g
3	eggs	3
$\frac{1}{4}$ cup	heavy or whipping (35%) cream	50 mL
$\frac{1}{4}$ cup	brandy	50 mL
2 tbsp	coarsely chopped fresh flat-leaf (Italian) parsley, sage, tarragon, chives or basil	25 mL
3 tbsp	all-purpose flour	45 mL
2 tsp	salt	10 mL
$\frac{1}{2}$ tsp	freshly ground black pepper	2 mL
1 tsp	ground nutmeg	5 mL
$\frac{1}{4}$ cup	shelled raw pistachios	50 mL
3 oz	pancetta, sliced	90 g
	Hot water	

1. In a food processor, combine chicken livers, eggs, cream, brandy and parsley; pulse until almost smooth. Sprinkle flour, salt, pepper and nutmeg over liver mixture and process until smooth. Add pistachios and pulse a few times to incorporate.

2. Press mixture into prepared loaf pan, smoothing top so that it is flat. Place pancetta across surface of liver mixture, completely covering the top. Wrap loaf pan tightly in two layers of foil and place in baking dish.

3. Place baking dish in preheated oven and pour in hot water until it comes halfway up the sides of the loaf pan. Bake for $1\frac{1}{2}$ hours. Let cool to room temperature, then cover tightly with plastic wrap and refrigerate for at least 3 hours, until thoroughly chilled, or for up to 3 days.

4. To serve, cut loaf into $\frac{1}{2}$-inch (1 cm) thick slices.

Easy Extras

▸ Add a finely chopped peeled pear or apple with the pistachios.

▸ Add a caramelized chopped onion or $\frac{1}{2}$ cup (125 mL) sautéed chopped wild (exotic) mushrooms with the pistachios.

Layered Salad

This salad is a spectacular addition to any buffet. It is endlessly variable, and its colors can be altered to fit any theme.

Tips

Serving this salad in a straight-sided glass bowl or trifle dish keeps the colorful layers visible.

Assemble in individual servings by layering the ingredients in large, squat glass tumblers.

Make Ahead

Assemble salad, cover top with damp paper towels and refrigerate for up to 2 hours before serving.

● **Glass bowl with straight sides or trifle dish**

2 cups	shredded red cabbage	500 mL
1	English cucumber, quartered lengthwise and sliced	1
3	large tomatoes, diced	3
1	head romaine lettuce, chopped	1
1½ cups	shredded carrots	375 mL
8 oz	goat cheese	250 g
²⁄₃ cup	walnut halves, coarsely chopped	150 mL
½ cup	blue cheese dressing	125 mL

1. Place cabbage in the bottom of glass bowl. Spread cucumber on top, followed by tomatoes, then romaine. Sprinkle carrots on top. Crumble goat cheese over carrots and top with walnuts. Serve with dressing on the side.

Easy Extras

▸ Add dried fruit, chopped fresh fruit, sliced red onions, steamed summer squash, chilled cooked potatoes, grilled vegetables or cooked diced chicken.

Variation

▸ Use Stone-Ground Mustard Vinaigrette (page 219) or Avocado Cucumber Dressing (page 222) in place of the blue cheese dressing.

Essential Recipes ● Salads and Dressings

Greek Salad

SERVES 6
or can be multiplied
up to 4 times

This crisp, crunchy salad is a nice palate cleanser and makes a light accompaniment to Spiced Lamb Kebabs (page 417) or Herb-Roasted Rack of Lamb (page 241). Opa!

Make Ahead

Salad can be made up to 1 day ahead if covered and refrigerated.

4	plum (Roma) tomatoes, cut into wedges	1
1	English cucumber, quartered lengthwise and thickly sliced	1
1	red onion, thinly sliced	1
1	green bell pepper, chopped	1
½ cup	pitted kalamata olives	125 mL
6 oz	feta cheese, crumbled	175 g
1 tbsp	chopped fresh oregano	15 mL
2 tbsp	extra virgin olive oil	25 mL
1 tbsp	freshly squeezed lemon juice	15 mL
	Salt and freshly ground black pepper	

1. In a salad bowl, combine tomatoes, cucumber, red onion, green pepper, olives and feta. Sprinkle with oregano, olive oil, lemon juice and salt and pepper to taste; toss to combine.

Easy Extras

▶ Add 2 sliced grilled chicken breasts.

Variations

▶ In place of the oregano, olive oil and lemon juice, use Basic Vinaigrette (page 218) or Creamy Basil Dressing (page 220).

▶ To stretch this salad, serve it on a bed of chopped romaine or in limestone lettuce cups.

▶ Add 1 cup (250 mL) chopped drained marinated artichoke hearts, rinsed drained canned chickpeas or cooked green beans. Top each serving with 2 drained oil-packed anchovy fillets.

▶ For a main-course salad, cook and chill 1 lb (500 g) short pasta, toss with an additional 2 tbsp (25 mL) olive oil and 1 tbsp (15 mL) lemon juice and add to the salad.

Classic BLT Salad

SERVES 6
or can be multiplied
up to 4 times

Serve this salad with
Mac and Cheese
(page 249) for a fun
retro lunch.

Tip

Serve with baguette
slices, crostini or
croutons.

Make Ahead

Cook and crumble
the bacon up to
2 days before. Wrap
in plastic wrap and
refrigerate. Let come
to room temperature
before using.

1	head iceberg lettuce, wilted outer leaves removed	1
$\frac{1}{3}$ cup	ranch dressing	75 mL
2	tomatoes, diced	2
1	avocado, diced	1
$\frac{1}{2}$ cup	thinly sliced red onion	125 mL
8 oz	bacon, cooked crisp and crumbled	250 g
$\frac{1}{2}$ tsp	freshly ground black pepper	2 mL

1. Remove core from lettuce and discard. Cut head into 6 wedges. Place each wedge on a salad plate and drizzle with dressing. Sprinkle with tomatoes, avocado, red onion, bacon and pepper.

Variations

▸ Use Roasted Garlic Dressing (page 221) or Creamy Basil Dressing (page 220) in place of the ranch dressing.

▸ Use romaine or butter lettuce in place of the iceberg lettuce.

▸ Make this a main-dish salad by adding $1\frac{1}{2}$ lbs (750 g) grilled chicken or shrimp.

Seared Ahi Tuna Salad

SERVES 6
or can be multiplied
up to 4 times

This salad is not only elegant, but nearly instant. The tuna in this salad is served warm, but if you prefer, you can chill it before slicing.

Tip

Serve this salad in large martini glasses. Dice tuna instead of slicing.

1 tbsp	canola oil	15 mL
1½ lbs	sushi-grade ahi tuna steaks	750 g
	Salt and freshly ground black pepper	
14 oz	mixed baby greens	420 g
1	recipe Basic Vinaigrette (page 218)	1

1. In a heavy skillet (preferably cast iron), heat oil over high heat. Sprinkle both sides of tuna with salt and pepper.

2. When oil is very hot, place tuna in skillet and sear, without moving, for 1 minute. Turn tuna and sear the other side. The tuna should still be quite cool and uncooked in the center. If you prefer, cook tuna for longer on each side. Let cool for 15 minutes before slicing.

3. Toss greens with dressing and divide among salad plates. Arrange tuna slices on top.

Easy Extras

▸ Add 1 tbsp (15 mL) soy sauce to the vinaigrette recipe.

▸ Cut 6 wonton wrappers in half diagonally and fry in oil until crisp. Use to garnish salad.

▸ Sprinkle salad with a few white and black sesame seeds.

Warm Lentil Salad

This classic French dish will win over even the most emphatic lentil-haters. Serve over a few leaves of butter lettuce for a nice presentation.

Make Ahead

This salad can be make up to 2 days ahead if covered and kept refrigerated.

1 lb	dry brown lentils, rinsed and picked over for debris or stones	500 g
1/3 cup	extra virgin olive oil	75 mL
1/4 cup	white balsamic vinegar	50 mL
2 tsp	Dijon mustard	10 mL
1	red onion, finely chopped	1
1	red bell pepper, finely chopped	1
1	large carrot, finely diced	1
1	clove garlic, minced	1
1/4 cup	finely chopped fresh flat-leaf (Italian) parsley	50 mL
1 tbsp	minced fresh thyme	15 mL
	Salt and freshly ground black pepper	

1. Bring a medium saucepan of water to a boil over high heat. Add lentils and reduce heat to medium. Cook, uncovered, for about 15 minutes or until lentils are soft but still firm in the center. Drain and rinse under cool running water.

2. In a large bowl, whisk together oil, vinegar and mustard. Add cooked lentils, red onion, red pepper, carrot, garlic, parsley and thyme, tossing to combine. Season to taste with salt and pepper. Serve warm, at room temperature or chilled.

Variation

▶ Green or black lentils would also work well in this salad.

Essential Recipes • Salads and Dressings

Basic Vinaigrette

¼ cup	champagne vinegar	50 mL
2 tsp	Dijon mustard	10 mL
¾ tsp	granulated sugar	3 mL
¾ cup	extra virgin olive oil	175 mL
	Salt and freshly ground black pepper	

The addition of mustard and sugar not only adds sweet and tart tastes, but also helps to keep the dressing from separating. This dressing is good on any type of salad: green, pasta, bean, grain or vegetable.

1. In a food processor or blender, pulse vinegar, mustard and sugar to combine. With the motor running, through the feed tube, gradually add oil in a steady stream; process until creamy.

2. Transfer to a bowl and season to taste with salt and pepper.

Tip

If your dressing separates, process briefly in a food processor or blender until creamy.

Easy Extras

▶ Add 1 to 2 tsp (5 to 10 mL) minced shallots or garlic.

▶ Add 1 tbsp (15 mL) chopped fresh herbs. Make the dressing on the day you use it, as the herbs won't stay fresh for long.

▶ Add 1 tsp (5 mL) dried herbs. Dressing made with dried herbs can be made up to 3 days in advance.

Make Ahead

This dressing can be made up to 1 week in advance if refrigerated in an airtight container. If oil has solidified, let stand at room temperature until it becomes liquid before serving.

Variations

▶ Replace the champagne vinegar with red wine vinegar, sherry vinegar, balsamic vinegar, rice vinegar, cider vinegar, lemon juice, lime juice or orange juice. If using lemon juice, use double the amount of sugar.

▶ For a milder taste, replace the olive oil with canola oil; for a subtly nutty taste, use walnut or hazelnut oil.

Stone-Ground Mustard Vinaigrette

**MAKES 1 CUP
(250 ML)**
or can be multiplied
up to 4 times

*This dressing is great
not only on leafy green
salads, but also on hot
or chilled seafood and
chicken. It's also tasty
drizzled on a warm
potato salad just before
serving.*

Tips

If you omit the shallot,
the dressing can be
made up to 1 week in
advance. You can finely
mince the shallot and
stir it in just before
serving if you like.

If you plan to use this
dressing on a spinach
salad, add 1 tsp (5 mL)
granulated sugar
to compensate for
the bitterness of the
spinach leaves.

You can use Dijon or
brown mustard if you
don't like the look of
mustard seeds.

Make Ahead

This dressing can be
made up to 3 days in
advance if refrigerated
in an airtight container.
If oil has solidified,
let stand at room
temperature until it
becomes liquid before
serving.

1	shallot, coarsely chopped	1
1/4 cup	balsamic vinegar	50 mL
2 tbsp	stone-ground mustard	25 mL
2 tbsp	freshly squeezed lemon juice	25 mL
3/4 cup	extra virgin olive oil	175 mL
	Salt and freshly ground black pepper	

1. In a food processor or blender, pulse shallot, vinegar, mustard and lemon juice to combine. With the motor running, through the feed tube, gradually add oil in a steady stream; process until creamy.

2. Transfer to a bowl and season to taste with salt and pepper.

Easy Extra

▶ Add 1 tbsp (15 mL) chopped fresh thyme or 1 tsp (5 mL) dried thyme.

Creamy Basil Dressing

This dressing isn't just for salads: use it for marinating chicken or for dipping crudités.

Tip

To preserve its bright, fresh taste, this dressing should be used the same day you make it.

Make Ahead

This dressing can be made up to 4 hours in advance if covered and refrigerated. If oil has solidified, let stand at room temperature until it becomes liquid before serving.

2	shallots, coarsely chopped	2
½ cup	loosely packed fresh basil leaves	125 mL
¼ cup	white balsamic vinegar	50 mL
2 tbsp	mayonnaise	25 mL
⅛ tsp	granulated sugar	0.5 mL
⅓ cup	extra virgin olive oil	75 mL
	Salt and freshly ground black pepper	

1. In a food processor or blender, pulse shallots, basil, vinegar, mayonnaise and sugar to combine. With the motor running, through the feed tube, gradually add oil in a steady stream; process until creamy.

2. Transfer to a bowl and season to taste with salt and pepper.

Easy Extra

▶ For a subtle lemony flavor, add 2 tsp (10 mL) grated lemon zest.

Variations

▶ Replace the white balsamic vinegar with cider vinegar or rice vinegar.

▶ Substitute sour cream for the mayonnaise.

Roasted Garlic Dressing

This dressing is perfect for pasta salads or can be used as a marinade for meats, chicken, seafood and vegetables.

Make Ahead

This dressing can be made up to 3 days ahead if refrigerated in an airtight container.

● **Preheat oven to 350°F (180°C)**

8	cloves garlic (unpeeled)	8
1 cup	extra virgin olive oil, divided	250 mL
1 tsp	grated lemon zest	5 mL
¼ cup	freshly squeezed lemon juice	50 mL
	Salt and freshly ground pepper	

1. Toss garlic cloves with 1 tsp (5 mL) of the olive oil and wrap tightly in foil. Roast in preheated oven for about 40 minutes or until soft and golden. Unwrap and let cool.

2. Squeeze the soft garlic from its peel and place in a food processor or blender. Add the remaining olive oil, lemon zest and lemon juice; process until smooth.

3. Transfer to a bowl and season to taste with salt and pepper.

Easy Extras

▸ Add 1 tbsp (15 mL) chopped fresh flat-leaf (Italian) parsley, basil, oregano or sage.

▸ If you plan to use this as a marinade, add a pinch of cayenne pepper.

Variation

▸ Add ½ tsp (2 mL) ancho chili powder and replace the lemon zest and juice with lime zest and juice.

Essential Recipes • Salads and Dressings

Avocado Cucumber Dressing

**MAKES 1 CUP
(250 ML)**
or can be multiplied
up to 4 times

This dressing is oh so creamy — without any cream! Make it at the peak of avocado season.

Tip

Make this deliciously different dressing no more than an hour or two before serving.

1	large avocado, peeled, pitted and coarsely chopped	1
1/2 cup	coarsely chopped peeled cucumber	125 mL
1 tbsp	fresh mint leaves	15 mL
2 tbsp	freshly squeezed lemon juice	25 mL
2 tsp	liquid honey	10 mL
	Salt and freshly ground black pepper	

1. In a food processor or blender, process avocado, cucumber, mint, lemon juice and honey until smooth, adding a little water as needed if dressing is too thick.

2. Transfer to a bowl and season to taste with salt and pepper.

Quick Chicken Stock

**MAKES ABOUT
6 CUPS (1.5 L)**
or can be multiplied
up to 4 times

*Homemade chicken
stock lends a richer
and more "chickeny"
taste, without adding
excess salt. The beauty
of making it from
scratch is that you will
have lots to freeze for
future uses.*

Tip

You can make a double
batch of this recipe in
a large stock pot. To
make four times the
recipe, use two stock
pots and make two
double batches at the
same time.

Make Ahead

Pour cooled stock into
airtight containers and
refrigerate for up to
4 days. Or pour into
ice cube trays; when
frozen, pop out cubes
and store in airtight
freezer bags for up to
2 months to add to
recipes whenever you
need it.

1	roasted chicken, carcass only, with meat removed	1
4	stalks celery, chopped	4
2	onions, chopped	2
2	large carrots, chopped	2
8	sprigs thyme	8
8	sprigs flat-leaf (Italian) parsley	8
4	whole black peppercorns	4
1	bay leaf	1

1. Place chicken carcass in an 8-quart (8 L) stock pot and add 5 quarts (5 L) water, celery, onions, carrots, thyme, parsley, peppercorns and bay leaf; bring to a boil over high heat. Reduce heat and simmer for $1\frac{1}{2}$ hours, skimming any foam and debris from the surface as needed.

2. Remove from heat and strain through a fine-mesh sieve or colander. If not using right away, let cool completely before refrigerating or freezing.

Quick Chicken Soup

After straining the stock, return it to the pot and add a chicken breast and leg, 1 sliced carrot, 1 sliced celery stalk and $\frac{1}{2}$ chopped onion. Bring to a gentle simmer over medium heat and simmer for about 30 minutes or until chicken is no longer pink inside. Using tongs, remove chicken and shred the meat, discarding skin and bones. Return chicken to soup, along with 1 tbsp (15 mL) chopped fresh parsley and 2 cups (500 mL) cooked pasta. Simmer until heated through.

Essential Recipes · Soups

French Onion Soup

This soup gets a deeper, richer, sweeter flavor the longer the onions are cooked, so don't try to make it faster! However, you can let the onions simmer up to twice as long before adding the flour; just watch carefully and monitor the heat so the onions don't burn.

Tip
You can cook multiple batches (up to four) of this recipe all together, but you'll need to increase the cooking time for the onions in step 1 by about 6 minutes for each additional batch to make sure they get wonderfully browned and sweet.

Make Ahead
After step 2, let soup cool, then transfer to an airtight container and refrigerate for up to 3 days or freeze for up to 1 month. Bring to a simmer over medium heat before continuing with step 3. You may need to add a little beef broth or water when reheating the soup, as it will thicken slightly.

- **Six 1 cup (250 mL) ramekins or ovenproof soup bowls**
- **Baking sheet**

3 tbsp	unsalted butter	45 mL
2 tbsp	olive oil	25 mL
4	large onions, thinly sliced	4
1½ tbsp	all-purpose flour	22 mL
½ tsp	salt	2 mL
¾ cup	dry white wine	175 mL
6 cups	reduced-sodium beef broth	1.5 L
½ tsp	freshly ground black pepper	2 mL
12	baguette slices, toasted	12
6 oz	Gruyère cheese, shredded	175 g

1. In a large heavy pot, heat butter and oil over low heat. Add onions and cook, stirring often, for about 40 minutes or until golden brown. Sprinkle with flour and salt; cook, stirring constantly, for 3 minutes.

2. Gradually stir in wine and cook, stirring constantly, for 3 minutes or until wine is reduced by about a third. Stir in broth, increase heat to high and bring to a boil. Reduce heat and simmer for 30 minutes.

3. Meanwhile, preheat broiler. Set ramekins on baking sheet and ladle soup into ramekins. Float two baguette slices in each ramekin and sprinkle with cheese.

4. Broil for about 1 minute, watching closely, until cheese is lightly golden.

Easy Extras

▶ Add 2 tsp (10 mL) chopped fresh thyme or a healthy grating of nutmeg to the onions while they are browning.

▶ Stir in ½ cup (125 mL) crumbled cooked bacon or finely diced cooked ham before ladling into ramekins.

Variations

▶ To intensify the flavor, use dry sherry in place of the wine.

▶ Replace the Gruyère cheese with Swiss, Emmental or Asiago.

▶ Substitute chicken or vegetable broth for the beef broth.

Wine and Cheese Tasting
Cheese Board (page 333), Bread and Cracker Assortment (page 333) and Fresh Fruit Assortment (page 334)

Friends' Game Night
Crudités with Cucumber Dip (page 340),
Chicken Pesto Pasta Salad (page 342) and
Cherry Tomato and Bocconcini Salad (page 342)

Oscar Night
Creamy Tomato Soup (page 346),
Shrimp and Pineapple Skewers (page 347),
Smoked Turkey on Sage Mini Scones (page 348) and
Chocolate Fondue with Fruit, Cookies and Marshmallows (page 349)

Super Bowl Party
Buffalo Wings (page 351), Artichoke Parmesan Dip (page 350) and Super Bowl Super Drinks (page 355)

Southern Charm
Fresh Peach Pie (page 366) and Classic Lemon Bars (page 365)

Creamy Mushroom Soup

Serve this delightfully creamy, earthy soup as a first course, or freeze batches of it to use in your Thanksgiving casserole in place of store-bought soup.

Make Ahead

Let soup cool, then transfer to airtight containers and refrigerate for up to 2 days or freeze for up to 2 weeks.

2 tbsp	unsalted butter	25 mL
2	shallots, minced	2
1	leek, white and pale green parts only, thinly sliced	1
1 lb	button mushrooms, minced	500 g
1 lb	cremini mushrooms, minced	500 g
1/4 cup	dry white wine	50 mL
4 cups	Quick Chicken Stock (page 223) or reduced-sodium chicken broth, heated	1 L
1/2 cup	heavy or whipping (35%) cream	125 mL
	Salt and freshly ground black pepper	

1. In a large skillet, melt butter over medium-high heat. Sauté shallots and leeks for about 3 minutes or until softened. Working in batches if necessary, add button and cremini mushrooms and sauté until they have released their moisture.

2. Return all mushrooms to pan, add wine and cook for about 8 minutes or until wine has almost completely evaporated. (The larger the skillet, the more quickly the wine will evaporate.)

3. Working in batches, transfer mushroom mixture to a blender and purée until almost smooth. Add hot stock and purée to desired consistency.

4. Pour soup into a medium saucepan and bring to a simmer over medium heat. Stir in cream and simmer, stirring often, until steaming. Do not let boil. Season to taste with salt and pepper.

Easy Extras

▸ Stir in 1/4 cup (50 mL) dry sherry before adding the cream.

▸ Garnish each serving with 1 tsp (5 mL) crème fraîche or sour cream thinned with a bit of water.

▸ Sprinkle each serving with a few sautéed mushroom slices or snipped chives.

Minestrone

This is *the* Italian comfort soup. It is endlessly versatile, and pleases any number of palates.

Make Ahead

Make soup up to 1 day ahead and refrigerate in an airtight container. Add basil after reheating.

2 tbsp	olive oil	25 mL
1	small onion, chopped	1
3	cloves garlic, finely chopped	3
1	can (14 oz/398 mL) tomatoes, with juice	1
6 cups	Quick Chicken Stock (page 223) or reduced-sodium chicken broth	1.5 L
2 cups	shredded cooked chicken	500 mL
1 cup	diced red-skinned potatoes	250 mL
1 cup	rinsed drained canned chickpeas	250 mL
1 cup	rinsed drained canned white beans	250 mL
1 1/2 cups	loosely packed Swiss chard, roughly chopped	375 mL
1/2 cup	cooked small tube pasta or macaroni	125 mL
1/4 cup	chopped fresh basil	50 mL
	Salt and freshly ground black pepper	
1/3 cup	coarsely grated Parmesan cheese	75 mL

1. In a large saucepan, heat oil over medium heat. Sauté onions for about 4 minutes or until softened. Add garlic and sauté for 2 minutes.

2. Break up canned tomatoes and add them, with their juice, to the onions. Add stock, chicken, potatoes, chickpeas and beans; bring to a boil. Reduce heat, cover and simmer for about 6 minutes or until potatoes are almost tender.

3. Stir in Swiss chard, pasta and basil; simmer just until chard wilts. Remove from heat and season to taste with salt and pepper.

4. Ladle into bowls and sprinkle generously with Parmesan.

Variations

▸ Replace the chicken with sliced cooked sausage.

▸ Use escarole or spinach in place of the Swiss chard.

Quick Bouillabaisse

It takes about 30 minutes to make this quick and delicious bouillabaisse packed with richly flavored seafood. The fennel makes a simple tomato-based soup so much more sophisticated.

Make Ahead

Make the broth up to 2 days ahead, strain, let cool to room temperature and refrigerate in an airtight container.

2 tbsp	olive oil	25 mL
4	cloves garlic, chopped	4
1	onion, chopped	1
1	bulb fennel, sliced	1
1	can (28 oz/796 mL) tomatoes, drained and chopped	1
4 cups	Quick Chicken Stock (page 223) or reduced-sodium chicken broth	1 L
	Salt and freshly ground black pepper	
18	small clams, scrubbed	18
6	crab claws	6
6	jumbo shrimp, peeled and deveined	6
6	sea scallops (about 1-inch/2.5 cm diameter), trimmed of hard side muscles	6
1 tbsp	chopped fresh flat-leaf (Italian) parsley	15 mL

1. In a large skillet, heat oil over medium heat. Sauté garlic, onion and fennel for 10 minutes or until light golden. Stir in tomatoes and stock; bring to a boil. Reduce heat and simmer for 20 minutes or until fennel is very tender.

2. Strain broth through a sieve into a medium saucepan, pressing on solids to release as much liquid as possible. Discard solids. Season broth to taste with salt and pepper. Bring to a boil over medium-high heat. Add clams, crab claws, shrimp, scallops and parsley; cover, reduce heat to low and cook for about 5 minutes or until clams have opened, crab claws are brightly colored and firm, shrimp is pink and opaque and scallops are firm and opaque. Discard any clams that do not open.

3. Ladle into bowls, making sure to portion the seafood evenly. Serve hot.

Easy Extra

▶ Try stirring a spoonful of grated orange zest in with the shellfish.

Essential Recipes • Soups

Shrimp and Clam Chowder

*Even if you can't take
your party to some
faraway fishing village,
you can eat as though
you were there. Good-
quality seafood can
span the distance.*

Tips

Hollow out small
round loaves of
sourdough bread to use
instead of bowls.

If multiplying this
recipe, you may need
to simmer the soup a
little longer to cook the
vegetables after adding
the milk in step 2.
Make sure the potatoes
are soft before adding
shrimp and clams.

Make Ahead

Soup can be made
1 day in advance if
refrigerated in an
airtight container. After
cooking the bacon,
remove it from the
pan and continue with
recipe. Refrigerate
bacon separately and
add to reheated soup
before serving.

1 tbsp	unsalted butter	15 mL
4	slices thick-cut bacon, chopped	4
1 cup	chopped onion	250 mL
½ cup	thinly sliced carrots	125 mL
½ cup	thinly sliced celery	125 mL
1 cup	diced red-skinned potatoes	250 mL
2 tsp	fresh thyme leaves	10 mL
3 tbsp	all-purpose flour	45 mL
2 cups	bottled clam juice, warmed	500 mL
2 cups	whole milk, warmed	500 mL
1½ cups	chopped deveined peeled tiger shrimp	375 mL
1½ cups	chopped fresh or canned clams	375 mL
	Salt and freshly ground black pepper	

1. In a large heavy saucepan, melt butter over medium-high heat. Sauté bacon for 5 minutes or until crisp. Add onion, carrots and celery; sauté for about 7 minutes or until onions are translucent. Add potatoes and thyme; sauté for 2 minutes. Sprinkle with flour and sauté for 2 minutes.

2. Gradually stir in clam juice. Reduce heat and simmer for about 5 minutes or until thickened. Add milk and simmer, stirring often, for 10 minutes. Stir in shrimp and clams; simmer for about 3 minutes or until shrimp is pink and opaque. Season to taste with salt and pepper.

Easy Extras

▸ Cut the kernels off an ear of corn and add with the potatoes for seafood and corn chowder.

▸ Stir in 1 tbsp (15 mL) chopped fresh dill or flat-leaf (Italian) parsley before serving.

Basic Quiche

SERVES 6
or can be multiplied
up to 4 times

*If you want to add
to this basic recipe
(see the variations,
at right), use a 9-inch
(23 cm) pie pan to
accommodate the
extra ingredients.*

Tip

If you would like to
make four quiches,
make and bake them
in two double batches,
baking a maximum of
two at a time. If you try
to bake more than two,
they likely won't cook
evenly.

Make Ahead

Let quiche cool to
room temperature,
wrap in plastic wrap
and refrigerate for up
to 2 days or freeze for
up to 2 weeks. Reheat
in a 350°F (180°C)
oven until heated
through (25 minutes
for refrigerated quiche,
40 minutes for frozen).

- **Preheat oven to 350°F (180°C)**
- **8-inch (20 cm) pie plate**

$\frac{1}{2}$	recipe Basic Pie Crust dough (page 261)	$\frac{1}{2}$
3	eggs	3
$\frac{1}{2}$ cup	heavy or whipping (35%) cream	125 mL
1 tsp	salt	5 mL
$\frac{1}{2}$ tsp	freshly ground black pepper	2 mL
Pinch	ground nutmeg	Pinch

1. On a lightly floured work surface, roll out dough to a $\frac{1}{8}$-inch (3 mm) thick circle. Place dough in pie plate, pressing lightly into bottom and sides. Trim any excess dough that hangs over edge. Crimp edges by pressing with a fork or pinching with your fingers. Using a fork, pierce bottom of crust about 8 times.

2. Cover dough with parchment paper or foil and fill with a cup (250 mL) of pie weights, dry beans or rice to weigh down the dough. Bake in preheated oven for about 12 minutes or until light golden. Remove from oven, leaving oven on.

3. In a bowl, beat eggs, cream, salt, pepper and nutmeg until well combined. Pour into pie crust and bake for about 40 minutes or until center is set. Serve hot, warm or at room temperature.

Variations

▸ *Quiche Lorraine:* Sprinkle the pie crust with $\frac{1}{2}$ cup (125 mL) crumbled cooked bacon, $\frac{1}{3}$ cup (75 mL) sautéed chopped onions and $\frac{1}{3}$ cup (75 mL) shredded Swiss cheese before pouring in the egg mixture.

▸ *Greek Quiche:* Sprinkle the pie crust with $\frac{2}{3}$ cup (150 mL) chopped thawed frozen spinach (with excess moisture pressed out), $\frac{1}{2}$ cup (125 mL) crumbled feta cheese, $\frac{1}{4}$ cup (50 mL) toasted pine nuts and 2 tbsp (25 mL) chopped kalamata olives before pouring in the egg mixture.

▸ *Breakfast Quiche:* Sprinkle the pie crust with $\frac{1}{2}$ cup (125 mL) crumbled cooked breakfast sausage, 2 plum (Roma) tomatoes, diced, and $\frac{1}{3}$ cup (75 mL) shredded Cheddar cheese before pouring in the egg mixture.

Basic Frittata

This is a lovely alternative to quiche at a brunch or early-afternoon event, or cut into small servings on a buffet.

Tip

You can double this recipe if you cook it in two separate skillets and place under the broiler one at a time. When the first one is done, cover loosely with foil to keep warm until the second one is done.

- **Preheat broiler**
- **10-inch (25 cm) nonstick ovenproof skillet**

12	eggs	12
1/4 cup	freshly grated Parmesan cheese	50 mL
	Salt and freshly ground black pepper	
2 tbsp	unsalted butter	25 mL
1	onion, finely chopped	1

1. In a large bowl, beat eggs, Parmesan, and salt and pepper to taste. Set aside.

2. In ovenproof skillet, melt butter over medium-high heat. Sauté onion for 4 minutes or until translucent. Pour in egg mixture, reduce heat to low and cook gently, lifting the edges of the set eggs to allow uncooked egg to run to the bottom of the pan, for 3 to 4 minutes or until mixture is mostly set but still runny on top.

3. Place skillet under preheated broiler and cook until frittata is golden brown on top and cooked through. Invert onto a platter to serve.

Variations

▸ For a lighter frittata, use 6 eggs plus 3/4 cup (175 mL) liquid egg whites.

▸ Add 1 cup (250 mL) cooked chopped spinach, squeezed dry, and 1/2 cup (125 mL) crumbled feta cheese to the beaten eggs. Use a larger skillet.

▸ Add 1 cup (250 mL) crumbled cooked bacon, sausage or diced ham and 1/4 cup (50 mL) shredded Monterey Jack or Cheddar cheese to the beaten eggs. Use a larger skillet. Before broiling, sprinkle an additional 1/4 cup (50 mL) cheese on top.

▸ Add 1/2 cup (125 mL) crumbled goat cheese and 3 tbsp (45 mL) chopped fresh herbs to the beaten eggs.

▸ Add 1 cup (250 mL) drained cooked fresh chorizo, 1/2 cup (125 mL) shredded Cheddar cheese, 1/2 cup (125 mL) diced green chile peppers and 1/4 cup (50 mL) sliced green onions to the beaten eggs. Use a larger skillet.

Halibut Fillets Baked in Parchment

SERVES 6
or can be multiplied
up to 4 times

*Cooking fish in
parchment is a great
way to control portions
and serve an impressive
main course at the
same time. Serve the
packets at the table
and let guests carefully
cut them open,
releasing the steam
and the wonderful
herbal aroma.*

- Preheat oven to 375°F (190°C)
- Six 14- by 12-inch (35 by 30 cm) pieces of parchment paper
- Baking sheet

3 tbsp	unsalted butter	45 mL
1	large onion, sliced	1
3	garlic cloves, thinly sliced	3
6	rosemary sprigs	6
6	thyme sprigs	6
6	oregano sprigs	6
½ cup	white wine	125 mL
6	skinless halibut fillets (each 5 to 6 oz/150 to 175 g)	6
	Salt and freshly ground black pepper	
2	lemons, sliced	2

1. In a large skillet, melt butter over medium heat. Sauté onions for about 5 minutes or until lightly golden. Add garlic and sauté for 2 minutes. Remove from heat.

2. Lay parchment paper on a clean work surface. Divide onion mixture and place in the center of each piece of parchment. Top with a sprig each of rosemary, thyme and oregano. Sprinkle wine over herbs.

3. Place fish fillets over herbs and sprinkle with salt and pepper. Place 1 to 2 slices of lemon on top of each fillet. Fold parchment loosely over fillet. Fold all ends underneath the packet to seal completely and keep steam inside. Place parcels on baking sheet.

4. Bake in preheated oven for 20 to 25 minutes or until fish is opaque and flakes easily with a fork.

Poached Salmon

This classic dish is perfect for a buffet, and can be served hot, warm or cold. Leaving the skin on the salmon will make it easier to move to a serving platter after cooking.

Tip

If you want to multiply this recipe, make a double batch at a time, putting 2 sides of salmon in a roasting pan at the same time. Don't double the amount of broth, just increase it to 10 cups (2.5 L). Double the rest of the ingredients.

Make Ahead

Salmon can be cooked up to 1 day ahead if wrapped well in plastic wrap and refrigerated. No need to reheat — it is delicious cold or at room temperature.

• **Large stovetop-safe roasting pan or fish poacher**

4	black peppercorns	4
4	thyme sprigs	4
4	flat-leaf (Italian) parsley sprigs	4
3	shallots, chopped	3
8 cups	reduced-sodium fish or chicken broth	2 L
1/2 cup	dry white wine	125 mL
2 tbsp	freshly squeezed lemon juice	25 mL
2 lb	side of salmon, skin on	1 kg
	Salt and freshly ground black pepper	
2	lemons, cut into wedges	2

1. Place roasting pan over 2 burners on the stovetop. Add peppercorns, thyme, parsley, shallots, broth, wine, lemon juice and enough water so that liquid is 3 inches (7.5 cm) deep. Bring to a simmer over medium heat.

2. Carefully place salmon in liquid, skin side down. Adjust heat so that liquid stays just below a simmer and poach for 8 to 10 minutes or until salmon is just cooked through but not flaky. Season to taste with salt and pepper. Serve with lemon wedges.

Easy Extras

▷ Drizzle finished salmon with pesto.

▷ Place finely sliced cucumber on salmon, overlapping the slices to resemble fish scales.

▷ Add a little lemon juice and a lot of chopped fresh dill to a good-quality tartar sauce and serve with hot, warm or cold salmon.

▷ Garnish hot salmon with Basic Compound Butter (page 251) or Mango Salsa (page 381).

▷ Serve cold salmon with Easy Roasted Garlic Aïoli (page 252).

▷ Make a cucumber sauce to serve over chilled salmon: In a food processor, combine 1 peeled and chopped cucumber, 1 cup (250 mL) sour cream, 1/4 cup (50 mL) freshly squeezed lemon juice, 2 tbsp (25 mL) chopped fresh dill and 1/4 tsp (1 mL) salt; process until just smooth.

Whole Roasted Chicken

SERVES 6
or can be doubled

Don't balk at the butter: it will make a crisp, browned chicken the likes of which you've never known.

Tips

Carefully separate the skin from the chicken and spread butter mixture underneath the skin.

To double this recipe, place 2 chickens side by side in a large roasting pan or use two large baking dishes that fit side by side on the same oven rack.

- **Preheat oven to 375°F (190°C)**
- **Roasting pan with rack**
- **Kitchen twine**

⅓ cup	unsalted butter, softened	75 mL
1 tbsp	chopped fresh rosemary	15 mL
1 tbsp	chopped fresh thyme	15 mL
1 tbsp	chopped fresh flat-leaf (Italian) parsley	15 mL
1 tsp	grated lemon zest	5 mL
5 lb	roasting chicken	2.5 kg
	Salt and freshly ground black pepper	

1. In a small bowl, combine butter, rosemary, thyme, parsley and lemon zest. Set aside.

2. Rinse chicken inside and out and pat dry with paper towels to remove excess moisture. Fold wings under and tuck under back. Rub chicken with butter mixture to coat, making sure to get under the skin. Rub any excess mixture inside the cavity.

3. Tie legs together with kitchen twine and place breast side up on rack in roasting pan. Sprinkle generously with salt and pepper.

4. Roast in preheated oven for 1 to 1½ hours or until a meat thermometer inserted in the thickest part of the thigh registers 165°F (74°C). Let rest for 5 minutes before carving.

Essential Recipes • Entrées

Pan-Seared Chicken Breasts

*Chicken breasts may
seem like an ordinary
thing to serve, but pan-
searing is the difference
between boring and
succulent.*

Tips

For a healthier version,
remove the skin before
cooking the chicken
breasts.

This recipe is a natural
with Basic Pan Sauce
(page 254).

To multiply this recipe,
sear chicken breasts
and place on a greased
rimmed baking sheet,
covering loosely with
foil until all chicken
is seared. Remove foil,
place in preheated
oven and proceed with
step 2.

- Preheat oven to 375°F (190°C)
- Large ovenproof skillet

1 tbsp	olive oil	15 mL
6	skin-on boneless chicken breasts	6
	Salt and freshly ground black pepper	

1. In ovenproof skillet, heat oil over medium-high heat. Generously season chicken with salt and pepper and place in skillet, skin side down. Pan-fry for about 6 minutes or until skin is crisp and golden brown.

2. Turn chicken over and place skillet in preheated oven. Bake for about 8 minutes or until chicken is no longer pink inside. Remove from oven, tent with foil and let rest for 3 minutes before serving.

Carnitas

Braising the pork before roasting gives these carnitas their great texture. Use as a filling for tacos, burritos, tostadas, taquitos and enchiladas.

Tips

Serve with chopped onion, chopped fresh cilantro, lime wedges and warm corn tortillas.

Use a large, heavy stockpot to make a double batch of this recipe. If multiplying three or four times, divide ingredients between two large pots. For step 3, place shredded pork in a single layer on baking sheets (make sure not to crowd them, or the meat will steam instead of roast) and roast one sheet at a time to ensure optimal browning.

Make Ahead

Braise the pork, shred and let cool completely. Store in an airtight container in the refrigerator for up to 2 days before roasting.

4 lb	boneless pork shoulder blade (butt) roast, trimmed of visible fat and cut into 3-inch (7.5 cm) cubes	2 kg
4	cloves garlic	4
1	orange, cut into wedges	1
1	onion, cut into wedges	1
8	black peppercorns	8
3	whole cloves	3
1	bay leaf	1
$\frac{1}{2}$ tsp	salt	2 mL
8 cups	reduced-sodium beef or chicken broth	2 L

1. Place pork, garlic, orange wedges, onion, peppercorns, cloves, bay leaf, salt and broth in a large pot. Add enough water to cover and bring to a boil over high heat. Reduce heat to low, cover and simmer, adding water as needed to keep meat submerged, for about $3\frac{1}{2}$ hours or until pork is so tender that it falls apart easily.

2. Preheat oven to 400°F (200°C).

3. Drain pork and discard other solids. Coarsely shred pork and spread on a baking sheet. Roast for about 20 minutes or until browned and crisp.

Essential Recipes • Entrées

Roasted Pork Loin

This roast pork makes an impressive main course for a dinner party, and is also wonderful thinly sliced for sandwiches.

Tips

Serve with soft rolls or slices of crusty bread.

Serve with Mango Salsa (page 381).

Sauté 2 thinly sliced onions in 1 tbsp (15 mL) olive oil until golden and caramelized. Stir in 2 tbsp (25 mL) apple butter and ½ tsp (2 mL) salt. Use to top sliced pork or to dress sandwiches.

Slice for sandwiches and top with Easy Roasted Garlic Aïoli (page 252) and arugula; with fig spread or chutney and crumbled Gorgonzola cheese; or with ricotta cheese and sun-dried tomato pesto.

- **Preheat oven to 425°F (220°C)**
- **Roasting pan with rack**

2 tbsp	chopped fresh thyme	25 mL
2 tbsp	chopped fresh oregano	25 mL
1 tbsp	chopped fresh rosemary	15 mL
2 tsp	salt	10 mL
1 tsp	garlic powder	5 mL
½ tsp	freshly ground black pepper	2 mL
2 tbsp	butter, softened	25 mL
3 lb	boneless pork loin roast	1.5 kg

1. In a small bowl, combine thyme, oregano, rosemary, salt, garlic powder, pepper and butter. Massage mixture into pork, covering the meat completely. Place pork on rack in roasting pan.

2. Roast in preheated oven for 1 to 1½ hours or until a meat thermometer inserted in the thickest part of the meat registers 155°F (68°C). Tent with foil and let rest for 10 minutes before slicing.

Classic Pot Roast

This comfort food can easily be started the morning of the party, or even the day before. Pot roast seems to get better every time it is reheated.

Tips

If you can't find pancetta or want to save money, you can replace it with thick-cut bacon.

To double this recipe, purchase a 6-lb (3 kg) roast and cook in a large Dutch oven, increasing the cooking time to cook all the way through (it will increase, but won't double). To multiply by three, use two 4½-lb (2.25 kg) roasts and cook in two Dutch ovens. To multiply by four, use two 6-lb (3 kg) roasts in two large Dutch ovens.

Make Ahead

Make this dish the day before and let cool for 30 minutes, then cover and refrigerate. Reheat in a 325°F (160°C) oven for 60 to 90 minutes, or until heated through.

- Preheat oven to 350°F (180°C)
- Dutch oven

3 lbs	boneless beef chuck (blade) roast	1.5 kg
	Salt and freshly ground black pepper	
8 oz	pancetta, coarsely chopped	250 g
2 cups	small onions, peeled	500 mL
4	stalks celery, cut into 1-inch (2.5 cm) pieces	4
2	large carrots, cut into 1-inch (2.5 cm) pieces	2
2 tbsp	chopped fresh thyme	25 mL
1	bay leaf	1
1½ cups	dry red wine	375 mL
2 cups	reduced-sodium beef broth (approx.)	500 mL
3 cups	cubed Yukon gold potatoes (2-inch/5 cm cubes)	750 mL

1. Sprinkle beef on all sides with salt and pepper.
2. Heat Dutch oven over medium-high heat. Sauté pancetta for about 4 minutes or until crisp. Using a slotted spoon, remove pancetta to a plate lined with paper towels.
3. Place roast in Dutch oven and brown on all sides. Remove roast to a plate.
4. Reduce heat to medium, add onions, celery, carrots, thyme and bay leaf to Dutch oven and sauté for about 5 minutes or until onions begin to turn golden. Add wine, stirring to scrape up any brown bits stuck to the bottom of the pan, and bring to a boil. Reduce heat and simmer vigorously for about 10 minutes or until liquid is reduced by half.
5. Return roast to Dutch oven and add broth until liquid comes two-thirds up the sides of meat. Cover and roast in preheated oven for 1½ hours. Add potatoes and pancetta, cover and roast for about 1 hour or until potatoes are tender. Discard bay leaf. Serve roast and vegetables drizzled with cooking liquid.

Hearty Beef Stew

*There's nothing better
than beef stew on a cold
winter's night. Be sure
to make this the day
before, as it improves so
much in the fridge.*

Tips

If you use mushrooms
that are larger than
1 inch (2.5 cm) across,
cut them in half.

If multiplying the
recipe three or four
times, use a large,
heavy stockpot. Scrape
up browned bits on
the bottom of the
pan between searing
batches of meat to
prevent burning. If you
don't have a very large
pot, make one double
and one single batch or
two double batches in
two separate large pots.

Make Ahead

After step 5, let
cool, transfer to an
airtight container and
refrigerate for up to 2
days or freeze for up to
2 weeks.

2 lbs	boneless beef chuck (blade) roast or eye of round steak, cut into 1½ inch (4 cm) cubes	1 kg
	Salt and freshly ground black pepper	
2 tbsp	all-purpose flour	25 mL
½ tsp	paprika	2 mL
1 tbsp	olive oil (approx.)	15 mL
1 tbsp	unsalted butter	15 mL
1½ cups	pearl onions, peeled	375 mL
1 cup	sliced carrots (½-inch/1 cm slices)	250 mL
1 cup	sliced celery (½-inch/1 cm slices)	250 mL
1½ cups	dry red wine	375 mL
1 tbsp	tomato paste	15 mL
2 cups	cubed red-skinned potatoes (1-inch/2.5 cm cubes)	500 mL
8 oz	mushrooms, about 1 inch (2.5 cm) across	250 g
1 tsp	dried thyme	5 mL
½ tsp	dried oregano	2 mL
1	bay leaf	1
3 cups	reduced-sodium beef broth (approx.)	750 mL
1 tbsp	minced fresh flat-leaf (Italian) parsley	15 mL

1. Season beef with salt and pepper. Combine flour and paprika and dust over beef, shaking off excess.

2. In a Dutch oven or a large heavy pot, heat oil over medium-high heat. Add beef, in batches if necessary, and sear on all sides, adding oil as needed between batches. Using a slotted spoon, remove beef to a plate.

3. Add butter to pot and reduce heat to medium. Sauté onions, carrots and celery for about 6 minutes, or until light golden.

4. In a small bowl, whisk together red wine and tomato paste. Add to vegetables and bring to a boil. Reduce heat and simmer for 8 minutes.

5. Return beef to pot, along with potatoes, mushrooms, thyme, oregano, bay leaf, and broth; cover and simmer for 1½ to 2 hours, or until beef is very tender.

6. Before serving, stir in parsley and season to taste with salt and pepper.

Osso Buco

*Tying kitchen twine
around the width of
each shank before
cooking will prevent
the meat from falling
off the bone while it's
cooking. This is a meal
no one will ever forget.*

Tips

For the best taste,
purchase good-quality
veal or beef broth.
Many gourmet markets
carry frozen broths.

Call your local butcher
to preorder veal shanks
cut into 2-inch (5 cm)
thick pieces.

You can make a double
batch of this recipe in
a large Dutch oven.
If multiplying by
three or four, use two
Dutch ovens. Scrape
up browned bits on
the bottom of the
pan between searing
batches of meat to
prevent burning.

- **Preheat oven to 350°F (180°C)**
- **Dutch oven**
- **Kitchen twine**

6	large veal shanks, about 2 inches (5 cm) thick	6
	Salt and freshly ground black pepper	
1/4 cup	all-purpose flour	50 mL
3 tbsp	olive oil	45 mL
3 tbsp	butter	45 mL
4	stalks celery, chopped	4
2	large carrots, chopped	2
2	onions, chopped	2
3 cups	veal or beef broth	750 mL
1 cup	dry red wine	250 mL
2 tbsp	tomato paste	25 mL
1	can (14 oz/398 mL) Italian-style tomatoes, with juice	1
1	bay leaf	1
1	recipe Gremolata (page 256)	1

1. Sprinkle veal shanks with salt and pepper, then dredge in flour, shaking off excess. Tie kitchen twine around the outside of each shank to hold it together while cooking.

2. In Dutch oven, heat oil and butter over medium-high heat. Brown shanks well on both sides, in batches as necessary. Remove shanks to a plate.

3. Add celery, carrots and onions to Dutch oven and sauté for about 6 minutes or until golden brown. Add broth, wine and tomato paste, whisking until tomato paste is incorporated. Increase heat to high and bring to a boil and cook until slightly thickened, about 15 minutes.

4. Break apart tomatoes and add to sauce. Add bay leaf. Return shanks to the pan. Cover and roast in preheated oven for about 3 hours or until meat is very tender. Discard bay leaf. Remove shanks and season cooking liquid with salt and pepper, then strain sauce, discarding solids.

5. Remove twine from shanks and serve with sauce and gremolata.

Variation

▸ Make this dish with lamb shanks instead of veal.

Veal Paillard

SERVES 6
or can be multiplied
up to 4 times

*This dish comes
together very quickly
and looks much fancier
than it actually is.*

Tips

Serve veal on top of
a bed of watercress,
arugula or romaine.

If multiplying this
recipe more than two
times, place cooked
veal on a baking sheet,
cover loosely with
foil and keep hot in a
175°F (80°C) oven as
you finish cooking the
remaining veal, then
proceed with step 3.

¼ cup	unsalted butter	50 mL
2 tbsp	olive oil	25 mL
2 tbsp	minced shallots	25 mL
1 tbsp	minced garlic	15 mL
1 tbsp	thinly sliced fresh chives	15 mL
2 tsp	grated lemon zest	10 mL
2 lbs	veal top round steaks, thinly sliced	1 kg
	Salt and freshly ground black pepper	
	Juice of 1 lemon	

1. In a large skillet, heat butter and oil over medium-high heat. Sauté shallots and garlic for 2 minutes. Add chives and lemon zest; sauté for 1 minute.

2. Sprinkle veal with salt and pepper. Add to skillet, in batches as necessary, and cook for 2 minutes. Turn and cook for about 1 minute or until cooked through. Sprinkle with lemon juice.

3. Remove veal to a serving platter and pour the flavored butter from the pan over the meat.

Variation

▸ Replace the lemon zest and juice with orange zest and juice.

Herb-Roasted Rack of Lamb

SERVES 6
or can be multiplied up to 4 times

This makes a stunning main course for any party. Cut into individual chops or cook and serve as a standing, or crown, rack of lamb.

Tips

To serve, cut into individual chops and stand chops on end with their bones in the air.

For a crown rack of lamb, before roasting, stand both racks on end with the bones sticking up and out. Form into a circle and tie with kitchen twine to secure. Remove the twine just before serving.

To double this recipe, use a large rimmed baking sheet in place of the baking dish. To multiply by three or four times, roast lamb in two batches on large baking sheets, covering the first one loosely with foil when finished while roasting the second.

- **Preheat oven to 375°F (190°C)**
- **Shallow baking dish or roasting pan**

½ cup	panko bread crumbs	125 mL
1 tbsp	minced fresh rosemary	15 mL
1 tbsp	minced fresh thyme	15 mL
2 tsp	garlic powder	10 mL
1 tsp	minced fresh chervil (optional)	5 mL
1 tsp	salt	5 mL
½ tsp	freshly ground black pepper	2 mL
2	racks of lamb (each about 1½ lbs/750 g)	2
2 tbsp	olive oil	25 mL
2 tbsp	Dijon mustard	25 mL

1. In a small bowl, combine panko, rosemary, thyme, garlic powder, chervil (if using), salt and pepper. Set aside.

2. Pat each lamb rack dry with paper towels and sprinkle with salt and pepper.

3. In a large skillet, heat oil over high heat. Sear lamb, in batches, on all sides until well browned. Remove from heat and brush tops of racks generously with mustard. Press panko mixture thickly into the mustard. Place lamb in baking dish.

4. Roast in preheated oven for 15 minutes for medium-rare, or until desired doneness. Cover loosely with foil and let rest for 10 minutes before slicing and serving.

Roasted Vegetables

SERVES 6
or can be multiplied
up to 4 times

Roasting is easy to do and adds great taste to a wide variety of vegetables. Add flavorings such as herbs, spices or garlic, for roast veggies that fit in with any party or meal.

Tips

Use a mixture of several vegetables from the list at right. Try to combine vegetables that cook at approximately the same rate: do not roast delicate beans with hearty squash, for instance. Instead, add the less dense vegetable after 20 to 30 minutes and finish roasting them together.

Served chilled or at room temperature, drizzled with Basic Vinaigrette (page 218), Creamy Basil Dressing (page 220) or Roasted Garlic Dressing (page 221).

- **Preheat oven to 400°F (200°C)**
- **Rimmed baking sheet, lined with foil**

2 lbs	vegetables, prepped (see table, at right)	1 kg
2 tbsp	olive oil	25 mL
	Salt and freshly ground black pepper	

1. Toss vegetables with oil, salt and pepper. Spread on prepared baking sheet and roast in preheated oven until vegetables begin to char on top and are cooked all the way through.

Easy Extras

▶ Before roasting, toss vegetables with a few cloves of minced garlic; 1 tbsp (15 mL) chopped fresh herbs or 1 tsp (5 mL) dried herbs; 1 tsp (5 mL) ancho or chipotle chile powder (for a Tex-Mex taste); 2 tbsp (25 mL) chopped fresh cilantro and $\frac{1}{2}$ tsp (2 mL) ground cumin (for Indian-style vegetables); or, for a little heat, a pinch or two of cayenne pepper or a diced jalapeño pepper.

▶ Garnish with 2 tsp (10 mL) grated lemon, lime or orange zest.

Vegetable	Prep
Artichokes	Use artichokes less than 4 inches (10 cm) across. Remove tough outer leaves and cut off top half of remaining leaves. Cut into quarters and cook in boiling water for about 8 minutes or until cooked halfway through before roasting.
Asparagus	Trim any tough ends. Asparagus can be left whole or cut to desired lengths.
Beets	Scrub outside very well and cut into wedges about 1 inch (2.5 cm) thick at the widest point.
Bell peppers	Remove stems, membranes and seeds. Cut into 1-inch (2.5 cm) strips.
Brussels sprouts	Trim ends and cut in half. Blanch for 2 minutes before roasting.
Carrots	Peel and cut into 1-inch (2.5 cm) pieces.
Cauliflower	Separate into florets.
Corn on cob	Cut into wheels or leave whole. Blanch for 2 minutes before roasting.
Eggplant	Cut into $\frac{1}{2}$-inch (1 cm) slices or 1-inch (2.5 cm) cubes. Toss with a little lemon juice to prevent browning.
Fennel bulb	Cut into $\frac{1}{2}$-inch (1 cm) slices.
Leeks	Cut in half lengthwise or cut into 1-inch (2.5 cm) slices.
Mushrooms	Leave whole or cut in half if bigger than 3 inches (7.5 cm).
Onions	Cut into wedges about 1 inch (2.5 cm) thick at the widest point.
Parsnips	Peel and cut into 1-inch (2.5 cm) pieces.
Potatoes	Cut large potatoes into 1-inch (2.5 cm) pieces. Small potatoes can be cut in half or into quarters.
Summer squash*	Cut into 1-inch (2.5 cm) thick slices.
Sweet potatoes and yams	Peel and cut into 1-inch (2.5 cm) pieces.
Winter squash**	Peel, seed and cut into 1-inch (2.5 cm) pieces

* Summer squashes include zucchini and yellow, pattypan and crookneck squash.
** Winter squashes suitable for roasting are butternut, acorn, buttercup, carnival, delicata, kabocha and pumpkin.

Sautéed Vegetables

SERVES 6
or can be multiplied
up to 4 times

1½ lbs	vegetables, prepped (see table, at right)	750 g
1 tbsp	olive oil or butter	15 mL
	Salt and freshly ground black pepper	

The trick to successfully sautéing vegetables is to blanch them first in a large pot of boiling water. After blanching, the vegetables are rinsed under cold running water to stop the cooking, at which point they can be refrigerated for up to 1 day before sautéing.

1. Bring a large pot of water to a boil over high heat. Blanch vegetables in boiling water (see table for cooking times).

2. Drain and rinse under cold running water until cool. If not using right away, refrigerate in an airtight container for up to 1 day.

3. In a large skillet, heat oil over medium-high heat. Sauté vegetables for about 4 minutes or until slightly golden and heated through.

Tips

Vegetables can be sautéed in either olive oil or butter, or a combination of both.

If multiplying the recipe, sauté each type of vegetable separately in batches that fit easily into the skillet for even cooking. Toss together before serving.

Easy Extras

▶ While sautéing the vegetables, add 1 tbsp (15 mL) chopped sun-dried tomatoes, minced garlic or chopped fresh herbs, or ¾ tsp (3 mL) dried herbs.

▶ Toss sautéed vegetables with 2 tsp (10 mL) grated lemon or orange zest; 2 tbsp (25 mL) toasted pine nuts or sliced almonds; or 1 tbsp (15 mL) freshly grated Parmesan cheese.

Vegetable	Prep	Blanching Time
Artichokes (less than 2 inches/5 cm wide)	Hearts only	2 minutes
Asparagus	Trim ends	8 to 45 seconds, depending on size
Broccoli	Cut into florets	10 seconds
Brussels sprouts	Trim ends, then halve	1 to 2 minutes
Carrots	Peel and slice	10 to 30 seconds
Cauliflower	Cut into florets	30 to 45 seconds
Corn on the cob	Cut into wheels	2 minutes
Green beans (large, Blue Lake)	Trim, then halve	2 minutes
Green beans (petite, haricots verts)	Trim	20 to 30 seconds
Peas in pod (sugar snap and snow peas)	Sauté whole	No blanching necessary
Potatoes	Peel (optional), then slice or dice	2 minutes
Summer squash*	Slice or dice	No blanching necessary

* Summer squashes include zucchini and yellow, pattypan and crookneck squash.

Basic Scalloped Potatoes

SERVES 6
or can be multiplied
up to 4 times

This filling, rich side dish is infinitely preferable to plain rice or a ho-hum pasta. Add a touch of grated nutmeg to the melted butter, if you like.

Tip

To multiply this recipe, make it in double batches and use a 13- by 9-inch (33 by 23 cm) baking dish. Be sure to check that the potatoes are cooked through to the center. You may need to increase the baking time by up to 20 minutes in the larger dish. If multiplying by three or four times, and baking more than one dish at a time, switch the placement of the baking dishes in the oven halfway through, to ensure even cooking.

- Preheat oven to 350°F (180(C)
- 9-inch (23 cm) square glass baking dish, buttered

2½ lbs	potatoes, peeled and very thinly sliced	1.25 kg
1 tbsp	all-purpose flour	15 mL
3 tbsp	unsalted butter, melted	45 mL
1¼ tsp	salt	6 mL
¼ tsp	freshly ground black pepper	1 mL
1¼ cups	half-and-half (10%) cream	300 mL

1. Bring a large pot of water to a boil over high heat. Add potatoes and boil for about 4 minutes or until barely yielding but still firm to the bite. Drain and set aside.

2. In a bowl, whisk together flour and melted butter until a thin paste forms.

3. Spread about a third of the potatoes on the bottom of prepared baking dish. Drizzle with a third of the butter mixture. Sprinkle with salt and pepper. Repeat layers two more times. Pour cream over the potatoes.

4. Bake in preheated oven for 35 to 40 minutes or until potatoes are cooked through and golden brown on top and are just starting to bubble around the edges. Serve hot.

Easy Extras

▸ Add 1½ cups (375 mL) shredded cheese, ½ cup (125 mL) per layer, to the potatoes. Any of your favorite cheeses will work: Cheddar, Monterey Jack, Gruyère, Swiss, Edam, Gouda, Colby, even pepper Jack.

▸ For a crispy top, combine ½ cup (125 mL) fresh or panko bread crumbs and 2 tbsp (2 mL) melted butter; scatter over the potatoes before baking.

▸ For a more sophisticated flavor, add a finely sliced fennel bulb or onion to the boiling water with the potatoes.

▸ Add ½ cup (125 mL) finely diced ham, pancetta or crumbled cooked sausage to the drained potatoes before assembling and baking the dish.

Basic Risotto

SERVES 6
or can be multiplied
up to 4 times

Arborio rice is the
shortest and plumpest
short-grain rice
available. Grown in
Italy, it has a very high
starch content and can
absorb lots of moisture
without getting gummy,
giving risotto its
distinctive, creamy
texture.

Tips

Never rinse rice before
using it for risotto, or
you will wash off the
starch.

Other types of rice that
work well for risotto
are carnaroli, baldo,
Padano and Roma.

In step 3, test rice
by dragging a spoon
through the center of
the pan: if the path
behind the spoon
remains dry without
filling with liquid, it's
time to add more stock.

If you're multiplying
the recipe, it will take a
little longer to cook in
step 4.

A double recipe can be
made in the same pan.
To multiply by three
or four times, divide
ingredients into two
large saucepans.

5 cups	Quick Chicken Stock (page 223) or reduced-sodium chicken broth (approx.)	1.25 L
1 tbsp	olive oil	15 mL
½ cup	finely chopped onion	125 mL
2 cups	Arborio rice	500 mL
1 cup	dry white wine	250 mL
¼ cup	freshly grated Parmesan cheese	50 mL
2 tbsp	unsalted butter	25 mL
	Salt and freshly ground black pepper	

1. In a saucepan, bring stock to a simmer over medium-high heat. Reduce heat and keep stock at a low simmer.

2. In a large saucepan, heat oil over medium-high heat. Sauté onion for about 5 minutes or until translucent. Add rice and cook, stirring frequently, for 3 minutes or until rice just smells fragrant. Add wine and bring to a boil. Boil, stirring very often, until wine is almost absorbed.

3. Reduce heat to medium and cook, stirring, while adding stock about ½ cup (125 mL) at a time, letting rice become nearly dry before adding more stock. Stir constantly to keep rice from sticking to the bottom of the pan.

4. Reduce heat as necessary to keep it at a simmer and continue adding stock and stirring for about 10 minutes or until rice is just al dente (a bit firm in the center of the grain). Add a bit more stock to finish, so that risotto has the consistency of creamy oatmeal. Remove from heat and stir in cheese and butter. Season to taste with salt and pepper. Serve hot.

Variations

▶ *Spring Risotto:* Add ¼ cup (50 mL) finely diced carrot while sautéing the onions. Add ¼ cup (50 mL) fresh green peas with the last addition of stock and cook just until bright green. Stir in ⅓ cup (75 mL) sliced green onions just before adding the Parmesan.

▶ *Fall Risotto:* Add 2 tsp (10 mL) fresh thyme leaves while sautéing the onions. Stir in 1 cup (250 mL) sautéed sliced mushrooms (button, cremini, shiitake, morel, oyster, porcini or any other kind) just before adding the Parmesan. (The mushrooms should not be sautéed with the onions because they turn risottos an unappetizing brown. Cooking them separately makes the end dish more attractive.)

Cheese Polenta

SERVES 6
or can be multiplied
up to 4 times

Polenta can be used in a variety of ways: serve it right away, or use it as a base for sautéed vegetables, stews or appetizers.

Tips

Make a polenta marinara by spreading polenta in a baking dish and spooning 1½ cups (375 mL) prepared marinara sauce over top; sprinkle with 1 cup (250 mL) shredded mozzarella cheese and bake at 350°F (180°C) for about 15 minutes or until cheese is bubbly.

Spread cooked polenta out on a greased rimmed baking sheet and chill until firm. Cut into desired shapes and fry on both sides in a little oil or butter. Serve polenta cakes under a sauce or main dish, or on the side instead of a biscuit or dinner roll.

Make Ahead

Finished polenta can be kept in the top half of a double boiler over barely simmering water for up to 4 hours.

6 cups	Quick Chicken Stock (page 223) or reduced-sodium chicken broth	1.5 L
1½ tsp	salt	7 mL
1½ cups	coarsely ground cornmeal	375 mL
¼ cup	freshly grated Parmesan cheese	50 mL
¼ cup	butter	50 mL
¾ tsp	freshly ground black pepper, or to taste	3 mL

1. In a large pot, bring stock and salt to a boil over high heat. Reduce heat to medium-high and gradually sprinkle in cornmeal, whisking constantly to get rid of any lumps, for 5 minutes. Reduce heat to low and simmer, stirring frequently with a large spoon, for about 1 hour or until mixture is the consistency of mashed potatoes.

2. Remove from heat and stir in Parmesan, butter and pepper.

Easy Extras

▸ Stir a drained 7-oz (212 g) can of diced green chile peppers, 1 cup (250 mL) shredded Monterey Jack cheese and 1 tbsp (15 mL) chili powder into the polenta before serving.

▸ Serve polenta topped with sautéed sliced wild (exotic) mushrooms and onions; sautéed spinach and bacon; or sautéed sliced bell peppers, onions and garlic sausage.

Variations

▸ Replace the Parmesan with crumbled Gorgonzola or goat cheese and add ¼ cup (50 mL) chopped dried figs or golden raisins.

▸ Grill chilled slices of polenta and serve topped with grilled eggplant, bell peppers and mushrooms.

Mac and Cheese

SERVES 6
or can be multiplied
up to 4 times

*You can take this
cheesy side dish to
new levels by adding
peppers, cooked meat
or flavorful spices, or
you can keep it simple.*

Tips

You can replace half
or all of the cheese
with any other good
melting cheese, such as
Monterey Jack, Gouda,
Edam, Gruyère,
mozzarella or fontina.

For a crunchy topping,
cut the amount of
cheese in half and,
instead of sprinkling
cheese on top, combine
$\frac{1}{2}$ cup (125 mL) coarse
fresh or panko bread
crumbs with 3 tbsp
(45 mL) melted butter
and sprinkle over top
before baking.

Make Ahead

Mac and Cheese can be
assembled through step
3 up to 1 day ahead.
Let cool, wrap in plastic
wrap and refrigerate.
Bake in a 350°F
(180°C) oven for about
35 minutes or until top
is golden and dish is
heated through.

- **Preheat oven to 375°F (190°C)**
- **13- by 9-inch (33 by 23 cm) baking dish, generously buttered**

1 lb	elbow macaroni	500 g
1 tbsp	unsalted butter	15 mL
1 tbsp	all-purpose flour	15 mL
1¼ cups	whole milk, heated	300 mL
2 cups	shredded sharp (old) Cheddar cheese	500 mL
Pinch	ground nutmeg	Pinch
	Salt and freshly ground black pepper	

1. Bring a large pot of salted water to a boil over high heat. Add macaroni, reduce heat slightly, and boil for about 6 minutes or until barely al dente but still firm. Drain and return to pot.

2. Meanwhile, in a medium saucepan, melt butter over medium heat. Add flour and cook, stirring constantly, for about 3 minutes or until paste is pale golden. Gradually pour in milk, whisking constantly to prevent lumps from forming. Reduce heat to low and simmer, stirring occasionally, for about 5 minutes or until thickened. Remove from heat. Add half the cheese, stirring constantly until cheese is melted and sauce is smooth. Add nutmeg and season to taste with salt and pepper.

3. Pour sauce over macaroni and stir to combine. Spread in prepared baking dish and sprinkle with the remaining cheese.

4. Bake in preheated oven for about 25 minutes or until cheese on top is golden and bubbly.

Easy Extras

▸ Add 1 cup (250 mL) diced ham or crumbled cooked bacon or sausage to the macaroni mixture before baking.

▸ Add 1 cup (250 mL) sautéed sliced mushrooms and $\frac{1}{2}$ cup (125 mL) sautéed chopped onions to the melted cheese sauce.

▸ Brown 8 oz (250 g) lean ground beef or turkey with $\frac{1}{2}$ tsp (2 mL) taco seasoning and add to the macaroni mixture along with a drained 4-oz (114 g) can of diced green chile peppers.

Cheese Soufflés

There's a myth that soufflés are impossible and finicky, but nothing could be further from the truth. They will deflate about 5 minutes after removal from the oven, so it is best to serve immediately.

Tip

Wash bowl and beaters well and dry completely before beating egg whites, as any trace of fat will keep the whites from achieving the necessary stiffness for a successful soufflé. Also be sure there are no bits of yolk in your egg whites or they won't stiffen.

- **Preheat oven to 400°F (200°C)**
- **Six 1cup (250 mL) ramekins, buttered**
- **Baking sheet**

5	eggs, separated, at room temperature	5
3 tbsp	all-purpose flour	45 mL
2½ tbsp	unsalted butter	32 mL
1 cup	milk, heated	250 mL
¼ cup	finely chopped fresh basil	50 mL
2 tsp	finely chopped fresh thyme	10 mL
½ tsp	paprika	2 mL
¼ tsp	salt	1 mL
Pinch	ground nutmeg	Pinch
	Freshly ground black pepper	
⅔ cup	finely grated Parmesan cheese	150 mL

1. In a large bowl, using an electric mixer, beat egg whites until soft peaks form. Set aside.

2. In a heavy saucepan, over medium heat, cook flour and butter, stirring constantly, for about 2 minutes or until foamy; do not let color. Remove from heat and let cool for a few seconds, then add hot milk all at once, whisking vigorously to blend well.

3. Return to medium heat and bring to a simmer, whisking constantly; simmer, whisking constantly, for about 5 minutes or until mixture is thick enough to coat the back of a spoon. Whisk in basil, thyme, paprika, salt, nutmeg and pepper to taste. Remove from heat and let cool for 5 minutes.

4. Whisk in egg yolks, one at a time. Whisk in one-quarter of the whipped egg whites. Quickly fold in the remaining whites and Parmesan. Pour into prepared ramekins, filling each three-quarters full. Place ramekins on a baking sheet.

5. Place baking sheet in oven and immediately reduce oven temperature to 375°F (190°C). Bake for about 20 minutes or until soufflés have puffed and tops have browned. Do not open the oven door during baking. Serve immediately, as the soufflés will deflate quickly.

Basic Compound Butter

*Compound butter is
simply butter with a
flavoring added to it.
Additions can vary to
suit whatever food it
is being served with.
Compound butter
is usually rolled
into a log about 1 to
2 inches (2.5 to 5 cm)
thick and wrapped in
waxed paper. Keep it
refrigerated, and pass
it at the table. Slices
add a delicate touch
to a serving of hot
vegetables, pasta, rice,
potatoes, fish, chicken
or even steak.*

Make Ahead

Compound butters can
be frozen for up to 2
months if wrapped well
in waxed paper, then
placed in a sealable
plastic bag. Let thaw
in the refrigerator for 3
hours before using.

½ cup	butter, slightly softened	125 mL
1	shallot, minced	1
2 tsp	grated lemon zest	10 mL
2 tsp	minced fresh flat-leaf (Italian) parsley	10 mL

1. In a small bowl, combine butter, shallot, lemon zest and parsley.
2. Spoon mixture onto a piece of waxed paper and form into a log 1 to 2 inches (2.5 to 5 cm) across. Roll up tightly and twist ends tightly to seal. Refrigerate for at least 1 hour, until chilled, or for up to 3 days.

Variations

▸ *Herbed Compound Butter:* Add 2 tsp (10 mL) of any chopped fresh herb you like. Rosemary, oregano, tarragon, dill, sage and thyme all work well.

▸ *Chili Compound Butter:* Replace the shallot with 1 clove very finely minced garlic and add 1 tsp (5 mL) chili powder. Serve with fish or chicken.

▸ *Chive Compound Butter:* Replace the parsley with 1 tbsp (15 mL) finely chopped fresh chives. Serve on baked potatoes.

▸ *Mint Compound Butter:* Add 2 tsp (10 mL) finely minced fresh mint. Serve with corn on the cob.

▸ *Horseradish Compound Butter:* Replace the lemon zest with 2 tbsp (25 mL) grated fresh horseradish or well-drained prepared horseradish. (Wrap horseradish in a kitchen or paper towel and squeeze to remove excess moisture before adding to butter.) Serve with red meat.

▸ *Peppercorn Compound Butter:* Replace the lemon zest with 1 tsp (5 mL) coarsely ground peppercorns. Use tricolor peppercorns for a prettier look.

Easy Roasted Garlic Aïoli

MAKES 1½ CUPS (375 ML)
or can be multiplied up to 4 times

Aïoli is a garlic mayonnaise that can sometimes be a bit strongly flavored. This one is made with roasted garlic for a more mellow taste. It's great on roasted chicken or pork sandwiches, it makes a grand dressing for seafood salads, and it adds a creamy garlic taste when stirred into soups — especially seafood soups, such as bouillabaisse.

Tip

Roasted garlic is sometimes available in the same section of the grocery store as pre-peeled garlic cloves. Using ¼ cup (50 mL) of it will make this sauce even faster.

● **Preheat oven to 350°F (180°C)**

1	head garlic	1
1 tsp	olive oil	5 mL
1 cup	mayonnaise	250 mL
¼ cup	freshly squeezed lemon juice	50 mL
1 tbsp	Dijon mustard	15 mL

1. Slice garlic head in half across the middle and place bottom half on a small square of foil. Drizzle with olive oil and replace top half. Wrap tightly with foil. Roast in preheated oven for about 40 minutes or until very soft and golden brown. Let cool.

2. Squeeze out garlic cloves and place in a food processor or blender. Add mayonnaise, lemon juice and mustard; purée until smooth.

Easy Extra

▸ Add 1 tbsp (15 mL) finely chopped fresh flat-leaf (Italian) parsley or chives.

Variation

▸ For a more intense garlicky taste, use 4 cloves of unroasted garlic and omit the olive oil.

Basic Cream Sauce

This basic sauce can be altered to suit any type of food, from mac and cheese to savory crêpes, and from fish to chicken to veggies.

Tip

If multiplying the recipe, use a larger saucepan with a heavy bottom, and stir more frequently to prevent burning on the bottom.

¼ cup	unsalted butter	50 mL
¼ cup	all-purpose flour	50 mL
2 cups	whole milk, heated	500 mL
	Salt	

1. In a medium saucepan, melt butter over medium heat. Stir in flour until mixture forms a smooth paste. Cook, stirring constantly, for 5 minutes. If flour starts to brown, reduce heat slightly.

2. Gradually pour in hot milk, whisking constantly until mixture is smooth and begins to thicken. Increase heat to high and bring to a boil. Reduce heat to low and simmer, stirring occasionally, for about 10 minutes or until thickened. Season to taste with salt.

Easy Extras

▸ Add 1 tsp (5 mL) grated lemon or lime zest to simmering sauce.

▸ Sauté 2 minced shallots in the butter before adding the flour.

▸ Add ¼ cup (50 mL) finely chopped sun-dried tomatoes to simmering sauce.

▸ Stir in 2 tbsp (25 mL) chopped fresh herbs (such as parsley, chives, basil, tarragon, oregano, chervil or thyme) at the end of cooking.

▸ Add 2 to 3 tbsp (25 to 45 mL) Dijon or stone-ground mustard at the end of cooking.

Variation

▸ *Cheese Sauce:* When cream sauce is finished cooking, remove from heat and add 1 cup (250 mL) shredded or grated cheese, such as Cheddar, Emmental, fontina, Gruyère, Jarlsberg, Manchego, raclette or Swiss, stirring until sauce is smooth.

Essential Recipes · Sauces

Basic Pan Sauce

Pan sauces are made with the drippings left over in a pan after you've cooked a piece of chicken, beef, pork or seafood. The fond, or browned bits stuck to the pan, add an effortless depth of flavor to a sauce. This recipe uses veal or beef broth with red wine for a rich sauce, but you could also use fish or chicken broth with white wine for a lighter sauce.

Tips

Purchase a good-quality veal or beef broth, as a broth with too much salt in it will ruin your sauce. There are excellent brands available frozen. These are usually concentrated, so follow the package directions to add an appropriate amount of water.

1 to 3 tsp	olive oil (if necessary)	5 to 15 mL
1	shallot, finely chopped	1
¾ cup	dry red wine	175 mL
1½ cups	veal or beef broth	375 mL
1	sprig thyme	1
	Salt and freshly ground black pepper	
2 tbsp	cold butter, cut into small cubes	25 mL

1. Use a pan left over from cooking that still has 2 to 3 tsp (10 to 15 mL) oil and juices in it. Add oil, if necessary, or pour out liquid if you have too little or too much. Place pan over medium-high heat. Sauté shallots for about 2 minutes or until they begin to brown.

2. Increase heat to high and pour in wine, stirring up any browned bits stuck to the bottom of the pan. Bring to a boil and cook for about 5 minutes or until about two-thirds of the wine has evaporated. Add broth and thyme and boil for about 7 minutes or until sauce is reduced by about half. Remove from heat and discard thyme. Season to taste with salt and pepper. Gently stir in butter, one piece at a time.

Variation

▸ Replace the wine with ½ cup (125 mL) bourbon, rum, whiskey or brandy and ¼ cup (50 mL) water.

Pistou

MAKES ½ CUP (125 ML)
or can be multiplied up to 4 times

Pistou is the French version of pesto, without nuts or cheese. It is traditionally served in Soupe au Pistou (the French version of minestrone), but it adds great taste to all types of soup. It can also be tossed with hot pasta or used as a spread for sandwiches or baguette slices.

Make Ahead
Transfer pistou to an airtight container and refrigerate for up to 1 day or freeze for up to 1 week.

2 to 6	cloves garlic, or to taste	2 to 6
2 cups	lightly packed fresh basil	500 mL
½ cup	olive oil, divided	125 mL
1 tbsp	grated lemon zest	15 mL

1. In a food processor, process garlic, basil and half the oil until smooth. With the motor running, through the feed tube, gradually add the remaining oil in a steady stream; process until incorporated.

2. Transfer to a bowl and stir in lemon zest.

Variations

▶ Use half basil and half flat-leaf (Italian) parsley.

▶ Add ¼ cup (50 mL) lightly packed fresh sage leaves.

▶ Turn this recipe into a pesto by adding ¼ cup (50 mL) each pine nuts and freshly grated Parmesan cheese.

▶ For a great sauce for fish, stir in 1 tbsp (15 mL) drained capers.

Gremolata

**MAKES ½ CUP
(125 ML)**
or can be multiplied
up to 4 times

*Gremolata is the tasty
garnish for Osso Buco
(page 239), but it can
be easily altered to suit
just about any dish (see
variations, at right).*

Make Ahead
Gremolata can be made
up to 1 day ahead
if refrigerated in an
airtight container.

¼ cup	grated lemon zest	50 mL
3 tbsp	minced flat-leaf (Italian) parsley	45 mL
1 tbsp	minced garlic	15 mL

1. In a small bowl, combine lemon zest, parsley and garlic.
   Let stand for 1 hour to blend the flavors.

Variations
▶ If making this recipe to serve with Osso Buco, you can
   add 1 tbsp (15 mL) minced anchovy fillets.

▶ Replace half the parsley with basil, mint or sage.

▶ For a garnish that will taste great with chicken or
   fish, replace half the lemon zest with 1 tbsp (15 mL)
   each orange zest and lime zest.

Western Hoedown

Cowhand Spareribs (page 368), Garlicky Grilled Corn on the Cob (page 370) and Bacon-Stuffed Twice-Baked Potatoes (page 371)

Pacific Northwest Coast
Roasted Wild Salmon (page 376) and Wild Rice Pilaf (page 378)

PLEASE JOIN US

DATE

TIME

PLACE

Hawaiian Luau
Island-Style Chicken (page 384) and Pineapple and Golden Raisin Rice Salad (page 385)

Mexican Fiesta
Roasted Chicken and Cheese Enchiladas (page 388), Spanish Rice (page 389) and Grilled Corn and Black Bean Salad (page 390)

Barcelona Bash
Seafood Paella (page 394) and Spiced Olives (page 392)

Red Bell Pepper Coulis

This easy sauce is great over seafood, chicken or even pasta, and is also delicious as a thin sandwich spread.

1 tbsp	olive oil	15 mL
1	jar (12 oz/375 mL) roasted red bell peppers, drained, rinsed and roughly chopped	1
1/3 cup	Quick Chicken Stock (page 223) or reduced-sodium chicken broth (approx.)	75 mL
	Salt and freshly ground black pepper	

1. In a medium saucepan, heat oil over medium-high heat. Sauté roasted peppers for about 3 minutes or until heated through. Add stock and bring to a simmer. Reduce heat and simmer, stirring frequently, for about 7 minutes or until peppers are very soft.

2. Transfer to a food processor or blender and process to the consistency of a thin tomato sauce. If necessary, add more stock, 1 tbsp (15 mL) at a time, and pulse to combine. Season to taste with salt and pepper.

Variations

▸ Add 1 tsp (5 mL) ancho chili powder or ground cumin with the roasted peppers for a Tex-Mex taste that is delicious on red meat or pork.

▸ Sauté 1 cup (250 mL) chopped onion in the oil before adding the peppers.

▸ If serving with seafood, try adding 1 tbsp (15 mL) freshly squeezed lemon juice or balsamic vinegar for a little tartness.

Essential Recipes • Sauces

Cucumber Chile Sauce

**MAKES 2 CUPS
(500 ML)**
or can be multiplied
up to 4 times

*This sauce is normally
served with fried
appetizers such as egg
rolls and wontons, but
it is also delicious with
chicken or fish.*

1 tbsp	granulated sugar	15 mL
½ cup	seasoned rice vinegar	125 mL
1½ tbsp	reduced-sodium soy sauce	22 mL
1½ tbsp	olive oil	22 mL
1	cucumber, peeled and finely chopped	1
1	small red onion, finely chopped	1
1	small serrano pepper, seeded and finely chopped	1
¼ cup	dry-roasted salted peanuts, chopped	50 mL
¼ cup	fresh cilantro, roughly chopped	50 mL
2 tsp	grated gingerroot	10 mL

1. In a bowl, combine sugar, vinegar and soy sauce, stirring until sugar is dissolved. Whisk in oil until combined. Stir in cucumber, red onion, serrano pepper, peanuts, cilantro and ginger. Cover and refrigerate for at least 1 hour, until chilled, or for up to 1 day.

Barbecue Sauce

**MAKES 2 CUPS
(500 ML)**
or can be multiplied
up to 4 times

*Barbecue sauces come
in an endless variety
and can be customized
to your taste. This is an
excellent basic recipe,
neither too sweet nor
too tangy.*

2 cups	ketchup	500 mL
1/3 cup	light (fancy) molasses	75 mL
1 tbsp	packed brown sugar	15 mL
2 tbsp	Worcestershire sauce	25 mL
1 tbsp	Dijon mustard	15 mL

1. In a medium saucepan, over medium heat, combine ketchup, molasses, brown sugar, Worcestershire sauce and mustard, stirring until sugar is dissolved. Increase heat and bring to a boil. Reduce heat and simmer, stirring frequently, for 15 minutes or until thickened.

Variations

▸ To make your sauce tangier, add 1 to 2 tbsp (15 to 25 mL) cider vinegar.

▸ To give your sauce more kick, add a few pinches of cayenne pepper or a few shakes of hot pepper sauce.

▸ For a sweeter sauce, add 1 to 2 tbsp (15 to 25 mL) liquid honey, pure maple syrup or additional brown sugar.

▸ For greater depth of flavor, add 1/4 cup (50 mL) whiskey or bourbon, or 1 tsp (5 mL) instant coffee or espresso granules.

Essential Recipes • Sauces

Peanut Sauce

This sauce is traditionally served with satay (spiced beef or chicken skewers), but is also great with seafood or over rice.

1 cup	creamy peanut butter	250 mL
2 tbsp	packed brown sugar	25 mL
3 tbsp	freshly squeezed lime juice	45 mL
2 tbsp	reduced-sodium soy sauce	25 mL
2 tsp	hot red chili paste	10 mL
¼ cup	dry-roasted salted peanuts	50 mL

1. In a food processor, purée peanut butter, brown sugar, lime juice, soy sauce and chili paste until smooth. Add a little warm water, if necessary, and process to desired consistency. Add peanuts and pulse a few times to coarsely chop and incorporate.

Variation

▸ To make a creamy peanut dressing perfect for a green salad, add ¼ cup (50 mL) olive oil before adding the peanuts. Add the oil gradually through the feed tube, with the motor running, and process until well incorporated.

Basic Pie Crust

**MAKES ENOUGH
DOUGH FOR
TWO 9-INCH
(23 CM) CRUSTS**

Tip

This recipe can easily
be doubled. If you need
more, make double
batches one at a time
to keep pastry tender
and flaky.

2¼ cups	all-purpose flour	550 mL
1 tsp	salt	5 mL
1 tsp	granulated sugar	5 mL
1 cup	cold unsalted butter, cut into small pieces	250 mL
¼ cup	ice water	50 mL

1. In a food processor, pulse flour, salt and sugar a few times to combine. Add butter and pulse until crumbly. Begin adding ice water, 1 tbsp (15 mL) at a time, pulsing after each addition until a loose dough forms.

2. Divide dough in half and form into two flattened balls. Wrap tightly in plastic wrap and refrigerate for at least 20 minutes, until chilled, or place plastic-wrapped dough in freezer bags with excess air squeezed out and freeze for up to 1 month.

Essential Recipes · Desserts and Dessert Sauces

Basic Crêpes

**MAKES
12 CRÊPES**
or can be multiplied
up to 4 times

*Crêpes can be rolled,
folded or stacked with a
wide variety of fillings
and sauces. And they're
not just for dessert —
there are also dozens of
savory fillings.*

Make Ahead

Wrap stacked, cooled
crêpes in plastic wrap
and refrigerate for up to
2 days or freeze for up
to 2 weeks.

- **10-inch (25 cm) crêpe pan or shallow nonstick skillet**

¼ cup	all-purpose flour	50 mL
¼ tsp	granulated sugar	1 mL
Pinch	salt	Pinch
1	egg	1
¾ cup	whole milk	175 mL
1½ tsp	vegetable oil	7 mL
1½ tsp	unsalted butter, melted	7 mL

1. In a food processor or blender, process flour, sugar, salt, egg, milk, oil and butter until smooth. Transfer to a bowl, cover and refrigerate for 1 hour.

2. Brush crêpe pan with a little vegetable oil and heat over medium heat. Pour in a small amount of crêpe batter and swirl to make a thin, even layer. Cook until set and barely golden, then carefully flip over and cook until set on the other side, about 1 minute total. Remove from pan and stack between pieces of waxed paper. Serve either alone or with a filling. Repeat with remaining batter.

Variations

- Fill crêpes with chocolate hazelnut spread (such as Nutella) and sliced bananas.

- Drizzle with honey or dust with confectioner's (icing) sugar.

- Simmer 3 cups (750 mL) chopped peeled pears or apples with ½ cup (125 mL) sweet wine or water and 2 tbsp (25 mL) packed brown sugar. Add a sprinkling of ground cinnamon and use as a delicious crêpe filling.

- For traditional Crêpes Suzette, drizzle warm caramel sauce over crêpes and sprinkle with a bit of grated orange zest. Fold into triangles and spoon hot Grand Marnier over top. Ignite Grand Marnier and serve.

Sponge Cake

Sponge cake provides the base for a variety of desserts, including trifle, madeleines, ladyfingers and strawberry shortcake. When cooked in a thin layer, sponge cake can also be used for jelly rolls.

Tip

This recipe can be doubled and baked in a 15- by 10-inch (38 by 25 cm) cake pan. Bake until a tester inserted in the center comes out clean. If you want to make more than one 10-inch (25 cm) cake, it's best to make the batter in separate batches and bake them one at a time, so they bake evenly. Don't let the batter sit after mixing, or it will deflate.

Make Ahead

Cake can be stored in an airtight container at room temperature for up to 2 days or wrapped tightly in plastic wrap, then in foil, and frozen for up to 2 months.

- Preheat oven to 325°F (160°C)
- 10-inch (25 cm) round cake pan, bottom lined with parchment paper

9	eggs, separated, at room temperature	9
1 cup + 2 tbsp	granulated sugar, divided	275 mL
1 cup	cake flour, sifted	250 mL

1. In a large bowl, using an electric mixer, beat egg yolks until creamy, about 4 minutes. Gradually add 1 cup (250 mL) of the sugar, beating continuously until mixture is creamy and pale yellow, about 5 minutes. Set aside.

2. In another large bowl, using an electric mixer with clean beaters, beat egg whites and the remaining sugar until stiff peaks form. Carefully fold into yolk mixture. Carefully fold in flour until just incorporated. Pour into cake pan.

3. Bake in preheated oven for about 25 minutes or until a tester inserted in the center comes out clean. Let cool completely in pan on a wire rack.

4. Run a thin metal spatula around the sides of the pan to loosen cake. Tap bottom gently, then invert onto a flat plate and peel off parchment paper.

Easy Extras

▸ Sprinkle cooled sponge cake generously with your favorite liqueur. Hazelnut, almond, orange, cherry or coconut flavors all work well. Or use rum, whiskey, brandy or bourbon.

Essential Recipes • Desserts and Dessert Sauces

Chocolate Ganache Cake

For the best-tasting ganache, use good-quality dark chocolate that is meant to be enjoyed on its own. Unsweetened (baking) chocolate is too bitter in such a simple topping.

Tips

Before chilling the final layer of ganache, decorate top of cake with small chocolate truffles, chocolate-covered cherries or other fancy chocolate candies. Place candies around edge of cake, spaced so that one candy is on each slice when cake is cut.

If using a hand mixer in step 2, sprinkle in flour mixture ¼ cup (50 mL) at a time, beating between each addition. Or add flour all at once, stirring with a wooden spoon until mostly incorporated, then beat until smooth with hand mixer.

This recipe can easily be doubled. Bake in two cake pans, rotating pans in the oven halfway through baking to ensure even cooking.

- Preheat oven to 325°F (160°C)
- 9-inch (23 cm) round cake pan, lined with parchment paper, paper sprayed with nonstick cooking spray
- Baking sheet, lined with waxed or parchment paper

Cake

1 cup	all-purpose flour	250 mL
½ tsp	baking powder	2 mL
½ tsp	baking soda	2 mL
½ tsp	salt	2 mL
6 oz	semisweet chocolate chips	175 g
1¼ cups	packed light brown sugar	300 mL
6 tbsp	unsalted butter, softened, divided	90 mL
1 tsp	vanilla extract	5 mL
2	eggs	2
½ cup	buttermilk	125 mL

Ganache

8 oz	good-quality dark chocolate, chopped	250 g
¾ cup	heavy or whipping (35%) cream	175 mL

1. *Cake:* In a bowl, combine flour, baking powder, baking soda and salt. Set aside.

2. Place chocolate chips in a microwave-safe bowl and heat on High for 30-second intervals, stirring in between, until chocolate is melted and smooth.

3. In a large bowl, using an electric mixer, beat together brown sugar, ¼ cup (50 mL) of the butter and vanilla. Add eggs, one at a time, beating well after each addition. Beat in melted chocolate. Beat in flour mixture alternately with buttermilk, making two additions of each, until mixture is smooth. Pour batter into prepared pan.

4. Bake in preheated oven for about 30 minutes or until a tester inserted in the center comes out clean. Let cool in pan on a wire rack for 30 minutes.

5. Remove cake from pan and peel off parchment paper. If necessary, slice off the uneven top of the cake to make it level. Turn cake upside down, so that the flat bottom of the cake becomes the top. Place on wire rack over prepared baking sheet.

6. *Ganache:* Place dark chocolate in a heatproof bowl. In a small heavy saucepan, heat cream over medium heat until it just begins to boil. Immediately remove from heat and pour over chocolate. Let stand for 5 minutes, then stir until chocolate is melted and mixture is smooth.

7. Pour half of the ganache over top and sides of cake to coat. Refrigerate until ganache is set, about 30 minutes.

8. In the small heavy saucepan, heat the remaining ganache over very low heat, stirring constantly, just until fluid. Pour over chilled cake, spreading to cover top and sides. Refrigerate until ganache is set, about 30 minutes.

Variations

▶ Before covering cake with ganache, sprinkle cake with 1/4 cup (50 mL) rum, brandy or bourbon, or coffee, coconut, raspberry, cherry, almond or hazelnut liqueur.

▶ To make a cake reminiscent of the famous Viennese Sachertorte, spread 1/3 cup (75 mL) apricot jam on top before adding ganache. Raspberry or strawberry jam or orange marmalade also work well.

Make Ahead

Prepare cake through step 5, cover and refrigerate for up to 1 day. Or, after ganache has completely set, wrap cake well in plastic wrap and freeze for up to 2 weeks. After thawing, dip a metal spatula in hot water and run over ganache to smooth.

Essential Recipes • Desserts and Dessert Sauces

Pound Cake

SERVES 8 TO 10
or can be doubled

*Pound cake is an
excellent base for many
desserts. It is much
denser than sponge
cake and takes the
addition of sauces very
well. Sliced pound cake
is good served with
fruit and ice cream,
and cubed pound
cake works well with
chocolate fondues.*

Tips

If using a hand mixer
in step 2, sprinkle in
flour mixture ¼ cup
(50 mL) at a time,
beating between
each addition. Or
add flour all at once,
stirring with a wooden
spoon until mostly
incorporated, then
beat until smooth with
hand mixer.

To double this recipe,
bake in two loaf pans,
rotating in the oven
halfway through
baking to ensure
even cooking. If you
need more than two,
it's best to make and
bake double batches
separately.

- **Preheat oven to 325°F (160°C)**
- **9- by 5-inch (23 by 12.5 cm) loaf pan, lined with parchment paper**

2 cups	cake flour	500 mL
¼ tsp	salt	1 mL
¼ tsp	cream of tartar	1 mL
1 cup	granulated sugar	250 mL
1 cup	unsalted butter, softened	250 mL
1 tsp	vanilla extract	5 mL
4	eggs	4
1	egg white	1

1. In a bowl, sift together flour, salt and cream of tartar. Set aside.

2. In another bowl, using an electric mixer, beat sugar and butter until very creamy, about 10 minutes. Beat in vanilla. Beat in eggs, one at a time, scraping down sides of bowl after each addition. Beat in egg white.

3. With mixer set to low speed, add flour mixture ½ cup (125 mL) at a time, beating until fully incorporated. Pour batter into prepared loaf pan, smoothing top.

4. Bake in preheated oven for 45 to 55 minutes or until a tester inserted in the center comes out clean. Let cool completely in pan on a wire rack.

Variation

▶ For an easy fruit cake, stir in 1 cup (250 mL) chopped mixed candied fruit, such as pineapple, cherries, citron, golden raisins, mango and ginger, after the flour mixture.

Butter Cookies

**MAKES
24 COOKIES**
or can be multiplied
up to 4 times

This basic cookie recipe can be altered to suit any occasion.

Tips

If using a hand mixer in step 2, sprinkle in flour mixture ¼ cup (50 mL) at a time, beating between each addition. Or add flour all at once, stirring with a wooden spoon until mostly incorporated, then beat until smooth.

If baking more than one baking sheet at a time, rotate pans in the oven halfway through to ensure even baking. Keep extra dough chilled until ready to bake.

Make Ahead

The wrapped dough log can also be sealed in a freezer bag and frozen for up to 1 month. Thaw in the refrigerator before proceeding with step 4.

The baked cookies can be stored in a cookie tin at room temperature for up to 5 days.

- **2 baking sheets, lined with parchment paper**

2 cups	all-purpose flour	500 mL
¾ tsp	baking powder	3 mL
¼ tsp	salt	1 mL
1 cup	granulated sugar	250 mL
1 cup	unsalted butter, softened	250 mL
1	egg	1
1½ tbsp	grated lemon zest	22 mL
1 tbsp	vanilla extract	15 mL

1. In a bowl, combine flour, baking powder and salt. Set aside.

2. In a large bowl, using an electric mixer, cream sugar and butter until light and fluffy, about 5 minutes. Beat in egg, lemon zest and vanilla. Beat in flour mixture, ½ cup (125 mL) at a time, until fully incorporated.

3. Form dough into a log about 2 inches (5 cm) thick and roll tightly in waxed paper. Refrigerate for at least 1 hour, until dough is chilled through, or for up to 2 days.

4. Preheat oven to 375°F (190°C).

5. Unwrap cookie dough and cut into ¼-inch (0.5 cm) thick slices. Place 2 inches (5 cm) apart on prepared baking sheets.

6. Bake for 10 to 12 minutes or until light golden around the edges. Transfer cookies to wire racks and let cool to room temperature.

Easy Extras

▸ Replace the lemon zest with lime or orange zest. If desired, you can also add ½ tsp (2 mL) lemon, lime or orange extract with the vanilla.

▸ Dip cooled cookies in melted dark, milk or white chocolate. Place on waxed paper until chocolate sets.

Variations

▸ Replace ⅓ cup (75 mL) of the flour with an equal amount of ground nuts.

▸ For spice cookies, omit the lemon zest and add ¼ cup (50 mL) finely chopped candied ginger and 2 tsp (10 mL) ground cinnamon with the egg.

Meringue Cookies

*This easy meringue
batter makes simply
delicious airy cookies,
but you can also bake it
into a variety of shapes
and sizes, to be used in
trifles or puddings, or
as cake decorations.*

Tips

Make more uniformly
shaped cookies by
placing batter in a large
pastry bag fitted with
a large star tip and
piping it onto prepared
baking sheets.

Egg whites increase
dramatically in
volume when beaten
for meringues, so if
you want to make
more than 36 cookies,
it's best to make one
recipe at a time so the
mixing bowl doesn't
overflow.

Make Ahead

Cookies can be made
up to 1 week ahead
if stored in a cookie
tin at a cool room
temperature.

- Preheat oven to 300°F (150°C)
- 2 baking sheets, lined with parchment paper

4	egg whites	4
1/2 tsp	cream of tartar	2 mL
1 cup	granulated sugar	250 mL

1. In a large bowl, using an electric mixer, whip egg whites and cream of tartar on high speed until soft peaks form, about 3 to 5 minutes. Reduce speed to medium and gradually add sugar, beating continuously and making sure each addition is thoroughly incorporated before adding more. Continue beating until peaks are stiff and glossy, about 5 minutes.

2. Dollop batter in scant 1/4 cup (50 mL) mounds on prepared baking sheets. (The meringues will not spread a great deal while baking, so they can be very close together.)

3. Bake in preheated oven, one sheet at a time or rotating baking sheets partway for even baking, for about 30 minutes or until meringues are firm and crisp throughout. Let cool completely on baking sheet on a wire rack.

Variations

- Fold 1 cup (250 mL) ground hazelnuts or almonds into the stiff egg whites before baking.

- After the cookies have cooled, dip the bottoms in melted dark, milk or white chocolate. Place on waxed paper, chocolate side down, until chocolate sets. Or dip the tops in melted chocolate, then into finely chopped nuts.

- Pipe batter into nest or donut shapes. After the meringues have baked and cooled to room temperature, they can be used as a base for fruit and whipped cream.

- Make a spectacular dessert by folding 1 cup (250 mL) ground hazelnuts into the meringue batter, then spread on prepared baking sheets in two or three 8-inch (20 cm) circles about 3/8 inch (9 mm) thick. Bake for about 20 minutes or until crisp. Let cool, then create a meringue "layer cake" with berries and whipped cream between the layers.

Dark Chocolate Truffles

MAKES ABOUT 18 TRUFFLES
or can be multiplied up to 4 times

Use a good-quality dark chocolate made for snacking. Unsweetened (baking) chocolate is too bitter for truffles. Serve these on decorative dessert plates or package them in wrapped boxes for guests to take home.

Make Ahead
Truffles can be prepared through step 2 and stored in an airtight container in the refrigerator for up to 1 month. Then all you need to do for beautiful truffles is scoop and roll.

- Baking sheet, lined with waxed paper

7 oz	good-quality dark chocolate, chopped into small pieces	210 g
½ cup	heavy or whipping (35%) cream	125 mL
2 tbsp	unsalted butter	25 mL

1. Place chocolate in a heatproof bowl and set aside.

2. In a small heavy saucepan, over medium heat, bring cream and butter to just under a boil. Remove from heat and pour over chocolate. Let stand for about 5 minutes, then whisk until smooth. Cover and refrigerate until firm, about 2 hours.

3. Using a melon baller or a teaspoon, scoop chocolate into 1-inch (2.5 cm) balls and place on prepared baking sheet. Lightly roll balls to make them rounder. Refrigerate until very firm.

Easy Extras

▶ Roll truffles in chopped nuts, unsweetened cocoa powder, shredded coconut, confectioner's (icing) sugar or chocolate sprinkles.

▶ Dip truffles in melted dark, milk or white chocolate. Add a few large flakes of sea salt to the truffles after dipping.

▶ Add 2 tsp (10 mL) liqueur to chocolate mixture. Cognac, brandy, orange liqueur, kirsch, rum, bourbon, almond liqueur and coffee liqueur are all good flavoring additions.

Fresh Berry Trifle

This great recipe uses a store- or bakery-bought cake and turns it into something spectacular. This dessert looks best when assembled and served in a trifle dish, to show off all the colorful layers. The creamy filling and the whipped cream can both be made up to 2 days ahead, making this dessert a snap to put together the day of your party.

Tips

If multiplying this recipe more than twice, make the pastry cream in double batches — any more than that and you'll risk scalding.

Use sponge cake, angel food cake, chocolate cake, carrot cake or any kind of cake you like.

Berries aren't in season? Use banana slices, orange segments, mango slices, pineapple cubes or kiwifruit slices.

• **Trifle dish or clear straight-sided bowl**

2 cups	whole milk	500 mL
5 tbsp	granulated sugar, divided	75 mL
3	egg yolks	3
1/8 tsp	salt	0.5 mL
1 cup	heavy or whipping (35%) cream, chilled	250 mL
1 tsp	vanilla extract	5 mL
1	10 to 12 oz (300 to 375 g) pound cake, cut into 1 to 2-inch (2.5 to 5 cm) cubes	1
3 tbsp	orange- or almond-flavored liqueur	45 mL
1/2 cup	raspberry jam	125 mL
1 cup	raspberries	250 mL
1 cup	blueberries	250 mL
1 cup	sliced strawberries	250 mL
1/4 cup	sliced almonds	50 mL

1. In a medium saucepan, over medium heat, combine milk and 2 tbsp (25 mL) of the sugar, stirring to dissolve sugar. Bring just to a boil and remove from heat.

2. In a medium heatproof bowl, whisk together egg yolks, 2 tbsp (25 mL) sugar and salt. While whisking briskly, gradually add 1/2 cup (125 mL) of the hot milk to warm the yolks. Pour yolk mixture gradually into the remaining milk, whisking to combine.

3. Place milk mixture over medium-low heat and cook, stirring constantly, until mixture is thick enough to coat the back of a spoon. Do not let simmer. Remove from heat and strain through a fine-mesh sieve into a bowl. Let cool for 10 minutes. Cover loosely and refrigerate for at least 1 hour, until chilled, or for up to 2 days.

4. In a chilled bowl, using an electric mixer, beat cream, vanilla and the remaining sugar until medium peaks form. Use immediately or cover and refrigerate for up to 2 days.

5. Place one-third of the cake cubes in trifle dish. Sprinkle with 1 tbsp (15 mL) liqueur. Spread one-third of the jam over cake layer and arrange one-third of the berries on top. Pour one-third of the custard mixture over berries. Repeat layers twice more. Top with whipped cream and sprinkle with almonds. Serve immediately or refrigerate for up to 1 hour.

Crème Brûlée

SERVES 8
or can be doubled

This dessert takes any party up a notch. Garnish with a few fresh berries.

Tips

If you want to save the expense of purchasing a vanilla bean, you can replace it with $1\frac{1}{2}$ tsp (7 mL) pure vanilla extract. You'll also save some time, because you won't have to let the cream steep for 15 minutes to infuse it with vanilla flavor.

If you cannot find turbinado sugar, granulated sugar will work fine.

This recipe can easily be doubled. If you need more, make it in double batches.

To flavor crème brûlée, stir 1 tbsp (15 mL) brandy, rum, Grand Marnier, kirsch, Kahlúa or bourbon into the hot cream.

Spice up your brûlée by adding $\frac{1}{2}$ tsp (2 mL) ground cardamom, cinnamon or nutmeg to the hot cream.

- Preheat oven to 325°F (160°C)
- Eight $\frac{2}{3}$-cup (150 mL) ramekins
- Large baking dish
- Kitchen torch (optional)

4 cups	heavy or whipping (35%) cream	1 L
$\frac{3}{4}$ cup	granulated sugar, divided	175 mL
1	vanilla bean, split in half lengthwise	1
12	egg yolks	12
	Boiling water	
	Turbinado sugar	

1. In a medium saucepan, over medium heat, combine cream, half the sugar and vanilla bean, stirring to dissolve sugar. Bring just to a simmer and remove from heat. Cover and let stand for 15 minutes. Remove vanilla bean, scrape out seeds and stir seeds into hot cream, discarding the bean.

2. Meanwhile, in a bowl, whisk together egg yolks and the remaining sugar until smooth. While whisking briskly, gradually add $\frac{1}{2}$ cup (125 mL) of the hot cream to warm the yolks. Pour yolk mixture gradually into the remaining cream, whisking to combine.

3. Pour mixture into ramekins and place in baking dish. Set dish in preheated oven, then fill dish with boiling water to reach halfway up the sides of the ramekins. Bake for about 40 minutes or until custard has just begun to set but is still jiggly in the center. Let cool to room temperature, about 40 minutes. Remove ramekins from baking dish, cover and refrigerate for at least 2 hours, until chilled, or for up to 1 day.

4. Just before serving, blot any moisture that has collected on the surface of the custard. Sprinkle a generous layer of turbinado sugar over each custard and let stand at room temperature for 10 minutes.

5. Using a kitchen torch, carefully heat sugar until it caramelizes. (Alternatively, place brûlée close under a broiler, rotating ramekins as necessary to encourage even browning.) Serve immediately.

Easy Extra

▸ Stir 2 tsp (10 mL) grated lemon, orange or lime zest into the cream mixture before pouring into ramekins.

Dark Chocolate Soufflé

*Serve this most elegant
of desserts with barely
sweetened whipped
cream and a little warm
caramel sauce.*

Tip

To double this recipe,
bake in two separate
soufflé dishes, side
by side in the oven
(don't try to rotate
them during baking,
though).

- Preheat oven to 375°F (190°C)
- 3-quart (3 L) soufflé dish, generously buttered

3/4 cup	whole milk	175 mL
1 tbsp	unsalted butter	15 mL
1 tsp	vanilla extract	5 mL
5 oz	good-quality dark chocolate, chopped into small pieces	150 g
5	eggs, separated, at room temperature	5
3 tbsp	granulated sugar	45 mL
2 tbsp	all-purpose flour	25 mL

1. In a small heavy saucepan, over medium-high heat, combine milk, butter and vanilla. Bring just to a boil and remove from heat. Add chocolate and let stand for 2 minutes, then stir until melted and smooth. Set aside.

2. In a bowl, using an electric mixer, beat egg yolks until light and pale in color, about 5 minutes. Add sugar and beat for 3 minutes. While whisking briskly, gradually add 1/4 cup (50 mL) of the chocolate mixture to warm the yolks. Pour yolk mixture gradually into the remaining chocolate mixture, whisking to combine. Sprinkle with flour and stir just to combine.

3. In a clean bowl, using an electric mixer with clean beaters, beat egg whites until soft peaks form. Carefully fold into chocolate mixture. Spoon batter into prepared soufflé dish.

4. Bake in preheated oven for 30 minutes or until puffed in the center. Serve immediately, as the soufflé will deflate quickly.

Variation

For individual chocolate soufflés, spoon batter into six generously buttered 2/3-cup (150 mL) ovenproof ramekins. Bake for 15 to 17 minutes.

French Vanilla Ice Cream

SERVES 6
or can be made
in batches for
more servings

*This recipe uses
the same technique
and ingredients as
the Crème Anglaise
(page 274), replacing
the vanilla extract with
a vanilla bean.*

Tip

If you need more
than one batch of this
recipe, it's best to make
a single batch at a time.

● **Ice cream maker, prepared according to manufacturer's instructions**

1 cup	heavy or whipping (35%) cream	250 mL
1/3 cup	granulated sugar, divided	75 mL
1	vanilla bean, split in half lengthwise	1
4	egg yolks	4

1. In a small saucepan, over medium heat, combine cream, half the sugar and vanilla bean, stirring to dissolve sugar. Bring just to a boil and remove from heat. Cover and let stand for 15 minutes. Remove vanilla bean, scrape out seeds and stir seeds into hot cream, discarding the bean.

2. In a bowl, whisk together egg yolks and the remaining sugar until smooth. While whisking briskly, gradually add 1/2 cup (125 mL) of the hot cream to warm the yolks. Pour yolk mixture gradually into the remaining cream, whisking to combine.

3. Place cream mixture over medium-low heat and cook, stirring constantly, until mixture is thick enough to coat the back of a spoon. Do not let simmer. Remove from heat and strain through a fine-mesh sieve. Let cool, then transfer to an airtight container and refrigerate for at least 2 hours, until chilled, or for up to 2 days.

4. Pour cream mixture into ice cream maker and freeze according to manufacturer's instructions.

Variations

▸ Stir 1 cup (250 mL) fresh banana purée into cream mixture before freezing.

▸ Place 1/2 cup (125 mL) dried cherries in a bowl and cover with 1/2 cup (125 mL) rum. Let stand for at least 2 hours or overnight. Drain cherries and add to cream mixture before freezing.

▸ Add 1/4 cup (50 mL) chopped candied ginger and 1 tsp (5 mL) ground cinnamon to cream mixture before freezing.

▸ Add 2/3 cup (150 mL) chopped fresh fruit, such as berries, peaches, pineapple, mango or oranges, to ice cream mixture halfway through freezing.

▸ Add 1/2 cup (125 mL) peanut butter, 1 tbsp (15 mL) at a time, to ice cream mixture halfway through freezing.

Crème Anglaise

MAKES 1½ CUPS (375 ML)
or can be multiplied up to 4 times

This is the *classic dessert sauce*, *traditionally served with pies, tarts and sweet soufflés.*

Tips

For quick crème Anglaise in a pinch, use melted vanilla ice cream.

If multiplying this recipe, keep an eye on the heat and adjust as necessary to keep it below a simmer.

1½ cups	heavy or whipping (35%) cream	250 mL
⅓ cup	granulated sugar, divided	75 mL
1 tbsp	vanilla extract	15 mL
4	egg yolks, at room temperature	4

1. In a small saucepan, over medium heat, combine cream, half the sugar and vanilla, stirring to dissolve sugar. Bring just to a boil and remove from heat.

2. In a bowl, whisk together egg yolks and the remaining sugar until smooth. While whisking briskly, gradually add ½ cup (125 mL) of the hot cream to warm the yolks. Pour yolk mixture gradually into the remaining cream, whisking to combine.

3. Place cream mixture over medium-low heat and cook, stirring constantly, until mixture is thick enough to coat the back of a spoon. Do not let simmer. Remove from heat and strain through a fine-mesh sieve. Use right away or let cool, transfer to an airtight container and refrigerate for at least 2 hours, until chilled, or for up to 2 days.

Raspberry Coulis

2½ cups	raspberries	625 mL
½ cup	granulated sugar	125 mL
1 tbsp	grated lemon zest	15 mL
2 tbsp	freshly squeezed lemon juice	25 mL

This is a beautiful red flash on the plate for which it is well worth tracking down fresh raspberries. Of course, you could easily substitute frozen.

1. In a food processor or blender, process raspberries, sugar, lemon zest and lemon juice until smooth. Strain through a fine-mesh sieve to remove the seeds.

Variations

▶ Replace the lemon zest and juice with orange zest and juice.

▶ Reserve about a third of the zest and stir in at the end to add flecks of color.

Tips

If you want to drizzle this sauce decoratively on dessert plates, place the strained sauce in a small saucepan and simmer for 5 to 7 minutes or until slightly thickened. For neat and easy drizzling, place cooled sauce in a plastic squeeze bottle.

Purchase a good-quality fudge sauce and drizzle both raspberry and fudge sauces over ice cream or chocolate cake.

Essential Recipes • Desserts and Dessert Sauces

Caramel Sauce

1½ cups	granulated sugar	375 mL
½ cup	water	125 mL
1 cup	heavy or whipping (35%) cream	250 mL
3 tbsp	unsalted butter	45 mL

Even though you can easily find jars of caramel sauce, making it yourself is such a triumph the first time you do it correctly. It has endless uses as a dip, a spread or a topping.

Tip

Be very careful when working with caramel, as it reaches extremely high temperatures and it may splatter when you add the cream.

Make Ahead

Caramel sauce will last for up to 2 weeks if refrigerated in an airtight container. It thickens as it cools, so you will need to warm it (microwaving works fine) before using.

1. In a large saucepan, over low heat, combine sugar and water, stirring constantly until sugar dissolves. Increase heat to medium-high and bring to a boil. Boil, without stirring, until sauce becomes a dark caramel color, about 20 minutes.

2. Meanwhile, in a small saucepan, heat cream and butter over medium heat until butter is melted and cream is hot.

3. Reduce heat under caramel sauce to low. Gradually pour in hot cream mixture, stirring constantly until sauce is smooth. Let cool to room temperature before serving.

Orange Cranberry Sauce

*This gorgeous fuchsia
sauce can be poured
over ice cream or used
as a zippy filling for
crêpes.*

Tips

You'll need about
10 oz (300 g)
cranberries to get
2½ cups (625 mL).
If you have a 12-oz
(340 g) bag, feel
free to add the extra
cranberries; the recipe
will work just fine.

Serve this instead of
your usual cranberry
sauce at Thanksgiving
dinner.

Make Ahead

This sauce can be made
up to 1 week ahead if
refrigerated in an airtight
container. Chilled sauce
will thicken. To thin,
stir in 1 to 2 tbsp (15 to
25 mL) orange juice
or water.

2½ cups	fresh cranberries	625 mL
¼ cup	packed light brown sugar	50 mL
¾ cup	pure maple syrup	175 mL
½ cup	thawed frozen orange juice concentrate	125 mL
¼ cup	water	50 mL

1. In a small saucepan, bring cranberries, brown sugar, maple syrup, orange juice concentrate and water to a simmer over medium heat. Simmer, stirring frequently, until most of the cranberries have burst open and sauce is thick, about 10 minutes.

Essential Recipes • Desserts and Dessert Sauces

Festive Punch

*Punch is great for kids'
or adult parties. This
one uses fruit frozen
into ice cubes for a
colorful beverage. To
add some alcohol for an
adult beverage, see the
variations at right.*

Tip

Distilled water freezes
clear, making the fruit
easier to see.

- **3 ice cube trays**
- **Large punch bowl**

1/3 cup	blueberries	75 mL
1/3 cup	sliced small strawberries	75 mL
1/3 cup	drained canned mandarin orange segments	75 mL
1 tbsp	small fresh mint leaves	15 mL
3 cups	unsweetened pineapple juice, chilled	750 mL
3 cups	ginger ale, chilled	750 mL
2 cups	cranberry juice, chilled	500 mL

1. Divide blueberries, strawberries, oranges and mint among ice cube trays. Fill trays with water (preferably distilled) and freeze until ready to use.

2. Just before serving, combine pineapple juice, ginger ale and cranberry juice in punch bowl. Float the ice cubes on top and serve one in each glass.

Variations

▶ Replace the ginger ale with a bottle of inexpensive Champagne or sparkling wine.

▶ Reduce the pineapple juice to 2 cups (500 mL) and add 1 cup (250 mL) rum or vodka.

▶ Place the fruit and mint leaves in a Bundt pan or angel food cake pan and fill pan with 3 inches (7.5 cm) of water, then freeze for one large ice ring. Dip pan into warm water to unmold ice ring.

▶ Freeze edible flowers in ice in place of the fruit.

Minted Ice Tea

SERVES 6
or can be multiplied
up to 4 times

This basic ice tea recipe can be altered to fit any party (see variations, at right).

6	mint tea bags	6
4 cups	boiling water	1 L
1/3 cup	granulated sugar	75 mL
4 cups	cold water	1 L
	Mint sprigs	

1. Place tea bags in a pitcher and pour in boiling water. Let steep for 4 minutes, then discard tea bags. Add sugar and stir to dissolve. Add cold water and refrigerate until chilled.
2. To serve, pour tea over ice and garnish with a mint sprig.

Variations

▶ Replace the sugar with liquid honey or a sugar substitute.

▶ Use half mint tea and half black tea, green tea or white tea.

▶ Replace the mint tea with a black tea flavored with spices or fruit.

▶ Use lavender tea in place of the mint tea and garnish with fresh sprigs of lavender.

Mulled Cider

This lightly alcoholic warm cider makes a great addition to any holiday party. Make it a few hours before the party so that it fills the air with a homey, spicy scent.

Tips

You can use a plain brandy or a good-quality apple brandy, such as Calvados.

Make this recipe non-alcoholic by replacing the brandy with more apple cider.

If using sweetened apple cider, omit the brown sugar.

6 cups	unsweetened apple cider	1.5 L
6	whole cloves	6
2	cinnamon sticks	2
1	bay leaf	1
3 tbsp	packed brown sugar	45 mL
1/4 tsp	ground cardamom	1 mL
1/4 tsp	grated nutmeg	1 mL
	Grated zest and juice of 1 orange	
3/4 cup	brandy (see tip, at left)	175 mL

1. In a saucepan, combine apple cider, cloves, cinnamon, bay leaf, brown sugar, cardamom, nutmeg, orange zest and orange juice; bring to a boil over high heat. Reduce heat and simmer for 15 minutes or until slightly reduced.

2. Strain to remove spices and zest, add brandy and serve.

Classic Champagne Cocktail

Add a touch of instant class to any party with this great cocktail. Serve before dinner or lunch, or even with brunch.

1	sugar cube	1
2	dashes angostura bitters	2
$\frac{1}{2}$ oz	cognac	15 mL
	Champagne, chilled	

1. Place sugar cube in the bottom of a Champagne flute. Pour in bitters, then add cognac. Top with Champagne, stir and serve immediately.

Fruity Champagne Cocktail

Champagne saucers are making a comeback, and this cocktail is the perfect drink to serve in one. For even more extravagance, add a raspberry, $\frac{1}{8}$ of a thin orange slice and $\frac{1}{4}$ of a thin lime slice.

2 tbsp	orange juice, chilled	25 mL
1 tbsp	unsweetened pineapple juice, chilled	15 mL
1 tbsp	cranberry juice, chilled	15 mL
2	dashes orange-flavored liqueur	2
	Champagne, chilled	

1. Pour orange juice, pineapple juice, cranberry juice and liqueur into a Champagne flute. Top with Champagne and serve immediately.

Essential Recipes • Beverages

Kir

Crème de cassis is a French liqueur made from black currants, and it makes a refreshing addition to white wine. Serve this drink before dinner or lunch.

½ oz	crème de cassis	15 mL
	Dry white wine, chilled	

1. Pour the crème de cassis into a wine glass and fill with white wine.

Dirty Martini

SERVES 1

Adding olive brine makes the liquid slightly cloudy or "dirty." A "dusty" martini is one with a teaspoon (5 mL) or less of brine.

	Ice	
2 oz	gin	50 mL
1 tbsp	brine from cocktail olives	15 mL
⅓ oz	extra-dry vermouth	10 mL
	Cocktail olive	

1. In a cocktail shaker filled with ice, combine gin, olive brine and vermouth. Shake and strain into a glass. Garnish with the olive.

Pink Lady

SERVES 1

The queen of all girly drinks! This pretty pink concoction uses egg whites to create a foamy top.

Tip

Egg white powder can be found in the baking section of well-stocked grocery stores or in larger health food stores.

	Ice	
½ oz	gin	15 mL
1 tbsp	freshly squeezed lemon juice	15 mL
2	dashes grenadine	2
1 tsp	egg white powder	5 mL
	Maraschino cherry	

1. In a cocktail shaker filled with ice, combine gin, lemon juice, grenadine and egg white powder. Shake and strain into a glass. Garnish with the maraschino cherry.

Planter's Punch

SERVES 1

Not just classic but downright old-fashioned, this drink is becoming popular again. It can be made in pitchers for easier serving.

	Ice	
1½ oz	dark rum	45 mL
1	dash angostura bitters	1
1 tbsp	freshly squeezed lemon juice	15 mL
2 tsp	light (white) corn syrup	10 mL
	Ice	

1. In a cocktail shaker filled with ice, combine rum, bitters, lemon juice and corn syrup. Shake and strain into a wine glass filled with ice. Serve with a straw.

Bahama Mama

SERVES 1

A great cocktail for a hot summer day, the Bahama Mama is full of complex flavors, as well as three kinds of alcohol. This drink can be made in pitchers for easier serving.

	Ice	
2 oz	dark rum	50 mL
½ oz	coconut-flavored liqueur	15 mL
½ oz	coffee-flavored liqueur	15 mL
½ cup	unsweetened pineapple juice	125 mL
1½ tsp	freshly squeezed lemon juice	7 mL
	Maraschino cherry	
	Small pineapple wedge	

1. In a cocktail shaker filled with ice, combine rum, coconut liqueur, coffee liqueur, pineapple juice and lemon juice. Shake and strain into a glass. Garnish with the maraschino cherry and pineapple wedge.

Blue Hawaiian

SERVES 1

A sweetly potent tropical drink evocative of grass skirts and tikis. Tradition demands that it be served with a paper umbrella. It can be made in pitchers for easier serving.

1 oz	white rum	25 mL
1 oz	blue curaçao	25 mL
2 tbsp	coconut cream	25 mL
¼ cup	unsweetened pineapple juice	50 mL
1 cup	ice cubes	250 mL
	Pineapple wedge	

1. In a blender, combine rum, curaçao, coconut cream and pineapple juice. Add ice and blend until smooth. Pour into a chilled glass and garnish with the pineapple wedge.

Fuzzy Navel

SERVES 1

The difference between a navel that is fuzzy and one that is hairy is the amount of vodka. Make yours hairy by adding an extra ounce (25 mL) of vodka. This drink can be made in pitchers for easier serving.

	Ice	
1 oz	vodka	25 mL
1 oz	peach schnapps	25 mL
²/₃ cup	orange juice	150 mL
	Orange slice	

1. In a cocktail shaker filled with ice, combine vodka, schnapps and orange juice. Shake and strain into a glass. Garnish with the orange slice.

Sea Breeze

SERVES 1

A refreshing drink for a warm day, this cocktail can be turned into its sweeter version, the Bay Breeze, by replacing the grapefruit juice with pineapple juice. It can be made in pitchers for easier serving.

	Ice	
1¹/₂ oz	vodka, chilled	45 mL
¹/₂ cup	cranberry juice, chilled	125 mL
2 tbsp	grapefruit juice, chilled	25 mL
	Lime slice	

1. Fill a highball glass with ice. Pour in vodka, cranberry juice and grapefruit juice. Garnish with the lime slice.

Essential Recipes • Beverages

White Russian

This great evening drink can be made with ¼ cup (50 mL) half-and-half (10%) cream or whole milk in place of the heavy cream, for a lighter drink. Or make it a Black Russian by leaving out the cream altogether and increasing the vodka to 2 ounces (50 mL).

	Ice	
1½ oz	vodka	45 mL
1 oz	coffee-flavored liqueur	25 mL
1 tbsp	heavy or whipping (35%) cream	15 mL

1. Fill an old-fashioned glass with ice. Pour in vodka and liqueur. Top with cream.

Mint Julep

There is much debate about whether or not the mint should be muddled (smashed) in this drink. If you like, you can use a large sprig of mint (unmuddled) in place of the (muddled) mint leaves. Serve in chilled tall skinny glasses.

8	fresh mint leaves	8
1 tsp	superfine sugar	5 mL
1 tbsp	cold water	15 mL
1½ oz	bourbon	45 mL
	Crushed ice	
	Club soda, chilled	

1. Place mint in the bottom of a tumbler. Add sugar and cold water. Muddle the mint with a wooden spoon until sugar is dissolved and mint is mashed. Add bourbon and fill glass with crushed ice. Top with club soda and serve immediately.

Rob Roy

SERVES 1

A Rob Roy is a Manhattan made with Scotch whisky. This drink makes me think of dark, smoky restaurants with leather booths and big fat steaks. Definitely an evening drink, suitable for before or after dinner.

	Ice	
1 1/2 oz	Scotch	45 mL
1 1/2 oz	sweet vermouth	45 mL
1 to 2	dashes angostura bitters	1 to 2
	Twist of orange peel	

1. In a cocktail shaker filled with ice, combine Scotch, vermouth and bitters. Shake and strain into a cocktail glass. Garnish with the orange peel.

Golden Cadillac

SERVES 1

This is a great after-dinner drink that has a special affinity with chocolate desserts.

	Ice	
1 oz	Galliano	25 mL
1 oz	white crème de cacao	25 mL
2 tbsp	heavy or whipping (35%) cream	25 mL

1. In a cocktail shaker filled with ice, combine Galliano, crème de cacao and cream. Shake and strain into a cocktail glass.

Theme Menus

~~~~~~

Champagne and Caviar Party

Wine and Cheese Tasting

Girls' Night In

Friends' Game Night

Oscar Night

Super Bowl Party

Backyard Campout

Southern Charm

Western Hoedown

Pacific Northwest Coast

Hawaiian Luau

Mexican Fiesta

Barcelona Bash

Italian Pasta Party

German Feast

Grecian Get-Together

Turkish Twilight

African Ivory Coast

Chinese Banquet

Garden Brunch

Everything in this menu can be made ahead and is delicious served at room temperature, making it perfect for a brunch or light lunch.

Menu

Chilled Melon Soup

SERVES 6
or can be multiplied up to 4 times

Serve this in dainty espresso cups or shot glasses for a refreshing liquid appetizer.

Tips

Garnish each bowl with a fresh mint leaf and a half slice of lime.

Make tiny honeydew melon balls from the remaining melon and float a few on top of the soup.

2	large English cucumbers, peeled and chopped	2
3 cups	chopped honeydew melon	750 mL
¼ cup	fresh mint leaves	50 mL
½ cup	crème fraîche	125 mL
¼ cup	liquid honey	50 mL
2 tbsp	freshly squeezed lime juice	25 mL
Pinch	freshly ground black pepper (optional)	Pinch

1. In a blender or food processor, purée cucumbers, melon, mint, crème fraîche, honey, lime juice and pepper (if using) until smooth. Transfer to a bowl and serve right away or cover and refrigerate for up to 4 hours.

Potato Onion Torte with Sausage

SERVES 6
or can be multiplied
up to 4 times

*This torte is even
better the next day. Its
versatility makes it a
great buffet dish, as it
can be served hot or at
room temperature.*

Tips

You can substitute
spicy sausage, ham,
prosciutto, pancetta
or bacon for the sweet
Italian sausage.

If making a double
batch, use a 13- by
9-inch (33 by 23 cm)
baking dish. If
multiplying the recipe
four times, use two 13-
by 9-inch (33 by 23
cm) baking dishes.

Make Ahead

This torte can be
prepared up to 2 days
ahead. Let it cool to
room temperature, then
cover and refrigerate
(without cutting it
into wedges). Serve
at room temperature
or cover loosely with
foil and reheat in a
300°F (150°C) oven
for 20 minutes or until
heated through.

- **Preheat oven to 350°F (180°C)**
- **8-inch (20 cm) springform pan, sprayed with nonstick cooking spray**

1 tbsp	olive oil	15 mL
1	large onion, thinly sliced	1
1½ lbs	boiling potatoes, peeled and very thinly sliced	750 g
6 tbsp	cold unsalted butter, diced, divided	90 mL
8 oz	sweet Italian sausage, cooked and crumbled	250 g
¼ cup	chopped fresh flat-leaf (Italian) parsley	50 mL
¼ cup	chopped fresh basil	50 mL
1 tbsp	fresh thyme leaves	15 mL
Pinch	salt	Pinch
Pinch	freshly ground black pepper	Pinch
1½ cups	shredded Monterey Jack cheese	375 mL
½ cup	freshly grated Parmesan cheese	125 mL

1. In a skillet, heat oil over medium heat. Sauté onions for about 12 minutes or until soft and golden. Remove from heat and set aside.

2. Cover the bottom of the prepared pan with one-third of the potato slices. Dot with 2 tbsp (25 mL) of the butter. Scatter half the onions, sausage, parsley, basil, thyme, salt and pepper over the potatoes. Top with half the Monterey Jack and Parmesan.

3. Place another third of the potato slices on top of the cheese and press down gently to compress. Dot with 2 tbsp (25 mL) butter. Scatter the remaining onions, sausage, parsley, basil, thyme, salt, pepper, Monterey Jack and Parmesan over the potatoes. Top with the remaining potatoes and press down gently. Dot with the remaining butter.

4. Bake in preheated oven for about 1 hour or until top is golden brown and crunchy. Let cool for 10 minutes before releasing springform pan. Cut into 6 wedges.

Niçoise Salad

SERVES 6
or can be multiplied
up to 4 times

This is a composed salad, meaning it is arranged on the plate rather than being tossed together. The dressing is served separately, so the salad can be served on a tray or platter instead of in a bowl. Oil-cured olives look like tiny prunes. They are salty and don't have the vinegar taste of brine-cured olives.

Tips

If you use a large green bean variety, such as Blue Lake, you will need to blanch them longer to achieve the same tender-crisp.

Limestone lettuce is also known as butter, Boston or Bibb lettuce. You can substitute any attractive lettuce you like.

Make Ahead

Chop everything that needs chopping 2 days before. Before refrigerating, wrap in damp paper towels, then in plastic wrap, to keep from drying out.

8 oz	petite green beans or haricot verts, trimmed	250 g
1	head limestone lettuce	1
3	cans (each 5 to 7 oz/150 to 210 g) chunk white tuna in water, drained	3
3	hard-cooked eggs, peeled and cut into wedges	3
3	plum (Roma) tomatoes, cut into wedges	3
1	fennel bulb, thinly sliced	1
1	large English cucumber, sliced	1
¾ cup	oil-cured or niçoise olives	175 mL
¾ cup	Niçoise Garlic Dressing (see recipe, below)	175 mL

1. Bring a medium pot of salted water to a boil over high heat. Blanch green beans for 2 minutes or until just tender but still crunchy. Using a slotted spoon, transfer green beans to a bowl or sink of ice water to stop the cooking process. Let stand until chilled; drain well.

2. Cover a serving tray or platter with lettuce leaves. Arrange tuna, eggs, tomatoes, fennel, cucumber, olives and green beans on top. Serve with dressing on the side.

Variations

▶ Make this salad ultra-fancy and replace the tuna with freshly seared ahi tuna.

Niçoise Garlic Dressing

2	cloves garlic	2
1/4 cup	seasoned rice vinegar	50 mL
1 tbsp	lemon juice	15 mL
2 tsp	Dijon mustard	10 mL
1/2 cup	extra virgin olive oil	125 mL
	Salt and freshly ground black pepper	

MAKES ABOUT 3/4 CUP (175 ML)
or can be doubled

This is a lovely garlicky dressing, but you can replace the garlic with shallots if you prefer a less pungent flavor.

Make Ahead

This dressing can be made the day before if refrigerated in an airtight container.

1. In a food processor or blender, pulse garlic, vinegar, lemon juice and mustard to combine. With the motor running, through the feed tube, gradually add oil in a steady stream; process until creamy. Transfer to a bowl and season to taste with salt and pepper.

Variation

▶ Add 6 anchovy fillets or 1 1/2 tsp (7 mL) anchovy paste with the garlic.

Salade Niçoise: A Perfect Plate

The term "niçoise," meaning "in the style of Nice," is a descriptive word for dishes that typically incorporate tomatoes, black olives, garlic and anchovies. Salade niçoise is the most popular of all such dishes. It has been suggested that ballet choreographer George Balanchine was responsible for the creation of the very first salade niçoise during his tenure in Monte Carlo. Niçoise salads are favored because they offer a little bit of every perfect taste and texture in each bite: crisp vegetables, filling protein from the tuna and eggs, starch from the potatoes and a good balance between sweet and tangy from the lemon juice and vinaigrette.

To be considered a true salade niçoise, the aforementioned hallmark ingredients should be included, but you can add any other ingredients that serve your fancy. And if potatoes seem a bit heavy for your salad, simply leave them out, as we did here.

The first time I ate salade niçoise was in a small café in Monte Carlo. The beautiful tiny purple olives were not pitted. I thought it must be a mistake, but when I asked my server about the pits, he simply replied, "Madame, that's your job." In the condiment section of your grocery store, most jars of niçoise olives now come pitted. I have since learned that they are much more difficult to pit than other olives, so make sure to read the label if you want to avoid the effort.

Fresh Berries with Mascarpone and Honey

SERVES 6
or can be multiplied
up to 4 times

Mascarpone is an Italian cheese made by draining moisture from heavy cream. The result is a very smooth and slightly sweet fresh cheese, without the tanginess of cream cheese.

8 oz	mascarpone cheese	250 g
3 tbsp	superfine sugar	45 mL
1/2 tsp	almond extract	2 mL
1 1/2 cups	sliced strawberries	375 mL
1/3 cup	blueberries	75 mL
1/3 cup	raspberries	75 mL
1/4 cup	sliced almonds	50 mL
1/4 cup	liquid honey	50 mL

1. In a small bowl, combine mascarpone, sugar and almond extract. Cover and refrigerate for at least 30 minutes, until chilled, or for up to 2 days.
2. Spoon mascarpone mixture into dessert glasses. Place strawberries, blueberries and raspberries on top. Sprinkle with almonds and drizzle with honey.

Variations

▶ Use chopped fresh peaches and nectarines, when in season.

▶ This is also wonderful with fresh figs, cut into wedges.

Aniseed Biscotti

**MAKES ABOUT
32 COOKIES**
or can be multiplied
up to 4 times

*Biscotti are great
cookies for dipping in
coffee, because of their
delightful crispness.*

Make Ahead

Store biscotti in an
airtight container at
room temperature for
up to 1 week.

The dough for the
biscotti can be made up
to 2 months in advance.
Wrap well in plastic
wrap, then place in a
freezer bag and freeze.
Thaw in the refrigerator
for 24 hours before
baking.

• **Preheat oven to 350°F (180°C)**
• **Large baking sheet, lined with foil, foil sprayed with
nonstick cooking spray**

2 cups	all-purpose flour	500 mL
2 tsp	baking powder	10 mL
1/2 tsp	salt	2 mL
1/3 cup	orange juice	75 mL
3/4 tsp	vanilla extract	3 mL
1 cup	granulated sugar	250 mL
1/2 cup	unsalted butter, softened	125 mL
2	eggs, at room temperature	2
1 tbsp	aniseed	15 mL

1. In a bowl, combine flour, baking powder and salt; set
aside.

2. In a small bowl, combine orange juice and vanilla.

3. In a large bowl, using an electric mixer, cream sugar
and butter until light and fluffy, about 5 minutes. Add
eggs, one at a time, beating well after each addition. Beat
in flour mixture alternately with orange juice mixture,
making two additions of each. Stir in aniseed.

4. Form dough into two 8- by 2-inch (20 by 5 cm) logs. Place
at least 4 inches (10 cm) apart on prepared baking sheet.

5. Bake in preheated oven for about 40 minutes or until
golden and firm. Let cool completely on baking sheet on
wire racks. Reduce oven temperature to 300°F (150°C).

6. Transfer cooled logs to a cutting board. Using a serrated
knife, cut logs diagonally into 1/2-inch (1 cm) thick slices.
Arrange slices on baking sheet.

7. Bake for about 40 minutes, turning a few times so they
brown evenly, until cookies are dry and lightly browned.
Remove from baking sheet and let cool on wire racks.

Picnic Boxed Lunch

You can have a picnic just about anywhere you can spread a blanket. Backyards, beaches, parks, patios — it really doesn't matter where.

Roasted Chicken Chopped Salad with Blue Cheese Vinaigrette

SERVES 6
or can be multiplied up to 4 times

There's so much variety and potential in this chopped salad, and it's an easy one to serve on a picnic blanket. Take liberties with the ingredients and personalize it however you please. Buy a roasted chicken at your grocery store to make this recipe quicker.

Make Ahead

Chopped salads can be prepped a day in advance if you store the ingredients separately in the refrigerator.

1	head romaine lettuce, chopped	1
6	green onions, sliced	6
3	tomatoes, diced	3
1	large carrot, diced	1
1	red bell pepper, finely chopped	1
1	yellow bell pepper, finely chopped	1
1	cucumber, peeled and diced	1
1	can (14 to 19 oz/398 to 540 mL) chickpeas, drained and rinsed	1
1 lb	fresh mozzarella cheese, diced	500 g
1 lb	bacon, cooked crisp and crumbled	500 g
2 cups	diced roasted chicken	500 mL
$\frac{1}{2}$ cup	sliced cooked or drained canned red beets	125 mL
$\frac{3}{4}$ cup mL	Blue Cheese Vinaigrette (see recipe, opposite)	175 mL

1. Divide romaine among serving plates. Arrange green onions, tomatoes, carrot, red pepper, yellow pepper, cucumber, chickpeas, mozzarella, bacon, chicken and beets attractively on top. Serve with dressing on the side.

Easy Extras

▶ This is the place to exercise your imagination. Add any ingredients that strike your fancy, such as artichoke hearts, corn kernels, edamame or other beans, almonds, pecans or sunflower seeds.

Blue Cheese Vinaigrette

½ cup	extra virgin olive oil	125 mL
¼ cup	crumbled blue cheese	50 mL
¼ cup	champagne vinegar or seasoned rice vinegar	50 mL
2 tsp	Dijon mustard	10 mL
¼ tsp	salt	1 mL
Pinch	freshly ground black pepper	Pinch

1. In a food processor or blender, pulse oil, blue cheese, vinegar, mustard, salt and pepper until creamy.

Variation

▸ The blue cheese can be replaced with feta, Gorgonzola or cream cheese.

MAKES 1 CUP (250 ML) or can be multiplied up to 4 times

Place servings of dressing in small containers with lids, such as Mason jars or disposable plastic condiment cups, and pack them with the salads so the dressing won't make the salad go to mush before you're ready to serve it.

Make Ahead

This dressing can be made up to 3 days in advance if refrigerated in an airtight container.

Ambrosia

SERVES 6
or can be multiplied
up to 4 times

Ambrosia, food of the gods, is a well-known traditional Southern dish that can be altered to suit any taste. It sits well overnight, and travels nicely.

1	can (11 oz/312 mL) mandarin orange segments in light syrup, drained	1
½	pineapple, peeled, cored and chopped	½
2 cups	red grapes, halved	500 mL
1 cup	sweetened shredded coconut	250 mL

1. In a bowl, combine oranges, pineapple, grapes and coconut. Cover and refrigerate for at least 45 minutes, until chilled, or overnight.

Easy Extra

▶ Sprinkle with ¼ cup (50 mL) golden raisins, dried cranberries or chopped pecans.

Variations

▶ If dainty champagne grapes are available, use them in place of the red grapes.

▶ Try diced apples, clementines or any stone fruit in this salad.

Herbed Parmesan Cheese Straws

*Quite possibly the most
addictive Southern
finger food, these cheese
straws absolutely
demand sweet tea
or lemonade as an
accompaniment. If
you're feeling brave,
add a pinch of cayenne
pepper to the cheese
straws.*

Tip

If multiplying this
recipe, make dough
in batches to keep it
from getting tough.
Bake strips in the
bottom and top thirds
of the oven, rotating
the sheets halfway
through.

Make Ahead

Store between layers
of waxed paper in an
airtight container at
room temperature for
up to 2 days.

- **Preheat oven to 350°F (180°C)**
- **2 baking sheets, sprayed with nonstick cooking spray**

$3/4$ cup	all-purpose flour	175 mL
$1/2$ cup	freshly grated Parmesan cheese	125 mL
$1/4$ cup	unsalted butter, cut into pieces and chilled	50 mL
$1/4$ tsp	salt	1 mL
Pinch	dried thyme	Pinch
Pinch	dried rosemary	Pinch
Pinch	freshly ground black pepper	Pinch
1 tbsp	milk	15 mL

1. In a food processor, pulse flour, Parmesan, butter, salt, thyme, rosemary and pepper until mixture resembles coarse meal. Add milk through the feed tube and pulse until dough comes together.

2. On a lightly floured surface, roll out dough to an 8-inch (20 cm) wide rectangle about $1/8$ inch (3 mm) thick. Cut into strips about 8 inches (20 cm) long by $1/4$ inch (0.5 cm) wide. Place strips at least 1 inch (2.5 cm) apart on prepared baking sheets.

3. Bake in preheated oven for about 15 minutes or until light golden. Let cool completely on baking sheets.

Variation

▸ These cheese straws can be made with any type of hard or semi-hard grated cheese, such as Gouda, Comté, Asiago or Gruyère.

Nutty Blondies

*These sweet squares
taste best if made
the day before. Add
anything you wish to
the batter: seeds, rolled
oats, nuts or even diced
dried fruit.*

Make Ahead

Store in an airtight
container at room
temperature for up to
3 days, or wrap tightly
in plastic wrap, then in
foil, and freeze for up to
2 months.

- **Preheat oven to 350°F (180°C)**
- **13- by 9-inch (33 by 23 cm) baking dish, buttered**

2 cups	firmly packed light brown sugar	500 mL
1 cup	melted butter	250 mL
2 tsp	baking powder	10 mL
1/4 tsp	salt	1 mL
1 1/2 tsp	vanilla extract	7 mL
2 cups	all-purpose flour	500 mL
2	eggs, beaten	2
1 1/2 cups	semisweet chocolate chips	375 mL
1/2 cup	chopped pecans	125 mL
1/2 cup	chopped walnuts	125 mL

1. In a large bowl, using a wooden spoon, cream brown sugar and butter. Stir in baking powder, salt and vanilla. Add flour alternately with eggs, making three additions of flour and two of eggs, stirring well after each addition. Stir in chocolate chips, pecans and walnuts. Spread in prepared baking dish.

2. Bake in preheated oven for 25 to 30 minutes or until a tester inserted in the center comes out clean. Let cool completely before cutting into squares.

Variation

▸ Use butterscotch or white chocolate chips in place of the chocolate chips.

Tips for Packing
a Picnic Lunch

1. Try to use small, individual-size collapsible coolers, which are not only easier to carry, but also conserve storage space when not in use.

2. If you are serving items that should stay chilled, you can freeze water bottles and use them as cooler packs, but first pour out about $\frac{1}{4}$ cup (50 mL) water to avoid exploding bottles. When you arrive at your picnic site, your food will still be chilled and you can use your melting water bottles as refreshing beverages throughout the day.

3. Buy disposable food storage containers (you can find environmentally friendly containers almost anywhere today) so you don't have to worry about losing a few in case guests want to take theirs home. The containers that make it back home with you can be washed and reused.

4. Consider packing individual-size portions of food so there is little to no fuss in organizing your food and doing last-minute chopping or plating. If you are serving something like a chopped salad, pour a little bit of dressing into the bottom of each container and pile the salad on top — this will be fine for an hour or two if refrigerated (but serve dressing on the side if assembling the night before). When it comes time to eat, guests can toss their salads and eat.

5. Insects can be annoying party-crashers, especially at picnics. Although there are many insect repellants out there, most of them are harsh and poisonous chemicals that can be dangerous, especially around your food. At the very least, their odors are not the most appetizing, and will detract from your careful food preparation. Effective and resourceful alternatives are bundles of fresh herbs, as many herbs are natural insect repellants. Sage, rosemary and basil can be tied together into small bunches and set around your picnic. They serve both as insect repellant and as naturally decorative centerpieces. Small mixtures of cinnamon, nutmeg, mace and caraway seeds in mesh bags are also effective repellants and work as potpourri as well.

Kids' Treasure Hunt

No utensils needed to eat these yummy treats, so they're perfect for kids.

Menu

Turkey Taco Wraps

SERVES 6
or can be multiplied up to 4 times

Kids big and small will enjoy this hand-held favorite. Jazz them up for more sophisticated palates with salsa verde, thinly sliced jicama or avocado, or cooked black or pinto beans.

1 tbsp	olive oil	15 mL
1 lb	ground turkey	500 g
1	package (1¼ oz/35 g) taco seasoning mix	1
6	8-inch (20 cm) tomato or spinach flour tortillas, halved	6
4	green onions, sliced	4
1	large tomato, diced	1
1	head romaine lettuce, shredded	1
1 cup	shredded Cheddar cheese	250 mL
¼ cup	chopped fresh cilantro	50 mL
	Sour cream and salsa	

1. In a large skillet, heat oil over medium-high heat. Brown turkey, crumbling with a wooden spoon, until no longer pink. Add taco seasoning and 2 tbsp (25 mL) water and cook for 1 minute. Remove from heat.

2. Roll each tortilla into a cone shape and fill with turkey, green onions, tomato, romaine, cheese and cilantro. Serve hot or warm, with salsa and sour cream.

Easy Extra

▸ Black olives make a great addition to these taco wraps.

Confetti Fruit Salad

This eye-catching salad can be altered in a myriad of ways, depending on your taste. Serve in small crystal bowls or in colored cocktail glasses.

Tip

To toast coconut, spread it on a baking sheet and place in a 350°F (180°C) oven, stirring occasionally for even browning, for about 5 minutes or until golden brown.

1	small honeydew melon	1
1	small seedless watermelon	1
1	small cantaloupe	1
1 cup	blueberries	250 mL
1/4 cup	sweetened shredded coconut, toasted	50 mL

1. Using a variety of melon ballers of different sizes, make honeydew, watermelon and cantaloupe balls. In a large bowl, toss melon balls with blueberries and coconut.

2. Serve right away or cover and refrigerate for up to 1 day.

Party Snack Mix

Serve this snack mix in cute single-serving bags.

Tip

This recipe can be easily altered to any child's taste. Use white chocolate chips or different types of nuts. Add your child's favorite candy.

6 cups	popped popcorn	1.5 L
1 cup	mini pretzel twists	250 mL
3/4 cup	diced dried tropical fruit mix	175 mL
1 cup	Cheddar cheese–flavored crackers	250 mL
1/2 cup	roasted salted almonds	125 mL

1. In a large bowl, combine popcorn, pretzels, dried fruit, crackers and almonds.

2. Serve right away or store in an airtight container at room temperature for up to 3 days.

Theme Menus • Kids' Treasure Hunt

Chocolate Cupcakes with Whipped Cream Filling

**MAKES
12 CUPCAKES**
or can be doubled

These filled cupcakes have the childhood appeal of store-bought plastic-wrapped cupcakes, but without the mystery ingredients! Prepare the cream and the cupcakes, and fill them as a party activity: just make sure to cover everyone with aprons.

Tips

Cupcake or muffin tin liners can be purchased in all different kinds of prints and colors.

If doubling the recipe, rotate the tins in the oven halfway through baking.

Make Ahead

The ganache can be made up to 5 days ahead if refrigerated in an airtight container. When ready to use, reheat, uncovered, in the microwave on High for 30-second intervals, stirring between intervals, until pourable.

- Preheat oven to 350°F (180°C)
- 12-cup muffin tin, lined with paper liners
- Piping bag fitted with a plain tip
- Baking sheet, lined with waxed paper

Cupcakes

1⅓ cups	all-purpose flour	325 mL
⅔ cup	granulated sugar	150 mL
⅔ cup	unsweetened cocoa powder	150 mL
1 tsp	baking powder	5 mL
1 tsp	baking soda	5 mL
½ tsp	salt	2 mL
3	egg whites	3
1 cup	water	250 mL
⅔ cup	mayonnaise	150 mL
⅓ cup	heavy or whipping (35%) cream	75 mL
2 tsp	vanilla extract	10 mL

Filling

⅔ cup	heavy or whipping (35%) cream	150 mL
⅓ cup	confectioner's (icing) sugar, sifted	75 mL
½ tsp	vanilla extract	2 mL

Ganache

½ cup	heavy or whipping (35%) cream	125 mL
3½ oz	dark chocolate, finely chopped	100 g
1 tbsp	unsalted butter, softened	15 mL

1. *Cupcakes:* In a large bowl, combine flour, sugar, cocoa, baking powder, baking soda and salt.

2. In another bowl, using an electric mixer, beat egg whites until frothy. Beat in water, mayonnaise, cream and vanilla until well blended. Pour into flour mixture and beat on low speed until smooth. Pour batter into prepared muffin tin.

3. Bake in preheated oven for 10 minutes or until a tester inserted in the center of a cupcake comes out clean. Let cool in tin on a wire rack for 10 minutes. Remove from tin and let cool completely on wire rack, about 30 minutes.

4. Using a small melon baller, scoop a hole from the top of each cupcake. Reserve this piece to use as a plug. Using your finger, press inside each cupcake to make the hole wider and deeper inside. Set aside.

5. *Filling:* In a bowl, using an electric mixer, whip cream until it begins to thicken. Add confectioner's sugar and vanilla; whip until stiff peaks form, about 2 minutes.

6. Fill piping bag with whipped cream. Pipe cream into cupcake holes. Use reserved cupcake pieces to top the whipped cream centers. Place filled cupcakes on prepared baking sheet.

7. *Ganache:* In a small heavy saucepan, heat cream over medium-low heat until it just starts to boil. Remove from heat and add chocolate. Let stand for 3 to 4 minutes or until chocolate is soft and melting. Add butter and stir until chocolate is smooth.

8. Dip the top of each cupcake in ganache. Return to baking sheet and refrigerate until chocolate is set and firm to the touch.

Make Ahead
The cupcakes can be made up to 1 day ahead if kept covered and refrigerated.

Treasure Hunt!

Here's how to create your own unique treasure hunt that your children and their friends will love!

1. Begin from the end and work backwards. Figure out where you're going to "bury" the treasure, and what that treasure might be. Chocolate coins wrapped in gold foil, a bucket or box of assorted toys, stickers and candy (you can usually find big goody bags filled with an assortment of toys and candy at local party stores) or other age-appropriate trinkets will be heartily appreciated by your guests.

2. Once you have chosen an end location, begin planning the overall route. Consider the space in your home, including the yard, how the clues will flow depending on the route, and how long and complicated you want the route to be.

3. After setting your route, decide on the clues: small riddles, reverse writing, fill-in-the-blank letters for words, describing the next location, etc. Don't make the overall route and clues too long and difficult, or the children may get bored and won't be motivated to continue until the end. If you want to make a longer treasure hunt, it's a good idea to create a "rest stop" halfway through, with snacks and drinks to re-energize the kids for the rest of the hunt.

4. It may seem obvious, but make sure none of the children are around as you set up, or the game is for naught! It's nice to have two adults, so one can distract and entertain the children while the other sets up the treasure hunt.

Neighborhood Block Party

This menu is also great for a family reunion, down-home weekend or end-of-summer party.

Menu

Spicy Garlic Shrimp

SERVES 6
or can be multiplied
up to 4 times

These shrimp make great finger-food appetizers. They can also be tossed with cooked pasta or rice for a flavorful main dish.

Tips

Try tossing shrimp with chopped fresh herbs, such as parsley, oregano, basil, mint or tarragon, when returning shrimp to the sauce.

If multiplying this recipe, sauté the shrimp in batches in step 1; don't crowd the skillet.

2 tbsp	olive oil, divided	25 mL
1 lb	jumbo shrimp, peeled and deveined	500 g
4	cloves garlic, minced	4
$\frac{1}{4}$ tsp	salt	1 mL
Pinch	hot pepper flakes	Pinch
Pinch	ground cumin	Pinch
Pinch	freshly ground black pepper	Pinch
$\frac{1}{4}$ cup	dry white wine	50 mL
1	lemon, cut into wedges	1

1. In a large skillet, heat 1 tbsp (15 mL) of the oil over high heat. Sauté shrimp for 2 to 3 minutes or until pink and opaque. Remove shrimp to a plate and keep warm.

2. Reduce heat to medium and add remaining oil to skillet. Add garlic, salt, hot pepper flakes, cumin and black pepper; sauté for about 3 minutes or until garlic is light golden. Increase heat to high, add wine and bring to a boil. Boil for about 5 minutes or until liquid has reduced by half. Add shrimp and remove from heat. Toss to coat with sauce.

3. Serve shrimp hot or at room temperature, garnished with lemon wedges.

Roasted Balsamic Chicken

SERVES 6
or can be multiplied
up to 4 times

*There really isn't
anything better than
perfectly roasted
chicken. Of course, you
can always buy your
favorite roasted chicken
from the grocery store.*

Tip

Make this recipe with
chicken thighs or
drumsticks in place
of the breasts. Buy
2 pieces per person,
and roast until juices
run clear when chicken
is pierced and a meat
thermometer inserted
in the thickest part
registers 165°F (74°C).

Make Ahead

The chicken can be
made a day ahead
if refrigerated in an
airtight container.
Reheat in a covered
baking dish in a 325°F
(160°C) oven until
heated through, about
18 minutes. To reheat
sauce, place in a small
saucepan over medium
heat and simmer for
3 minutes.

- **Preheat oven to 375°F (190°C)**
- **Rimmed baking sheet, sprayed with nonstick cooking spray**

¾ cup	olive oil	175 mL
¾ cup	balsamic vinegar	175 mL
6	cloves garlic, minced	6
1	large onion, finely chopped	1
2 tbsp	chopped fresh rosemary	25 mL
2 tbsp	chopped fresh flat-leaf (Italian) parsley	25 mL
2 tsp	salt	10 mL
2 tsp	freshly ground black pepper	10 mL
6	bone-in skin-on chicken breasts	6
2 cups	Quick Chicken Stock (page 223) or reduced-sodium chicken broth	500 mL
2 tsp	granulated sugar	10 mL

1. In a bowl, combine oil, vinegar, garlic, onion, rosemary, parsley, salt and pepper. Add chicken, turning to coat all sides. Cover and refrigerate for at least 2 hours or overnight, turning once.

2. Remove chicken from marinade. Strain marinade and reserve. Place chicken on prepared baking sheet, skin side up.

3. Roast chicken in preheated oven for about 35 minutes or until chicken is no longer pink inside and a meat thermometer inserted in the thickest part registers 165°F (74°C).

4. Meanwhile, in a medium saucepan, combine reserved marinade, stock and sugar; bring to a boil over high heat. Reduce heat to medium-high and boil for about 10 minutes or until reduced by half.

5. Spoon sauce over chicken and serve hot.

Variation

▶ This same marinade and method can be used with 1 large (5- to 6-lb/2.5 to 3 kg) or 2 small (2½- to 3-lb/1.25 to 1.5 kg) whole roasting chickens. Roast a large chicken for 2 to 2½ hours, or two small chickens for 1 to 1¾ hours, until a meat thermometer inserted in the thickest part of the thigh registers 165°F (74°C).

Red and Green Garden Salad with Sourdough Croutons and Creamy Vinaigrette

SERVES 6
or can be multiplied up to 4 times

Alter this versatile salad by substituting whatever vegetables are at their peak. The croutons and dressing complement just about anything.

Make Ahead

Assemble the salad in its serving bowl the evening before your party, lay a damp paper towel over top and cover with plastic wrap. Keep refrigerated until ready to serve. Toss with dressing and croutons right before serving.

3	plum (Roma) tomatoes, cut into wedges	3
1	head red leaf lettuce, chopped	1
1	small head radicchio, chopped	1
½	cucumber, sliced	½
½ cup	Creamy Vinaigrette (see recipe, opposite)	125 mL
1 to 2 cups	Sourdough Croutons (see recipe, opposite)	250 to 500 mL

1. In a large bowl, combine tomatoes, red leaf lettuce, radicchio and cucumber. Toss with dressing and croutons just before serving.

Variation

▸ For garlic croutons, replace the salt with garlic salt.

Creamy Vinaigrette

⅓ cup	extra virgin olive oil	75 mL
2 tbsp	seasoned rice vinegar	25 mL
2 tsp	freshly squeezed lemon juice	10 mL
2 tsp	Dijon mustard	10 mL
	Salt and freshly ground black pepper	

**MAKES ABOUT
½ CUP (125 ML)**
or can be multiplied
up to 4 times

1. In a food processor or blender, process oil, vinegar, lemon juice, mustard and salt and pepper to taste until smooth.

2. Use right away or transfer to an airtight container and refrigerate for up to 4 days. If oil has solidified, let warm to room temperature and shake well before using.

Easy Extras

▸ Add a clove of garlic or ¼ cup (50 mL) fresh basil leaves to the dressing before blending. If making ahead, do not add garlic or fresh herbs until up to 2 hours before serving.

This dressing can be made in just minutes and tastes so much more delicious than any store-bought dressing. Feel free to add and substitute depending on what you have on hand. Other vinegars, flavored oils or seasonings can all work well.

Sourdough Croutons

¼ cup	extra virgin olive oil	50 mL
2 cups	cubed white sourdough bread	500 mL
	Salt and freshly ground black pepper	

**MAKES 2 CUPS
(500 ML)**
or can be multiplied
up to 4 times

1. In a large skillet, heat oil over medium heat. Sauté bread cubes until golden brown on all sides. Transfer to a plate lined with paper towels and let cool. Season to taste with salt and pepper.

Easy Extra

▸ Toss croutons with ½ tsp (2 mL) of any type of dried herb before cooking.

Once you begin making your own croutons, you'll never want to purchase them again. They add an easy homemade touch to any salad.

Make Ahead

Croutons can be made up to 2 days ahead if stored in an airtight container at room temperature.

Pasta with Green Beans and Sweet Peppers

SERVES 6
or can be multiplied up to 4 times

Gemelli means "twin" in Italian and resembles twisted rope. Cellentani is a hollow, corkscrew-shaped pasta. Penne is a tube-shaped pasta with diagonally cut ends. Any of the three makes a beautiful salad. This dish can be served hot, at room temperature or chilled.

Tip

If you can't find gemelli or cellentani, fusilli, radiatore, rotelli or ziti are all good substitutions.

1 lb	gemelli, cellentani or penne pasta	500 g
¼ cup	olive oil, divided	50 mL
12 oz	petite green beans or haricots verts, trimmed and halved	375 g
1	small red onion, thinly sliced	1
2	yellow bell peppers, thinly sliced	1
½ cup	chopped fresh basil	12 mL
	Salt and freshly ground black pepper	

1. Bring a large pot of salted water to a boil over high heat. Cook pasta according to package directions. Drain and toss with 1 tbsp (15 mL) of the olive oil. Set aside.

2. Meanwhile, bring a medium pot of water to a boil over high heat. Cook green beans until just tender, about 2 minutes. Drain under cool running water and set aside.

3. In a large skillet, heat the remaining oil over medium-high heat. Sauté onion for about 7 minutes or until soft and translucent. Add yellow peppers and sauté for 2 minutes. Add green beans, basil and salt and pepper to taste. Sauté until green beans are heated through, about 2 minutes.

4. Toss vegetables with pasta.

Who Doesn't Like Macaroni and Cheese?

The cheesy, starchy goodness known as mac and cheese evokes the feeling of home with one bite. It's no wonder that people of all culinary persuasions seem to love this dish. It is said that the name of the pasta, macaroni, originated in Italy when an early sovereign, upon trying the dish, exclaimed, "Maccheroni!" meaning "How very dear!" It has been served in Italian homes, restaurants and inns for more than 500 years.

Macaroni and cheese slowly made its way to North America around the 18th century, but was not popularized until 1802, when the third president of the United States, Thomas Jefferson, served it for the first time in the White House.

If you want to jazz up your macaroni and cheese, there is a variety of tried-and-true riffs on the basic combination. Instead of using the traditional Cheddar cheese, try using another great melting cheese, like a nutty Gruyère or a mild Gorgonzola. You can also sprinkle in some fresh herbs (thyme and tarragon work well) or cubed smoked ham. Or, just before serving, crumble warm cooked bacon over the top of a casserole dish full of macaroni and cheese and broil it until just browned on top. Another trick for dressing up your macaroni and cheese is to spread it evenly in a casserole dish, top it off with seasoned bread crumbs and bake it in the oven.

Rustic Apple Pie

SERVES 6
or can be multiplied up to 4 times

Master this simple, versatile pie and you'll be glad you did. The crust is fail-safe and works for innumerable fillings.

Tips

Make this recipe much simpler by using premade pie dough, found in your grocer's refrigerated section.

Buy apples already sliced in your grocer's produce section, and don't worry about the peels — a little skin never hurt anyone, and after all, this pie is "rustic."

Serve with cream, freshly whipped with a touch of sugar.

Make Ahead

The dough can be made and rolled out up to 3 days in advance if wrapped well with plastic wrap and stored in the refrigerator.

The pie can be made up to 2 days ahead. Store at room temperature in an airtight container or wrapped in plastic wrap.

- 10-inch (25 cm) pie plate

Crust

1 1/3 cups	all-purpose flour	325 mL
2 tbsp	granulated sugar	25 mL
1/2 tsp	salt	2 mL
7 tbsp	cold unsalted butter, cut into small pieces	105 mL
1	egg yolk	1
3 tbsp	ice water	45 mL

Filling

2 lbs	Granny Smith or pippin apples, peeled and thinly sliced	1 kg
2 tbsp	freshly squeezed lemon juice	25 mL
1/2 tsp	ground cinnamon	2 mL
3	eggs	3
1/2 cup	packed light brown sugar	125 mL
1/2 cup	heavy or whipping (35%) cream	125 mL
1/2 tsp	vanilla extract	2 mL
1/2 cup	raspberries	125 mL

1. *Crust:* In a food processor, pulse flour, sugar, and salt a few times to combine. Add butter and pulse until mixture resembles coarse cornmeal.

2. Whisk together egg yolk and water and sprinkle over flour mixture. Pulse just until mixture comes together to form a dough. Press dough into a ball and wrap in plastic wrap. Refrigerate for 30 minutes.

3. Meanwhile, preheat oven to 400°F (200°C). On a lightly floured work surface, roll out dough to 1/8 inch (3 mm) thick. Carefully place dough in pie plate. Cut off any overhanging dough and crimp edges.

4. *Filling:* Sprinkle apple slices with lemon juice and cinnamon and arrange in pastry shell.

5. In a bowl, using an electric mixer, beat eggs and brown sugar until pale and creamy. Beat in cream and vanilla. Pour over apples.

6. Bake for 20 minutes. Reduce heat to 350°F (180°C) and bake for 25 minutes or until filling is set. Let cool before garnishing with raspberries and slicing.

Birthday for a Special Mom

This subtly sophisticated menu will be a special treat for any treasured women in your life ... or treasured men, too.

Menu

Shaved Artichoke and Bibb Lettuce Salad

SERVES 6
or can be multiplied up to 4 times

This beautiful salad features the unexpected addition of raw artichoke.

Make Ahead

Without the artichoke, the dressing can be made up to 1 day ahead if kept refrigerated in an airtight container.

	Juice of 2 lemons, divided	
1	large artichoke	1
1	clove garlic	1
¼ cup	extra virgin olive oil	50 mL
1 tbsp	Dijon mustard	15 mL
	Salt and freshly ground black pepper	
1	head Bibb lettuce, roughly torn	1
1	bunch radishes, thinly sliced	1
¼ cup	fresh tarragon, roughly chopped	50 mL
2 oz	Parmigiano-Reggiano cheese, shaved	60 g

1. In a small bowl, combine the juice of 1 of the lemons with 1 cup (250 mL) cold water. Snap off outer leaves of artichoke and pare down to the heart. Scoop out choke with a spoon and place heart in prepared lemon water.

2. In a food processor or blender, process the remaining lemon juice, garlic, oil and mustard until creamy. Season to taste with salt and pepper.

3. Divide lettuce, radishes and tarragon among salad plates.

4. Remove the artichoke heart from the water and, using a vegetable peeler, slice very thinly. Place artichoke in dressing and toss to coat. Spoon over salads. Garnish with shaved cheese.

How to Clean an Artichoke

Although preparing an artichoke might seem like a daunting task, it's not as difficult as it looks, and it's always worth the effort. It can be quite relaxing if you have more than one to do. Nothing is more delicious than a perfectly cooked fresh artichoke. Use it as a bowl for a crab salad or caviar and crème fraîche, or just fill it with a mustard-infused mayonnaise for dipping, which you can easily make with bottled condiments. Another dipping possibility is warm garlic oil with fresh thyme, which is my favorite way to show off this versatile vegetable for a lunch appetizer.

Here are some simple steps to cleaning an artichoke:

1. Cut ¾ inch (2 cm) off the top of the artichoke and remove the very end of the stem.
2. Peel the outermost layer of the stem from the end up; when you get to the round of the artichoke, continue peeling off the small, hard bottom leaves.
3. With a pair of scissors, cut off the tips of each leaf around the whole artichoke.
4. Cut the artichoke in half through the heart and scoop out the chokes (the fuzzy purple and white insides). Or, if you're planning to use it as a bowl, pry apart leaves to expose the pale green leaves in the center. Pull out these leaves, then scrape out the choke with a spoon. Squeeze lemon juice inside to keep it from browning.
5. Steam the artichokes for 45 to 60 minutes, depending on the size. When they have completely changed color to a bright green and you can easily pull out the leaves, the artichoke is ready. For added flavor, cook your artichokes in a court-bouillon: Add some lemon juice, white wine vinegar or another acidic liquid to a pot of water, along with the aromatics of your choice (such as herbs, spices or peppercorns) to create a flavorful cooking liquid.

Chicken Eggplant Rollups

*These rollups are
much easier than
making lasagna, but
no less impressive.
Use crumbled Italian
sausage instead of or in
addition to the chicken,
if you wish.*

Tip

Rotisserie-roasted
chickens have great
flavor and are perfect
for this recipe.

Make Ahead

Prepare through
step 4, cover and
refrigerate for up to
1 day. Bake just before
serving, increasing the
baking time by about
5 minutes.

- Preheat oven to 350°F (180°C)
- 13- by 9-inch (33 by 23 cm) baking dish, sprayed with nonstick cooking spray

1 tbsp	olive oil (approx.)	15 mL
2	large eggplants, cut lengthwise into $\frac{1}{4}$-inch (0.5 cm) thick slices	2
1	jar (24 oz/750 mL) prepared marinara sauce	1
2 cups	shredded cooked chicken	500 mL
2 cups	shredded mozzarella cheese, divided	500 mL
$\frac{1}{4}$ cup	chopped fresh basil	50 mL
1 tbsp	chopped fresh oregano	15 mL
	Salt and freshly ground black pepper	

1. In a large skillet, heat oil over medium-high heat. Cook eggplant slices, in batches as necessary, for 3 to 4 minutes or until light golden on each side. Transfer to a plate lined with paper towels and let cool. Add more oil between batches as necessary.

2. Spoon some marinara sauce into prepared baking dish so it just covers the bottom.

3. In a bowl, combine chicken, $1\frac{1}{2}$ cups (375 mL) of the mozzarella, basil and oregano. Season to taste with salt and pepper.

4. Divide chicken mixture among eggplant slices and roll up. Place in baking dish, seam side down, and spoon the remaining marinara sauce over top. Sprinkle with the remaining mozzarella.

5. Bake in preheated oven for 20 minutes or until cheese on top is melted and golden brown.

Asiago Asparagus

SERVES 6
or can be multiplied
up to 4 times

Asparagus is an elegant addition to any menu. This recipe is quick and delicious.

Tip

Thin asparagus needs much less time to cook — pencil-thin stalks cook in 20 seconds. Thicker asparagus has stringy, woody ends; snap off the ends and use a vegetable peeler to peel the outer layer of the stalk.

Make Ahead

Blanch the asparagus up to 1 day before and store in an airtight container in the refrigerator.

1½ lbs	asparagus, tough ends trimmed and stalks peeled	750 g
2 tbsp	unsalted butter	25 mL
2 tbsp	olive oil	25 mL
	Salt and freshly ground black pepper	
½ cup	shredded Asiago cheese	125 mL

1. Bring a large pot of salted water to a boil over high heat. Blanch asparagus for 20 to 60 seconds, depending upon size, until tender-crisp. Drain and immediately plunge into a bowl or sink of ice water for a minute or two to stop the cooking process. Drain.

2. In a large skillet, heat butter and olive oil over medium-high heat until butter is melted and foamy. Add asparagus and sauté for about 3 minutes or until heated through. Season to taste with salt and pepper.

3. Arrange asparagus on a serving dish and pour the melted oil and butter from the pan over top. Sprinkle with Asiago.

Theme Menus • Birthday for a Special Mom

Orzo Salad with Fresh Herbs

Orzo is rice-shaped pasta about twice the size of a grain of rice. It makes an excellent and unusual substitute for rice, and works especially well in salads.

Tip

Riso (rice-shaped pasta, smaller than orzo), *acini di pepe* ("peppercorns"), *conchigliette* ("tiny conch shells"), *seme di melone* ("melon seeds"), *tripolini* ("little bows") or any miniature pasta can be used in place of the orzo.

Make Ahead

Orzo can be cooked up to 2 days ahead if drained, tossed with a little olive oil and refrigerated in an airtight container.

1 lb	orzo pasta	500 g
¼ cup	extra virgin olive oil	50 mL
2 tbsp	freshly squeezed lemon juice	25 mL
	Salt and freshly ground black pepper	
2 cups	chopped drained marinated artichoke hearts	500 mL
2 tbsp	finely chopped red onion	25 mL
1 tbsp	chopped fresh flat-leaf (Italian) parsley	15 mL
1 tbsp	chopped fresh dill	15 mL
	Grated zest of 1 lemon	

1. Bring a large pot of salted water to a boil over high heat. Cook pasta according to package directions. Drain and rinse under cool running water. Drain well.

2. In a large bowl, whisk together oil and lemon juice and toss with the pasta. Season to taste with salt and pepper. Stir in artichoke hearts, onion, parsley, dill and lemon zest. Serve at room temperature or chilled.

Ice Cream Terrine with Raspberry Sauce

SERVES 6 TO 8
or can be multiplied
up to 4 times

The perfect warm-weather dessert for any elegant meal. Garnish with fresh raspberries, whipped cream and mint leaves for an even more festive look.

- 9- by 5-inch (23 by 12.5 cm) loaf pan, lined with 2 layers of plastic wrap, allowing 4 inches (10 cm) of plastic to hang over the sides

1 pint	chocolate sorbet	500 mL
1 pint	vanilla ice cream	500 mL
1 pint	raspberry sorbet	500 mL
1 cup	chopped walnuts	250 mL
1	package (12 oz/340 g) frozen unsweetened raspberries, thawed	1
½ cup	granulated sugar	125 mL

1. Place chocolate sorbet in refrigerator for 15 minutes to soften.

2. Spread chocolate sorbet evenly in bottom of prepared loaf pan. Freeze for 15 minutes. Meanwhile, place vanilla ice cream in the refrigerator to soften.

3. Spread ice cream evenly on top of chocolate sorbet and freeze for 15 minutes. Meanwhile, place raspberry sorbet in the refrigerator to soften.

4. Spread raspberry sorbet evenly on top of ice cream. Sprinkle with walnuts and fold plastic wrap over top, pressing walnuts gently into surface of sorbet. Freeze for at least 2 hours or, for longer storage, overwrap tightly in foil, then place in a freezer bag and freeze for up to 3 weeks.

5. Meanwhile, in a food processor or blender, process raspberries and sugar until smooth. Pour through a strainer, pressing to extract as much sauce as possible from the solids. Discard solids. Use right away or place sauce in an airtight container and refrigerate for up to 3 days.

6. To serve, use the plastic overhang to lift the terrine from the pan. Remove the plastic wrap. Slice into servings and drizzle with raspberry sauce.

Variation

▸ The walnuts can be replaced with any of your favorite nuts, or with candied nuts.

Afternoon Tea

This menu would also work well for a sweet sixteen party or a retirement lunch for a co-worker. All of the recipes can be easily packed up to serve nearly anywhere.

Menu

Miniature Egg Salad Sandwiches

SERVES 6
or can be multiplied up to 4 times

Make Ahead
Egg salad can be made up to 2 days ahead if refrigerated in an airtight container.

6	eggs, hard-cooked, cooled, peeled and halved	6
3 tbsp	mayonnaise	45 mL
2 tsp	Dijon mustard	10 mL
	Salt and freshly ground pepper	
1	stalk celery, minced	1
¼ cup	minced red onion	50 mL
8	slices dark rye bread, crusts removed	8
1 cup	curly salad greens (such as frisée)	250 mL

1. Place egg yolks in a small bowl. Add mayonnaise, mustard and salt and pepper to taste. Mash with a fork until smooth.

2. Finely chop egg whites and stir into yolk mixture. Stir in celery and red onion.

3. Spread egg mixture on 4 pieces of bread. Top with salad greens and cover with remaining bread. Slice each sandwich in half, then cut each half into three "fingers."

Easy Extra
▸ Cook a couple of strips of bacon until crisp, crumble and stir into the egg salad.

Variation
▸ Just about any bread will work instead of the rye.

Italian Pasta Party
Antipasti Platter (page 398) and Penne with Pancetta and Winter Greens (page 401)

Grecian Get-Together
Garlic-Roasted Leg of Lamb (page 411) and Rice with Tomatoes and Peppers (page 412)

Turkish Twilight
Spiced Lamb Kebabs (page 417), Roasted Eggplant and Peppers (page 418)
and Carrot, Onion and Tomato Couscous (page 419)

African Ivory Coast
Grilled Cornish Game Hens with Lemon and Yogurt (page 424), Spiced Zucchini and Pepper Kebabs (page 423), Couscous with Raisins and Caramelized Onions (page 426) and Lemon Cumin Cookies (page 427)

Chinese Banquet
Ginger Shrimp Pot Stickers with Hot Mustard Dipping Sauce (page 428)

Cheddar Cumin Scones
with Black Forest Ham

**MAKES
6 SCONES**
or can be multiplied
up to 4 times

Make Ahead

Scones can be made up
to 2 weeks in advance
if wrapped tightly
in plastic wrap and
frozen, or up to 2 days
in advance if stored in
an airtight container at
room temperature. Slice
in half and add ham
before serving.

- **Preheat oven to 425°F (220°C)**
- **Baking sheet, sprayed with nonstick cooking spray**

2 cups	all-purpose flour	500 mL
1 tbsp	baking powder	15 mL
¾ tsp	salt	3 mL
½ tsp	freshly ground black pepper	2 mL
¼ tsp	ground cumin	1 mL
¼ cup	cold unsalted butter, cut into small pieces	50 mL
¾ cup	shredded Cheddar cheese	175 mL
½ cup	whole milk	125 mL
⅓ cup	heavy or whipping (35%) cream	75 mL
6 oz	Black Forest ham, thinly sliced	175 g

1. In a large bowl, sift together flour, baking powder, salt, pepper, and cumin. Using your fingertips or a pastry blender, blend in butter until mixture resembles coarse meal. Add Cheddar cheese and toss to coat. Sprinkle with milk and cream, stirring with a fork until just combined.

2. Turn out onto a floured work surface and knead lightly until the mixture forms a dough. Roll out dough into a ¾-inch (2 cm) thick square and cut into six 2½-inch (6 cm) squares. Place at least 1 inch (2.5 cm) apart on prepared baking sheet.

3. Bake in preheated oven for 12 to 15 minutes or until golden. Remove from baking sheet and let cool to room temperature on a wire rack.

4. Slice scones in half. Place 1 oz (30 g) ham on bottom half and cover with top half.

Variations

▹ Try replacing the ham with sliced turkey.

▹ Omit the cumin and cheese. Just after blending in the butter, add ¾ cup (175 mL) dried cranberries and ¼ tsp (1 mL) grated orange zest, then proceed as directed.

▹ Spread cut sides of scones with stone-ground mustard, if desired.

Crustless Cucumber and Tomato Sandwiches

Make Ahead

Sandwiches can be
made up to 1 hour
ahead if covered with
damp paper towels
and kept at room
temperature.

4 oz	whipped cream cheese	125 g
8	slices whole-grain white bread, crusts removed	8
	Salt and fresh ground black pepper	
½ cup	thinly sliced English cucumber	125 mL
2	tomatoes, thinly sliced	2
1 cup	watercress (optional)	250 mL

1. Spread cream cheese on 4 slices of bread and sprinkle
   with salt and pepper to taste. Arrange cucumber and
   tomatoes on top of cream cheese. Add watercress and top
   with remaining bread slices. Slice each sandwich in half,
   then cut each half diagonally into three pieces.

Variation

▶ Just about any bread will work for these sandwiches.

Butter Shortcakes with Berries and Cream

SERVES 6
or can be multiplied up to 4 times

Homemade shortcake, sweet berries and real whipped cream make this dessert an extraordinary treat.

Tip

To add subtle depth to this delicious dessert, add 1 tbsp (15 mL) of your favorite liqueur to the cream as you whip it.

- Preheat oven to 400°F (200°C)
- 2-inch (5 cm) round cookie cutter
- Baking sheet, lined with parchment paper

1²⁄₃ cups	all-purpose flour	400 mL
2 tsp	packed light brown sugar	10 mL
1 tsp	baking powder	5 mL
¼ cup	cold unsalted butter, cut into small pieces	50 mL
1	egg	1
⅓ cup	whole milk	75 mL
⅓ cup	heavy or whipping (35%) cream	75 mL
1 tbsp	granulated sugar	15 mL
1 cup	strawberries, sliced	250 mL
1 cup	raspberries, blueberries or a combination	250 mL

1. In a bowl, combine flour, brown sugar and baking powder. Using your fingers, rub in butter until mixture looks like coarse meal.

2. In a small bowl, whisk together egg and milk. Using a fork, stir into flour mixture until a soft dough forms.

3. Turn dough out onto a heavily floured surface and knead for 1 minute. Roll out dough to about 1 inch (2.5 cm) thick. Using the cookie cutter, cut out 6 rounds of dough, gathering up and rerolling the scraps, if necessary. Place at least 1 inch (2.5 cm) apart on prepared baking sheet.

4. Bake in preheated oven for 15 minutes or until golden. Let cool on baking sheet.

5. Meanwhile, in a clean bowl, using an electric mixer, whip cream and granulated sugar until soft peaks form, about 5 minutes. Cover and refrigerate until ready to serve, for up to 1 day.

6. Split shortcakes in half and place bottom halves on dessert dishes. Spoon berries and whipped cream on bottom halves. Cover with top halves and serve immediately.

Variation

▶ Make this recipe with whatever fruits are available and ripe: peaches, nectarines, mangos, kiwis, bananas, apricots, blackberries, tangerines or oranges.

Chocolate-Dipped Strawberries

SERVES 6
or can be multiplied
up to 4 times

Nothing is prettier that these beautiful chocolate-striped strawberries.

Tips

Instead of melting chocolate in the microwave, you can melt it in a heatproof bowl set over hot, not boiling water.

If you're multiplying the recipe, set the bowl of melted chocolate over a saucepan or bowl of warm water to make sure it doesn't set before you've drizzled all of the berries. Just be careful water doesn't drip into the chocolate

- Baking sheet, lined with waxed paper

7 oz	good-quality dark chocolate, chopped	210 g
1 tsp	shortening, divided	5 mL
18	large strawberries, rinsed and patted dry	18
7 oz	good-quality white chocolate, chopped	210 g

1. Place dark chocolate in a small microwave-safe bowl. Add $1/2$ tsp (2 mL) shortening and heat on High for 30-second intervals, stirring in between, until chocolate is melted and smooth.

2. Holding strawberries over the bowl of dark chocolate to catch drips, dip a fork into chocolate and drizzle back and forth over each strawberry to make stripes. Place on prepared baking sheet.

3. Place white chocolate in a small microwave-safe bowl. Add $1/2$ tsp (2 mL) shortening and heat on High for 30-second intervals, stirring in between, until chocolate is melted and smooth.

4. Holding dark chocolate–striped strawberries over the bowl of white chocolate to catch drips, dip a fork into white chocolate and drizzle back and forth over each strawberry to make stripes. Return to prepared baking sheet.

5. If serving within 8 hours, place strawberries in a cool spot to set; otherwise, wrap loosely in plastic wrap and refrigerate for up to 1 day.

Variation

▶ If strawberries are not in season, you can make these with dried apricots or chopped mango or pineapple. Pat fresh fruit dry before drizzling chocolate to make sure it sticks.

Choosing a Fine Tea

There are innumerable varieties of tea, including black, green, oolong, white, specialty and herb. Black and green teas may increase the body's antioxidant activity by up to 45% and are said to contain antibacterial agents that help fight off gum disease and cavities.

Black tea, most popular among Westerners, is made with leaves that have gone through a fermentation process before they are steamed and dried. Although the flavors of black tea vary greatly depending on the size of the leaf, it has a more dominant and aggressive flavor than those of green and oolong teas.

Green tea, most popular among Asians, is produced from leaves that are not fermented but only steamed and dried. The flavor is slightly bitter and has a hint of a fresh leafy taste.

Oolong tea is produced from partially fermented leaves and has a flavor and aroma that fall between those of black and green teas.

White tea, which used to be the most widely sought-after tea in China, is now one of the least popular teas. The leaves are fermented lightly and naturally, and produce a very pale color and almost flavorless brew.

Specialty teas can be flavored with various spices or floral additions, such as anise, cinnamon, cardamom, clove, ginger, nutmeg, vanilla, jasmine, lavender, orange or lemon peel or chrysanthemum blossoms.

Herbal teas are not considered real teas because they are not made from tea leaves but from an assortment of dried herbs, flowers or spices.

When determining what sort of tea will be best for your party, think about the various flavors and aromas that appeal to you and your guests, and which tea will best complement your menu. For opinionated tea-drinkers, loose-leaf teas are preferred. They yield a stronger and more aromatic flavor, although they tend to be more expensive than tea in individual serving bags.

Champagne and Caviar Party

This menu is meant for socializing. Place serving trays in different locations around your party space to encourage guest mingling.

Menu

Prosciutto-Wrapped Mango

SERVES 6 or can be multiplied up to 4 times

This is a very quick, easy recipe that you can make in less than 5 minutes.

Make Ahead
Assemble these the morning of your party; keep refrigerated in an airtight container until serving.

2	ripe mangos, firm but not hard	2
4 oz	thinly sliced prosciutto, cut lengthwise into 1-inch (2.5 cm) strips	125 g
18	fresh mint leaves	18

1. Peel mangos and cut into long slices. Wrap a strip of prosciutto around each mango slice and garnish each with a mint leaf.

Variation
▶ If mangos are not available, make this with honeydew melon instead.

Caviar on Blini with Crème Fraîche

SERVES 6
or can be multiplied
up to 4 times

This grownup, cocktail party–worthy treat is sure to impress. Just a touch of an exotic ingredient like caviar goes a long way to dress up humble blini.

Make Ahead

Blinis can be made up to 2 weeks in advance if layered in waxed paper, wrapped tightly in plastic wrap and frozen, or up to 4 days ahead if kept refrigerated. Reheat in a 300°F (150°C) oven until just warm before serving.

1/2 cup	all-purpose flour	125 mL
1/4 cup	buckwheat flour	50 mL
1/4 tsp	baking soda	1 mL
1/4 tsp	salt	1 mL
2	eggs, separated	2
1/2 cup	milk	125 mL
3 tbsp	unsalted butter, melted	45 mL
1 tbsp	vegetable oil	15 mL
2 oz	black paddlefish caviar	60 g
1/2 cup	crème fraîche	125 mL
1 tbsp	chopped fresh chives	15 mL

1. In a large bowl, whisk together all-purpose flour, buckwheat flour, baking soda and salt.

2. In a small bowl, whisk together egg yolks, milk and butter. Whisk into dry ingredients and set aside.

3. In another bowl, using an electric mixer, beat egg whites until they hold soft peaks. Fold into flour mixture.

4. Heat a nonstick skillet over medium-high heat. Lightly brush pan with a little oil. Working in batches, spoon in a generous tablespoon (15 mL) of batter for each blini. Cook for about 1 minute or until surface bubbles. Flip and cook for 1 minute. Transfer to a serving dish. Repeat with remaining batter, brushing skillet with oil between batches as necessary.

5. Serve blini topped with caviar, crème fraîche and chives.

Variations

▸ Serve with thinly sliced smoked salmon for a more filling appetizer.

▸ Garnish with finely minced red onion or hard-cooked egg instead of the caviar.

Lobster Ceviche with Grilled Fennel

Serve this elegant dish in martini glasses for great visual impact.

Tip

Be sure to lightly steam the lobster to rare doneness so it doesn't get tough and rubbery once marinated in the lime and lemon juice.

1 lb	shelled steamed lobster meat, cut into 1/2-inch (1 cm) pieces (see tip, at left)	500 g
1/4 cup	freshly squeezed lime juice	50 mL
1/4 cup	freshly squeezed lemon juice	50 mL
2	fennel bulbs, fronds removed and bulbs thinly sliced	2
1/3 cup	extra virgin olive oil, divided	75 mL
	Salt and freshly ground black pepper	
1/4 cup	thinly sliced green onions	50 mL
1	large English cucumber, halved lengthwise and thinly sliced	1
Pinch	granulated sugar (optional)	Pinch
1/3 cup	chopped fresh mint	75 mL
	Thin strips of lemon and lime zest	

1. In a non-reactive bowl, combine lobster, lime juice and lemon juice. Cover and refrigerate for 1 1/2 hours.

2. Preheat barbecue grill to high (or heat a grill pan over medium-high heat). Brush fennel slices with half the oil and sprinkle with salt and pepper to taste. Grill for 1 to 2 minutes per side, turning once, until tender.

3. Remove lobster mixture from refrigerator and stir in grilled fennel, the remaining oil, green onions and cucumber. Taste and adjust seasoning with salt and pepper, if desired. If taste is too tart, stir in granulated sugar. Cover and refrigerate for 30 minutes.

4. Serve garnished with mint, lemon peel and lime zest.

How to Cook a Live Lobster

Please be warned that if you are a card-carrying member of PETA, you may want to avoid these cooking instructions. I grew up in San Francisco, where, down at the piers by the San Francisco Bay, you could buy freshly caught Dungeness crab. I thought crab was heaven on earth until I discovered lobster. In the summers, we went to Catalina Island, where we bought live spiny lobsters and my father broiled them to perfection. When I grew up, I went east and experienced Maine lobster, thereby achieving nirvana. I later attended a French cooking school and learned the most efficient and humane way to prepare the lobster for his destiny:

1. Start with a large stockpot of vigorously boiling water. Add lots of sea salt, freshly squeezed lemon juice, a bay leaf and white peppercorns.
2. Place your live lobster on a cutting board and hold the back and tail down firmly with one hand. Wear a glove if you are squeamish.
3. With your free hand, hold a large, sharp knife vertically so the tip is barely touching the neck of the lobster. With one quick motion, plunge the knife into the back of the lobster's neck, then carefully drop the lobster head-first into the boiling water. Cover the pot with a tight-fitting lid.
4. Boil the lobster for about 9 to 10 minutes per pound (500 g), no longer. Respect the lobster by not overcooking it. Serve with clarified butter.

Bay Shrimp Crostini

SERVES 6
or can be multiplied
up to 4 times

Tip

Use packaged crostini to cut the prep time in half.

Make Ahead

Baked crostini can be stored in an airtight container at room temperature for up to 2 days.

• **Preheat oven to 350°F (180°C)**

1	French baguette, cut diagonally into ¼-inch (0.5 cm) thick slices	1
5 tbsp	olive oil, divided	75 mL
12 oz	bay shrimp, peeled, deveined and cooked	375 g
12	cherry or pear tomatoes, cut into small wedges	12
2 tbsp	thinly sliced fresh basil	25 mL
	Salt and fresh ground black pepper	

1. Using a pastry brush, lightly brush both sides of bread slices with 4 tbsp (60 mL) of the oil. Place on baking sheets and bake in preheated oven for about 8 minutes or until light golden brown. Let cool.

2. In a bowl, toss together shrimp, tomatoes, basil and the remaining oil. Place spoonfuls of the shrimp mixture on top of crostini.

Death-by-Chocolate Cookies

Theme Menus • Champagne and Caviar Party

**MAKES
24 COOKIES**
or can be multiplied
up to 4 times

*A real chocolate lover's
cookie!*

Tips

Double the recipe and
make gift packages of
cookies for your guests
to take home.

If baking multiple
batches, bake one sheet
at a time. Let baking
sheets cool between
batches.

Make Ahead

Store cookies between
layers of waxed paper
in an airtight container
at room temperature
for up to 4 days or in
the freezer for up to
1 week.

- Preheat oven to 350°F (180°C)
- 2 baking sheets, sprayed with nonstick cooking spray
  or lined with parchment

8 oz	good-quality dark chocolate (70% to 80% cacao), chopped	250 g
1½ cups	all-purpose flour	375 mL
3 tbsp	unsweetened cocoa powder	45 mL
¼ tsp	baking powder	1 mL
¼ tsp	salt	1 mL
1 cup	granulated sugar	250 mL
⅓ cup	unsalted butter, softened	75 mL
2	eggs	2
1½ tsp	vanilla extract	7 mL
1 cup	white chocolate chips	250 mL
1 cup	chopped walnuts (optional)	250 mL

1. Place dark chocolate in a microwave-safe bowl and heat on High for 30-second intervals, stirring in between, until chocolate is melted and smooth. Set aside.

2. In a bowl, stir together flour, cocoa powder, baking powder and salt. Set aside.

3. In another bowl, using an electric mixer, beat sugar and butter until well combined. Add eggs, one at a time, beating well after each addition. Continue beating until mixture is pale and creamy, about 5 minutes. Beat in melted chocolate and vanilla until just blended. Fold in flour mixture. Fold in white chocolate chips and walnuts (if using).

4. Form dough into balls of about 2 tbsp (25 mL) each and place 2 inches (5 cm) apart on prepared baking sheets, flattening cookies with your hand to 3 inches (7.5 cm) across.

5. Bake in preheated oven for 10 to 12 minutes or until cooked through. Let cool completely on baking sheets on wire racks.

Wine and Cheese Tasting

This menu was designed with white wines in mind. To serve six people, purchase one bottle of Chardonnay or Pinot Grigio, one bottle of Chenin Blanc, Fumé Blanc or Sauvignon Blanc, and one bottle of Gewürztraminer or Riesling. Take advantage of your local wine merchant's knowledge and ask for suggestions.

For an elegant end to the evening, serve small glasses of port with a little bite of Roquefort, Gorgonzola, Stilton or another fine blue cheese.

Menu

Spiced Nuts with Dried Fruit

SERVES 6 TO 8
or can be multiplied up to 4 times

Use your favorite nuts and dried fruits in this recipe.

Tips

The spiced fruits and nuts should be served warm for the best flavor.

If you use salted nuts, you may omit the salt.

2 tbsp	canola oil	25 mL
1/3 cup	whole almonds	75 mL
1/3 cup	whole cashews	75 mL
1/4 cup	whole pistachios	50 mL
1/4 cup	dates, pitted and halved	50 mL
1/4 cup	dried apricots, cut into quarters	50 mL
1/4 cup	dried cranberries	50 mL
1/2 tsp	ground cumin	2 mL
3 tbsp	roughly chopped fresh cilantro	45 mL
1 1/2 tsp	grated orange zest	7 mL
Pinch	cayenne pepper	Pinch
	Salt and freshly ground black pepper	

1. In a large skillet, heat oil over medium heat. Add almonds, cashews, pistachios, dates, apricots, cranberries and cumin; toss to coat with oil. Toast, stirring constantly, until apricots and nuts begin to change color and smell toasty.

2. Remove pan from heat and stir in cilantro, orange zest and cayenne. Season to taste with salt and pepper.

Cheese Board

SERVES 6 TO 8
or can be multiplied
up to 4 times

*Serve mild-tasting
cheeses, as strongly
flavored ones will
overpower most wines.
Buy very good-quality
cheeses and let
them come to room
temperature before
serving.*

Tip

Make use of the cheese
counter in your local
gourmet store. Ask them
to help you choose a
good hard cheese, a
soft ripened cheese,
a soft goat cheese and
a semi-hard cheese.

4 oz	Asiago, Parmigiano-Reggiano, Grana Padano, dry Monterey Jack or Gruyère cheese, very coarsely crumbled	125 g
4 oz	Brie, Bûcheron, Camembert or Pavé d'Affinois cheese	125 g
4 oz	chèvre or Boursin cheese	125 g
4 oz	aged Cheddar or Swiss cheese, sliced	125 g

1. Arrange cheeses on a serving plate or cheese board with small knives and spreaders.

Bread and Cracker Assortment

SERVES 6 TO 8
or can be multiplied
up to 4 times

*Bread and crackers
serve a dual purpose:
they cleanse the palette
while also serving as a
vessel for the cheese.*

Tip

Look for sweet tortas
from Spain. These
are fried flatbread
crackers with honey
and aniseed, and are
delightfully flavorful.

1	baguette, sliced	1
1	small loaf walnut bread, sliced	1
1	package (4$\frac{1}{2}$ oz/128 g) water crackers	1
1	package (3$\frac{1}{2}$ oz/100 g) grissini (thin breadsticks) or crostini	1

1. Arrange breads and crackers in a shallow bowl or basket.

Theme Menus • Wine and Cheese Tasting

Fresh Fruit Assortment

The perfect foil to a rich cheese, crisp fruit is essential to a wine and cheese party.

Tips

If fresh figs aren't available, then dried figs or even a small bowl of fig jam or compote are good substitutions.

Quince paste is another readily available substitute for fresh figs, and is a traditional paring with wine and cheese.

2	Bosc or Anjou pears, sliced	2
2	Gala or Fuji apples, sliced	2
1 tbsp	freshly squeezed lemon juice	15 mL
1 tbsp	water	15 mL
1	bunch red or green grapes	1
12	fresh figs, such as Adriatic or Calimyrna (green), Turkey (brown) or Mission (purple-black), halved lengthwise	12

1. Place pear and apple slices in two separate bowls. Combine lemon juice and water; lightly sprinkle over cut fruit to prevent it from turning brown; toss to coat evenly. Arrange pears, apples, grapes and figs on a board or platter.

Baby Greens Salad

SERVES 6 TO 8
or can be multiplied
up to 4 times

Use this recipe as a base and add any vegetables you like, or some grilled shrimp for protein.

⅓ cup	olive oil	75 mL
2 tbsp	white balsamic vinegar	25 mL
2 tsp	Dijon mustard	10 mL
1	shallot, minced	1
	Salt and freshly ground black pepper	
12 oz	baby salad greens	375 g
1	English cucumber, sliced	1
1½ cups	cherry tomatoes, halved	375 mL

1. In a large salad bowl, whisk oil, vinegar and mustard until creamy. Stir in shallot and season to taste with salt and pepper. Add greens, cucumber and tomatoes; toss to coat.

A Party of Three Wines

Buying the right kinds of wine for a party can seem overwhelming, especially if you aren't pairing it with a specific meal but are just looking for a variety that will suit both food and guests. First off, it's good to know this rule of thumb: when in doubt, serve white wine with fish and chicken and red wine with red meats (the flavor profiles just work better this way, trust me).

It's important to have wine that complements your food but doesn't overpower it — you want your guests to feel that the wine is enhancing their meal. If you are having trouble choosing wines, ask a knowledgeable wine merchant to help you out. A wine steward can help you find good-quality, affordable wines that will suit budget and guests. There are many excellent $10 to $15 bottles of wine from California, Canada, Australia or France.

But, honestly, wine is about what you like to taste. I have personally never met a bottle of red wine I didn't like. (I wonder if my editor will let that line stay in.)

For this wine-tasting menu, I'd start with a very cold Fumé Blanc, move on to a Chardonnay and serve a Pinot Grigio with the salad. Try topping the salad with some sautéed garlicky shrimp or cubes of a lovely Serrano ham.

Or as Julia Child always toasted, bon appétit!

Girls' Night In

Serve this menu when you have the girls over for movie night, or when your teenage daughter invites her friends for a sleepover.

Menu

Rock Shrimp Salad Wraps

SERVES 6
or can be multiplied up to 4 times

These wonderfully tart and crunchy wraps make for perfect, filling finger food. Or turn the shrimp mixture into a main-course salad, and serve over a bed of chopped lettuce.

Make Ahead

You can prepare all the ingredients for this salad the day before, store everything in separate airtight containers in the refrigerator and toss together right before serving.

2	cloves garlic	2
1/3 cup	extra virgin olive oil	75 mL
3 tbsp	freshly squeezed lime juice	45 mL
Pinch	cayenne pepper, or to taste	Pinch
	Salt and freshly ground black pepper	
1 1/2 lbs	cooked rock shrimp	750 g
4	green onions, thinly sliced	4
2	stalks celery, thinly sliced	2
1	small jicama, peeled and diced	1
1/4 cup	finely chopped fresh mint	50 mL
1/4 cup	finely chopped fresh cilantro	50 mL
1	head limestone or butter lettuce	1

1. In a food processor or blender, process garlic, oil, lime juice and cayenne until creamy. Season to taste with salt and pepper.

2. In a large bowl, combine shrimp, green onions, celery, jicama, mint and cilantro. Add dressing and toss to coat.

3. Serve shrimp mixture with lettuce leaves on the side to use as wrappers.

Variation

▸ Replace the shrimp with 2 cups (500 mL) shredded cooked chicken.

White Bean Rosemary Dip with French Baguette

SERVES 6
or can be multiplied
up to 4 times

This is a popular dip in Tuscany. It also makes a great sandwich spread with roasted turkey or vegetables.

Tip
Slice the fresh baguette just before serving.

Make Ahead
Dip can be made up to 4 days ahead if refrigerated in an airtight container.

3 cups	rinsed drained canned small white beans	750 mL
2 tbsp	chopped fresh flat-leaf (Italian) parsley	25 mL
2 tsp	chopped fresh rosemary	10 mL
1/4 tsp	salt	1 mL
Pinch	freshly ground black pepper	Pinch
Pinch	cayenne pepper, or to taste	Pinch
3 tbsp	plain yogurt	45 mL
2 tbsp	freshly squeezed lime juice	25 mL
1	French baguette, sliced	1

1. In a food processor or blender, process beans, parsley, rosemary, salt, black pepper, cayenne, yogurt and lime juice until smooth. Serve with sliced baguette.

Variation
▶ Replace the white beans with chickpeas (garbanzo beans) or black beans for a different taste.

Theme Menus ● Girls' Night In

Five More Things to Do with a Can of White Beans

1. Make soup: Drain and purée beans and stir into 2 cups (500 mL) chicken broth. Bring to a simmer over medium heat. Season to taste with salt and freshly ground black pepper.
2. Make a quick side dish: Sauté beans in a skillet until warm, add some freshly squeezed lemon juice, season to taste with salt and freshly ground black pepper, and serve a bed of creamy beans topped with a cooked salmon fillet.
3. Fix breakfast: Sauté beans with minced garlic and chopped onions and red and green bell peppers. Season to taste with salt and freshly ground black pepper. Pour in lightly beaten eggs and scramble eggs for a vegetable hash.
4. Prepare an easy entrée: For a white bean gratin, purée half the beans and stir in the remaining whole beans. Fold in sautéed minced garlic and chopped onions, and season to taste with salt and freshly ground black pepper. Spread in a casserole dish, top with shredded Gruyère cheese and bread crumbs, and scatter unsalted butter, cut into small pieces, over top. Bake at 375°F (190°C) for 15 minutes or until golden brown.
5. Make a hearty stuffing: Use the puréed dip as a stuffing for lamb chops. Butterfly the chops and spread the bean dip all over the inside. Roll the lamb up and, using kitchen twine, tie the chop so that the bean purée is contained. Bake at 350°F (180°C) until lamb reaches desired doneness.

Spinach and Ricotta-Stuffed Mushrooms

SERVES 6
or can be multiplied
up to 4 times

*These are so good you
might want to make
twice as many —
they'll go like candy.
You can try this basic
recipe with lots of
other fillings: other soft
cheeses, minced garlic,
pesto or sun-dried
tomatoes, for example.*

- **Preheat oven to 375°F (190°C)**
- **13- by 9-inch (33 by 23 cm) baking dish, sprayed with olive oil cooking spray**

1	package (5 oz/150 g) baby spinach	1
18	white or brown mushrooms (each about 2 inches/5 cm across)	18
	Olive oil cooking spray	
1	egg, lightly beaten	1
1⅓ cups	ricotta cheese	325 mL
⅓ cup	fine plain dry bread crumbs	75 mL
	Salt and freshly ground black pepper	
¾ cup	shredded mozzarella cheese	175 mL

1. Place spinach in a microwave-safe glass bowl and sprinkle with 1 tbsp (15 mL) water. Cover with waxed paper or vented plastic wrap and microwave on High for 30-second intervals until spinach has just wilted. Remove cover and let cool.

2. Remove stems from mushrooms and place caps upside down in prepared baking dish. Spray mushrooms lightly with cooking spray.

3. In a bowl, combine egg, ricotta and bread crumbs. Season to taste with salt and pepper.

4. Place spinach on several layers of paper towels or a clean kitchen towel and roll up, twisting to squeeze out excess liquid. Finely chop spinach. Add to ricotta mixture and stir to combine.

5. Fill mushrooms with ricotta mixture. Press mozzarella into the filling.

6. Bake in preheated oven for 8 minutes or until cheese is golden and filling is hot.

Variations

▶ You can use ½ cup (125 mL) finely chopped fresh basil in place of the spinach. Don't bother to cook it; just add it to the ricotta filling.

▶ Add ½ cup (125 mL) crumbled cooked spicy Italian sausage to the stuffing mixture.

Raspberry Lemon Sorbet

SERVES 6
or can be multiplied
up to 4 times

Served with almond or pirouette cookies, this dessert makes quite a statement.

Tips

The raspberries can be replaced by the same amount of frozen pitted cherries, chopped mangos or strawberries, for a different taste.

You can freeze this in an ice cream maker if your machine is suitable for sorbets.

2	packages (each 12 oz/340 g) unsweetened frozen raspberries	2
¾ cup	granulated sugar	175 mL
	Grated zest of 1 lemon	
2 tbsp	freshly squeezed lemon juice	25 mL
2 tbsp	water	25 mL

1. In a food processor or blender, purée raspberries, sugar, lemon juice and water until smooth. Add lemon zest and pulse 2 or 3 times to combine.

2. Transfer to an airtight container and freeze for at least 1 hour, until firm, or for up to 1 month. Let stand at room temperature for 10 minutes if it is too hard to scoop.

Friends' Game Night

Easy to make, easy to eat — the perfect party food for guests who are actively engaged in playing cards, board games, dominoes or charades, or even watching a movie.

Menu

Crudités with Cucumber Dip

SERVES 6
or can be multiplied up to 4 times

This is a very quick, easy recipe that you can make in less than 10 minutes.

Tip
Serve with pita chips or breadsticks in addition to the crudités.

1	large English cucumber, peeled and coarsely chopped	1
1/3 cup	coarsely chopped sweet onion	75 mL
1 1/2 cups	plain whole-milk yogurt	375 mL
	Salt and freshly ground black pepper	
6	stalks celery, cut into sticks	3
3	large carrots, cut into sticks	3
1	red or yellow bell pepper, cut into strips	1
1 cup	sugar snap peas, trimmed	250 mL

1. In a food processor or blender, pulse cucumber, onion and yogurt until mixture is somewhat smooth but still has some small chunks of cucumber. Transfer to an airtight container and refrigerate for at least 1 hour, until chilled, or overnight.

2. Arrange celery, carrots, bell pepper and sugar snap peas on a serving tray and serve with dip on the side.

Variation

▸ For a creamier dip, replace the yogurt with sour cream, or use half sour cream and half yogurt.

Mini Pepperoni Pizzas

SERVES 6
or can be multiplied
up to 4 times

These little pizzas are as easy as can be. Don't be shy about using convenient prepared foods, like the pitas and pizza sauce, to save some time on the day of the party. Jazz them up with a flavored sauce, different cheeses or a drizzle of pesto over the top.

Tips

For a more traditional pizza, purchase $1\frac{1}{2}$ lbs (750 g) prepared pizza dough and divide into 18 small balls. Roll out on a floured work surface to $\frac{1}{8}$ inch (3 mm) thick, add toppings and bake as directed.

Make these little pizzas with any of your favorite toppings. Try pesto, cooked bay shrimp and mozzarella cheese, or diced pineapple and Canadian bacon.

• **Preheat oven to 425°F (220°C)**

18	mini pitas (about 3 inches/7.5 cm)	18
$\frac{1}{2}$ cup	pizza sauce	125 mL
2 cups	shredded mozzarella cheese	500 mL
$\frac{1}{2}$ cup	thinly sliced small mushrooms	125 mL
8 oz	pepperoni, cut into thin strips	250 g

1. Top mini pitas with pizza sauce, mozzarella, mushrooms and pepperoni. Arrange on a baking sheet.

2. Bake in preheated oven for 4 to 5 minutes or until cheese starts to bubble and brown.

Cherry Tomato and Bocconcini Salad

Bocconcini are balls of mozzarella the size of large marbles. You can use cubed fresh mozzarella if it proves difficult to find. Serve this easy-to-make salad with sliced French bread or garlic crostini.

1 lb	bocconcini or fresh mozzarella cheese, drained and cubed	500 g
4 cups	cherry tomatoes	1 L
1 cup	kalamata or oil-cured olives (optional)	250 mL
1/2 cup	fresh basil leaves, chopped	125 mL
1/4 cup	extra virgin olive oil	50 mL
	Salt and freshly ground black pepper	

1. In a bowl, combine bocconcini, tomatoes, olives (if using), basil and oil. Season to taste with salt and pepper.

Variations

▸ Stretch this recipe by adding lots of sliced blanched asparagus or broccolini.

▸ This recipe can easily be made into a pasta salad by adding 1 lb (500 g) pasta, cooked and cooled.

Chicken Pesto Pasta Salad

This is a great recipe for using up leftovers. Shred last night's chicken and use any vegetables you happen to have around.

Tip

Instead of basil pesto, you can use sun-dried tomato pesto, walnut pesto, mint pesto or whatever else strikes your fancy.

1 lb	rigatoni, mostaccioli, penne or ziti pasta	500 g
2 tbsp	olive oil	25 mL
1/2 cup	basil pesto	125 mL
2 cups	shredded cooked chicken	500 mL
1/3 cup	sliced roasted red bell peppers	75 mL
1	can (14 to 19 oz/398 to 540 mL) chickpeas, drained and rinsed	1
	Salt and freshly ground black pepper	
5 oz	baby spinach	150 g

1. Bring a large pot of salted water to a boil over high heat. Cook pasta according to package directions.

2. Drain pasta, place in a large bowl and toss with oil. Add pesto and toss to coat. Stir in chicken, roasted peppers and chickpeas. Season to taste with salt and pepper. Cover and refrigerate for at least 1 hour, until chilled, or for up to 2 days.

3. Add spinach and toss to combine.

Spiced Popcorn Party Mix

SERVES 6
or can be multiplied
up to 4 times

• **Preheat oven to 325°F (160°C)**
• **2 large baking dishes or roasting pans, sprayed with nonstick cooking spray**

2	egg whites	2
2 tbsp	granulated sugar	25 mL
1 tbsp	paprika	15 mL
1 tsp	kosher salt	5 mL
$\frac{1}{4}$ tsp	cayenne pepper	1 mL
Pinch	ground cumin	Pinch
8 cups	freshly popped popcorn (unsalted and unbuttered)	2 L
2 cups	pretzel sticks	500 mL
1 cup	golden raisins	250 mL
1 cup	roasted salted almonds	250 mL
1 cup	roasted salted cashews	250 mL

1. In a large bowl, whisk together egg whites, sugar, paprika, salt, cayenne and cumin. Add popcorn, pretzels, raisins, almonds and cashews; toss to thoroughly coat.

2. Spread evenly in prepared baking dishes and bake in preheated oven for about 16 minutes or until coating is crisp.

3. Cover about 3 feet (90 cm) of a kitchen counter with waxed paper. Spread popcorn mixture on waxed paper and let cool completely. Store in an airtight container at room temperature for up to 3 days.

Oscar Night

Academy Awards night is big deal at my house. Friends come over, and I cook a lot of food. We drink Champagne, and we watch the show all day and all night. The next day, we have an "Oscar" hangover from watching for so long. (It couldn't be the Champagne!)

My best friend, Michael, a brilliant designer, has even been known to make Oscar Cheese. That's right: Cheddar cheese sculpted into a perfect Oscar statuette. Bette Davis would have howled! Oscar Night is not just the biggest night in Hollywood; it has become a worldwide tradition.

The recipes in this menu are all designed to be cooked before your guests arrive, and to be eaten with your fingers, if you like, in front of the television. I don't want you to miss a minute of the show!

Menu

My Favorite Blue Cheeses

Blue cheeses can be crumbly or creamy, with a taste ranging from mildly nutty to very earthy and salty. There are many excellent blues to choose from.

- Cashel Blue is an Irish cheese that gets creamier and richer-tasting as it ages.
- Fourme d'Ambert, one of France's oldest cheeses, is also one of my favorites. It's creamy enough to spread and has a mild taste.
- Gorgonzola Dolcelatte, from Italy, is a mild, buttery cheese that becomes stronger as it ages.
- Hook's Original Blue, from Wisconsin, is sweet, sharp and very intense.
- Humboldt Fog, from California, is a goat's milk blue (very light on the "blue"). It is moist and crumbly, with a lemony tang.
- Point Reyes Blue is another excellent California blue cheese, creamy and semi-firm in texture.
- Roquefort, as dictated by European law, is aged in caves in the Roquefort-sur-Soulzon area of France. It's crumbly, very tangy and strong.
- St. Agur Blue, a medium-strong French cheese, is pleasing to most palates.
- Stilton is *the* English cheese. Moist and firm, it gets smoother and more buttery as it ages.
- Valdeón is produced in Spain. Creamy, nutty and intensely flavored, it is also salty and just a little bit gritty.

Crab and Blue Cheese Bundles

SERVES 6
or can be multiplied up to 4 times

If you think you're making enough of these, double it — they go faster than hotcakes. Crabmeat comes in four basic varieties: lump or jumbo lump, *the solid white meat from the back legs;* backfin, *from the body and legs, with good color;* special, *which is shredded; and* claw meat, *small reddish-brown pieces of meat from the claws. Choose lump or backfin meat for this recipe.*

Make Ahead

Make these little bundles a day ahead and refrigerate in an airtight container. Reheat in a 325°F (160°C) oven before serving.

- Candy/deep-fry thermometer

12 oz	cooked lump crabmeat	375 g
¼ cup	crumbled blue cheese	50 mL
2 tbsp	finely chopped chives	25 mL
2 tbsp	mayonnaise	25 mL
2 tbsp	cream cheese, softened	25 mL
	Salt and freshly ground black pepper	
18	wonton wrappers	18
	Vegetable or canola oil	

1. In a bowl, combine crab, blue cheese, chives, mayonnaise and cream cheese. Season to taste with salt and pepper.

2. Place a generous teaspoon (5 mL) of crab mixture in the center of each wrapper, then lightly moisten the inside edges with water. Gather edges together to make little sacks and pinch to seal.

3. In a deep, heavy saucepan, heat 3 inches (7.5 cm) of oil over medium heat until it registers 350°F (180°C) on thermometer. Working in batches, fry crab bundles until golden, about 4 minutes. Using tongs or a slotted spoon, remove bundles to a plate lined with paper towels to drain before serving.

Variation

▸ You can make this dish with lobster or bay shrimp meat instead of the crab.

Creamy Tomato Soup

*This can be served
in demitasse cups
or espresso cups for
an easily portable
appetizer — you won't
even need spoons.*

Tip
Serve with breadsticks
or crostini perched on
the edge of each small
cup or bowl.

Make Ahead
This soup can be
refrigerated in an
airtight container for up
to 2 days or frozen for
up to 2 weeks. Thaw
in the refrigerator for
2 days before serving.
Reheat gently over
medium heat and keep
warm over low heat
until ready to serve.

1 tbsp	olive oil	15 mL
1	large leek, white and pale green parts only, sliced	1
1	stalk celery, chopped	1
1/2 cup	chopped onion	125 mL
3 cups	Quick Chicken Stock (page 223) or reduced-sodium chicken broth	750 mL
1	can (28 oz/796 mL) tomatoes	1
1/3 cup	heavy or whipping (35%) cream, at room temperature	75 mL
	Sea salt and freshly ground black pepper	
6	chives, snipped	6

1. In a large pot, heat oil over medium-high heat. Sauté leek, celery and onion for about 5 minutes or until onion is soft. Add stock and tomatoes; bring to a boil. Reduce heat to low, cover and simmer for 30 minutes.

2. Using an immersion blender, or in a food processor or blender in batches, purée soup until smooth. Return to the pot, if necessary, and stir in cream. Reheat over medium heat, stirring occasionally, until steaming. Season to taste with salt and pepper. Serve garnished with chives.

Shrimp and Pineapple Skewers

SERVES 6
or can be multiplied
up to 4 times

Grilled skewers make a filling but simple addition to your party menu. They're a cinch to prepare, and they'll go further towards satisfying hunger than a cheese puff would.

Tips
These skewers can also be cooked on a barbecue grill or on a foil-lined rimmed baking sheet under a broiler.

Serve these hot, warm or chilled.

Make Ahead
These skewers can be made up to 1 day in advance if stored in an airtight container in the refrigerator.

- **18 short wood or bamboo skewers (or 9 long ones, broken in half), soaked in water for 15 minutes**

2	cloves garlic, minced	2
1	small jalapeño pepper, seeded and minced	1
2 tbsp	chopped fresh cilantro	25 mL
1/2 tsp	salt	2 mL
Pinch	cayenne pepper	Pinch
3 tbsp	freshly squeezed lime juice	45 mL
3 tbsp	olive oil	45 mL
1 lb	jumbo shrimp, peeled and deveined	500 g
1/2	pineapple, peeled, cored and cut into 1 1/2-inch (4 cm) cubes	1/2

1. In a bowl, combine garlic, jalapeño, cilantro, salt, cayenne, lime juice and oil. Add shrimp and pineapple, tossing to combine. Let stand for 10 minutes.

2. Meanwhile, heat a grill pan over high heat.

3. Remove shrimp and pineapple from marinade, discarding marinade. Thread one piece of pineapple and one shrimp onto each skewer. Grill, in batches as necessary, for 1 to 2 minutes per side, turning once, until shrimp are pink and opaque.

Smoked Turkey on Sage Mini Scones

These crumbly, buttery scones are a delightful substitute for the usual white-bread finger sandwiches. Try other herbs for flavoring, or try folding in 1/2 cup (125 mL) shredded cheese with the milk.

Tip

Scones can be made up to 2 weeks in advance if wrapped tightly in plastic wrap and frozen, or up to 2 days in advance if stored in an airtight container at room temperature. Slice in half and fill before serving.

- **Preheat oven to 425°F (220°C)**
- **Baking sheet, sprayed with nonstick cooking spray**

2 cups	all-purpose flour	500 mL
1 tbsp	baking powder	15 mL
1/4 tsp	salt	1 mL
1/4 cup	cold unsalted butter, cut into small pieces	50 mL
1/3 cup	whole milk	75 mL
1/3 cup	heavy or whipping (35%) cream	75 mL
1 tbsp	finely chopped fresh sage	15 mL
1/4 cup	Dijon mustard	50 mL
2 tbsp	mayonnaise	25 mL
8 oz	smoked turkey breast, thinly sliced	250 g

1. In a large bowl, sift together flour, baking powder and salt. Using your fingertips or a pastry blender, blend in butter until mixture resembles coarse meal. Sprinkle with milk and cream, stirring with a fork until just combined.

2. Turn out onto a floured work surface and sprinkle with sage. Knead briefly, just until the mixture forms a dough. Roll out dough to a 3/4-inch (2 cm) thick square and cut into twelve 1 1/2-inch (4 cm) squares. Place at least 1 inch (2.5 cm) apart on prepared baking sheet.

3. Bake in preheated oven for 10 to 12 minutes or until golden. Remove from baking sheet and let cool to room temperature.

4. Combine mustard and mayonnaise. Slice scones in half, spread with a little mustard mixture and fill with sliced turkey.

Chocolate Fondue with Fruit, Cookies and Marshmallows

SERVES 6
or can be multiplied
up to 4 times

This dessert is one of my favorites. Guests young and old will love the chance to dip everything within reach into chocolate. Use cookies, fruits or cubes of cake as dipping tools — if you can dip it, you can eat it.

Tip

For extra decadence, look for fancy handmade square marshmallows available at some gourmet markets.

1	red apple, sliced	1
1 tbsp	freshly squeezed lemon juice	15 mL
2 cups	strawberries	500 mL
6	dried pineapple rings, halved	6
12	dried apricots	12
12	amaretti cookies	12
12	large marshmallows, preferably handmade (see tip, at left)	12
1½ cups	heavy or whipping (35%) cream	375 mL
1 lb	good-quality dark chocolate, finely chopped	500 g

1. Toss apple slices in lemon juice to prevent browning.

2. Place apple slices, strawberries, dried pineapple and apricots, cookies and marshmallows on a serving tray.

3. In a large, heavy saucepan, over medium heat, bring cream just to a boil. Immediately remove from heat and stir in chocolate until melted. Pour into a fondue pot or other heavy serving bowl. Keep warm over a tea light candle to serve.

Variations

▸ You can also use fresh or dried pears or mangos, orange segments or sliced bananas.

▸ Try cubed pound cake or angel food cake.

▸ Flavor the cream with 1 tsp (5 mL) vanilla, almond, coconut or orange extract before adding the chocolate.

Melting Chocolate

Though many people find melting chocolate to be a daunting task, it doesn't have to be. There is no need to pull out the double boiler or start worrying about how you're going to scrub burned chocolate off your pot. Melting chocolate is easy! All you need is a microwave-safe glass bowl, some good-quality chocolate chips or chocolate pieces and a microwave. To get perfectly melted chocolate, put the bowl of chocolate bits into the microwave and begin melting on High in 30-second intervals. Every 30 seconds, remove the bowl and stir the chocolate to prevent scorching. This should take 1 to 2 minutes, depending on how much chocolate you're melting. Yes, it's really that easy!

If you're dipping a large number of cookies or strawberries, for example, keep the chocolate warm in a fondue pot over a candle or in a small slow cooker on Low.

Super Bowl Party

Whether you and your friends have been out on the field yourselves or simply want to slouch on the couch to watch the big game on TV, you need fortification!

Menu

Artichoke Parmesan Dip

SERVES 6
or can be multiplied up to 4 times

This dip is also great served cold or at room temperature.

Tips

Serve with thick-cut potato chips, breadsticks or baguette slices.

If multiplying this recipe, you can prepare multiple batches at once, but it's best to heat it in single batches so you can serve one at a time, replacing empty dishes with new, warm dip.

- Preheat oven to 400°F (200°C)
- 4-cup (1 L) gratin dish or 8-inch (20 cm) square ovenproof dish

1	can (14 oz/398 mL) artichoke hearts, drained	1
6 oz	whipped cream cheese	175 g
1/2 cup	freshly grated Parmesan cheese, divided	125 mL
1/2 cup	sour cream	125 mL
1/4 tsp	dried thyme	1 mL
	Salt and freshly ground black pepper	

1. In a food processor, purée artichoke hearts, cream cheese, half the Parmesan, sour cream and thyme until nearly smooth. Season to taste with salt and pepper.

2. Spoon into ovenproof dish and sprinkle with the remaining Parmesan. Bake in preheated oven for 18 minutes or until cheese is golden brown and dip is heated through.

3. Serve warm or let cool, transfer to an airtight container and refrigerate for up to 2 days. Warm in the microwave for 1 minute before serving.

Buffalo Wings

SERVES 6
or can be multiplied up to 4 times

These wings are so great that you might want to make a double recipe. They are even good cold, right out of the fridge. I won't tell.

Tip
Be a traditionalist and serve these wings with celery sticks.

Make Ahead
You can make these wings the day before, toss with sauce, let cool completely and store in an airtight container in the refrigerator. To reheat, spread wings out in a single layer on a baking sheet and place in a 350°F (180°C) oven until hot, about 10 minutes.

• **Candy/deep-fry thermometer**

1 tbsp	salt	15 mL
1 tbsp	paprika	15 mL
1/2 tsp	freshly ground black pepper	2 mL
1/4 tsp	cayenne pepper	1 mL
2 lbs	chicken wings, rinsed and patted dry	1 kg
3 tbsp	hot pepper sauce, such as Frank's Louisiana or your favorite, or to taste	45 mL
3 tbsp	butter	45 mL
	Vegetable oil	
1 cup	blue cheese dressing	250 mL

1. In a large bowl, combine salt, paprika, black pepper and cayenne. Add chicken wings and toss to coat. Set aside.

2. In a small saucepan, over low heat, cook hot pepper sauce and butter until butter has melted. Stir to combine and remove from heat.

3. In a heavy saucepan that is at least 5 inches (12.5 cm) deep, heat 2 inches (5 cm) of oil over medium heat until it registers 350°F (180°C) on thermometer. Working in batches, fry wings until skin is crisp and juices run clear when chicken is pierced, about 8 minutes. Using tongs or a slotted spoon, remove wings to a plate lined with paper towels to drain.

4. Toss wings in hot sauce mixture. Serve with blue cheese dressing on the side.

Twenty-Minute Chili

Chilis are extremely forgiving, and, once simmered for at least 20 minutes, the flavors get along marvelously. Virtually any legume, vegetable or meat can be added.

Tip
Serve with warm tortillas or tortilla chips.

Make Ahead
This chili can be made up to 3 days in advance if refrigerated in an airtight container — and it improves with time. Reheat in a large, covered pot over medium heat, stirring frequently.

2 tbsp	olive oil	25 mL
1	large onion, chopped	1
3	cloves garlic, minced	3
1½ lbs	lean ground beef	750 g
1	can (14 to 19 oz/398 to 540 mL) red, pinto or kidney beans, drained and rinsed	1
1	can (28 oz/796 mL) crushed tomatoes, with juice	1
1	can (14 oz/398 mL) tomato sauce	1
3 tbsp	chili powder, or to taste	45 mL
2 tsp	paprika	10 mL
1 tsp	ground cumin	5 mL
1 tsp	dried oregano	5 mL
	Salt and freshly ground black pepper	
	Chopped red onion, tomato and cilantro	
	Shredded Cheddar cheese	

1. In a large pot, heat oil over medium heat. Sauté onion for about 5 minutes or until golden. Add garlic and sauté for 1 minute. Add beef and cook, stirring often to break up the bigger bits, for about 6 minutes or until meat is crumbled and no longer pink inside.

2. Add beans, crushed tomatoes, tomato sauce, chili powder, paprika, cumin, oregano and salt and pepper to taste; bring to a boil. Reduce heat and simmer, stirring occasionally, for 20 minutes to let flavors blend.

3. Serve hot with red onion, tomato, cilantro and cheese on the side.

Roast Beef Sandwiches with Horseradish Sauce

SERVES 6
or can be multiplied
up to 4 times

Depending on the type of party you are hosting, you might want to serve these on sliced baguette for smaller sandwiches.

Tip

Use as much or as little horseradish in the sauce as suits your taste.

Make Ahead

The horseradish sauce can be made up to 2 days in advance if kept covered and refrigerated.

The beef can be roasted the day before if kept covered and refrigerated. Let stand at room temperature for 30 minutes before slicing.

- **Preheat oven to 450°F (230°C)**
- **Shallow roasting pan or baking dish with a rack set inside**

2 lb	boneless beef tri-tip roast	1 kg
2 tsp	dried thyme	10 mL
	Salt and freshly ground black pepper	
1½ cups	sour cream	375 mL
2 to 4 tbsp	prepared horseradish, or to taste	25 to 50 mL
1 tbsp	freshly squeezed lemon juice	15 mL
6	grinder rolls, split	6

1. Rub surface of beef generously with thyme, salt and pepper. Place roast, fat side up, on rack in roasting pan. Roast in preheated oven for 20 to 25 minutes or until a meat thermometer inserted in the thickest part of the roast registers 140°F (60°C) for medium-rare, or until desired doneness. Transfer to a cutting board, tent loosely with foil and let rest for 10 minutes.

2. Meanwhile, in a small bowl, combine sour cream, horseradish and lemon juice. Season to taste with salt and pepper.

3. Thinly slice tri-tip across the grain and serve on rolls with horseradish sauce on the side.

Cheesecake Squares with Chocolate Cookie Crust

SERVES 8 TO 12
or can be multiplied
up to 4 times

Cut these decadent little desserts into bite-size pieces for easy eating.

Tip

To multiply this recipe, make double batches in a 13- by 9-inch (33 by 23 cm) pan and increase baking time to 45 to 50 minutes. If you need to make more than one double batch, make and bake them separately for even baking.

Make Ahead

Cheesecake can be made up to 3 weeks in advance if wrapped tightly in plastic wrap, then wrapped in foil and frozen. Let thaw in the refrigerator for 24 hours before serving.

- **Preheat oven to 325°F (160°C)**
- **9-inch (23 cm) square cake pan, lined with parchment paper so that paper "handles" stick out 3 inches (7.5 cm) from 2 opposite sides**

24	chocolate wafer cookies, ground into crumbs	24
1/4 cup	unsalted butter, melted	50 mL
4	eggs	4
1 cup	granulated sugar	250 mL
1 tsp	vanilla extract	5 mL
8 oz	cream cheese, softened	250 g

1. In a small bowl, combine crushed cookies and butter. Press into bottom of prepared cake pan. Set aside.

2. In another bowl, using an electric mixer, beat eggs, sugar and vanilla until smooth. Beat in cream cheese. Pour mixture over crust.

3. Bake in preheated oven for 40 minutes or until cheesecake is set and no longer jiggles in the middle. Let cool to room temperature in pan on a wire rack. Cover with plastic wrap and refrigerate for at least 2 hours, until chilled, or for up to 3 days.

4. Carefully lift cheesecake from the pan, using the parchment paper handles. Set on a clean work surface and cut into squares. Serve cold.

Easy Extras

▸ Decorate the tops of the cheesecake squares with jam or marmalade, caramel sauce, fresh berries or a sprinkling of chopped nuts.

Pineapple Bombs

4 cups	pineapple juice	1 L
16 oz	Southern Comfort	500 mL
8 oz	Triple Sec	250 mL
3 cups	ice cubes	750 mL
	Thin pineapple wedges	

1. In a large spill-proof container, combine pineapple juice, Southern Comfort, Triple Sec and ice. Close the lid and shake well, until liquid is chilled.
2. Strain into a large pitcher. Taste and add more pineapple juice, if desired. Serve with pineapple wedges.

Pink Pixie Punch

Tip
Freeze lemon slices
ahead of time so you
have frosty garnishes.

6 cups	ice cubes	1.5 L
2	bottles or cans (each 12 oz/341 mL) light-colored beer	2
16 oz	vodka	500 mL
1	can (4 oz/125 mL) frozen pink lemonade concentrate, thawed	1
24 to 32 oz	lemon-lime soda, or to taste	750 mL to 1 L
	Thin lemon slices	

1. Fill a large punch bowl halfway with ice. Add beer, vodka, lemonade and 24 oz (750 mL) of the lemon-lime soda; stir until well combined. Taste and add more soda, if desired.
2. Garnish punch bowl with lemon slices. Serve with a ladle.

Super Bowl Super Drinks

Have you ever noticed that at many sports-themed parties, beer seems to be the only alcoholic beverage available? Sometimes only a cocktail will do for the big game. Here are a couple of cocktails that will work well with this menu. (To be honest, after you've had one, they'll work with any menu!)

Backyard Campout

This menu isn't just for kids! Adults will enjoy it just as much — especially if you serve cold beer, or brandied hot coffee for chilly nights. Two of these recipes are fun to make over a campfire or barbecue pit, but you can also make them in your kitchen.

Menu

Campfire-Roasted Hot Dogs and Sausages on a Stick

SERVES 6
or can be multiplied up to 4 times

If you or your guests were Scouts, this will be second nature. Some great variations for food roasted on sticks are cocktail wieners for little people, sturdy fruit such as pineapple or mangos, or gourmet sausages.

Tip

Instead of using sticks, straighten out 6 wire coat hangers (make sure they're not coated), bending one end back on itself to make a looped handle.

• Two $\frac{1}{2}$-inch (1 cm) thick sticks, at least 2 feet (60 cm) long

6	hot dog wieners or precooked sausages	6
6	hot dog buns	6
	Mustard, ketchup and sweet pickle relish	
1½ cups	shredded Cheddar cheese	375 mL
½ cup	chopped red onion	125 mL

1. Skewer wieners on sticks and cook over a campfire until lightly charred. Place in buns and add toppings as desired.

Variation

▸ You can also cook wieners on a rack over a fire or barbecue pit, or on a grill.

Barbecue Baked Beans

SERVES 6
or can be multiplied
up to 4 times

You can buy beans in a can and nestle the can in the ashes of the campfire to heat, or you can blow your guests away with homemade beans. An added plus is that your house will smell utterly divine for days.

Tips

You can also make these with pinto beans.

If you do not have a Dutch oven or cast-iron skillet, you can make this in a large, heavy saucepan; in step 3, instead of using the oven, simmer over very low heat for 2 hours, stirring occasionally, or transfer to a casserole dish with a lid.

- Preheat oven to 325°F (160°C)
- Small Dutch oven or large, deep cast-iron skillet

4	slices bacon	4
1	onion, chopped	1
3 cups	rinsed drained canned white beans	750 mL
1	can (8 oz/227 mL) tomato sauce	1
2/3 cup	reduced-sodium beef broth	150 mL
1/4 cup	packed dark brown sugar	50 mL
1/4 cup	light (fancy) molasses	50 mL
1/4 cup	barbecue sauce	50 mL
1 tbsp	cider vinegar	15 mL

1. Heat Dutch oven over medium-high heat. Add bacon and cook until crispy. Transfer to a plate lined with paper towels, leaving fat in the pan. Let bacon cool, then crumble.

2. Reduce heat to medium, add onions to bacon fat and sauté for about 4 minutes or until light golden. Stir in beans, tomato sauce, broth, brown sugar, molasses, barbecue sauce and vinegar; increase heat to high and bring to a boil, stirring frequently.

3. Cover and bake in preheated oven for 2 hours, stirring occasionally. Stir in crumbled bacon.

4. Serve hot or let cool, transfer to an airtight container and refrigerate for up to 3 days. Reheat in a heavy pan over your fire, barbecue or grill.

Veggies with Ranch Dressing Dip

SERVES 6
or can be multiplied
up to 4 times

Also called crudités, a vegetable tray is the best way to fill in the cracks at an event, for very little effort or money.

4	stalks celery, cut into sticks	4
4	large carrots, cut into sticks	4
1 cup	sugar snap peas, trimmed	250 mL
1 cup	cherry tomatoes	250 mL
1 cup	julienned peeled jicama	250 mL
1 cup	ranch dip or dressing	250 mL

1. Arrange vegetables on a serving dish. Pour dressing into a small bowl and place on serving dish. Cover and refrigerate until ready to serve.

Caramel Marshmallow Popcorn Balls

SERVES 6
or can be multiplied
up to 4 times

These are even more delicious than Rice Krispies Treats. As with every good party recipe, there is endless potential for variations here. Dried fruits, other nuts or a teaspoon (5 mL) of almond, coconut or vanilla extract would be good additions.

Tips

Place popcorn balls in cupcake liners for easy storage and serving. Store in an airtight container at room temperature for up to 1 day.

Only make double batches at a time, to make sure the syrup cooks properly and so you'll have enough time to shape the balls before they firm up too much.

● **Large baking sheet, sprayed with nonstick cooking spray**

6 cups	popped popcorn (unsalted and unbuttered)	1.5 L
3 cups	mini marshmallows, divided	750 mL
1/4 cup	granulated sugar	50 mL
1/4 cup	packed light brown sugar	50 mL
6 tbsp	half-and-half (10%) cream	90 mL
1/4 cup	unsalted butter	50 mL
1/3 cup	sweetened shredded coconut (optional)	75 mL
1/2 cup	salted roasted peanuts (optional)	125 mL

1. Spread popcorn on prepared baking sheet.

2. In a medium saucepan, combine 2 cups (500 mL) of the marshmallows, granulated sugar, brown sugar, cream and butter. Bring to a boil over medium heat. Reduce heat and simmer for 10 minutes. Let cool slightly.

3. Pour marshmallow mixture over popcorn, tossing to coat. Sprinkle with the remaining marshmallows, coconut (if using) and peanuts (if using) and toss to combine. Let cool for 10 minutes. Rub your hands lightly with oil and form the mixture into 12 balls. Return to prepared baking sheet.

S'mores

SERVES 6
or can be multiplied
up to 4 times

This cooking method will eliminate blackened and charred marshmallows and the inevitable tears from a marshmallow lost to the flames. Let everyone make their own personalized s'mores: provide extra ingredients such as sliced bananas, peanut butter or strawberry jam.

Tip

You can also make these in a 400°F (200°C) oven. Wrap in foil, place on a baking sheet and bake for about 10 minutes or until marshmallows are gooey.

• **Six 12-inch (30 cm) pieces of foil**

2	bars (each 1½ oz/45 g) milk or dark chocolate, broken into squares	1
12	graham crackers	12
12	marshmallows	12

1. Place a few pieces of chocolate and two marshmallows between two graham crackers. Wrap each sandwich tightly in foil. Place on a rack over a fire (or on a grill) and cook for about 5 minutes, turning once, until marshmallows are gooey.

S'mores and More

While I have never been a Girl Scout, I somehow managed to discover s'mores. My father was a camper, a hunter and a fisherman. He loved the great outdoors. My mother loved the Hilton. So as a compromise, my family spent many nights camping in our backyard. My mother had her bathroom, and my father had his tent and canteen.

Telling ghost stories under the stars, I learned how great food tastes when cooked outdoors. Over what was left of the barbecue's coals, my sisters and I learned the art of making classic s'mores: two halves of a graham cracker, one perfect square of a Hershey's chocolate bar and a warm, soft, slightly toasted and almost gooey marshmallow.

Though you may be tempted not to mess with perfection, it's always fun to add your own twist on any delicious treat. Here are a few suggestions to get you started:

- Smear some seedless raspberry jam on the graham crackers before assembling the s'mores, for an extra sweet and tangy boost to the already rich dessert.
- Thinly slice a banana and add a couple of slices to the s'mores sandwich. There's something about chocolate and bananas that really clicks.
- For the truly sophisticated s'mores eater, dip the marshmallow in warmed Cointreau.
- For highly evolved palates, offer a variety of chocolates instead of the usual Hershey's bars; bittersweet (dark) chocolate, white chocolate or any fancy flavored varieties (flavored with ginger or hot pepper, for instance) make interesting additions.
- Try cinnamon-flavored graham crackers or British-style biscuits, such as McVitie's.

Southern Charm

When you're packing for a picnic, perishables need to be kept chilled in an ice chest until you're ready to serve. In this menu, the only perishables are the chicken and the potato salad. Pack the peach salsa separately and add it to the chicken before serving. The cornbread, lemon bars and pie can be brought as is — no need to pack them in the ice chest. If you are short on space in your ice chest, open plastic water bottles and pour out about an inch (2.5 cm) of water, then freeze. Place the frozen water bottles in the bottom of the ice chest instead of ice or ice packs.

Menu

Quick Fried Chicken with Peach Salsa

SERVES 6
or can be multiplied up to 4 times

Serve this chicken hot, cold or at room temperature. It's great on a picnic.

Tip
If making this for a picnic, slice chicken breasts into 1-inch (2.5 cm) wide strips before breading and frying. Double the coating ingredients and decrease the cooking time to 2 to 3 minutes per side.

½ cup	all-purpose flour	125 mL
3	eggs, lightly beaten	3
1¼ cups	panko bread crumbs	300 mL
1 tsp	paprika	5 mL
½ tsp	salt	2 mL
½ tsp	freshly ground black pepper	2 mL
¼ tsp	dried oregano	1 mL
¼ tsp	onion powder	1 mL
6	boneless skinless chicken breasts (each about 5 oz/150 g)	6
⅓ cup	canola or other vegetable oil	75 mL
3 cups	Peach Salsa (see recipe, opposite)	750 mL

1. Place flour on a dinner plate. Place eggs in a bowl. In another bowl, combine bread crumbs, paprika, salt, pepper, oregano and onion powder.

2. Slice each chicken breast into two thin pieces widthwise, as you would to butterfly it, but cutting all the way through. Dredge chicken in flour, shaking off excess. Dip chicken in egg, then press into bread crumb mixture, shaking off excess. Discard any excess flour, egg and bread crumb mixture.

3. In a large skillet, heat oil over medium-high heat. Cook chicken, in batches, for 5 minutes per side, or until golden brown and no longer pink inside.

4. Serve with peach salsa spooned on top.

Tip

If multiplying this recipe, use two skillets to speed up the cooking and be sure to replace the oil and wipe out the pan between batches if it gets too dark with lots of browned bits. You may need to adjust the heat if doing multiple batches to make sure the chicken cooks evenly. Add oil as necessary when multiplying batches.

Make Ahead

You can prepare this chicken up to 2 days ahead if cooled completely and stored in an airtight container in the refrigerator.

Peach Salsa

3	large peaches, peeled and diced	3
2	plum (Roma) tomatoes, diced	3
1 cup	diced pineapple	250 mL
2 tbsp	chopped fresh cilantro	25 mL
2 tbsp	freshly squeezed lime juice	25 mL
	Salt and freshly ground black pepper	

1. In a non-reactive bowl, combine peaches, tomatoes, pineapple, cilantro and lime juice. Season to taste with salt and pepper. Serve immediately or cover and refrigerate for up to 6 hours.

MAKES ABOUT 3 CUPS (750 ML) or can be multiplied up to 4 times

What's more Southern than sweet, fresh peaches?

Zesty Cornbread

Cornbread is simple and satisfying, the classic down-home side — only this one has a kick! Up the cayenne for even more spice.

Tip

If multiplying the recipe, make double batches at a time, bake in a 13- by 9-inch (33 by 23 cm) pan and increase the baking time to 45 to 50 minutes.

Make Ahead

Cornbread can be made up to 4 days in advance if wrapped tightly in foil and refrigerated. Reheat, loosely covered, in a 300°F (150°C) oven until warmed through.

Cornbread can be made up to 4 weeks in advance if wrapped tightly in foil, placed in a freezer bag and frozen. Thaw overnight in the refrigerator before reheating, loosely covered, in a 300°F (150°C) oven until warmed through.

- Preheat oven to 375°F (190°C)
- 9-inch (23 cm) square baking pan, greased

2⅓ cups	cornmeal	575 mL
1 cup	all-purpose flour	250 mL
⅓ cup	granulated sugar	75 mL
1 tbsp	baking powder	15 mL
½ tsp	baking soda	2 mL
½ tsp	salt	2 mL
⅛ tsp	cayenne pepper, or to taste	0.5 mL
Pinch	freshly ground black pepper	Pinch
½ cup	unsalted butter, softened	125 mL
1½ cups	buttermilk	375 mL
4	eggs	4

1. In a food processor, combine cornmeal, flour, sugar, baking powder, baking soda, salt, cayenne and black pepper; pulse to blend. Add butter and pulse until mixture resembles coarse meal.

2. In a large bowl, whisk together buttermilk and eggs. Add cornmeal mixture and stir with a fork until just moistened. Pour batter into prepared pan, smoothing top.

3. Bake in preheated oven for 40 minutes or until a tester inserted in the center comes out clean. Let cool completely in pan on a wire rack.

Easy Extra

▶ Stir ⅔ cup (150 mL) shredded jalapeño Jack cheese into the batter before pouring it into the pan.

Hush Puppies

SERVES 6 TO 8
or can be multiplied
up to 4 times

Tips

If self-rising cornmeal mix isn't available, substitute $1\frac{1}{2}$ cups (375 mL) yellow cornmeal, 2 tbsp (25 mL) baking soda and $\frac{3}{4}$ tsp (3 mL) salt, and add $\frac{1}{3}$ cup (75 mL) more all-purpose flour.

If you're making multiple batches of Hush Puppies, be sure to adjust the heat to keep the oil at the correct temperature when frying and scoop out any small pieces periodically to avoid a burnt flavor in the oil.

• **Candy/deep-fry thermometer**

2 cups	self-rising cornmeal mix (see tip, at left)	500 mL
3 tbsp	all-purpose flour	45 mL
2 tbsp	finely sliced green onions	25 mL
1 cup	milk	250 mL
1	egg, lightly beaten	1
	Vegetable oil	
	Salt and freshly ground black pepper	

1. In a large bowl, combine cornmeal mix, flour and green onions.

2. In a separate bowl, whisk together milk and egg. Whisk into cornmeal mixture until well incorporated. Let stand for 5 minutes.

3. In a deep, heavy saucepan, heat 3 inches (7.5 cm) of oil over medium-high heat until it registers 375°F (190°C) on thermometer. Working in batches, drop batter by tablespoonfuls (15 mL) into the hot oil and fry, turning frequently, until golden brown, about 5 minutes. Don't overcrowd the pan. Using tongs or a slotted spoon, remove fritters to a plate lined with paper towels to drain. Season to taste with salt and pepper. Serve immediately.

Variation

▸ Add $\frac{1}{3}$ cup (75 mL) grilled sweet corn kernels or 2 tbsp (25 mL) lightly sautéed minced jalapeño peppers to the batter before frying.

Hush Puppies

What are hush puppies and where did they come from?

Hush puppies are delicious little bits of fritters traditionally made from cornmeal, milk, water and chopped onions. While the origins are still a bit unclear, one historian says that plantation cooks used to deep-fry extra batter and feed it to the dogs to keep them quiet during dinner. Murmurs of "Hush, puppy" came from the kitchen.

Growing up in San Francisco, I had never eaten hush puppies, so when I got a job on a Mississippi riverboat, I learned to cook and appreciate them.

Hush puppies are a traditional Southern snack and appetizer, and if you have time they're a great addition to the Southern Charm menu.

Lemon Dill Potato Salad

SERVES 6
or can be multiplied
up to 4 times

The creaminess of this potato salad comes from the russet potatoes, which are cooked until they begin to fall apart.

Tip

Garnish with slices of hard-cooked eggs or a sprinkle of paprika.

3	large russet potatoes, peeled and cut into 1-inch (2.5 cm) cubes	3
1 tbsp	grated lemon zest	15 mL
3 tbsp	freshly squeezed lemon juice	45 mL
2 tbsp	olive oil	25 mL
1/4 tsp	salt	1 mL
1/4 tsp	freshly ground black pepper	1 mL
2	stalks celery, diced	2
1/2 cup	minced red onion	125 mL
1/2 cup	diced English cucumber	125 mL
4	green onions, thinly sliced	4
2 tbsp	chopped fresh dill	25 mL
1/3 cup	mayonnaise	75 mL

1. Bring a large pot of water to a boil over high heat. Add potatoes and reduce heat to medium. Boil potatoes for about 15 minutes or until soft and just beginning to fall apart. Drain and set aside.

2. In a large bowl, whisk together lemon zest, lemon juice, oil, salt and pepper. Add potatoes and stir to combine. Gently stir in celery, red onion and cucumber. Cover and refrigerate for at least 30 minutes, until chilled, or for up to 2 days.

3. Just before serving, stir in green onions, dill and mayonnaise. Taste and adjust seasoning with salt and pepper, if desired.

Classic Lemon Bars

SERVES 6 TO 8
or can be multiplied
up to 4 times

*Here's another recipe
that is just made for
picnics. Lemon bars
travel nicely and
can be served at any
temperature, and the
zesty lemon flavor is
the perfect way to end
any meal.*

Tip
If multiplying this
recipe, make double
batches at a time and
bake in a 13- by 9-inch
(33 by 23 cm) baking
dish, increasing the
baking time by 5 to
10 minutes.

Make Ahead
These lemon bars can
be made up to 3 days
in advance if stored in
an airtight container at
room temperature.

- **Preheat oven to 350°F (180°C)**
- **8-inch (20 cm) square baking dish, buttered**

Crust

1 1/2 cups	cake flour	375 mL
1/3 cup	confectioner's (icing) sugar	75 mL
Pinch	salt	Pinch
3/4 cup	cold unsalted butter, cut into small pieces	175 mL

Filling

3	eggs	3
1 1/2 cups	granulated sugar	375 mL
3 tbsp	cake flour	45 mL
1 tbsp	grated lemon zest	15 mL
1/4 cup	freshly squeezed lemon juice	50 mL
2 tbsp	confectioner's (icing) sugar	25 mL

1. *Crust:* In a large bowl, sift together flour, confectioner's sugar and salt. Using a pastry cutter or two knives, cut in butter until mixture resembles coarse meal. Press into bottom of prepared baking dish. Bake in preheated oven for 20 minutes or until light golden brown. Transfer to a wire rack, leaving oven on.

2. *Filling:* Meanwhile, in a bowl, using an electric mixer, beat eggs, granulated sugar, flour, lemon zest and lemon juice until creamy and smooth. Pour over the still-warm crust.

3. Bake for 20 to 25 minutes or until filling is set. Let cool completely in dish on wire rack. Sift confectioner's sugar over top before cutting into bars.

Variation
▶ Sliced almonds make a beautiful alternative topping, instead of the confectioner's sugar; you'll need about 1/4 cup (50 mL).

Fresh Peach Pie

Serve slices of pie with a scoop of vanilla bean ice cream for a dreamy dessert.

● **Preheat oven to 400°F (200°C)**

4 lbs	peaches	2 kg
¾ cup	granulated sugar	175 mL
¼ cup + 1 tbsp	all-purpose flour	65 mL
	Grated zest of 1 lemon	
1 tbsp	freshly squeezed lemon juice	15 mL
¼ tsp	ground nutmeg	1 mL
	Never-Fail Pie Crust for a 9-inch (23 cm) double-crust pie (see recipe, opposite), chilled	
2 tbsp	unsalted butter, cut into small pieces	25 mL
1	egg yolk	1
2 tbsp	water	25 mL

1. Cut a shallow X into the skin on the bottom of each peach. Bring a large pot of water to a boil over high heat. Working in batches, blanch peaches for 45 seconds. Using a slotted spoon, transfer peaches to a large bowl or sink of ice water to stop the cooking process. When cool, blot dry with paper towels.

2. Starting from the X, peel skin from peaches. Cut peaches lengthwise into ½-inch (1 cm) thick slices and place in a large bowl. Add sugar, flour, lemon zest, lemon juice and nutmeg; toss well to coat and let stand for 5 minutes.

3. Pour peach mixture into bottom pie crust. Dot with butter.

4. Whisk together egg yolk and water. Brush the edge of the bottom crust with egg wash. Lay the top crust on top. Press the edges of the crusts together to seal, and trim the overhang to ½ inch (1 cm). Fold the overhang under and crimp the edges decoratively. Brush the top crust with the remaining egg wash and cut a few slits on top to vent steam. Place pie on a baking sheet.

5. Bake in preheated oven for 30 minutes. Reduce oven temperature to 375°F (190°C) and cover the edges of the pie with foil to keep them from burning. Bake for about 30 minutes or until crust is deep golden brown and filling is bubbly. Let cool completely on a wire rack.

Variation

▶ Substitute 4 cups (1 L) sliced strawberries (about 2 lbs/ 1 kg) for the peaches.

Never-Fail Pie Crust

- **One or two 9-inch (23 cm) pie plates**

2 cups	all-purpose flour	500 mL
1 tbsp	granulated sugar	15 mL
1/2 tsp	salt	2 mL
1/2 cup	cold unsalted butter, cut into small pieces	125 mL
1/4 cup	cold vegetable shortening, cut into small pieces	50 mL
5 tbsp	ice water (approx.)	75 mL

1. In a food processor, pulse flour, sugar, salt, butter and shortening until mixture resembles coarse meal. Sprinkle with 4 tbsp (60 mL) ice water and pulse until most of the dough comes together and forms a ball. If dough remains crumbly, sprinkle with the remaining ice water and pulse briefly, just until dough comes together.

2. Divide dough in half and form into flattened balls. Cover with plastic wrap and refrigerate for at least 1 hour, until chilled, or for up to 3 days.

If Making a Double-Crust Pie

3. On a floured work surface, roll out one piece of dough to a 14-inch (35 cm) circle. Fold dough in half, and in half again, to make moving it easier. Place dough over pie plate, unfold and gently press into pan. Trim edges, leaving a 1/2-inch (1 cm) overhang.

4. On a floured piece of waxed paper, roll out second piece of dough to a 14-inch (35 cm) circle. Transfer to a baking sheet.

5. Cover both the baking sheet and the pie plate with plastic wrap and refrigerate for at least 30 minutes, until chilled, or for up to 3 days.

If Making 2 Single-Crust Pies

3. On a floured work surface, roll out one piece of dough to a 14-inch (35 cm) circle. Fold dough in half, and in half again, to make moving it easier. Place dough over pie plate, unfold and gently press into pan. Trim edges, leaving a 1/2-inch (1 cm) overhang.

4. Repeat with the second piece of dough and another pie plate.

5. Cover both pie plates with plastic wrap and refrigerate for at least 30 minutes, until chilled, or for up to 3 days.

MAKES ENOUGH FOR 1 DOUBLE-CRUST
or 2 single-crust pies

Make Ahead
Dough can be stored in a freezer bag or airtight container in the freezer for up to 1 month. Thaw in the refrigerator for 24 hours before rolling out and baking.

Western Hoedown

You can have a hoedown in a barn, backyard, meeting hall or anyplace you like. Hoedown is a state of mind —there's no need for the wide open prairie. Hand out bandanas to your guests, throw a little hay on the floor, put some country and western dance music on the stereo, and you've got a party!

Menu

Cowhand Spareribs

SERVES 6
or can be multiplied up to 4 times

Spareribs are from the belly of the pig. One slab weighs about 2 to 3 lbs (1 to 1.5 kg). Purchase the largest slabs, with the least amount of visible fat, you can find.

Tips
These ribs can also be roasted in a 400°F (200°C) oven for 20 to 25 minutes or until meat pulls away from the bone.

This recipe uses a dry rub. If you like, serve with your favorite barbecue sauce on the side.

5 to 6 lbs	pork spareribs (about 2 slabs)	2.5 to 3 kg
2 tsp	garlic salt	10 mL
2 tsp	packed dark brown sugar	10 mL
1 tsp	paprika	5 mL
1 tsp	ancho chile powder	5 mL
1 tsp	ground cumin	5 mL
1 tsp	dry mustard	5 mL
1 tsp	freshly ground black pepper	5 mL

1. Place spareribs in a pot of boiling salted water large enough to submerge them completely (if you don't have a pot this large, cut slabs in half). Immediately turn heat down to low (just under a simmer) and cook, uncovered, for 1 hour or until fork-tender. Drain ribs and let cool slightly.

2. Meanwhile, in a bowl, combine garlic salt, brown sugar, paprika, chile powder, cumin, mustard and pepper. Pat ribs dry and rub both sides with spice mixture. Place in an airtight container and refrigerate for at least 2 hours or overnight. Let stand at room temperature for 30 minutes.

3. Meanwhile, preheat barbecue grill to medium-high.

4. Grill spareribs, turning often, for 16 to 20 minutes or until well browned on both sides and meat pulls away from the bone.

The History of Barbecue Sauce

The true origins of barbecue sauce have been greatly disputed, and are foggy at best. Many people believe it originated with Native Americans, who passed it on to colonialists in the 1600s while teaching them the art of slow-cooking meats. Barbecue sauce was solely vinegar-based until the 19th century, when the tomato was finally liberated from the widespread misconception that it was poisonous. Barbecue sauce was first commercially produced in 1926 by the Louis Maull Company, but wasn't nationally distributed until 1948, by the well-known Heinz Company.

These days, it seems that every enthusiast with a grill has created his or her own sauce variation, with different degrees of sweetness, spiciness, tang or smoke. Barbecue sauce is a very personal thing — be prepared to defend your preference.

For example, in Texas, barbecue sauce is a savory tomato-based sauce spiked with hot chiles and smoky spices such as cumin; it is generally thin and spicy-hot. If you were to mosey over to South Carolina, you'd find a completely different type of sauce: a mustardy, vinegar-laden, heavily peppered sauce that could set your nostrils aflame — in a good way. Continuing over to Tennessee, more specifically to singin'-the-blues Memphis, the local sauce occupies a middle ground between the conflicting Texas versus Carolina styles. A barbecue sauce from Memphis is definitely tomato-based, but is sweetened with brown sugar, tangy with vinegar and spiced just right, with a smoky base. Whatever sauce suits your fancy — sweet, spicy, tangy, thick, thin, acidic, mild or bold — there is a sauce out there with your name on it. Every sauce recipe is different, so a barbecue is a good forum for narrowing down the greats.

When purchasing bottled sauces, doctoring to taste is key. Cut any cloying sweetness with red wine vinegar or a fresh squeeze of lemon juice; add a spoonful of brown sugar if the acidity is too overpowering.

Garlicky Grilled Corn on the Cob

SERVES 6
or can be multiplied up to 4 times

Be sure not to remove the corn husks all the way when preparing this buttery portable side dish. They'll blacken as you grill and will help the corn stay moist underneath.

Tip

You can also roast the corn on a rimmed baking sheet in a 425°F (220°C) oven for 25 minutes or until tender.

Make Ahead

You can butter and wrap the corn in its husks the day before. Refrigerate until ready to grill.

- **Preheat barbecue grill to medium-high**

6 tbsp	butter	90 mL
2	cloves garlic, mashed	2
6	ears corn, husks peeled back and silks removed	6
	Salt and freshly ground black pepper	

1. Mash together butter and garlic. Rub over corn kernels and sprinkle with salt and pepper to taste. Fold husks back over corn to cover.

2. Grill corn, turning often, for about 20 minutes or until tender.

Easy Extra

▸ Fresh herbs are a delicious addition. Try adding 1 tbsp (15 mL) chopped fresh chives, mint, sage, thyme or tarragon to the butter.

Bacon-Stuffed Twice-Baked Potatoes

SERVES 6
or can be multiplied up to 4 times

These potatoes are real man food, and will win the affection of anyone who tries them. Use a different kind of cheese or a different meat for variation — Gouda and Spanish ham would be a great pair.

Make Ahead

The potatoes can be filled and stored in an airtight container in the refrigerator for up to 2 days. Increase the baking time to 20 minutes.

- **Preheat oven to 375°F (190°C)**
- **Rimmed baking sheet**

8	medium russet potatoes	8
1 tbsp	olive oil	15 mL
1/3 cup	milk, warmed	75 mL
4	green onions, finely chopped	4
1 lb	bacon, cooked crisp and crumbled	500 g
1 1/2 cups	shredded Cheddar cheese, divided	375 mL
2/3 cup	sour cream	150 mL
	Salt and freshly ground black pepper	

1. Pierce each potato once with a small, sharp knife. Rub potatoes with oil and place directly on oven rack. Bake in preheated oven for about 40 minutes or until easily pierced with a knife. Let cool slightly before handling. Reduce oven temperature to 350°F (180°C).

2. Cut 2 of the potatoes in half and scoop out flesh, discarding peel. Place potato flesh in a bowl and set aside.

3. Slice a large X in the top of the remaining 6 potatoes. Hold a potato at each end and press so that the X opens up. Carefully scoop out about half of the flesh, being careful not to tear the skin. Add to potato in bowl.

4. Add milk to potato flesh in bowl and, using an electric mixer, beat until creamy. Stir in green onions, bacon, 1 cup (250 mL) of the cheese and sour cream. Season to taste with salt and pepper.

5. Spoon filling back into potato skins, heaping the filling high. Sprinkle with the remaining cheese. Place on baking sheet and bake for about 10 minutes or until cheese is melted.

Wagon Train Biscuits

**MAKES
12 BISCUITS**
or can be multiplied
up to 4 times

*These are large biscuits,
but light as a cloud.*

Tip
Serve with butter or
honey. Or both!

Make Ahead
The dough for these
biscuits can be made
up to 1 month ahead.
Cut biscuits into
desired shapes, wrap
in plastic wrap, then
in foil, and freeze.
Thaw overnight in the
refrigerator. Let stand
at room temperature
for 30 minutes before
baking.

- Preheat oven to 425°F (220°C)
- Baking sheet, lightly sprayed with nonstick cooking spray
- 3-inch (7.5 cm) round cookie cutter

2 cups	all-purpose flour	500 mL
1 tbsp	baking powder	15 mL
1 tsp	salt	5 mL
1/2 tsp	cayenne pepper (optional)	2 mL
3/4 cup	cold unsalted butter, cut into small pieces	175 mL
3/4 cup	heavy or whipping (35%) cream	175 mL

1. In a large bowl, sift together flour, baking powder, salt and cayenne (if using). Using your fingertips or a pastry blender, blend in butter until mixture resembles very coarse meal. Sprinkle with cream, stirring with a fork until just moistened.

2. Turn out onto a lightly floured work surface and briefly knead until dough comes together. Roll out dough to about 1 inch (2.5 cm) thick. Cut out biscuits with the cookie cutter. Gather together scraps, reroll and cut to make 12 biscuits total. Place 1 inch (2.5 cm) apart on prepared baking sheet

3. Bake in preheated oven for about 20 minutes or until golden brown. Let cool for a few minutes before serving.

Don't Mess with Texas Brownies

SERVES 8 TO 10
or can be multiplied
up to 4 times

A real chocolate-lover's treat! Double (or triple) this recipe to give away brownies to guests as favors, or to keep in the freezer for a chocolate emergency.

Tip

If multiplying this recipe, make double batches at a time and bake in a 13- by 9-inch (33 by 23 cm) baking pan, increasing the baking time by 5 to 10 minutes.

Make Ahead

These brownies freeze very well. Let cool completely, wrap in plastic wrap and then in foil, and freeze for up to 1 month.

- Preheat oven to 325°F (160°C)
- 8-inch (20 cm) square baking pan, lightly sprayed with nonstick cooking spray

8 oz	good-quality dark chocolate, chopped	250 g
1/2 cup	all-purpose flour	125 mL
3 tbsp	unsweetened cocoa powder	45 mL
1/4 tsp	baking powder	1 mL
1/4 tsp	salt	1 mL
1 cup	granulated sugar	250 mL
1/3 cup	unsalted butter	75 mL
4	eggs	4
1 1/2 tsp	vanilla extract	7 mL
1 cup	milk chocolate chips	250 mL
1 cup	chopped walnuts (optional)	250 mL

1. Place dark chocolate in a microwave-safe bowl and heat on High for 30-second intervals, stirring in between, until chocolate is melted and smooth. Set aside.

2. Meanwhile, in a bowl, combine flour, cocoa powder, baking powder and salt. Set aside.

3. In a large bowl, using an electric mixer, cream sugar and butter until light and fluffy. Add eggs, one at a time, beating well after each addition. Continue beating until mixture is pale and creamy, about 5 minutes. Beat in melted chocolate and vanilla until just blended. Fold in flour mixture. Fold in chocolate chips and walnuts (if using). Pour batter into prepared pan, smoothing top.

4. Bake in preheated oven for 35 minutes or until a tester inserted in the center comes out clean. Let cool completely in pan on a wire rack before cutting into squares.

Pacific Northwest Coast

The Pacific Northwest is famous for fantastic fresh seafood. Bring a little bit of the coast into your home with this menu.

Menu

Diver Scallop Skewers

SERVES 6
or can be multiplied up to 4 times

Diver scallops, which are gathered by hand, are generally larger, with firmer flesh and less sediment, than standard scallops, which are dredged. These scallops make a great eat-with-your-fingers appetizer.

Tip
For best results, look for scallops that are about 1½ inches (4 cm) across. If your scallops are closer to 1 inch (2.5 cm) in size, buy 18 instead of 12.

• **12 short wood or bamboo skewers, soaked in water for 15 minutes**

12	large basil leaves	12
3 oz	thinly sliced prosciutto, cut into ½-inch (1 cm) strips	90 g
12	medium diver scallops (see tip, at left), trimmed of hard side muscles	12
2 tbsp	olive oil	25 mL
	Salt and freshly ground black pepper	
1	lemon, cut into 6 wedges	1

1. Wrap a basil leaf and a strip of prosciutto around each scallop and secure with a skewer. Brush with oil and sprinkle with salt and pepper.

2. Heat a grill pan over high heat. Grill scallops, turning once, for 1 to 2 minutes per side or until firm and opaque. Serve with lemon wedges.

Variations

▸ You can substitute pancetta for the prosciutto.

▸ Large or jumbo shrimp are a nice alternative to the scallops.

Spinach, Apple and Pancetta Salad

This salad seems simple, but the combination of flavors is stunning. Serve as a sweet and leafy palate cleanser at the end of the meal, or as a starter.

Make Ahead

Make the dressing up to 2 days in advance and store in an airtight container in the refrigerator.

1	Gala or Fuji apple, chopped	1
1 tbsp	freshly squeezed lemon juice	15 mL
1/3 cup	olive oil, divided	75 mL
6 oz	pancetta, finely diced	175 g
2 tbsp	sherry vinegar	25 mL
1 tbsp	Dijon mustard	15 mL
12 oz	baby spinach	375 g
1/2 cup	finely sliced red onion	125 mL
	Salt and freshly ground black pepper	

1. Toss apple in lemon juice to prevent browning. Set aside.

2. In a skillet, heat 2 tsp (10 mL) of the oil over high heat. Sauté pancetta for 5 minutes or until browned. Transfer to a plate lined with paper towels to drain.

3. In a large salad bowl, whisk together the remaining oil, vinegar and mustard until creamy. Add spinach and toss to coat. Add onion, apple and pancetta and toss to combine. Season to taste with salt and pepper.

Variations

▸ Use 6 slices of bacon in place of the pancetta.

▸ Use a pear in place of the apple.

Roasted Wild Salmon

*Sometimes it's the
simplest preparations
that make the best
meals. This is a prime
example: buy the
freshest salmon, use
plenty of fresh herbs,
and you'll have an
effortless, delicious
entrée. Reserve a few
sprigs of herbs to
scatter over the salmon
for presentation.*

Tips

If serving on a buffet,
purchase a side of
salmon with the skin
still on, then slice into
single-serving pieces
through the flesh,
without cutting into
the skin. This makes
an attractive way to
serve the salmon,
and helps you judge
accurate portions. Be
sure to have a wide
metal spatula available
for guests to help
themselves.

You can use six 5-oz
(150 g) salmon fillets if
a side of salmon is not
available.

A mini or small food
processor works best
for processing the
butter spread.

- **Preheat oven to 450°F (230°C)**
- **Large rimmed baking sheet, oiled**

2	lemons, cut into ¼-inch (0.5 cm) slices	2
1	side of wild-caught or organically raised salmon (2 lbs/1 kg)	1
2	shallots	2
1 tbsp	fresh rosemary leaves	15 mL
1 tbsp	coarsely chopped fresh chives	15 mL
1 tsp	granulated sugar	5 mL
6 tbsp	butter, softened	90 mL
	Salt and freshly ground black pepper	

1. Place lemon slices on prepared baking sheet. Place salmon on top of lemon slices, skin side down.

2. In a mini chopper or food processor, pulse shallots, rosemary, chives, sugar and butter until shallots and rosemary are finely chopped.

3. Coat the top of the salmon with butter mixture. Roast in preheated oven for 15 to 20 minutes, depending upon thickness, until fish is opaque and flakes easily with a fork.

Wild Salmon

Salmon is widely popular for good reason. The gorgeous pink flesh and distinctly sophisticated flavor have drawn many to this unfishy fish. Although some are intimidated by wild salmon, there is nothing to be afraid of; wild salmon has a more concentrated flavor and comes in a bolder shade of ruby. Concerns about farmed salmon — both health-related and environmental — are reason enough to take a walk on the wild side. Overcrowding and inadequate breeding tanks have caused rampant pollution and encourage non-native parasites. Look for wild salmon in your markets and give it a try.

I lived in a cabin on a creek in Sequim, Washington, for a time, at the very end of my hippie years. Washington is salmon country. We ate salmon morning, noon and night. None of the fish was wasted. The skin was made into belts and shoes, and the flesh was, obviously, devoured. Boiling the heads to soften the insides makes the most delicious salmon mousse.

In the morning, I would drink my coffee next to the creek and watch one determined salmon after another battle its way upstream to spawn. Once in a while, a salmon would get stuck on a rock — not hurt, just stuck — and I always helped them with a nudge back into the water. A Native American who lived next door would tell me that I was interfering with nature. I told her, "No, I'm saving for the future."

To learn more about this remarkable fish, visit www.wildsalmon.com.

Fish Poaching Pans

A *poissonière* is a long, narrow pan for poaching fish. They often have a rack with handles that allow the fish to be lifted from the hot liquid. A roasting pan of sufficient size can also be used. Poachers are usually made of stainless steel but are also available (at an enormous price) in copper. Get a poacher that is long enough to set across two burners at once; most poachers measure 18 to 22 inches (45 to 55 cm) in length. They can be purchased at restaurant supply stores.

Wild Rice Pilaf

SERVES 6
or can be multiplied
up to 4 times

Wild rice is nutty and chewy — and not even a rice at all, but actually a long-grain marsh grass. Serve it as a gorgeous alternative to plain white or brown rice.

Tips

Wild rice should be cooked covered. However, unlike cooking white or brown rice, you can lift the lid from time to time to stir and check on the cooking.

If multiplying the recipe, sauté the mushrooms, onions and red peppers in batches in step 2, then add them all back to the pan before adding rice. If making more than 2 batches, you may need to mix in the rice in a large pot.

Make Ahead

This dish can be made the day before if refrigerated in an airtight container. Reheat in a covered baking dish in a 325°F (160°C) oven for 20 minutes.

4 cups	Quick Chicken Stock (page 223) or reduced-sodium chicken broth	1 L
2 cups	wild rice	500 mL
1/4 cup	unsalted butter, divided	50 mL
8 oz	mushrooms, finely chopped	250 g
1/2 cup	minced red onion	125 mL
1	red bell pepper, finely chopped	1
2 tbsp	chopped fresh flat-leaf (Italian) parsley	25 mL
	Salt and freshly ground black pepper	

1. In a large pot, bring stock to a boil over high heat. Stir in wild rice and return to a boil. Reduce heat to low, cover and simmer for about 45 minutes or until about half the kernels have burst open.

2. Meanwhile, in a large skillet, melt 2 tbsp (25 mL) of the butter over medium-high heat. Sauté mushrooms and red onion for 3 minutes or until light golden. Add red pepper and parsley; sauté for 2 minutes or until pepper is soft.

3. Drain any excess liquid from rice and stir in mushroom mixture and the remaining butter, fluffing the rice. Season to taste with salt and pepper.

Pear Bread Pudding

SERVES 6
or can be multiplied
up to 4 times

*This sweet dessert is
out of this world when
served with warm
caramel sauce.*

Tips

Italian-style loaf bread
works best for this
recipe. A standard
sandwich bread doesn't
have enough backbone
to hold up during
baking.

If making a double
batch of this recipe,
bake it in a lasagna
or roasting pan
and increase the
baking time to 55 to
60 minutes. If you
need more servings,
make double batches
and rotate baking
dishes in the oven
partway through to
ensure even baking.

• 13- by 9-inch (33 by 23 cm) glass baking dish or ceramic casserole, generously buttered

½ cup	all-purpose flour	125 mL
½ cup	granulated sugar	125 mL
1 tsp	ground cinnamon	5 mL
4	eggs, beaten	4
1 cup	heavy or whipping (35%) cream	250 mL
¼ cup	butter, melted	50 mL
1 tsp	almond extract	5 mL
½ tsp	vanilla extract	2 mL
1 lb	firm ripe pears, peeled and chopped	500 g
1	loaf Italian bread, crusts removed, cut into 1-inch (2.5-cm) pieces (about 4 cups/1 L)	1
⅔ cup	caramel sauce, warmed	150 mL

1. In a large bowl, using an electric mixer, beat flour, sugar, cinnamon, eggs, cream, butter, almond extract and vanilla until well combined. Fold in pears and bread.

2. Pour into prepared baking dish, cover loosely with foil and let stand for 15 minutes. Meanwhile, preheat oven to 325°F (160°C).

3. Bake, covered, in preheated oven for 30 minutes. Remove foil and bake for about 15 minutes or until top is golden brown.

4. Scoop into dessert dishes and drizzle with caramel sauce.

Easy Extras

▶ Garnish each serving with a few raspberries or sliced almonds.

▶ Stir in 1 cup (250 mL) semisweet chocolate chips, white chocolate chips or butterscotch chips with the pears.

Variation

▶ Make this with apples or 2 cups (500 mL) berries instead of the pears.

Hawaiian Luau

Luaus are traditional Hawaiian celebrations held to mark significant events such as the return of tribal warriors, a family member home from a long journey or a child's coming of age. These celebrations were given the name "luau" only about 150 years ago; before that, the feasts were called 'aha 'aina. The food and rituals at these 'aha 'aina were highly symbolic to native Hawaiians. Each food served held its own significance: some dishes represented strength and courage, while others represented virtues and ambitions the participant wanted to obtain.

Today, luaus are sometimes still held to celebrate special events, though now the draw of live entertainment, hula dancers and fire-breathers packs in the crowds. Many of the foods usually served at luaus today are not really indigenous to Hawaii: bananas, coconuts, sweet potatoes, taro, pork and chicken were introduced by Polynesian settlers.

Buy coconut sorbet and macadamia nut cookies to round out this popular menu.

Menu

Coconut Shrimp with Mango Salsa

SERVES 6
or can be multiplied up to 4 times

These sweet and savory shrimp can be served on any occasion, for a kid- and adult-friendly meal.

Tip
Use ready peeled and deveined shrimp from the seafood or frozen section of your grocery store.

● **Candy/deep-fry thermometer**

1 cup	unsweetened shredded coconut	250 mL
2/3 cup	all-purpose flour	150 mL
1/2 tsp	baking soda	2 mL
1/4 tsp	salt	1 mL
1/4 tsp	cayenne pepper	1 mL
1	egg, lightly beaten	1
1/3 cup	ginger ale or beer	75 mL
12 oz	large shrimp, peeled and deveined	375 g
	Vegetable or canola oil	
1 1/2 cups	Mango Salsa (see recipe, opposite)	375 mL

1. Place coconut in a stainless steel bowl. In another bowl, whisk together flour, baking soda, salt, cayenne, egg and ginger ale until smooth.

2. Dip shrimp in batter, then dredge in coconut, pressing slightly to help coconut stick. Discard any excess coconut and flour mixture.

3. In a deep, heavy saucepan, heat 3 inches (7.5 cm) of oil over medium-high heat until it registers 350°F (180°C) on thermometer. Working in small batches, fry shrimp for 3 to 5 minutes or until golden brown. Using tongs, remove shrimp to a plate lined with paper towels to drain.

4. Serve shrimp with mango salsa spooned over top.

Mango Salsa

2	mangos, peeled and diced	2
1	jalapeño pepper, seeded and minced	1
1	clove garlic, minced	1
¼ cup	minced sweet onion	50 mL
2 tbsp	chopped fresh cilantro	25 mL
½ tsp	grated lime zest	2 mL
2 tbsp	freshly squeezed lime juice	25 mL

1. In a bowl, combine mangos, jalapeño, garlic, onion, cilantro, lime zest and lime juice. Use right away or cover and refrigerate for up to 1 day.

Variation

▸ You can substitute 1 cup (250 mL) diced papaya or pineapple chunks for the mango.

Tip

If you're multiplying the recipe, be sure to adjust the heat to keep the oil at the correct temperature when frying and use a fine-mesh metal sieve to scoop out any small pieces periodically to avoid a burnt flavor in the oil.

MAKES ABOUT 1½ CUPS (375 ML) or can be multiplied up to 4 times

Fresh salsa is one of life's great joys. Adjust the recipe to your taste, changing it according to what's in season.

Tips

To prevent burns, wear disposable gloves while seeding and mincing jalapeños.

Although the taste of fresh mango is best, 1 cup (250 mL) diced thawed frozen mango can be used in a pinch.

Instead of making this from scratch, you can buy your favorite salsa and add chopped mango and fresh cilantro.

Oven-Roasted Kalua Pork

Traditionally, Kalua pork is a whole pig, slow-roasted in a pit dug in the ground. Here's an easier way to achieve the same delicious result. Serve the meat on its own or on buns, with barbecue sauce.

Tip

To double this recipe, use a 6- to 7-lb (3 to 3.5 kg) roast and increase the roasting time by about 1 hour. To triple it, use two 5-lb (2.5 kg) roasts; they will be fork-tender in about $4\frac{1}{2}$ hours. To multiply by four, use two 6- to 7-lb (3 to 3.5 kg) roasts and increase the roasting time by about 1 hour.

Make Ahead

Pork can be roasted and shredded a day in advance and stored in an airtight container in the refrigerator. Reheat, loosely covered with foil, in a 300°F (150°C) oven until warmed through, about 15 minutes.

- **Preheat oven to 325°F (160°C)**
- **Roasting pan**

2 tsp	ancho chile powder	10 mL
2 tsp	salt	10 mL
2 tsp	coarsely ground black pepper	10 mL
2 tbsp	olive oil	25 mL
2 tsp	Worcestershire sauce	10 mL
1 tsp	liquid smoke	5 mL
1 tsp	hot pepper sauce	5 mL
4 lb	boneless pork shoulder blade (butt) roast, trimmed of visible fat	2 kg

1. In a small bowl, combine ancho chile powder, salt, black pepper, oil, Worcestershire sauce, liquid smoke and hot pepper sauce to make a paste.

2. Rub paste over entire surface of pork. Wrap pork securely in two layers of foil, keeping seams up so the juices stay inside. Place in roasting pan.

3. Roast in preheated oven for $4\frac{1}{2}$ hours or until fork-tender. Let cool for 10 minutes before unwrapping. Slice pork or pull meat apart with forks.

Kalua Pig Roast

It's one of those party ideas that many people contemplate but few are brave enough to attempt on their own: the island-style roast of a whole pig, known in Hawaii as Kalua pig. Kalua pig is roasted slowly — over the course of many hours — in an *imu*, a traditional underground oven. The construction of an *imu* is in itself a task: digging a hole at least 5 by 3 feet (150 by 90 cm) and 3 feet (60 cm) deep, for starters. The design of the oven, which is lined with hot rocks and banana and tea leaves, allows it to slowly roast the pig over the course of a day, requiring as many as 12 hours, depending on the size of the pig. And, of course, sourcing a whole pig takes some hunting as well. For the adventurous, instructions for preparing a traditional Kalua pig are available on a number of websites and in some cookbooks, such as *Retro Luau* by Richard Perry.

Want to try cooking a real Kalua pig? Start at least 7 days in advance by contacting your local meat market and asking them to order you a whole pig. Ask for the pig to be dressed, which means all the internal organs have been removed and the inside is cleaned. The dressed pig will weigh about 70% of the whole pig's weight, so if you order a 60-pound (27 kg) pig you will be buying a 42-pound (19 kg) dressed pig. That might sound like an enormous amount of meat, but after cooking you will have slightly less than 20 pounds (9 kg) of cooked meat. The smaller the pig, the less meat you'll end up with, because smaller pigs have a higher percentage of skin and bone.

For obvious reasons, roasting a whole pig is something many hosts would rather outsource to a caterer, as the typical home cook is able to keep plenty busy with side dishes and decor for such a gathering. Check with local caterers or butchers for recommendations for experienced pig-roast professionals. There are also many recipes available online (check www.epicurious.com) that circumvent the need for an *imu* by wrapping a cut of pork (a much more reasonable choice for smaller gatherings) in banana leaves and roasting it in a regular oven, then seasoning it with liquid smoke to attempt to replicate the rich, smoky flavor of Kalua pig.

Island-Style Chicken

Luau time! Get that island flavor in an easy dish everyone will enjoy. Of course, you can adapt this to suit any kind of chicken you prefer. Double the sauce for 2 roaster birds, or use all drumsticks for a finger-food event.

Tips

Instead of grilling, this chicken can be baked on a foil-lined baking sheet in a 350°F (180°C) oven.

Use 2 chicken drumsticks or thighs per person in place of the breasts. Allow extra cooking time for dark meat pieces, and grill until juices run clear when chicken is pierced with a fork.

Make Ahead

The sauce can be made a day in advance. Let cool completely, transfer to an airtight container and refrigerate.

For even more flavor, after basting the chicken, let it marinate overnight in an airtight container in the refrigerator.

• **Preheat barbecue grill to high**

1½ cups	packed dark brown sugar	375 mL
1½ cups	ketchup	375 mL
1 cup	orange juice	250 mL
1 cup	cider vinegar	250 mL
1 cup	unsweetened pineapple juice	250 mL
2 tbsp	cornstarch	25 mL
6	boneless skinless chicken breasts (each about 5 oz/150 g)	6

1. In a non-reactive saucepan, combine brown sugar, ketchup, orange juice and vinegar. Bring to a boil over medium heat, stirring constantly. Reduce heat to medium-low.

2. In a small bowl, stir pineapple juice and cornstarch until smooth. Whisk into hot sauce and simmer, stirring constantly, for about 6 minutes or until mixture thickens and becomes smooth.

3. Baste chicken with sauce and grill for 6 to 8 minutes or until golden brown. Turn chicken, baste and grill for 5 minutes or until no longer pink inside. Remove from heat and keep warm.

4. Return remaining sauce to saucepan and bring to a boil over high heat. Reduce heat and simmer for about 15 minutes or until thickened. Serve chicken drizzled with sauce.

Pineapple and Golden Raisin Rice Salad

SERVES 6
or can be multiplied up to 4 times

This salad is sweet, punchy and crunchy, and is the perfect palate cleanser after fatty meat and fried coconut shrimp. Vegetarians and omnivores alike will come back for seconds.

Tip

If fresh pineapple is not available, you can use drained canned crushed pineapple.

Make Ahead

The salad and dressing can be made up to 1 day in advance if refrigerated separately in airtight containers. If the oil in the dressing solidifies, let it stand at room temperature until it becomes liquid. If it has separated, whisk to combine. Toss salad with dressing an hour before serving and let warm to room temperature.

1 1/2 cups	long-grain white rice	375 mL
2/3 cup	thinly sliced green onions	150 mL
2/3 cup	thinly sliced celery	150 mL
1/2 cup	golden raisins	125 mL
1/3 cup	chopped pineapple	75 mL
1/3 cup	chopped fresh flat-leaf (Italian) parsley	75 mL
2 tbsp	olive oil	25 mL
2 tbsp	unsweetened pineapple juice	25 mL
2 tbsp	freshly squeezed lemon juice	25 mL
	Salt and freshly ground black pepper	

1. In a large saucepan, bring 3 cups (750 mL) water to a boil over high heat. Add rice, reduce heat to low, cover and simmer for 15 minutes. Let stand, covered, for 10 minutes, then transfer rice to a large bowl and let cool to room temperature.

2. Add green onions, celery, raisins, pineapple and parsley to rice, stirring to combine.

3. In a small bowl, whisk together oil, pineapple juice and lemon juice until creamy. Season to taste with salt and pepper. Pour into rice mixture and toss to coat.

Theme Menus • Hawaiian Luau

Mexican Fiesta

~~~~~~

The fresh, spicy flavors of Mexican food make it a party favorite. Add a purchased dessert for an easy finish to this great menu. Or make this easy pineapple dessert: Peel, core and slice 1 pineapple. Place slices on a baking sheet and sprinkle with ¼ cup (50 mL) loosely packed brown sugar. Broil until sugar liquefies and bubbles. Let cool to room temperature (or cover with plastic wrap and refrigerate for up to 1 day) and serve with scoops of coconut sorbet.

Menu

Carne Asada for Breakfast

Carne asada, meaning "roasted meat," originated in Mexico as a way to use tougher cuts of meat, such as skirt and flank steak, by marinating them in fresh local ingredients such as lime juice, cilantro, chile peppers, garlic, onion and different spices. Today, the popularity of carne asada has spread throughout North America.

Since carne asada is simply a marinated and grilled meat, there is no one specific recipe to follow, only basic guidelines. Stick with common Mexican flavors like those mentioned above, but feel free to use any acidic ingredient (like citrus juice or vinegar), spicy or pungent chiles or spices, plenty of salt and lots of freshly ground pepper. Carne asada is especially great in a regular meal rotation because tough cuts of meat are more economical, and it can be used in small amounts in a number of dishes, such as tacos, burritos, tostadas and nachos, or by itself with a side of grilled vegetables and rice.

Having collectively run several big catering kitchens in Los Angeles, my experienced kitchen helpers taught me about carne asada. We'd get the flat-top grill smoking-hot in the morning and use up the marinated meat from the previous night's party, serving it with fried eggs and tortillas. Later in the day, it's especially well accompanied by ice-cold beer.

Carne Asada

SERVES 6
or can be multiplied
up to 4 times

You can easily double this grilled steak and use the leftovers to make sandwiches the next day — it's worth the effort.

Tip

Serve with warm corn or flour tortillas, Salsa Fresca (page 391) and lime wedges.

6	cloves garlic, minced	6
1	bunch cilantro, stems removed, leaves roughly chopped (about 1 cup/250 mL loosely packed)	1
1	onion, chopped	1
1 cup	freshly squeezed lime juice	250 mL
	Grated zest and juice of 1 orange	
1 tsp	salt	5 mL
$\frac{1}{2}$ tsp	freshly ground black pepper	2 mL
2 lbs	beef skirt steak	1 kg

1. In a large non-reactive container, combine garlic, cilantro, onion, lime juice, orange zest, orange juice, salt and pepper. Add steak and turn to coat. Cover and refrigerate for at least 8 hours or for up to 24 hours, turning a few times.

2. Meanwhile, preheat barbecue grill to high (or heat a large grill pan over high heat).

3. Remove steak from marinade, discarding marinade. (If using a grill pan, cut steak into pieces that will fit in the pan.) Grill for about $2\frac{1}{2}$ minutes per side, turning once, for medium-rare, or until desired doneness. Transfer to a cutting board and let rest for 5 minutes. Slice meat across the grain into thin strips.

Making Your Fiesta Easier

Visit a local Mexican market for freshly made salsa, tortilla chips, enchiladas, tamales, carnitas and just about anything else you want to serve. Order the food two or three days in advance. Round out your menu with refried beans and grilled corn, and serve fruit sorbets for dessert.

Roasted Chicken and Cheese Enchiladas

Using a roasted chicken from your grocery store makes this recipe come together quickly. Serve with sour cream and chopped fresh cilantro.

Make Ahead

The enchiladas can be assembled and partially baked up to 1 day ahead. Bake in preheated oven for 15 minutes. Let cool, cover with foil and refrigerate. Reheat, uncovered, in a 325°F (160°C) oven until cheese begins to bubble and brown on top and filling is heated through.

Cooled cooked enchiladas can be wrapped tightly in plastic wrap, then in foil, and frozen for up to 2 weeks. To reheat, thaw in the refrigerator for 24 hours before removing foil and plastic wrap. Replace foil to loosely cover and bake in a 325°F (160°C) oven for 20 to 25 minutes or until heated through.

- **Preheat oven to 350°F (180°C)**
- **Two 8-inch (20 cm) square baking dishes or one 13- by 9-inch (33 by 23 cm) baking dish, sprayed with nonstick cooking spray**

2	cans (each 19 oz/540 mL) red enchilada sauce	2
12	corn tortillas	12
2¼ cups	shredded roasted chicken	550 mL
3 cups	shredded Monterey Jack cheese	750 mL
½ cup	thinly sliced green onions	125 mL
1 cup	shredded Cheddar cheese	250 mL

1. In a medium saucepan, warm enchilada sauce over low heat. Dip a tortilla in sauce and put on a plate. Place about 3 tbsp (45 mL) shredded chicken, 2 tbsp (25 mL) Monterey Jack and a few green onions down the center. Roll up tightly and place seam side down in prepared baking dishes. Repeat with the remaining tortillas, dividing evenly between dishes if necessary.

2. Pour the remaining sauce over enchiladas. Sprinkle with Cheddar cheese and the remaining Monterey Jack and green onions. Cover loosely with foil.

3. Bake in preheated oven for 15 minutes. Uncover and bake for about 6 minutes or until cheese begins to bubble and brown on top. Let stand for 5 minutes before serving.

Easy Extra

▸ Sprinkle a few black olive slices inside each enchilada.

Spanish Rice

SERVES 6 TO 8
or can be multiplied
up to 4 times

For a special treat, and to achieve a beautiful golden color, add a pinch of exotic saffron. Leftover rice makes a great filling for burritos.

Make Ahead

Rice can be prepared through step 2 up to 1 day ahead. Let cool, transfer to an airtight container and refrigerate. Reheat in a covered casserole or baking dish in a 325°F (160°C) oven for 15 to 20 minutes or until heated through, then stir in the cilantro and green onions.

$1/4$ cup	olive oil	50 mL
1	large red onion, finely chopped	1
4	cloves garlic, minced (optional)	4
$1 1/4$ cups	medium-grain white rice	300 mL
1	can (8 oz/227 mL) reduced-sodium tomato sauce	1
2 cups	water	500 mL
1 tsp	salt	5 mL
$1/2$ tsp	ground cumin	2 mL
$1/4$ tsp	dried oregano	1 mL
Pinch	freshly ground black pepper	Pinch
$1/4$ cup	chopped fresh cilantro (optional)	50 mL
1	bunch green onions, chopped	1

1. In a large skillet, heat oil over medium heat. Sauté onion for about 5 minutes or until soft. Add garlic (if using) and sauté for 1 minute or until fragrant. Stir in rice and sauté for 2 minutes or until fragrant.

2. Stir in tomato sauce, water, salt, cumin, oregano and pepper; bring to a boil. Reduce heat to low, cover and simmer for about 20 minutes or until rice is tender.

3. Stir in cilantro (if using) and green onions.

Easy Extras

▶ Sauté $1/2$ cup (125 mL) corn kernels or thawed frozen peas or 2 stalks celery, finely diced, with the garlic.

Grilled Corn and Black Bean Salad

Grilling the corn adds a great smoky taste to this vegetable-packed salad, and the pepitas (pumpkin seeds) are crunchy and salty. Goat or feta cheese can be substituted for the queso fresco.

Tips

You can also grill the corn in a grill pan over medium-high heat.

Make this salad easier by replacing the grilled corn with a 14-oz (398 mL) can of golden corn kernels, drained.

Make Ahead

This salad can be prepared through step 3 up to 2 days in advance if refrigerated in an airtight container.

● **Preheat barbecue grill to high**

2	ears corn, husks and silk removed	2
1 tbsp	butter, softened	15 mL
2	cans (each 14 to 19 oz/398 to 540 mL) black beans, drained and rinsed	2
1	red onion, minced	1
1	large cucumber, peeled and diced	1
1½ cups	cherry tomatoes, halved	375 mL
2 tbsp	olive oil	25 mL
2 tbsp	freshly squeezed lime juice	25 mL
	Salt and freshly ground black pepper	
½ cup	crumbled queso fresco	125 mL
¼ cup	roasted salted pepitas (green pumpkin seeds)	50 mL

1. Rub corn with butter and roll in waxed paper to cover. Place on a microwave-safe plate and microwave on High for 5 minutes or until tender.

2. Meanwhile, in a bowl, combine beans, red onion, cucumber and tomatoes. Add olive oil and lime juice, tossing to combine. Season to taste with salt and pepper. Set aside.

3. Carefully unwrap corn and grill for about 4 minutes, turning often, until corn has char marks on all sides. Let cool for 10 minutes. Cut kernels off the cob and add to bean mixture.

4. Sprinkle queso fresco and pepitas over the top just before serving.

Salsa Fresca

MAKES ABOUT 2½ CUPS (625 ML)
or can be multiplied up to 4 times

Also known as pico de gallo, salsa fresca is best eaten the day it is made.

Tips

Check with your local Mexican deli to see if they make their own fresh tortilla chips. If they're available, serve them with the salsa fresca.

If you are sensitive to hot peppers, wear rubber or latex gloves when cutting the jalapeño.

4	large tomatoes, diced	4
1	red onion, finely chopped	4
1	jalapeño pepper, seeded and minced (optional)	1
½ cup	finely chopped fresh cilantro	125 mL
1 tbsp	freshly squeezed lime juice	15 mL
Pinch	ground cumin	Pinch
	Salt	

1. In a bowl, combine tomatoes, red onion, jalapeño (if using), cilantro, lime juice and cumin. Season to taste with salt. Serve immediately or cover and refrigerate for up to 8 hours.

Variation

▶ Up the heat by adding another jalapeño or a minced serrano chile.

Barcelona Bash

Serve this meal in the Spanish style: for a late lunch, which is the main meal in Spain, usually served about 3:00 in the afternoon. Dinners are lighter and later, often as late as 10:00 in the evening during the summer months.

Menu

Spiced Olives

SERVES 6 TO 8
or can be multiplied
up to 4 times

Manzanilla, Arbequina and Empeltre olives are all excellent Spanish varieties to use in this recipe. If these aren't available, large unstuffed green olives or kalamata olives will do.

Make Ahead

Spiced olives can be made up to 1 week ahead if refrigerated in an airtight container.

2 cups	large Spanish olives	500 mL
1	large clove garlic, thinly sliced	1
1	large bay leaf, crumbled	1
1 tbsp	chopped fresh thyme	15 mL
1/2 tsp	paprika	2 mL
1/4 tsp	freshly ground black pepper	1 mL
	Grated zest of 1 orange	
1 tbsp	freshly squeezed orange juice	15 mL
1 tbsp	olive oil	15 mL

1. In a bowl, combine olives, garlic, bay leaf, thyme, paprika, pepper, orange zest, orange juice and oil.

Variations

▶ Replace the thyme with rosemary and the orange zest and juice with lemon zest and juice.

▶ Toss small cubes of a Spanish cheese with the olives for a nice twist.

Ensalada de Atún

SERVES 6
or can be multiplied
up to 4 times

Ensalada de atún *is
a Spanish salad made
with fresh tuna, but
to save time, you can
make it with the best-
quality canned chunk
white tuna you can find.*

Make Ahead
The tuna can be
cooked the day before
if stored in an airtight
container in the
refrigerator. Or the
salad can be assembled
the day before, covered
and refrigerated
overnight and spooned
into lettuce cups right
before serving.

3 tbsp	olive oil, divided	45 mL
1 lb	albacore tuna, cut into ³⁄₄-inch (2 cm) pieces	500 g
1	head limestone or butter lettuce	1
2	stalks celery, thinly sliced	2
1⁄3 cup	thinly sliced red onion	75 mL
1⁄4 cup	roasted red bell peppers, finely chopped	50 mL
2 tbsp	capers, rinsed and drained	25 mL
2 tbsp	freshly squeezed lemon juice	25 mL
1⁄4 tsp	salt	1 mL
Pinch	freshly ground black pepper	Pinch

1. In a large skillet, heat 1 tbsp (15 mL) of the oil over medium-high heat. Cook tuna, in batches as necessary, for about 4 minutes, turning carefully with a spatula, until seared on all sides. Remove from heat.

2. Place whole leaves of lettuce on individual salad plates to make lettuce "cups."

3. In a large bowl, combine tuna, celery, red onion, roasted peppers, capers, lemon juice, salt and pepper. Divide salad among lettuce cups.

Theme Menus • Barcelona Bash

Seafood Paella

The name "paella" comes from the wide, flat-bottomed pan paella is traditionally cooked and served in. If you don't have a paella pan, use the widest, flattest skillet you have.

Tips

To clean and debeard mussels, scrub them under cool running water with a stiff brush. If any of the feathery beard remains, pull it off. Mussels and clams should close up while you clean them. If they don't, tap lightly on the shell with your fingernail. If they still don't close, discard them.

You can double or triple this recipe if you divide all ingredients equally between two large paella pans or two 12-inch (30 cm) skillets. If tripling, increase the simmering time in step 3 to 14 minutes.

5 cups	Quick Chicken Stock (page 223) or reduced-sodium chicken broth	1.25 L
1/4 tsp	saffron threads	1 mL
1/4 cup	olive oil, divided	50 mL
1	red onion, thinly sliced	1
1	green bell pepper, thinly sliced	1
5	cloves garlic, chopped	5
2 cups	medium-grain white rice	500 mL
3/4 tsp	salt	3 mL
1/4 tsp	freshly ground black pepper	1 mL
1 lb	mussels, scrubbed and debearded (see tip, at left)	500 g
1 lb	clams, scrubbed	500 g
4	tomatoes, chopped	4
1/2 cup	fresh flat-leaf (Italian) parsley, chopped	125 mL
1 lb	large or jumbo shrimp, peeled and deveined	500 g
2	lemons, cut into wedges	2

1. In a large pot, bring stock and saffron to a boil over high heat. Reduce heat and simmer until ready to use.

2. In a large paella pan or skillet, heat 2 tbsp (25 mL) of the oil over medium-high heat. Sauté red onion and green pepper for 5 minutes or until soft. Reduce heat to medium, add garlic and sauté for 2 minutes or until garlic is golden. Transfer onion mixture to a bowl and set aside.

3. Return pan to medium-high heat and heat the remaining oil. Sauté rice for about 4 minutes or until light golden and fragrant. Stir in onion mixture, salt and pepper. Pour in stock mixture, reduce heat to low, cover and simmer for about 12 minutes or until liquid is nearly absorbed.

4. Uncover pan and place mussels, clams, tomatoes and parsley on top of the rice mixture. Cover tightly and simmer over very low heat for 7 minutes. Add shrimp, cover tightly and simmer for 3 to 4 minutes or until clams and mussels open and shrimp are pink and opaque. Discard any mussels and clams that do not open. Serve with lemon wedges.

Why Saffron is the Most Precious Spice in the World

Everybody knows that saffron is the most expensive spice in the world, but why? Saffron is the red and yellow stigma from a small purple crocus flower. It is aromatic and possesses a unique pungent flavor, making it the preferred ingredient for simultaneously enhancing the flavor and color of popular dishes such as bouillabaisse, risotto and, my favorite, paella. It's the cultivation and harvesting process that makes saffron so expensive: it takes about 12,000 stigmas to produce about 1 oz (30 g) of saffron, and each and every one of the stigmas, or threads, is hand-picked and carefully laid out to dry.

In stores, saffron can be found in two forms: ground or as whole threads. It may seem like you're getting more for less if you buy the powdered form, but it loses flavor easily and is usually blended with other staining spices, such as turmeric. Although saffron is pricy, a little bit goes a long way. You need only a small pinch of about 3 to 4 threads for an entire dish. Too much saffron yields a slightly medicinal flavor. For optimal color and flavor, crush the threads gently between your fingertips just before using.

On my first trip to Barcelona, I found relatively inexpensive saffron in a famous old marketplace near my hotel. I decided it would be the perfect gift from Spain for all my friends back home. I envisioned us making paella while drinking Tintos and Riojas. The fantasy was so compelling that the next thing I knew, I was buying 20 inexpensive paella pans to go with the 20 jars of incredibly inexpensive saffron. Then I found myself at the Federal Express office, trying to figure out how to send the 20 pans home, since they wouldn't fit in my suitcases — they weighed a ton and the airlines weren't sympathetic. Luckily, the saffron was well received, and when I divided the cost of the shipping bill among all the pans and saffron, it was still cheaper than buying them at home. Well, almost.

Patatas Bravas

These spicy, crunchy little potatoes are addictive.

Tips

Alter the heat of these tasty potatoes by using more or less hot pepper sauce.

If you're multiplying the recipe, be sure to adjust the heat to keep the oil at the correct temperature when frying and use a fine-mesh metal sieve to scoop out any small pieces periodically to avoid a burnt flavor in the oil.

- **Candy/deep-fry thermometer**

	Vegetable oil	
3	russet potatoes, cut into 1-inch (2.5 cm) cubes	3
	Salt and freshly ground black pepper	
½ cup	ketchup	125 mL
½ cup	mayonnaise	125 mL
1 tbsp	paprika	15 mL
½ tsp	dried thyme	2 mL
¼ tsp	onion powder	1 mL
¼ tsp	hot pepper sauce, or to taste	1 mL
2 tbsp	chopped fresh flat-leaf (Italian) parsley	25 mL

1. In a deep, heavy saucepan, heat 2½ inches (6 cm) of oil over medium heat until it registers 325°F (160°C) on thermometer. Working in batches, fry potatoes until partially cooked, about 8 minutes. Using a slotted spoon, remove potatoes to a plate lined with paper towels to drain. Remove pan from heat, leaving oil in the pan. Let stand for 20 minutes. Season potatoes to taste with salt and black pepper.

2. Meanwhile, in a bowl, combine ketchup, mayonnaise, paprika, thyme, onion powder and hot pepper sauce. Set aside.

3. Return pan to medium-high heat and heat oil to 350°F (180°C). Working in batches, fry potatoes until golden brown, about 8 minutes. Using a slotted spoon, remove potatoes to a plate lined with paper towels and let drain for 1 minute. Add to sauce and toss to coat. Sprinkle with parsley and serve immediately.

Oranges with Red Wine

This is a light, elegant dessert especially suited to a warm evening.

Tips

Toast nuts in a single layer on a baking sheet in a 350°F (180°C) oven for 7 to 10 minutes. Slide nuts onto paper towels to cool.

Serve over sliced pound cake with a dollop of freshly whipped cream.

If you're multiplying the recipe, increase the boiling time for the syrup by 3 to 4 minutes for each time recipe is multiplied.

1	bottle (750 mL) dry Spanish red wine	1
1 cup	granulated sugar, divided	250 mL
1	cinnamon stick (about 4 inches/10 cm long), broken in half	1
6	large oranges	6
3 tbsp	sliced almonds, toasted	45 mL

1. In a large saucepan, bring wine, all but 1 tbsp (15 mL) of the sugar and cinnamon stick to a boil over medium-high heat, stirring until sugar dissolves. Boil, stirring occasionally, for about 20 minutes or until liquid has reduced by about two-thirds. Discard cinnamon stick. Let cool completely, then transfer to an airtight container and refrigerate for 40 minutes, until cold, or for up to 1 day.

2. Grate zest from 2 of the oranges. In a small bowl, combine orange zest and the remaining sugar.

3. Slice the peel and white pith from all the oranges. Cut into segments and place in a large bowl. Drizzle with wine syrup and sprinkle with sugared orange zest and almonds.

Theme Menus • Barcelona Bash

Italian Pasta Party

Serve this meal with lots of fresh, crusty bread and Chianti in straw-covered bottles.

Menu

Antipasti Platter

SERVES 6
or can be multiplied up to 4 times

This dish is colorful and delicious. Serve with long, skinny breadsticks.

Tip

You can use nearly anything you like in an antipasti platter: marinated mushrooms, celery sticks or small chunks of Parmesan cheese all work great.

Make Ahead

The platter can be put together a day ahead of time if tightly covered in plastic wrap and refrigerated.

1 lb	fresh mozzarella cheese (bocconcini), drained and sliced	500 g
5 oz	dry salami, thinly sliced	150 g
5 oz	prosciutto, thinly sliced	150 g
1½ cups	marinated green and black olives	375 mL
1	jar (7 oz/210 mL) marinated artichoke hearts, drained and halved	1
1	jar (7 oz/210 mL) fire-roasted red bell peppers, drained and sliced	1
1 tbsp	extra virgin olive oil	15 mL
	Coarse sea salt flakes and freshly ground black pepper	

1. Arrange mozzarella, salami, prosciutto, olives, artichoke hearts and roasted peppers attractively on a small serving platter or tray. Drizzle olive oil over mozzarella slices. Sprinkle everything with salt and pepper.

Shrimp and Cannellini Bean Salad

SERVES 6
or can be multiplied
up to 4 times

For a pretty presentation, spoon servings of this salad into cups made of limestone lettuce or radicchio leaves.

2 tbsp	chopped fresh flat-leaf (Italian) parsley	25 mL
1/4 cup	extra virgin olive oil	50 mL
3 tbsp	freshly squeezed lemon juice	45 mL
2 tsp	Dijon mustard	10 mL
1/4 tsp	salt	1 mL
Pinch	freshly ground black pepper	Pinch
1 1/2 lbs	medium shrimp, peeled, deveined and cooked	750 g
2	cans (each 14 to 19 oz/398 to 540 mL) cannellini or white kidney beans, drained and rinsed	2
1	fennel bulb, thinly sliced, with 2 tbsp (25 mL) chopped fronds	1
1	red onion, thinly sliced	1
1	yellow bell pepper, finely chopped	1
1	red bell pepper, finely chopped	1

1. In a bowl, whisk together parsley, oil, lemon juice, mustard, salt and pepper until creamy. Set aside.

2. In a large bowl, combine shrimp, beans, fennel bulb, red onion, yellow pepper and red pepper. Add dressing and toss to coat. Cover and refrigerate for at least 40 minutes, until chilled, or for up to 2 hours. Garnish with fennel fronds before serving.

Roasted Cauliflower Linguini

This dish is rich and
delicious. Roasting the
cauliflower gives it a
slightly sweet, nutty
taste that is perfectly
complemented by the
salty bacon.

Tips

If you prefer, you can
use 3 thinly sliced
medium leeks, white
and pale green parts
only, in place of the
green onion.

You can replace the
pastry with the same
amount of chopped
fresh sage.

- Preheat oven to 375°F (190°C)
- Rimmed baking sheet, sprayed with nonstick cooking spray

1	head cauliflower, cut into florets	1
6 tbsp	olive oil, divided	90 mL
	Salt and freshly ground black pepper	
1½ lbs	linguini pasta	750 g
1	red onion, thinly sliced	1
4	cloves garlic, minced	4
1½ cups	heavy or whipping (35%) cream	375 mL
1 cup	Quick Chicken Stock (page 223) or reduced-sodium chicken broth (approx.)	250 mL
¼ cup	freshly grated Parmesan cheese	50 mL
Pinch	ground nutmeg	Pinch
1 lb	bacon, cooked crisp and crumbled	500 g
2 tbsp	chopped fresh flat-leaf (Italian) parsley	25 mL
	Additional freshly grated Parmesan cheese	

1. On prepared baking sheet, toss cauliflower with 2 tbsp (25 mL) of the oil and spread out in a single layer. Season to taste with salt and pepper. Roast in preheated oven for 30 minutes, turning several times, until golden. Set aside and keep warm.

2. Meanwhile, in a large pot of boiling salted water, cook linguini according to package directions. Drain and toss with 2 tbsp (25 mL) of the oil. Return to the pot and keep warm.

3. In a medium saucepan, heat the remaining oil over medium heat. Sauté red onion for about 5 minutes or until starting to turn golden. Add garlic and sauté for 2 minutes. Add cream, stock, Parmesan and nutmeg; increase heat to medium-high and bring to a boil. Immediately turn off heat and stir until cheese is melted and sauce is smooth. Season to taste with salt and pepper.

4. Add cauliflower, bacon and parsley to linguini. Pour in cream sauce and toss to coat, adding more stock if linguini appears dry. Serve sprinkled with Parmesan.

Variation

▶ Add 1 cup (250 mL) thawed frozen petit green peas with the garlic.

Penne with Pancetta and Winter Greens

SERVES 6
or can be multiplied up to 4 times

This simple pasta dish can be adjusted at your whim. Bacon and ham are good substitutes for pancetta, as are chopped cooked chicken or crumbled sausage.

Tip

Swiss chard has thick, wrinkly, shiny, dark green leaves and has a slightly bitter taste, though most of the bitterness is lost in cooking. There are varieties with red, white, orange and yellow stems, which add beautiful color to this dish. Escarole also has a slightly bitter taste, but has brighter green leaves.

Make Ahead

This pasta can be made up to 2 days in advance if covered tightly and refrigerated. To reheat, place in a casserole dish, sprinkle with grated Parmesan cheese and heat in a 375°F (190°C) oven for 15 to 20 minutes or until top is lightly golden and pasta is heated through.

1 lb	penne or ziti pasta	500 g
1/4 cup	olive oil, divided	50 mL
12 oz	pancetta, diced	375 g
2	bunches Swiss chard or escarole, chopped (about 12 cups/3 L)	2
1/2 cup	freshly grated Parmesan cheese	125 mL
	Salt and freshly ground black pepper	

1. In a large pot of boiling salted water, cook penne according to package directions. Drain and toss with 2 tbsp (25 mL) of the oil. Return to pot and keep warm.

2. Meanwhile, in another large pot, heat the remaining oil over medium heat. Sauté pancetta for about 4 minutes or until crispy. Using a slotted spoon, transfer to a plate lined with paper towels.

3. Add chard to the oil remaining in pot, cover, reduce heat to low and cook until wilted, about 2 minutes.

4. In a large serving bowl, toss together penne, pancetta, chard and Parmesan. Season to taste with salt and pepper.

Variation

▸ Mature spinach is a good substitute for the winter greens, but cut the cooking time down to 1 minute.

White Chocolate Ricotta Tart

SERVES 6
or can be multiplied
up to 4 times

Ricotta makes a dessert much like cheesecake, but not so heavy on the palate. It bakes into an airy-light filling that will be welcome after a meal of pasta and cured meats.

Tip

If you have any bits of dough left over, you can roll them out and cut them into flower shapes to decorate the top of the tart before baking.

• **8-inch (20-cm) tart pan with removable bottom**

$1/2$	recipe Basic Pie Crust dough (page 261)	$1/2$
2	eggs	2
2 cups	ricotta cheese	500 mL
2 tbsp	granulated sugar	25 mL
$1/2$ tsp	vanilla extract	2 mL
$3^1/_2$ oz	white chocolate, grated	100 g
	Grated zest of 2 lemons	

1. On a floured work surface, roll out pie dough to a $1/8$-inch (3 mm) thick circle. Press into tart pan, trimming edge even with pan, cover with plastic wrap and refrigerate for at least 45 minutes, until chilled, or for up to 2 days.

2. Preheat oven to 375°F (190°C).

3. In a bowl, whisk together eggs, ricotta, sugar and vanilla. Fold in chocolate and lemon zest. Pour into chilled tart shell.

4. Bake for 35 to 40 minutes or until top is golden brown and center is slightly puffed. Let cool completely in pan on a wire rack.

Homemade Ricotta

- **Cheesecloth**
- **Very large sieve or colander**
- **Instant-read thermometer**

| 1 gallon | whole milk | 4 L |
| 1 quart | buttermilk | 1 L |

1. Rinse a large piece of cheesecloth in cold water and fold it 5 to 6 times, for a piece about 1 foot (30 cm) square. Place in sieve.

2. In a large saucepan, combine whole milk and buttermilk. Place over high heat, stirring as it rises in temperature to ensure that it does not burn on the bottom. When the mixture gets warm (you will be able to see the curds slowly develop), stop stirring, but scrape the bottom of the pan occasionally to prevent sticking. When the mixture registers 175°F to 180°F (79°C to 82°C) on thermometer, remove from heat and carefully ladle the whey (or liquid) into the sieve.

3. After ladling the whey, ladle the curds into the sieve, being careful not to break up and crush the curds. The whey will begin to drain, leaving behind firm curds. When the draining has slowed, tie the edges of the cloth together to make a bag and tie it to the faucet or to a wooden spoon set across the opening of a large bowl to allow the remaining liquid to drain out of the bag.

4. Once the draining has stopped completely, after about 15 minutes, untie the bag, scoop the ricotta into airtight containers and refrigerate for up to 5 days.

MAKES 4 CUPS (1 L)

One winter, I was lucky enough to work as a culinary producer on Michael Chiarello's television show NapaStyle. Michael is one of the best cooks in the world, and is one of my favorite people. He loves to make homemade ricotta. I'm a city girl, so I was hesitant to try, but Michael taught me that it's not only easy, but fun, too. Look for more of Michael's recipes and cookbooks on his website, www.napastyle.com.

German Feast

A German feast is a great theme for a man's birthday or a hearty winter supper.

Menu

Lentil Stew

**SERVES 6 AS
A MAIN COURSE**
or 12 as a soup
course or can be
multiplied up to
4 times

*Serve this stew with
thick slices of fresh
crusty bread. It's so rib-
sticking, the guys won't
even notice the slew of
healthy vegetables.*

Make Ahead

This stew can be made
up to 3 days ahead
if refrigerated in an
airtight container. It
will get better the longer
it sits. Reheat in a heavy
saucepan over medium
heat, stirring frequently
to prevent burning,
until heated through.

1¼ cups	dry brown lentils, rinsed and picked over for debris or stones	300 mL
2½ cups	reduced-sodium beef broth	625 mL
1 tbsp	tomato paste	15 mL
2	carrots, diced	2
2	stalks celery, diced	2
1	onion, finely chopped	1
1	large red-skinned potato, diced	1
¼ cup	chopped fresh parsley	50 mL
1 lb	smoked sausages, cut into 1-inch (2.5 cm) thick slices	500 g
	Cider vinegar	
	Salt and freshly ground black pepper	
	Sour cream	

1. In a medium pot, combine lentils, broth and tomato paste. Add enough water to generously cover lentils by 2 inches (5 cm). Bring to a boil over high heat. Reduce heat and simmer for about 30 minutes or until lentils are tender but still intact.

2. Add carrots, celery, onion and potato; simmer, stirring occasionally, for 30 minutes. Stir in parsley and sausage. Season to taste with vinegar, salt and pepper.

3. Ladle into bowls and garnish each bowl with a dollop of sour cream.

Seared Pork Chops

SERVES 6
or can be multiplied
up to 4 times

Serve these pork chops over a bed of Red Cabbage with Apples (page 406). This cooking method keeps the chops moist and cooks them speedily.

Tips

This recipe can be made with boneless or bone-in pork chops. If the pork chops are small, get 2 per person.

Pork is much leaner today than it has been in the past, so it is important not to overcook it. Remove it from the heat as soon as just a hint of pink remains inside.

6	pork chops, 1 to 1½ inches (2.5 to 4 cm) thick	6
¼ cup	all-purpose flour	50 mL
¼ tsp	salt	1 mL
¼ tsp	freshly ground black pepper	1 mL
¼ tsp	ground coriander	1 mL
1 tbsp	olive oil	15 mL

1. Pat pork chops dry with paper towels. On a plate, combine flour, salt, pepper and coriander. Dredge pork chops in flour mixture on both sides and set aside. Discard any excess flour mixture.

2. In a large heavy skillet, heat oil over high heat. Cook pork chops for 2 to 4 minutes, turning once, until browned on both sides. Reduce heat to low, cover and cook for 3 to 4 minutes. Turn pork chops, cover and cook for 3 to 4 minutes or until just a hint of pink remains inside.

Theme Menus • German Feast

Red Cabbage with Apples

This cabbage dish is perfect with the seared pork (page 405), and will prove wrong those who think they hate cabbage. The sweetened apples are the ideal complement.

4	slices bacon, cut into 1-inch (2.5 cm) strips	1
1	onion, thinly sliced	1
3	green apples, chopped	3
1	head red cabbage, thinly sliced	1
1/4 cup	packed brown sugar	50 mL
2/3 cup	red wine	150 mL
3 tbsp	cider vinegar	45 mL
1 tsp	caraway seeds (optional)	5 mL
	Salt and freshly ground black pepper	

1. In a large heavy saucepan, sauté bacon over medium-high heat until about halfway cooked. Add onion and sauté for about 3 minutes or until soft.

2. Stir in apples, cabbage, brown sugar, wine, vinegar and caraway seeds (if using); bring to a boil. Reduce heat to low, cover and simmer, stirring occasionally, for 1 hour or until cabbage is very tender and most of the liquid has evaporated. (If there is still quite a bit of liquid in the pan after 1 hour, let simmer uncovered until liquid is gone.) Season to taste with salt and pepper.

Spaetzle with Butter and Sage

Spaetzle is a delicious, irregularly shaped fat noodle or dumpling, common in Germany and often found in Austria, Switzerland, Hungary and even parts of France and Italy. It's comfort food in its truest form, and an extremely versatile side.

Tips

You need a colander with larger holes that will allow the dough to be pressed through and form into dumplings. A fine-holed or wire-mesh colander won't work. Specially designed spaetzle presses and ricers are available at kitchenware stores.

To use leftovers, heat a little butter in a skillet and sauté the spaetzle until hot.

• **Colander, spaetzle press or ricer (see tip, at left)**

3 cups	all-purpose flour	750 mL
½ tsp	salt	2 mL
¼ tsp	freshly ground black pepper	1 mL
4	eggs	4
2 cups	low-fat milk	500 mL
2 tbsp	finely chopped fresh sage	25 mL
2 tbsp	chopped fresh flat-leaf (Italian) parsley	25 mL
⅓ cup	unsalted butter, softened	75 mL

1. In a large bowl, combine flour, salt and pepper. Add eggs, milk, sage and parsley, stirring until mixture comes together as a smooth, thin dough.

2. Bring a large pot of salted water to a boil over high heat. Hold colander over pot and press half the dough through the holes and into the water. Using a slotted spoon or a shallow sieve, scoop out spaetzle as it floats to the surface. Place in a shallow bowl and keep warm. Repeat with remaining dough, making sure water returns to a boil between batches. Toss with butter before serving.

Theme Menus • German Feast

Pear Kuchen

This traditional German dessert takes a bit of effort but is well worth it. Serve it with vanilla bean ice cream.

Tip

If you don't have a stand mixer, you can use an electric hand mixer, but it will take a bit of elbow grease and a good 10 minutes to mix the dough in step 2. If your mixer seems to be struggling, switch to a wooden spoon to avoid burning out the motor.

- Preheat oven to 400°F (200°C)
- Instant-read thermometer
- 13- by 9-inch (33 by 23 cm) glass baking dish
- 10-inch (25 cm) springform pan, buttered and dusted with flour

Dough

1/3 cup	whole milk	75 mL
1/3 cup	granulated sugar, divided	75 mL
1	package (1/2 oz/7 g) active dry yeast	1
1 1/2 cups	all-purpose flour, divided	375 mL
1	egg	1
1	egg yolk	1
1/2 tsp	salt	2 mL
1/2 tsp	vanilla extract	2 mL
1/2 tsp	almond extract	2 mL
7 tbsp	unsalted butter, softened	105 mL

Pear Topping

4	ripe but firm Bosc pears, peeled and chopped	4
1/3 cup	packed dark brown sugar	75 mL
3 tbsp	unsalted butter, melted	45 mL
3 tbsp	coarsely chopped almonds	45 mL
2 tbsp	all-purpose flour	25 mL
1/2 tsp	ground cinnamon	2 mL

1. *Dough:* Place milk in a microwave-safe bowl and heat on High for 15-second intervals until temperature reaches 110°F to 120°F (43°C to 49°C) on an instant-read thermometer. Stir in 1 tsp (5 mL) of the sugar. Sprinkle yeast over mixture and let stand until foamy, about 5 minutes.

2. Transfer milk mixture to a clean mixer bowl. Using an electric stand mixer fitted with a paddle attachment, beat in 1/3 cup (75 mL) of the flour. Beat in egg, egg yolk, the remaining sugar, salt, vanilla and almond extract. Gradually beat in the remaining flour. Beat in butter until a soft and sticky dough forms, about 3 minutes.

3. Transfer dough to a lightly oiled bowl and cover with plastic wrap. Let rise in a warm, draft-free place until doubled in size, about 1 1/2 hours.

4. *Topping:* In baking dish, toss pears with brown sugar and butter. Bake in preheated oven for about 30 minutes or until golden brown. Sprinkle with almonds, flour and cinnamon, stir to combine and set aside.

5. Reduce oven temperature to 350°F (180°C). Punch down dough and place in prepared springform pan, pressing it into the bottom. Cover with plastic wrap and let rise in a warm, draft-free place for 30 minutes.

6. Arrange pear mixture on top of dough, leaving a $\frac{1}{2}$-inch (1 cm) border around the edge. Bake for 35 to 40 minutes or until deep golden brown. Let cool on a wire rack until barely warm to the touch before releasing sides of pan.

Variation

▸ Use pecans, walnuts or hazelnuts in place of the almonds.

Dark Beer: It's Not Bitter, It's Rich and Deep!

What could go better with a large German feast than an icy-cold glass of refreshing dunkel beer? Dunkel, which means "dark," is one of the most popular types of beer in Germany today. It's no surprise that a country with so many varieties of deliciously rich and hearty dishes would be drawn to complementary beers.

There are two general categories of dunkels: dark wheat beers and dark lagers. The dark wheat beers usually have flavor profiles of toffee, nuts, chocolate, coffee and spicy hops. There are three basic types of dark lagers: Münchner, Franconian dunkles and schwarzbier. Munchner is a malted, lightly hopped beer that has traditionally been the standard beer of Munich. Franconian dunkles is a very heavily hopped, bitter, dark malted beer; in Germany, it is usually called "Dunkles Export." Schwarzbier is a very dark, opaque beer with notes of licorice and a slightly burnt flavor, similar to that of a stout.

Look for imported German beers at a well-stocked liquor store. Before chilling bottles in a tub of ice, slip a plastic bag around the beer — or around the entire six-pack — to preserve the labels.

Grecian Get-Together

Greek food is rich with the flavors of garlic, rosemary and oregano. This menu is perfectly suited to buffets, as all of these dishes taste great at room temperature.

Menu

Hummus with Pita Chips

SERVES 6 TO 8
or can be multiplied up to 4 times

Tahini is a paste made from ground sesame seeds and is used widely throughout the Mediterranean and Middle East.

Make Ahead
Hummus can be made up to 3 days in advance if refrigerated in an airtight container.

Pita chips can be made up to 4 days in advance if stored in an airtight container at room temperature.

3 cups	rinsed drained canned chickpeas	750 mL
¼ cup	tahini	50 mL
¼ cup	freshly squeezed lemon juice	50 mL
1 tsp	salt	5 mL
Pinch	freshly ground black pepper	Pinch
½ cup	extra virgin olive oil, divided	125 mL
6	pitas, each cut into 8 wedges	6

1. In a food processor, combine chickpeas, tahini, lemon juice, salt and pepper; process until smooth. With the motor running, through the feed tube, gradually pour in ⅓ cup (75 mL) of the oil; process until incorporated. Hummus should have the consistency of thin paste. If it is too thick, add a little water until desired consistency is reached.

2. Preheat oven to 375°F (190°C). Brush both sides of pita wedges with the remaining oil. Place on a baking sheet and bake for about 8 minutes or until crispy. Let cool for at least 5 minutes before serving with the hummus.

Easy Extras
▸ Personalize hummus by adding 2 tbsp (25 mL) puréed roasted garlic or 1 tbsp (15 mL) chopped fresh herbs.

Garlic-Roasted Leg of Lamb

SERVES 6
or can be doubled

There are few things as elegant and easy as roasted leg of lamb. Ask your butcher to bone and butterfly a leg of lamb for you if it isn't available in the meat aisle of your grocery store.

Tips

As the lamb rests after cooking, the internal temperature will continue to rise by about 5°F (3°C), so remove it from the oven when it is slightly less than the desired doneness.

If you have a large roasting pan, you can double the recipe.

Make Ahead

Lamb can be seasoned and tied a day ahead if wrapped tightly in plastic wrap and refrigerated.

- Preheat oven to 450°F (230°C)
- Roasting pan or large baking dish, sprayed with nonstick cooking spray
- Kitchen twine

3 lb	boneless leg of lamb, butterflied	1.5 kg
8	cloves garlic, minced	8
1/4 cup	olive oil	50 mL
	Grated zest of 1 lemon	
1/4 cup	freshly squeezed lemon juice	50 mL
3 tbsp	chopped fresh rosemary	45 mL
2 tbsp	chopped fresh flat-leaf (Italian) parsley	25 mL
1 tbsp	chopped fresh oregano	15 mL
1 tbsp	fennel seeds (optional)	15 mL
1 tsp	salt	5 mL
1/2 tsp	freshly ground black pepper	2 mL

1. Lay lamb flat on a clean work surface. In a small bowl, combine garlic, oil, lemon zest, lemon juice, rosemary, parsley, oregano, fennel seeds (if using), salt and pepper. Rub generously over both sides of lamb. Starting at the narrowest end, roll lamb up, smooth side out, and tie in several places with kitchen twine.

2. Place lamb in prepared roasting pan and place in preheated oven. Immediately reduce oven temperature to 325°F (160°C) and roast for about 2 hours, until a meat thermometer inserted in the thickest part registers 135°F (57°C) for medium-rare, or until desired doneness. Untie lamb, tent with foil and let rest for 10 to 15 minutes before slicing.

Rice with Tomatoes and Peppers

This is a typical rice dish from the Thessaly region of Greece. In Greece, it is known as bourani.

Make Ahead
Rice can be made up to 2 days ahead if refrigerated in an airtight container. Reheat in a covered casserole dish in a 325°F (160°C) oven for about 20 minutes or until warmed through.

⅓ cup	extra virgin olive oil	75 mL
1	small onion, finely chopped	1
2	cloves garlic, minced	2
1	red bell pepper, cut into thin strips	1
1	yellow bell pepper, cut into thin strips	1
1½ cups	long-grain white rice	375 mL
⅔ cup	chopped fresh flat-leaf (Italian) parsley	150 mL
3 cups	hot water	750 mL
⅓ cup	tomato sauce	75 mL
	Salt and freshly ground black pepper	

1. In a large saucepan, heat oil over medium heat. Sauté onions for about 4 minutes or until soft. Add garlic, red pepper and yellow pepper; sauté for 3 minutes or until peppers have just softened.

2. Stir in rice, parsley, hot water and tomato sauce; bring to a boil. Reduce heat to low, cover and simmer for about 20 minutes or until water is absorbed and rice is tender. Let stand, covered, for 5 minutes. Fluff with a fork. Season to taste with salt and pepper.

Easy Extras
▶ Add a little squeeze of lemon juice while fluffing the rice.

▶ Add a little chopped fresh oregano or rosemary with the parsley.

Roasted Mushrooms and Eggplant

*The combination of
lemon juice, olive oil,
oregano and thyme
gives vegetables a
classic Greek flavor.*

Make Ahead
The vegetables can be
roasted the day before
and refrigerated in an
airtight container. Bring
to room temperature
before serving.

- **Preheat oven to 425°F (220°C)**
- **Large shallow roasting pan**

1/3 cup	olive oil	75 mL
1 tsp	dried thyme	5 mL
1 tsp	dried oregano	5 mL
	Juice of 1 lemon	
	Salt and freshly ground black pepper	
1	large red onion, cut into 8 wedges	1
18	white or brown mushrooms, stems trimmed	1
2	eggplants, cut into 1 1/2-inch (4 cm) pieces	2

1. In a large bowl, whisk together olive oil, thyme, oregano and lemon juice. Season to taste with salt and pepper.

2. Separate onion layers and add to oil mixture. Add mushrooms and eggplants, tossing to combine. Pour into roasting pan, spreading out in a single layer.

3. Roast in preheated oven for about 20 minutes or until eggplant is cooked through and onions are beginning to char.

Easy Extras
- Halved plum (Roma) tomatoes are a great addition, as are thickly sliced bell peppers and artichoke hearts.

Semolina Orange Cake with Almonds

SERVES 6 TO 9
or can be multiplied up to 4 times

This is a very sweet, dense cake that tastes best served slightly warm.

Tip
Serve with slightly sweetened whipped cream or vanilla ice cream.

Make Ahead
Semolina cake tastes much better if made the day before. Wrap well and store at room temperature for up to 1 day. Refrigerate it if you need to keep it for 2 days. Warm in a 275°F (140°C) oven for 15 minutes before serving.

- **Preheat oven to 350°F (180°C)**
- **9-inch (23 cm) square baking pan, buttered**

2¼ cups	all-purpose flour	550 mL
¾ cup	fine semolina	175 mL
2 tsp	baking powder	10 mL
¼ tsp	salt	1 mL
1 tbsp	grated orange zest	15 mL
½ cup	orange juice	125 mL
3	eggs, separated	3
2 cups	granulated sugar, divided	500 mL
1 cup	unsalted butter	250 mL
⅔ cup	chopped almonds	150 mL
1 tbsp	orange-flavored liqueur	15 mL

1. In a large bowl, whisk together flour, semolina, baking powder and salt. Stir in orange juice until mixture is smooth. Set aside.

2. In a clean bowl, using an electric mixer, beat egg whites, gradually adding ¼ cup (50 mL) of the sugar, until stiff peaks form. Set aside.

3. In another bowl, using an electric mixer, cream egg yolks, ¼ cup (50 mL) sugar, butter and orange zest until pale in color. Add to flour mixture, stirring to combine. Fold in beaten egg whites. Pour batter into prepared pan and sprinkle with almonds.

4. Bake in preheated oven for about 40 minutes or until deep golden brown and a tester inserted in the center comes out clean.

5. Meanwhile, in a small heavy saucepan, over low heat, combine the remaining sugar and 1 cup (250 mL) water, stirring until sugar has dissolved. Add liqueur and bring to a boil over medium-high heat. Reduce heat and simmer for about 8 minutes or until slightly thickened.

6. Pour syrup over cake while both are still fairly hot. Let cool completely in pan on a rack before slicing and serving.

Ouzo Mojito

Tip

To make simple syrup, combine equal amounts of water and granulated sugar in a small saucepan and simmer over low heat, stirring until sugar has dissolved. Increase heat to medium and let simmer until thick. Let cool and store in an airtight container at room temperature for up to 1 week.

4	fresh mint leaves	4
	Crushed ice	
¾ cup	club soda	175 mL
2 oz	ouzo	50 mL
2 tbsp	simple syrup (see tip, at left)	25 mL

1. In the bottom of a chilled glass, muddle mint until crushed and fragrant. Fill the glass halfway with ice.

2. In a cocktail shaker filled with ice, combine club soda, ouzo and simple syrup. Shake until thoroughly combined and chilled, strain into glass and stir.

Ouzo, Past and Present

Ouzo is an anise-flavored liqueur that is widely consumed in Greece. Traditionally, it is served neat in a shot glass, or with a little water. When ouzo is served neat, it is completely clear, but when it is mixed with water or served over ice, it turns a milky, opalescent color.

When I first graduated from cooking school, I got a job cooking shrimp in a small fish market. The owner of the shop, Tasso, was from Greece. His wife was American (and his mistress was Mexican). His mother also worked there; she was a real stickler about how I peeled the shrimp. Most days, I tried to stay in the back kitchen, cooking boatloads of shrimp, as it seemed the safest place. Naturally, given the dynamics of this place, disagreements and fights were common. The worst problem with the fighting was that it made lunch late, and that made Tasso really angry because he took his nap after lunch, and he hated to take his nap late, because, as you can imagine, he truly needed his rest.

One of my tasks was to serve lunch. It didn't take me long to figure out that a few shots of ouzo before lunch simmered everyone down, and they came to the table as peaceful as lambs.

Recently, Jennifer, an intern in my kitchen, asked me if I liked ouzo. Back came the memories of those sleepy afternoons. Jen updated classic neat ouzo for me with this refreshing cocktail.

Turkish Twilight

Decorate your party space with rich silk pillows in jewel tones and serve dinner on a low table without chairs.

Menu

Zucchini Walnut Dip with Lavosh Crackers

SERVES 6
or can be multiplied up to 4 times

This dip is also great with crudités of celery and cauliflower, or spread inside a pita filled with fresh vegetables.

Tips

This dip can be served right away or chilled.

If multiplying the recipe, increase cooking time in the microwave by about 1 minute per batch.

Make Ahead

Dip can be made up to 3 days ahead if refrigerated in an airtight container.

2	zucchini, sliced	2
1	clove garlic, chopped	1
1/4 cup	chopped red onion	50 mL
1/4 cup	chopped walnuts	50 mL
1/2 cup	plain yogurt	125 mL
2 tbsp	olive oil	25 mL
1 tbsp	freshly squeezed lemon juice	15 mL
1/2 tsp	paprika	2 mL
	Salt	
1	package (5 oz/150 g) lavosh crackers or other flatbread	1

1. Place zucchini in a microwave-safe bowl, cover with plastic wrap and heat on High for 1 minute or until tender.

2. Transfer to a food processor or blender and add garlic, red onion, walnuts, yogurt, oil, lemon juice and paprika. Process until evenly ground but still slightly chunky. Season to taste with salt.

3. Serve dip with lavosh crackers.

Spiced Lamb Kebabs

SERVES 6
or can be multiplied
up to 4 times

The addition of cinnamon gives this dish a wonderfully exotic taste.

Tips

Kebabs can be served as sandwiches with flatbread.

If you prefer your lamb cooked to medium, broil or grill for 7 to 8 minutes; medium-well for 9 to 10 minutes; well for 11 to 12 minutes.

• **Twelve 12-inch (30 cm) metal or wooden skewers**

2½ lb	boneless leg of lamb	1.25 kg
¼ cup	olive oil	50 mL
1 tsp	ground cumin	5 mL
1 tsp	freshly ground black pepper	5 mL
½ tsp	ground cinnamon	2 mL
Pinch	cayenne pepper	Pinch
1	red onion, cut into large pieces	1

1. Trim fat from lamb and cut into 1½-inch (4 cm) cubes.

2. In a sealable plastic bag, combine oil, cumin, black pepper, cinnamon and cayenne. Add lamb, seal and toss to coat. Refrigerate for at least 2 hours or overnight, shaking bag occasionally to redistribute marinade.

3. Preheat broiler, or preheat barbecue grill to medium-high. If using wooden skewers, soak them in water for 10 minutes.

4. Separate onion into pieces of 2 to 3 layers. Remove lamb from marinade, discarding marinade. Thread lamb and onion onto skewers, with 3 slices of onion between each piece of lamb. If broiling, place on a foil-lined rimmed baking sheet. Broil or grill for 5 to 6 minutes, turning to sear all sides, until medium-rare, or until desired doneness.

Easy Extras

▸ Add other vegetables with the onions: cubes of zucchini, sliced bell peppers or small pieces of eggplant would work well. Salt eggplant generously, drain for at least 1 hour and rinse well before using.

Theme Menus • **Turkish Twilight**

Roasted Eggplant and Peppers

SERVES 6
or can be multiplied
up to 4 times

*This makes a great
hot side dish, or it
can be served at room
temperature over
chilled greens for a
delicious salad.*

Tip

If multiplying this
recipe, make sure
vegetables are in a
single layer, and rotate
pans in oven.

Make Ahead

Vegetables can
be cooked a day
in advance and
refrigerated in an
airtight container.
Reheat in a 325°F
(160°C) oven for 15
minutes before serving.

- Preheat oven to 450°F (230°C)
- 13- by 9-inch (33 by 23 cm) shallow baking dish

4	cloves garlic	4
2 tbsp	fresh oregano	25 mL
1/2 tsp	salt	2 mL
1/2 tsp	freshly ground black pepper	2 mL
3 tbsp	olive oil	45 mL
2 tbsp	freshly squeezed lemon juice	25 mL
1	large eggplant, cut into 1/4-inch (0.5 cm) slices	1
1	red bell pepper, cut into 8 long strips	1
1	yellow bell pepper, cut into 8 long strips	1
1	green bell pepper, cut into 8 long strips	1

1. In a food processor or blender, process garlic, oregano, salt, pepper, oil and lemon juice until smooth and creamy.

2. Place vegetables in a single layer in baking dish and brush with garlic mixture. Turn and brush the other side.

3. Roast in preheated oven for about 22 minutes or until eggplant is nicely browned on top and peppers begin to char.

Carrot, Onion and Tomato Couscous

Couscous (kuskus in Turkish) is fine granules of pasta made from semolina, and is an endlessly adaptable food.

Tip

This dish can be served hot, warm or at room temperature.

Make Ahead

This side can be made up to 2 days ahead if refrigerated in an airtight container.

2 cups	couscous	500 mL
½ cup	finely diced carrot	125 mL
1 cup	cherry tomatoes, quartered	250 mL
½ cup	finely chopped red onion	125 mL
½ cup	finely chopped fresh flat-leaf (Italian) parsley	125 mL
2 tbsp	olive oil	25 mL
	Salt and freshly ground black pepper	

1. In a medium saucepan, bring 3 cups (750 mL) water to a boil. Stir in couscous and carrot, then remove from heat, cover and let stand for 5 minutes.

2. Add tomatoes, red onion, parsley and olive oil; gently toss to coat. Season to taste with salt and pepper.

Almond Apricot Tart

This simple tart is baked on a baking sheet, not in a pie pan, so it has a thicker crust than most tarts, making it much easier to serve.

Tips

You can use dried apricots if fresh are unavailable. Cut 16 dried apricots in half and place in a small bowl. Pour in enough boiling water to cover, cover bowl and let stand for 30 minutes. Drain and use as directed.

Make Ahead

Tart can be prepared through step 3 and frozen for up to 2 weeks. Place baking sheet directly in freezer for at least 2 hours, then remove the tart and wrap securely in plastic wrap, then in foil. Store flat inside freezer. Bake from frozen in a 350°F (180°C) oven for 55 to 60 minutes.

Tart can be baked up to 1 day ahead if stored in an airtight container at room temperature.

• **Preheat oven to 400°F (200°C)**

3½ oz	almond paste	100 g
3 tbsp	granulated sugar	45 mL
3 oz	cream cheese	90 g
1	egg yolk	1
1 tsp	vanilla extract	5 mL
¼ tsp	ground cinnamon	1 mL
½	recipe Basic Pie Crust dough (page 261)	½
3 tbsp	sliced almonds	45 mL
10	large apricots, quartered	10
⅓ cup	liquid honey	75 mL

1. In a food processor, purée almond paste and sugar until very smooth. Add cream cheese, egg yolk, vanilla and cinnamon; process until smooth.

2. On a floured work surface, roll out dough to a 14-inch (35 cm) circle. Place on a heavy baking sheet (some dough can hang over the edges of the sheet).

3. Spoon cream cheese filling over dough, leaving a 2-inch (5 cm) border. Scatter almonds and apricots over filling. Fold edges of dough up and over filling, leaving 6 inches (15 cm) of filling open at the center. Press edges to make a sealed border for the tart. Drizzle honey over apricots.

4. Bake in preheated oven for about 40 minutes or until crust is golden brown and filling is bubbly. Let cool on baking sheet on a wire rack. Serve warm or at room temperature.

Variation

▸ Chopped fresh plums, nectarines or peaches are good substitutions for the apricots. You'll need about 3 cups (750 mL).

How to Make Faux Turkish Coffee

Turkish coffee is a very strong coffee made in a special long-handled open brass or copper pot called a *jezve* or *ibrik*. However, a saucepan will work just as well. Using a high-quality, finely ground coffee, combine about 2 scant tablespoons (25 mL) for each cup (250 mL) of water, add sugar, ground cinnamon, cardamom or nutmeg to taste and bring to a boil three times, letting it cool very briefly between each boil. Strain through a fine-mesh sieve into a serving carafe. Serve immediately after the third boil, preferably in small espresso cups. Remind your guests that the bubbles and froth that collect on the coffee's surface are said to bring good kismet to whoever gets a little in their cup.

Turkish Treats

At your next party, serve up a few Turkish treats, such as warm roasted pumpkin seeds, roasted corn kernels and chickpeas, halvah with pistachios, Turkish delight in various flavors, sesame sticks and dried figs. All of these yummy snacks are available at import stores and online.

African Ivory Coast

The exotic tastes of Africa make the perfect menu for a bon voyage or welcome back party.

Menu

Cucumber Salad with Feta and Mint

SERVES 6
or can be multiplied up to 4 times

This salad is wonderfully crunchy, subtly tart and refreshingly minty.

Tip

Serve this salad soon after assembling it so the cucumber stays crisp.

Make Ahead

Chop the fennel, green onions and cucumbers up to 1 day ahead of time. Wrap separately in damp paper towels, place in sealable plastic bags and refrigerate to keep fresh.

1	fennel bulb, including top fronds	1
$\frac{1}{4}$ cup	extra virgin olive oil	50 mL
2 tbsp	freshly squeezed lemon juice	25 mL
	Salt and freshly ground black pepper	
8	green onions, thinly sliced	8
2	large cucumbers, quartered lengthwise and sliced $\frac{1}{4}$ inch (0.5 cm) thick	2
2	bunches watercress	2
8 oz	feta cheese, crumbled	250 g
$\frac{1}{4}$ cup	chopped fresh mint	50 mL

1. Wash fennel bulb and remove fronds. Chop $\frac{1}{4}$ cup (50 mL) of the feathery fronds and set aside. Thinly slice bulb and set aside.

2. In a small bowl, whisk together oil and lemon juice. Season to taste with salt and pepper.

3. In a large serving bowl, combine fennel fronds and bulb, green onions, cucumbers, watercress, feta and mint. Add dressing and toss to coat. Serve immediately.

Spiced Zucchini and Pepper Kebabs

SERVES 6
or can be multiplied
up to 4 times

*These kebabs are a
perfect side dish to
accompany the Grilled
Cornish Game Hens
with Lemon and Yogurt.*

Make Ahead
Assemble the skewers
a day before and
refrigerate in an airtight
container. Grill or
broil them just before
serving.

● **Eighteen 12-inch (30 cm) wood or bamboo skewers**

½ cup	olive oil	125 mL
2 tbsp	soy sauce	25 mL
1 tbsp	red wine vinegar	15 mL
4	cloves garlic, minced	4
2 tsp	chopped fresh thyme	10 mL
1 tsp	salt	5 mL
½ tsp	freshly ground black pepper	2 mL
2 tsp	Dijon mustard	10 mL
3	zucchini, cut into 1-inch (2.5 cm) rounds	3
1	red bell pepper, cut into 1-inch (2.5 cm) squares	1
1	green bell pepper, cut into 1-inch (2.5 cm) squares	1
1	yellow bell pepper, cut into 1-inch (2.5 cm) squares	1

1. In a large bowl, whisk together oil, soy sauce and vinegar until emulsified. Whisk in garlic, thyme, salt, pepper and mustard. Add zucchini and red, green and yellow peppers; toss to coat. Cover and refrigerate for at least 1 hour, until chilled, or overnight.

2. Soak skewers in water for 30 minutes. Meanwhile, preheat barbecue grill to medium-high or preheat broiler.

3. Thread one slice of each color pepper onto each skewer. Follow with a slice of zucchini. Repeat two more times. If broiling, place on a baking sheet. Grill or broil for about 10 minutes, turning and brushing occasionally with marinade, if desired, until peppers just begin to char.

Waiting for Willy

This African Ivory Coast menu was inspired by a memorable trip to Africa. A dish similar to the Spiced Zucchini and Pepper Kebabs was served to me in a tiny café one afternoon. I was waiting for my guide to come back and take me to the local airport. While waiting, I sat at one of the two tables and thought, Sure, I can eat. Baskets and plates of perfectly prepared food arrived. The cumin smelled like perfume. Warm flatbreads and grilled meat — antelope, actually — rounded out my meal. Soon, Willy, my guide, arrived. I was surprised that he was on foot, and carrying a broom.

"Willy," I asked, "how will we get to the airport?"

"We are here," Willy replied. And at that moment, in the sky, I saw a plane. Willy walked ten steps to the nearby field. The plane landed, quickly and safely. We were there.

"Willy," I asked, "what's the broom for?"

"In case, Madame, I have to chase the elephants away," he said.

Of course.

Grilled Cornish Game Hens with Lemon and Yogurt

The unexpected spiciness of the cumin and cinnamon and the sweetness of the raisins make this dish very memorable. Try this same spicy-sweet combination on other poultry too.

Tip

These hens can also be baked in a large roasting pan in a 300°F (150°C) oven. There's no need to turn them, but do baste every 7 minutes or so until golden brown and cooked through.

- Preheat barbecue grill to medium-low
- Kitchen twine

Stuffing

2 tbsp	unsalted butter	25 mL
1	large onion, finely chopped	1
2 tsp	ground cinnamon	10 mL
1 tsp	ground cumin	5 mL
2/3 cup	fresh or panko bread crumbs	150 mL
1/2 cup	golden raisins	125 mL
1/4 cup	sliced almonds	50 mL
2 tbsp	olive oil	25 mL
2 tbsp	liquid honey	25 mL
2 tbsp	hot water	25 mL
2 tbsp	chopped fresh cilantro	25 mL
2 tbsp	chopped fresh mint	25 mL
	Salt and freshly ground black pepper	
6	rock Cornish game hens	6

Baste

1/3 cup	unsalted butter	75 mL
1/3 cup	liquid honey	75 mL
1 tsp	ground cinnamon	5 mL
1/2 tsp	ground cumin	2 mL
1/2 tsp	salt	2 mL
1/2 tsp	freshly ground black pepper	2 mL

Sauce

1 cup	plain whole-milk yogurt	250 mL
1 tbsp	granulated sugar	15 mL
	Grated zest of 2 lemons	

1. *Stuffing:* In a skillet, melt butter over medium-high heat. Sauté onion for about 5 minutes or until soft and translucent. Add cinnamon and cumin; sauté for 2 minutes.

2. In a bowl, combine onion mixture, bread crumbs, raisins and almonds. Set aside.

3. In a small bowl, stir together oil, honey and hot water until honey is dissolved. Pour over onion mixture and stir well. Stir in cilantro and mint. Season to taste with salt and pepper.

4. Rinse game hens under cold running water and pat dry. Divide the stuffing among the hens. Tie the legs together with kitchen twine. Set aside.

5. *Baste:* In a medium saucepan, over medium heat, combine butter, honey, cinnamon, cumin, salt and pepper, stirring until butter melts, honey dissolves and baste is heated through.

6. Brush hens with baste and grill, turning and basting frequently, for about 40 minutes or until hens are golden brown and juices run clear when thighs are pierced with a knife.

7. *Sauce:* Meanwhile, in a bowl, combine yogurt, sugar and lemon zest.

8. Serve hens with sauce on the side for dipping.

Make Ahead

The stuffing can be prepared up to 1 day ahead and refrigerated in an airtight container.

The Exotic Scent of Cumin

During my childhood, my mother was always cooking from international cookbooks. Yet I can remember the first time I tasted cumin: it was in her beef taco filling. My family loved Mexican food — or at least what we thought was Mexican food. It was the 50s; back then, cumin, or comino, was something very exotic, found only in Asian or Middle Eastern markets. We always bought it in San Francisco's Chinatown. Today, you can find cumin on any grocery store spice shelf.

If you trace cumin's history back to Biblical times, it appears that cumin made its way from the Middle East to Africa as precious cargo bobbing on a ship across the Indian Ocean, or tied to camels walking a spice trail.

Cumin is the dried fruit, a tiny seed, of a plant in the parsley family. The seed looks similar to a caraway seed. You can buy cumin seeds whole or ground. They come in three colors: amber, the most popular; white; and black, the most intense and peppery. The black seed is my favorite. Once you have smelled cumin, you won't forget its smoky quality. And as all cooks know, a hint of smoke in a dish creates an added depth of flavor. I use a lot of cumin in my cooking.

Couscous with Raisins and Caramelized Onions

SERVES 6
or can be multiplied up to 4 times

This couscous has a beautiful saffron color and a sweet taste from the raisins and caramelized onions.

Make Ahead

This recipe can be made a day ahead and refrigerated in an airtight container. Reheat in a covered baking dish in a 325°F (160°C) oven for 15 to 20 minutes, or until heated through.

● **Preheat oven to 325°F (160°C)**

1/3 cup	sliced almonds	75 mL
6 tbsp	unsalted butter, divided	90 mL
1	onion, finely chopped	1
1/2 cup	raisins	125 mL
2 tbsp	packed light brown sugar	25 mL
1 tbsp	finely minced gingerroot	15 mL
1 tsp	ground cinnamon	5 mL
4 cups	Quick Chicken Stock (page 223) or reduced-sodium chicken broth	1 L
Pinch	saffron threads	Pinch
2 cups	couscous	500 mL
1 tbsp	chopped fresh mint	15 mL
	Salt and freshly ground black pepper	

1. Spread almonds in a single layer on a baking sheet. Bake in preheated oven for about 10 minutes or until they just begin to turn golden. Immediately transfer almonds to a plate lined with paper towels. Set aside.

2. In a medium saucepan, melt 1/4 cup (50 mL) of the butter over medium-high heat. Sauté onion for about 7 minutes or until soft. Add raisins, brown sugar, ginger and cinnamon. Sauté for about 6 minutes or until onions begin to caramelize. Remove from heat, cover and set aside.

3. In a large saucepan, bring stock to a boil over high heat. Add saffron and the remaining butter; reduce heat and simmer for 2 minutes. Remove from heat and add couscous; cover and let stand for 5 minutes. Stir in almonds, onion mixture and mint. Season to taste with salt and pepper.

Lemon Cumin Cookies

**MAKES
24 COOKIES**
or can be multiplied
up to 4 times

*The cumin gives these
lemony cookies an
unexpectedly warm,
spicy taste.*

Tip
If multiplying the
recipe, bake cookies
one sheet at a time to
ensure even baking.

Make Ahead
The dough can be
frozen for up to 2
months if wrapped
in waxed paper and
placed in a plastic
freezer bag. Thaw
overnight in the
refrigerator before
slicing.

The baked cookies can
be stored in a cookie jar
at room temperature for
up to 5 days.

1 ½ cups	all-purpose flour	375 mL
1 tsp	baking soda	5 mL
¼ tsp	salt	1 mL
1 ½ cups	granulated sugar	375 mL
½ cup	unsalted butter, softened	125 mL
2	egg yolks	2
	Grated zest and juice of 2 lemons	
1 ½ tsp	ground cumin	7 mL

1. In a bowl, sift together flour, baking soda and salt. Set aside.

2. In a large bowl, using an electric mixer, cream sugar and butter until light and fluffy. Gradually beat in egg yolks, lemon zest, lemon juice and cumin. Fold in flour mixture until a soft dough forms.

3. Turn dough out onto a piece of waxed paper and roll into a log about 2 inches (5 cm) thick. Twist ends of waxed paper to seal. Refrigerate for at least 1 hour, until dough is stiff, or for up to 4 days.

4. Preheat oven to 325°F (160°C) and spray a baking sheet with nonstick baking spray.

5. Unwrap cookie dough and cut into ¼-inch (0.5 cm) slices. Place about 2 inches (5 cm) apart on prepared baking sheet.

6. Bake for 10 minutes or until edges begin to brown. Let cool for 10 minutes on baking sheet, then transfer to a wire rack to cool completely.

Chinese Banquet

Purchase steamed or fried rice from your local Chinese restaurant to round out this menu. You'll also want to get fortune cookies to serve for dessert, along with green tea ice cream.

Menu

Ginger Shrimp Pot Stickers with Hot Mustard Dipping Sauce

SERVES 6 TO 8
or can be multiplied up to 4 times

Pot stickers are easier than you might think, and these might even be more delicious than pot stickers you've had in restaurants!

Tip
Refrigerated or frozen wonton wrappers can be found in most well-stocked grocery stores.

- Candy/deep-fry thermometer

8 oz	bay shrimp, cooked and roughly chopped	250 g
2	green onions, finely chopped	2
1	clove garlic, minced	1
1	egg white	1
2 tbsp	chopped fresh cilantro	25 mL
1 tsp	grated gingerroot	5 mL
1/2 tsp	salt	2 mL
1/4 tsp	freshly ground black pepper	1 mL
Pinch	cayenne pepper	Pinch
1	package (8 oz/250 g) wonton wrappers	1
	Vegetable or canola oil	
2/3 cup	Hot Mustard Dipping Sauce (see recipe, opposite)	150 mL

1. In a bowl, combine shrimp, green onions, garlic, egg white, cilantro, ginger, salt, black pepper and cayenne.

2. Place wonton wrappers on a clean work surface. Place a heaping teaspoon (5 mL) of shrimp mixture in the center of each wrapper. Lightly dampen inside edges of wrapper with water and gather up and over filling into a little bundle, squeezing edges together lightly.

3. In a deep, heavy saucepan, heat 3 inches (7.5 cm) of oil over medium heat until it registers 375°F (190°C) on thermometer. Working in batches, fry pot stickers until golden brown, about 3 minutes. Using tongs or a slotted spoon, remove pot stickers to a plate lined with paper towels to drain.

4. Serve with Hot Mustard Dipping Sauce.

Variation

▶ Substitute cooked ground chicken for the shrimp, if you prefer.

Make Ahead
The filling can be made up to 1 day ahead if refrigerated in an airtight container.

Hot Mustard Dipping Sauce

¼ cup	Dijon mustard	50 mL
¼ cup	sour cream	50 mL
2 tbsp	soy sauce	25 mL
1 tsp	hot pepper sauce	5 mL
	Salt and freshly ground black pepper	

1. In a small bowl, whisk together mustard, sour cream, soy sauce and hot pepper sauce until smooth. Season to taste with salt and black pepper.

MAKES ABOUT ⅔ CUP (150 ML) or can be multiplied up to 4 times

The spice in this sauce is a perfect complement to the rich, filling pot stickers.

Make Ahead
This sauce can be made up to 4 days ahead if refrigerated in an airtight container.

Theme Menus · Chinese Banquet

Spicy Soy Ribs

*Ask your butcher to cut
a slab of pork ribs in
half across the bones,
for a more appetizer-
friendly size.*

Tip

If multiplying this
recipe, you can spread
a double batch of ribs
on a rimmed baking
sheet; just make sure
they're in a single layer.
If you need to make
more batches, cook
them separately.

Make Ahead

The sauce can be
prepared up to
3 days in advance
and refrigerated in an
airtight container.

The ribs can be cooked
halfway the day before,
then covered and
refrigerated. Toss
with the sauce and cook
the rest of the
way the next day.

- Preheat oven to 350°F (180°C)
- 13- by 9-inch (33 by 23 cm) shallow glass baking dish, lined with foil

1	slab baby back ribs (about 2 lbs/1 kg)	1
1/2 cup	packed light brown sugar	125 mL
2/3 cup	hoisin sauce	150 mL
1/3 cup	soy sauce	75 mL
1/4 cup	rice vinegar	50 mL
1/4 cup	tomato paste	50 mL
2 tsp	garlic powder	10 mL
1 tsp	cayenne pepper, or to taste	5 mL
1/2 tsp	ground ginger	2 mL
2 tsp	sesame seeds, toasted	10 mL
3	green onions, sliced	3

1. Slice ribs between the bones to separate. Place in prepared baking dish and bake in preheated oven for 40 minutes.

2. Meanwhile, in a small bowl, combine brown sugar, hoisin, soy sauce, vinegar, tomato paste, garlic powder, cayenne and ginger.

3. Remove ribs from oven and pour sauce over ribs, tossing to coat. Return to oven and bake for about 40 minutes, tossing in sauce every 10 to 15 minutes, until meat is very tender.

4. Sprinkle ribs with sesame seeds and green onions before serving.

How to Choose and Use a Cleaver

In Chinese cooking, one of the most essential, yet intimidating tools is the cleaver, best described as an ax-like knife. If you find yourself doing a lot of Chinese-style cooking, or butchering large quantities of meat, a cleaver is indispensable. Cleavers aren't just good for chopping food: the flat sides can be used to pound and tenderize meat and to smash ginger or garlic, and the bottom of the handle can be used as a pestle to grind herbs and spices.

Cleavers come in three different weights, each with different functions, so choose the cleaver that best fits your needs:

- Lightweight cleavers are used for slicing, cutting soft food and deboning.
- Medium-weight cleavers do just about everything — except cutting through especially hard bone, like beef or pork bones.
- Heavyweight cleavers are used to chop very cleanly and easily through bones.

Cleaver blades can be made of either carbon steel or stainless steel. Carbon is the preferred type, because it is stronger and cheaper than stainless steel. The downside to carbon steel blades is that they are much heavier than stainless steel blades, which can make them difficult to use, and they tend to rust.

Although you might wonder how safe fingers or even hands are in the presence of such a massive tool, learning to guide the broad center of the blade, pressing with the knuckles of a relaxed fist, can prevent most mishaps.

When cleaning your cleaver, wash it with hot, soapy water, dry it thoroughly and apply a thin layer of mineral oil (other oils will go rancid) to each side of the blade. This is the best way to keep the blade from rusting.

Years ago, I assisted Martin Yan at some department store cooking demonstrations for his television show. Martin only uses a cleaver — no other knife, ever! If you want to learn to use a cleaver well, watch Martin Yan (visit his website at www.yancancook.com). He also sells an excellent starter-size cleaver.

Tilapia with Five-Spice Butter

SERVES 6
or can be multiplied
up to 4 times

This quick dish works just as well with striped bass, snapper or orange roughy in place of the tilapia.

Tip

If multiplying this recipe, keep batches of tilapia warm after step 4 by placing it in a single layer on a rimmed baking sheet and covering it loosely with foil. Place it in a 185°F (90°C) oven until ready to serve, up to 20 minutes.

¼ cup	unsalted butter, softened	50 mL
1 tbsp	finely chopped fresh chives	15 mL
1 tsp	Chinese five-spice powder	5 mL
¼ tsp	salt	1 mL
¼ tsp	freshly ground black pepper	1 mL
6	skinless tilapia fillets (each about 5 oz/150 g)	6
2 tbsp	cornstarch	25 mL
3 tbsp	peanut or vegetable oil	45 mL

1. In a small bowl, combine butter, chives, five-spice powder, salt and pepper.

2. Place a sheet of waxed paper about 6 inches (15 cm) long on a clean work surface. Scrape butter mixture onto waxed paper and form into a short log. Roll up tightly and refrigerate until hard, about 1 hour. Twist ends to seal and keep refrigerated for up to 2 days.

3. Rinse tilapia and pat dry with paper towels. Sprinkle with salt and pepper, then dust lightly with cornstarch on both sides.

4. In a large skillet, heat oil over medium-high heat until the surface begins to ripple slightly. Add tilapia, in batches as necessary, and cook for 2 to 3 minutes or until bottom is golden. Turn and cook the other side for 2 minutes.

5. Unwrap butter and slice into 6 pieces. Garnish each fillet with a round of butter.

Broccolini and Mushrooms in Oyster Sauce

SERVES 6
or can be multiplied up to 4 times

Don't let the name "oyster sauce" scare you: it's a richly flavored sauce with no fishy taste that is used widely in Cantonese cooking. Buy a good-quality brand without MSG.

Tips

This recipe calls for small shiitake mushrooms. If they're not available, use a larger size and cut them into pieces.

To save time on preparing the food for this menu, purchase a broccoli and mushroom dish from your favorite local Chinese restaurant.

8 oz	small shiitake mushrooms, each 1 to 2 inches (2.5 to 5 cm) across, stems removed	250 g
8 oz	small button mushrooms	250 g
1 lb	broccolini, cut into 2-inch (5 cm) lengths	500 g
2 tbsp	cornstarch, divided	25 mL
1	jalapeño pepper, seeded and minced	1
2 tsp	minced gingerroot	10 mL
1 tbsp	black bean sauce with garlic	15 mL
1½ tsp	granulated sugar	7 mL
¾ tsp	salt	3 mL
2 tbsp	oyster sauce	25 mL
6 tbsp	peanut or vegetable oil, divided	90 mL

1. In a bowl, toss shiitake mushrooms, button mushrooms and broccolini with 2 tbsp (25 mL) water. Sprinkle with 1 tbsp (15 mL) of the cornstarch and toss to coat. Set aside.

2. In a small bowl, combine jalapeño, ginger and black bean sauce. Set aside.

3. In another small bowl, whisk together the remaining cornstarch, sugar, salt, ½ cup (125 mL) water and oyster sauce until cornstarch is dissolved. Set aside.

4. In a wok or large skillet, heat 3 tbsp (45 mL) of the oil over high heat. Add mushroom mixture and sauté for 2 minutes or until mushrooms are tender. Transfer to a large serving dish and set aside.

5. In the wok, heat the remaining oil over high heat. Add jalapeño mixture and cook, stirring constantly, for 1 minute. Add cornstarch mixture and cook, stirring constantly, for about 1 minute or until sauce thickens and begins to boil. Drizzle over mushroom mixture and serve hot.

Variation

▶ Use broccoli, petite green beans or asparagus in place of the broccolini in this recipe.

Part 3

Quick Reference Guide to Entertaining

Quick Reference Guide
to Entertaining

Alcohol

How much alcohol do you need for the party? In general, count on two drinks per person for the first hour and one drink per person for each additional hour of the party. That said, you know your friends; it could go higher or lower depending on the crowd. People tend to drink more chilled white wine in the summer and more red wine in the winter, though some are loyal to their favorite year-round. To further complicate matters, if you offer a partial or full bar, some guests will choose cocktails over wine or beer. And some guests might drink too much, necessitating some safety precautions on the part of the host. For more on figuring it all out, see the Beverages section, beginning on page 167, including several bar-related charts that are helpful for planning and shopping purposes. See also **nonalcoholic beverages**.

Aperitif *(aperitivo)*

Simply put, these are alcohol's answer to the hors d'oeuvre: they're meant to stimulate the appetite before a meal. Aperitifs can be enjoyed on their own or with light appetizers. Some popular aperitifs include dry Champagne or Champagne cocktails, which you can make with an inexpensive Champagne (finer bottles should always be appreciated unadulterated) and any of a number of additions; see page 281 for some recipes. Try adding a splash of flavored syrup, such as grenadine; a liqueur, such as amaretto or crème de cassis; or a juice, such as pomegranate, cranberry, blood orange or grapefruit. Other popular aperitifs include

France's Lillet, Dubonnet and pastis; Italy's Campari; Greece's ouzo; and Spain's sherry. Many hosts find that a glass of wine or a favorite cocktail, such as a martini, does the job too. It's best to avoid drinks that are overly sweet or filling before a meal.

Appetizers

Whether you call them appetizers, starters, hors d'oeuvres or *amuses-bouche*, these diminutive savory bites are usually big on flavor, igniting the appetite by offering a preview of the full meal to come. Or they can be grouped to make up the entire savory side of a cocktail party menu. Serve them with cocktails, mocktails, beer or wine. For some popular categories of appetizers, see **bruschetta**, **canapés** and **crostini**. Plated appetizers that require a fork and a knife or spoon are usually served as a first course once guests are seated at the table. For easy appetizers that you can make or purchase, see Easy Hors d'Oeuvres (page 159) and Even Easier Appetizers (page 162). For appetizer recipes, see pages 204–212 and the party menus, beginning on page 288.

Baker's labels

From **party favors** to hostess gifts, there's nothing more personal than a gift from your kitchen. Package them in style with printed baker's labels or gift tags. Creative, computer-savvy types can design and print their own at home on printer-friendly self-adhesive labels. Or you can outsource customized labels, printed with your name and, if you choose, the name of the specialty you're sharing: your grandmother's classic pound cake, your addictive cheese straws or that sought-after toffee you make for the holidays. Browse the designs available from Felix Doolittle (www.felixdoolittle.com), My Own Labels (www.myownlabels.com); and Sweet Paper Lane (www.sweetpaperlane.com).

Beer

Once considered to be somewhat déclassé, beer now has its own set of aficionados, much as wine does. And it's no wonder: with hundreds of types to choose from, each with its own history and taste, beer has become a very complex category. Beer's two main varieties, lager and ale, are tougher to distinguish than they once were, as their characteristics have become blurred: lagers aren't always light, and ales aren't always amber. Draft (or draught) beer is served straight from the keg or cask; some purists prefer it this way, as opposed to bottled or canned versions. See All About Beer, page 176, and the Beer Glossary (page 177).

Beverages

Beverages are among the essential elements for entertaining — you can't have a party without them. See the section devoted to beverages, beginning on page 167. See also **alcohol**, **beer**, **coffee**, **nonalcoholic beverages**, **tea** and **wine**.

Broth or stock

Broth, whether chicken, vegetable, mushroom, beef or even clam juice, is an important ingredient in cooking, used in everything from soups and stews to risotto to poached fish or chicken. Simply substituting broth for water when cooking rice, couscous, orzo and other basics can elevate standard sides to party-worthy accompaniments. While broth and stock

are basically interchangeable terms, "broth" seems to be the word of choice for package labels at the store. Make broth at home by simmering meats and/or vegetables in water and reserving the flavored liquid while discarding the solids. Some home cooks make broth in large batches and freeze it in smaller containers or even in ice cube trays (once frozen, the cubes can be transferred to a freezer bag) for use in a variety of recipes. Store-bought bouillon cubes are available in several varieties; these are reconstituted in boiling water to make broth quickly.

Brunch

Eating breakfast a little later in the day combines the best of both worlds: delicious breakfast foods, only not so terribly early. Brunch should kick off sometime between 10:30 and noon and wrap up by early- to mid-afternoon. Such a meal can be used to fete a number of occasions, though it's probably most popular for Mother's Day. See the Garden Brunch menu (page 292).

Bruschetta

Although the term is often used interchangeably with **crostini**, another Italian toast-based appetizer, bruschetta is technically distinguished by the fact that the bread is grilled, rather than toasted, and is then rubbed with garlic and drizzled with olive oil before being topped with, traditionally, chopped tomatoes and herbs.

Buffet

Buffet is a style of service that allows guests to serve themselves from a spread arranged on your table or sideboard. In addition to the food, the china and flatware are set up on the buffet for self-service. A buffet is a great choice when you're entertaining larger groups, especially if you're short-handed on help, because it's much easier than serving guests individually. Don't forget, though, that you'll need to make sure foods stay at the correct temperatures, and you'll need to replenish trays. Make sure you have adequate help for keeping the buffet fresh. See the section devoted to buffets, beginning on page 151.

Canapés

Hailing from France, this large category of appetizers consists of sliced bread, toast, pastry or crackers topped with a savory mixture or spread. See also **bruschetta** and **crostini**.

Caterers

Putting the food portion of your party safely in the hands of a professional caterer is sometimes the best way to go; it all depends on balancing the party you want to throw with your time, talents, interests and resources. A caterer might organize the entire party for you, perhaps even including flowers and beverages, or might simply offer drop-off food-only service. *Catersource* (www.catersource.com), a magazine for professional caterers, offers a search engine on its website to help you locate a caterer in your area. See Hiring a Caterer, page 104.

CDs

Every party needs music. If you haven't yet jumped on the **MP3** bandwagon, and aren't planning to, then you'll need a good selection of party albums on CD, and hopefully a multi-disc changer to save yourself the trouble of playing **DJ**. Amazon (www.amazon.com or www.amazon.ca) is a great resource for purchasing music. It also features MP3 downloads, so there are helpful audio previews. Overstock.com (www. overstock.com) is another great website for discounted CD purchases. If you're not much of a virtual shopper, many music stores now include setups that allow you to listen before you buy.

Centerpieces and flowers

Centerpieces aren't limited to the traditional flowers and candles — they can be arrangements of whole fruits, vegetables or breads that you'll use later, or they can be theme-related items, such as framed photos of the guest of honor. Be creative, but think about logistics, too: centerpieces that are too tall can make cross-table conversations more difficult to carry on, and centerpieces that are too large can take up valuable serving space on the table. See Centerpieces (page 68) and Flowers (page 69).

Chafing dishes

A chafing dish is used to warm food on the buffet table, keeping hot food hot for the duration of the party. It consists of a food container with heat under it; a dish of water sometimes separates the food container from the heat source, to keep the food from burning. Caterers typically use large stainless steel chafing dishes, but they're available in a number of sizes and designs. See the sources listed in **cookware and other equipment**. Ace Mart Restaurant Supply (www.acemart. com) alone offers more than a dozen types of chafing dishes. You can also rent them from party supply stores.

Cheese

Don't underestimate cheese's importance for entertaining: it can be used as the world's easiest and most widely appealing appetizer (put it on a board with a slicer and some crackers, and you're done); as part of a cheese and fruit display for a buffet or cocktail party; as an ingredient in salads, soups and main courses; and even as a European-style after-dinner offering. If you don't have a well-stocked local cheese shop or a gourmet food market with an extensive cheese section, you'll find what you need online through the Artisanal Cheese Center (www.artisanalcheese.com), which offers a fantastic selection of cheeses for international shipping and a knowledgeable staff to assist you. See the Cheese Glossary (page 164); Cheese, Wine and Fruit Pairings (page 159); and the Wine and Cheese Tasting menu (page 332).

Children

Entertaining children requires special planning for food, drink and activities that are tailored for the younger set. While you'll probably want to prepare less complicated food than you would for a gathering of grownups, you'll do well to spend a little more time planning the entertainment. See Kids' Party Themes (page 28); Kids on Location (page 52); Children's Party Games (page 194); and the Kids' Treasure Hunt menu (page 304). If you'd rather leave children out, that's fine, too, but make sure that all guests are on the same page — if one couple pays for a sitter, they'll be disappointed to spend the evening with other people's kids. See Adults Only (page 86).

China and flatware

For most parties, you'll likely need to use what you have in terms of china and flatware. Give your decor a new angle with creative table settings that include chargers, colorful napkins and maybe even coordinating but unique salad plates or dessert plates. If what you have simply won't work, consider **party rentals**. See China, Flatware and Glassware (page 65).

Cocktail parties

Cocktail parties are a popular choice for larger groups and for smaller spaces where a sit-down menu would be more difficult to pull off. Choose the hour carefully if you don't plan to serve food hearty enough to stand in for a full meal, and select your menu offerings smartly: with bite-size foods, it's easy to get carried away with making miniature pie crusts for mini quiches and other labor-intensive appetizers. See Cocktail Parties (page 158); the Champagne and Caviar Party menu (page 326); and the Wine and Cheese Tasting menu (page 332).

Cocktails

Cocktails undoubtedly make the festivities more festive; many people regularly enjoy a glass of wine with dinner, but a martini or a margarita really feels like something special. To find cocktail recipes online, try Barfliers (www.barfliers.com), which includes user ratings for each recipe and a photo of the type of glass you should serve it in; Bols (www.bolscocktails.com), which features a recipe database searchable by ingredients, method or type of glass; and Epicurious (www.epicurious.com), a favorite database for food recipes that also has trendy cocktail recipes from *Bon Appétit* and *Gourmet* magazines, among other sources. See the Beverages section, beginning on page 167, and the cocktail recipes on pages 281–287.

Coffee

A must-have for breakfasts and brunches, coffee also makes a nice after-dinner offering, allowing guests to distance themselves from the alcoholic drinks they might have enjoyed earlier in the evening. Because of its bitterness and acidity, coffee also pairs perfectly with most desserts, cutting through their richness. To make a great brew, begin with whole-bean coffee (store it in a dark, airtight container, never in the freezer or fridge), and grind it in a coffee grinder (inexpensive countertop versions are available at most kitchenware and home goods stores) just before using. Use 1 tablespoon (15 mL) coffee grounds per cup (250 mL) — you might need to experiment to find the perfect balance, as some water will be lost in the brewing process. Use tap water to brew coffee *only* if yours tastes good enough to drink straight; otherwise, use filtered water. While home espresso machines are fun to have on hand for café-style drinks, in my experience most of them are a little slow for doling out cappuccinos to an entire dinner party. See Coffee (page 180).

Compound butter
(beurre composé)

Compound butter is made from butter beaten with other ingredients to flavor it; some popular choices are garlic, herbs and cheese. The butter can then be formed into a log, wrapped in plastic wrap and refrigerated until just before the party. Slice the log and let it sit at room temperature for at least 15 minutes before serving. Compound butters make a festive accompaniment to corn on the cob, mashed potatoes, crusty bread and even steak — a pat on the top will melt into a decadent sauce. Or toss compound butter with cooked pasta or rice for an appealing side dish.

Convection oven

Convection ovens have a fan that constantly circulates the hot air inside when it's on, with different settings for convection baking and convection roasting. Many cooks prefer convection ovens for roasting meats and baking, citing more even browning and quicker cooking times than conventional ovens. If your oven has convection capabilities, take note that you might need to reduce the heat by 25°F to 50°F (10°C to 20°C) for many recipes, and you'll definitely want to reduce the cooking time, so check for doneness often as you begin to experiment.

Cookware and other equipment

When you need cookware and other kitchen equipment, you have many choices. Cook's Illustrated (www.cooksillustrated.com) and Epicurious (www.epicurious.com) both offer select reviews, while NexTag (www.nextag.com) will help you find the store with the best prices. Although they can be pricy, Williams-Sonoma (www.williams-sonoma.com) and Sur La Table (www.surlatable.com) carry top-of-the-line cookware, bakeware and other tools of the trade. Plus, they have storefronts across the United States (and Williams-Sonoma has several locations in Canada), which means you can handle the equipment before purchasing it — key for finding knives that fit your hands well and cookware with the weight and feel you're looking for. Websites that cater to the home cook include Chefs (www.chefscatalog.com) and Cooking.com (www.cooking.com). Discounted cookware is often available at Tuesday Morning (www.tuesdaymorning.com), TJ Maxx (www.tjmaxx.com), HomeSense (www.homesense.ca) and Costco (www.costco.com or www.costco.ca). See also **restaurant supply stores** and Equipment Basics (page 112).

Cream

Cream can range from 5% to 40% milk fat (MF), and the percentages and how the cream is labeled vary depending on whether you're buying it in the United States or Canada. If you want to make whipped cream, you'll need to purchase heavy whipping cream (37% to 40% MF, sometimes simply labeled "heavy cream"), or light whipping cream (30% to 36% MF) if you're in the United States; if you're in Canada, purchase whipping cream (35% MF). If you buy an aerosol can as a shortcut for whipped cream, be sure to read the label carefully, as some are fake non-dairy products (and therefore not recommended). Light cream (known as table cream in Canada) typically contains about half the fat, so you can't expect it to whip up, but it's a good choice for use in recipes where that's not an issue. Serve half-and-half (which is half milk and half cream, and has about 10% MF) or light cream with coffee or black tea when entertaining; it's richer than whole milk, lending a silkiness that makes the resulting beverages worthy of a special occasion.

Crostini

These little Italian toasts with savory toppings are a flexible, easy and always popular party appetizer. Crostini are similar to **bruschetta** (crostini are toasted and two-bite-size, while bruschetta is technically grilled and is usually larger), and are essentially the same thing as **canapés** — when canapés are prepared on toast. Crostini can be pre-assembled with a topping or simply set out with the topping or a variety of toppings so guests can help themselves. To save time, have the bakery run your bread loaves through a slicer; $1/4$ to $1/2$ inch (0.5 to 1 cm) thick is ideal. Some popular toppings include roasted tomatoes or peppers, olive tapenade, sautéed greens, sautéed mushrooms, cheeses (especially soft ones, such as fresh goat cheese), puréed white beans and pâtés, but nearly any small-scale savory topping is fair game. See the recipe for Bay Shrimp Crostini (page 330).

Crudités

This is a French term for vegetables served as an appetizer. While crudités are usually served raw, some hosts do choose to blanch the vegetables briefly before serving them with a spread, which is nice for vegetables like broccoli, cauliflower or asparagus. Other possibilities for a crudités platter include baby carrots or carrot sticks, celery sticks, bell pepper strips, bite-size pear or cherry tomatoes, jicama sticks, sugar snap peas, snow peas, cucumber spears, endive leaves and radishes. Serve crudités with your favorite creamy dip, hummus, aïoli or vinaigrette. See Creating a Crudités Display (page 155) and the recipe for Crudités with Cucumber Dip (page 340).

Decor

Decor is how you lend your location a special ambiance especially for the party. It usually begins with decluttering and a little furniture rearranging to make room for the crowd, and ends with finishing touches such as lighting candles. In between, you'll need to pull together the linens, centerpieces, flowers and tabletop items like serving dishes and utensils, glassware, china, flatware and party favors. Don't forget about the exterior of your house: a well-lit front porch with a pretty wreath or garland related to the party theme or season lets guests know they have the right place and date. Less obvious elements such as lighting and temperature also help set the scene for a relaxing gathering. See the chapter on decor, beginning on page 58.

Desserts

What's a party without a little something sweet? Purchased or homemade, simple or elaborate, desserts are welcome at any party — and can even constitute its entire menu (served with coffee, tea or other after-dinner drinks) for a post-concert gathering or other desserts party. For inspiration, see the dessert recipes on pages 261–277 and in the party menus, beginning on page 288.

Digestif (digestivo)

These after-dinner drinks, believed to aid digestion, are often heavier and higher in alcohol than their before-dinner counterparts, **aperitifs**. Some popular options include cognac, whiskey, Scotch, brandy and fortified wines such as port, Madeira and sherry (the last is popular as both an aperitif and a digestif). As the host, you will need to decide whether or not it's smart to offer such a potent nightcap toward the end of a party; guests who will soon be driving home might be better off with a cup of **coffee** or **tea**.

DJ

If you want your party to include dancing but don't want to hire a live band, look into getting a DJ for nonstop dance music geared toward your crowd's tastes and energy level. Many DJs can also provide lighting, games, karaoke and banter. You can find a local DJ through the American Disc Jockey Association (www.adja.org) or the Disk Jockey in Canada Network (www.djin10. tripod.com). See Music (page 187).

Dress

If you're hosting a costume party or another bash that requires special attire (a swimsuit for a pool party or athletic shoes for outdoor games, for instance), you should indicate that on the invitation so all guests come prepared. Some hosts even put "dressy casual" on the invitation to clarify the dress for a typical party, but the party theme, location and time

of day often provide sufficient guidance. A breakdown of different types of party dress can be found online at The Emily Post Institute (www.emilypost.com). See Letting Guests Know What to Wear (page 95).

Dutch oven

This large, tightly covered pot is sometimes called a French oven. Often made of enameled cast iron, which is perfect for long, slow cooking times, Dutch ovens are used for braising and stewing, and should be able to go from stovetop to oven (heat-resistant handles are a must). They're ideal for pot roasts, stews, baked beans (see the recipe for Barbecue Baked Beans, page 357) and more. Dutch ovens are available in a variety of bright colors from Lodge (www.lodgemfg. com) and Le Creuset (www.lecreuset.com), among other companies; better prices can often be found at discount stores. Choose a fun color, because they can also be brought to the table for serving. For more on cookware see Equipment Basics (page 112).

Enjoying your own party

It's simple but true: if you're having fun, so will your guests. The surest way to enjoy your own party is to be prepared ahead of time and to have enough help. That way, most of the work will be done before anyone arrives, allowing you to feel like a guest at your own party — in other words, to eat, drink and socialize along with everyone else. Sticking to a menu that's not fussy and can be prepared mostly in advance helps a great deal, as does enlisting a guest or two to help refill trays and wineglasses. See Enjoying Your Own Party (page 12).

Entertainment

Sure, it's an essential party element, but sometimes the right mix of guests and a little background music provide all the entertainment a party needs. At other times, you'll want to bring in the clowns — or maybe just a carefully chosen party game. For more suggestions, see the chapter on entertainment, beginning on page 184.

Etiquette

Entertaining brings up all kinds of etiquette questions. For instance, what does "black tie optional" really mean? The Emily Post Institute (www.emilypost.com) is a great resource for answers to common etiquette quandaries, including some related to entertaining and attending parties. For your home library, a copy of the updated *Emily Post's Etiquette* by Peggy Post will more fully answer questions on manners for practically any situation.

Flour

For most purposes, I prefer unbleached all-purpose flour as my pantry staple. Whole wheat flour is great for adding fiber and nutrition, and is becoming increasingly popular because of this, but store it airtight in the fridge or freezer, as it goes rancid more quickly than all-purpose flour. I like blending a little whole wheat flour in with all-purpose flour for pancakes or waffles with a little more substance. A white version of whole wheat flour has recently become available (it's made from a variety of wheat that's naturally white, rather than reddish) and many health-conscious bakers are experimenting with it and giving it great reviews. Cake or pastry flour has less protein, making for tender results, while bread flour has extra gluten for yeast bread baking. If you can't find the flour you want locally, contact King Arthur Flour (www. kingarthurflour.com), a producer of high-quality flours and much more; the website

is a baker's dream, with ingredients, baking mixes, bakeware, recipes and more.

Food allergies

The incidence of food allergies is on the rise. While some food allergies elicit rashes or other minor reactions, others can be deadly. It's always best to err on the side of caution; if a guest lets you know that he or she is allergic to, for instance, nuts or shellfish, keep them off the menu entirely, and take care to avoid cross-contamination in the kitchen. Read the list of ingredients on any packaged items you use and, for anything you're unsure about, consult with the guest directly. Also avoid using peanut oil or other hidden ingredients that could cause problems. When inviting people over for the first time, ask if they have any food allergies or dietary limitations when they call or email to RSVP. See also **gluten-free diets** and Accommodating Special Diets (page 109).

Food processor

It's hard to believe that this kitchen appliance has been widely available only since the 1970s — what did party hosts do without it? Cuisinart was the original, but several companies now make food processors. A good food processor can make short work of kitchen prep by chopping, slicing, shredding, grinding and puréeing ingredients with the flip of a switch. Look for one with an S-shaped blade for chopping, plus metal disks that can be inserted for slicing or shredding large quantities in seconds (think enough carrots for a carrot cake or mozzarella for that big lasagna). Choose a food processor with a large enough work bowl for your cooking habits; while you might not need the giant 20-cup (5 L) version, a 3-cup (750 mL) size is probably too small if you entertain regularly.

Food safety

It's always important to use the best food-safety practices when you cook, and it's especially important to do so when you're handling large quantities of perishables, as when you're entertaining. Food safety begins with a clean kitchen and continues with your shopping trip: selecting the best and freshest meats, poultry, seafood, eggs and dairy, and transporting them home safely and getting them into the refrigerator quickly. But it also involves safe handling during preparation, safe cooking temperatures, safe serving practices and safe storage of leftovers. Bacteria tend to breed in the danger zone of 40°F to 140°F (4°C to 60°C) — and you'll notice that room temperature falls squarely within that range. See Prepping Your Kitchen (page 120), and the sections that follow covering personal hygiene, food shopping, food storage, thawing food, handling food, and meat, poultry and seafood, as well as Handling Leftovers (page 163).

Games

Games, whether a backyard game of bocce or a fireside round of charades, can be a great icebreaker for a party, helping shy guests relax and enjoy themselves. Games also offer a change of pace after a meal. Even small groups of old friends can enjoy a game as a diversion. It's a good idea for every host to have a party game or two in mind as possible entertainment in case the conversation tapers off — or winds on and needs redirecting. See Tabletop Diversions (page 186) and Games (page 191).

Garnishing

Garnishes are an easy way to elevate the presentation of your food. Garnishes should be edible, simple and, in most cases, related to the flavors in the dish you're serving. Individual plates may be garnished, as may large platters of food for the buffet or for passing around the table family-style. When in doubt, don't forget the classic garnish of a fresh herb such as parsley; you'll likely have some left over from cooking. Small clumps of grapes or wedges of citrus fruits are also reliable accents. Many of the recipes in Part 2 include suggested garnishes. See Garnishing (page 150).

Glassware

Plastic cups are okay for entertaining outdoors, but glassware is preferable for all other situations. It sometimes seems like every drink requires its own custom glass, but you don't have to build an addition to house all that glassware. There are all-purpose **wineglasses** that can adequately hold whites, rosés and reds, not to mention sangria, margaritas, daiquiris and more. Double old-fashioned cocktail glasses are great all-purpose vessels for drinks ranging from gin and tonic to Scotch on the rocks. Do purchase any specialty glassware you'll make frequent use of, such as martini glasses — reusable means Earth-friendly and you won't save much by going with **party rental** glasses if you'll be renting them regularly (though that's a great option for one-time events). See Barware and Glasses (page 171).

Gluten-free diets

If a guest lets you know that he or she is on a gluten-free diet, what can you serve? As a bit of background, gluten is a protein in flour; those on gluten-free diets are usually sensitive to or allergic to wheat. If one of your guests is on a gluten-free diet, consult with him or her ahead of time to make sure there are appropriate choices on the menu. Some people are so allergic to gluten that a speck of flour can make them ill for days, so you need to be sure to avoid cross-contamination in the kitchen between items they can eat and items they cannot. Wheat, rye, barley and oats are typically off-limits. A steak dinner served with potatoes and vegetables would generally be fine, while bread and pasta are out (unless you use a specially formulated version, such as those made with rice).

Guests

Who's on the list? Who's not? Let your reason for the party — the occasion or the guest of honor — be your guide. Not everyone can come every single time, and they probably don't even want to. For all issues guest-related, from determining the party list to issuing the invitations to bidding them goodnight when *you're* ready, turn to the chapter on guests, beginning on page 82.

Heirloom produce

Heirloom produce is grown from seeds that have been saved from open-pollinated, often homegrown plants. Such seeds have remained in circulation by being passed down through families from one generation to the next. Heirloom fruits and vegetables are selected for flavor, texture and interest that surpass their perfect-looking commercial counterparts, which are selected for marketability (thick-skinned tomatoes that resist cracking as they ripen, for instance) and the ability to withstand shipping well. As a result, heirloom varieties offer a much wider spectrum of sizes, colors, shapes and flavors than most of us are used to seeing at the supermarket. Heirlooms are enjoying renewed popularity among chefs, home gardeners and some farmers. Look for heirloom produce at farmers' markets and in specialty markets, or grow your own. Seed Savers Exchange (www.seedsavers.org) offers hundreds of varieties of heirloom seeds

for the home gardener. For entertaining, heirloom tomatoes can make a gorgeous contribution to an *insalata Caprese*, for instance; other heirlooms can make colorful, delicious additions to a variety of dishes, especially when you want to highlight a single seasonal ingredient.

Herbs

Herbs — such as basil, cilantro and rosemary, to name a few — are the leaves of their eponymous plants. They make fragrant additions to a number of dishes, and learning how to use herbs can help you elevate otherwise standard fare. Because herbs are almost always better fresh, it's helpful to maintain a small herb garden (they can even be grown successfully in a pot on the patio or on a very sunny windowsill) to ensure that you'll have all the fresh herbs you need during the growing season. Most supermarkets also stock fresh herbs in the produce section. Dried herbs are great for certain uses, but they have a more concentrated flavor, so you'll need to dial down the amount significantly when replacing fresh with dried in a recipe (use roughly one-third the amount). However, for some recipes, such as basil pesto, substituting dried herbs simply won't work. For online herb sources, see the **spices** listing, which features websites that sell both herbs and spices. See Seasoning with Herbs and Spices (page 144).

Honey

We're all used to clover honey, but honey is now commercially available in a variety of flavors stemming from the type of flower the nectar was gathered from. Look for thyme, lavender or chestnut honeys, for instance. The flavors can be quite assertive, so don't use such specialty honeys interchangeably with clover honey in recipes. But stronger honeys are terrific for drizzling on crostini spread with fresh goat cheese, and in other uses where their unique flavors can be highlighted. Milder honeys, such as clover, are ideal for use in hot tea, in sweets and as a glaze for pork or for vegetables such as sweet potatoes and carrots. See also Crystallized Honey (page 146).

Ice

Don't skimp here! Plan on needing $1\frac{1}{2}$ to 2 pounds (750 g to 1 kg) per person at your party, plus 40 to 50 pounds (18 to 23 kg) to fill any large tubs or coolers you're using to chill drinks. See Ice (page 173).

Immersion blender

The most popular use for this hand-held, wand-like blender is to purée soups right in the pot. Many immersion blenders also have a whisk attachment that can be used to whip cream or egg whites. Devotees like the versions that have a detachable motor, as the rest of it can be put in the dishwasher. But with or without a detachable motor, they're easy to use and a snap to clean. Invest in one with a strong motor, and you'll rarely turn to your regular blender again.

Invitations

You can extend party invitations by phone, using the Internet or with a traditional paper version. For online invitations that can be delivered via email, visit websites like www. evite.com and www.sendomatic.com. You can make your own paper invitations with some stationery and a laser printer or a steady hand, plus embellishments such as stamps, punches and ribbons from stores like Michaels (www. michaels.com) or Target (www.target.com). Purchased invitations range from casual fill-ins to custom-printed ones; look for a variety

of options wherever you buy stationery. Some custom stationery retailers worth checking out include Dauphine Press (www.dauphinepress.com), French Blue Papers (www.frenchblueonline.com) and InvitationBox.com (www.invitationbox.com). See Extending the Invitation (page 87).

Knives

It's safer to work with sharp knives than with dull ones. Using good-quality knives and taking good care of them — including hand-washing, regular sharpening and proper storage — will keep you chopping quickly, safely and accurately when prepping for a party. See Knives (page 112).

Kosher foods

Kosher foods are those that conform to Jewish dietary laws. These laws have to do not only with the types of foods that can be eaten, but also with how those foods are combined and prepared. As with all diets, some people are much stricter than others, so it's best to consult with guests ahead of time about how you can best accommodate them. Sticking with a meatless meal is sometimes easiest, because then you don't have to worry about purchasing kosher meats or avoiding the combination of meat and dairy within the menu.

Liability

It may be a sad sign of the times, but party hosts do need to think about liability. Addressing problem areas ahead of time can help guests avoid accidents, and that's certainly preferable to dealing with questions after the fact about who's responsible. Keep exterior pathways and steps free of snow, ice and other debris, and make sure they're well lit. Inside, area rugs should be anchored by non-slip pads, stairwells should have sturdy handrails, and electrical or phone cords should be rerouted or taped down so they don't present a tripping hazard. When you're entertaining at another location, make sure that any issues of liability are spelled out in the contract, and ask the manager what can be done to prevent accidents or injuries ahead of time. See Who's Responsible? (page 47).

Location

Where you'll throw your party is among the first decisions you'll make when planning a gathering. Your home isn't always the best place; don't forget about the many free venues where you and friends can gather, such as parks, beaches and botanical gardens. There are also a number of locations you can rent — from the back room at your favorite neighborhood bistro to an art gallery. See the chapter on location, beginning on page 38.

Marinade

A marinade is the liquid mixture used to marinate, or soak, foods before they're cooked, for added flavor and sometimes also to tenderize them. Marinades usually have an acidic ingredient, such as vinegar or lemon juice, as well as flavorful components such as herbs or spices. They're commonly used on meats, poultry and vegetables. A marinade can be similar to a vinaigrette (I've been known to make a big batch and use some to toss with a salad and some for marinating) or it can be a brine (think of brining a Thanksgiving turkey before roasting). For safety, food should be marinated in a glass or ceramic dish in the refrigerator. To avoid cross-contamination, any marinade that has been used to marinate meat, poultry or fish must be boiled before it can be used for basting. See Meat (page 133) and the recipes

for Grilled Cornish Game Hens with Lemon and Yogurt (page 424) and Carne Asada (page 387).

Measuring

Stock your kitchen with dry measures (the standard metal measuring cups that can be leveled off at the top) and liquid measures (the standard Pyrex measuring cups with graduated lines on the sides), as well as a set of sturdy measuring spoons. Measuring correctly will ensure successful execution of your recipes, particularly when you're baking. See **mise-en-place** and Measuring (page 138), which includes several helpful charts.

Menu balance

Planning out a menu is a balancing act: you need to balance each dish's temperature, flavors, visual appeal, texture, ingredient variety and nutritional value. A balanced menu ensures that the meal is appealing as a whole, without being overly heavy or redundant, and offers a variety of tastes and textures. The menus in this book (beginning on page 288) are already balanced for you. See Creating a Balanced Menu (page 107).

Mise-en-place

This French term means having all ingredients organized, and many premeasured, before you begin cooking, just as you may have seen on a number of cooking shows. Mise-en-place is a great technique when you're preparing complex recipes, saving you from making mistakes in haste as you're cooking. See How to Mise en Place (page 147).

MP3s

An MP3 is a digital audio file that can be downloaded to a computer or MP3 player (such as an iPod); a home computer equipped with a CD burner can burn MP3 files to CDs. MP3s can be purchased singly or by the album on such websites as www.itunes.com, www.mp3.com and www.amazon.com or www.amazon.ca.

Music

Nearly every party needs music. The only exceptions are those that involve watching the small screen, such as a party planned around a sporting event or movie. For gatherings where music will be in the background, an iPod is a handy tool — with very little effort, you can create a custom playlist from **MP3s** for each event. A great group of **CDs** and a CD changer can also stand in as **DJ**. See the Music section, beginning on page 187.

Name tags

Name tags aren't necessary for smaller gatherings, but they're very helpful when you're hosting more than a dozen guests, particularly if many of them don't already know one another. See Introductions and Name Tags (page 185).

Nonalcoholic beverages

Always offer nonalcoholic options when you're hosting a party; their presence ensures that there's something for everyone, and it encourages people to pace themselves. See **coffee**, **tea** and Nonalcoholic Beverages (page 178).

Nonstick spray

Granted, nonstick spray can leave a stubborn, sticky residue if you don't wash it out of casserole dishes and bakeware quickly enough, but it is essential for certain uses. I always use nonstick spray when baking cakes, particularly Bundt cakes, to ensure that they will come out of the pan in one piece. For baking, the best luck I've had is with a product called Baker's Joy (www.bakersjoy.com). Pam, another favorite, works well for such uses as spraying foil that will cover a lasagna (spray side down), making sure that any melted cheeses and other toppings stay where they should. Where vegetable oil will do the trick, such as in the bottom of a skillet, I prefer the real thing to nonstick spray.

Oil

Olive oil is a pantry staple for good reason: it can be heated high enough for sautéing, yet it's flavorful enough to use raw. Generally speaking, I save expensive olive oil for use in salad dressings and dips, where its flavor will really come through. Extra virgin olive oil is from the olives' first pressing and has the lowest acidity available on the market; the brighter the color, the more flavorful the oil will usually be. I use lighter (in color), less expensive olive oil for sautéing and in cooked foods. Frying is usually best done with canola oil. If you use peanut oil or any other nut oil, make sure that none of your guests has a related **food allergy**, as the presence of such nut oils is impossible to detect visually in the finished dish. Truffle oil (usually a truffle-flavored olive oil) can be used to accent dishes with mushrooms in them; drizzle a bit over mushroom risotto, for instance. Sesame oil is great in Asian and Middle Eastern dishes and dips. Hazelnut oil can be a nice addition to salads. While olive oil can be stored in the pantry, many flavored oils should be refrigerated unless you'll use them fairly quickly.

Olives

Marinated olives make a great before-dinner nibble to go with cocktails or wine. Olives are also a popular addition to a number of dishes in the always-popular Mediterranean cuisine. Greece's kalamata olives are a very dark purple; they're a staple in Greek salad (along with feta, red onion and tomatoes). Niçoise olives, from Provence, are small and range from brown to black; they're used in *salade niçoise*, among many other dishes. Green olives are often sold pitted and stuffed with pimientos or other ingredients; this is the sort you'd use in a martini. Many upscale markets offer a selection of marinated olives in the deli section; pick some up to add to a spread of appetizers.

Party favors

Although they're not expected for grownup gatherings as they are for children's birthday parties, everyone loves a present, whether they're young or older. Party favors can offer a tabletop diversion before the meal is served, acting as an icebreaker of sorts. Party favors also make guests feel as if their presence was anticipated and appreciated; as a memento, party favors make the celebration more memorable. Make sure to choose favors that further your theme and décor designs. See Party Favors (page 75).

Party rentals

What do you do when you don't have enough place settings or wineglasses? What about when you need a tent for the backyard? Or water misters or heaters for a too-hot or too-cold patio seating area? Party rental companies are the go-to source for party items that aren't practical for purchasing. See Rental IQ (page 66).

Party supplies

If you're having trouble finding cocktail napkins that go with your party theme, or you want to purchase a dozen inexpensive cowboy hats to distribute to guests at a Western-themed party, there's no better destination than a party supply retailer. While general stores like Target or Walmart can provide many of the pieces, party supply retailers *exist* to fill the needs of hosts, from decor items to paper products to party favors. Just browsing can give you many great ideas. One of the largest is Oriental Trading Company (www.orientaltrading.com); it has thousands of party items, many geared toward children, plus tabletop decor, craft supplies, costumes and favors. Plum Party (www.plumparty.com) has more sophisticated, grownup offerings in addition to children's party supplies; it also has eco-friendly products, including compostable corn-based disposable plates, flatware and cups. Amols (www.amols.com) has supplies, decorations and favors at discount prices. Paper Mart (www.papermart.com) has gift bags, boxes, ribbons, papers and balloons. Party America (www.partyamerica.com) has locations across the United States and a great online store, too. Other party supply sites include Partypro.com (www.partypro.com); Party Secret (www.partysecret.com); and Party Supplies Online (www.partysuppliesonline.com).

Pasta and noodles

Everyone loves noodles — it's no wonder they're represented in a number of world cuisines (Italian, naturally, but also various other European and Asian cuisines). Pastas come in literally hundreds of shapes, from the ubiquitous spaghetti to orecchiette ("little ears"). These days, whole-grain pastas are gaining momentum, mostly for health reasons, as they pack an extra dose of fiber; read package labels carefully, as health benefits vary among brands and types. Fresh pastas, now available in most supermarkets, are made with eggs; while they're highly perishable, they can be frozen if you don't plan to use them right away. Rice noodles have long been popular in Asian cuisines, but brown rice pasta is a new addition to the whole-grain pasta selection that is wonderful in a variety of healthful diets, including **gluten-free diets**. In Italy, pasta is served as a first course; in North America, though, we often make an entrée of it. Pastas and noodles also make a great side dish — try orzo, spaetzle or gemelli. Long pastas, such as angel hair, are commonly served as an accompaniment to chicken, eggplant or veal parmigiana.

Pastry tools

Devoted bakers have their own arsenal of kitchen tools. Among them are pastry bags with decorative tips, although many cooks simply use a snipped freezer bag to pipe frosting or filling (a ricotta cheese mixture into manicotti, for example).

Pie weights are useful for blind baking, or prebaking, a pie crust before filling it, to prevent a soggy bottom. The pie weights keep the sides of the crust from shrinking or collapsing during baking. While bead-like pie weights are available commercially, some people just use a pound (500 g) of dried beans: line the crust with foil or parchment paper and fill it with beans, pushing them up against the sides of the crust. After prebaking the crust, cool and save the beans to reuse as pie weights (store them in a resealable plastic bag in the pantry).

Other pastry tools include pastry brushes, pastry wheels and a hand-held pastry blender used to mix fats into flour for pie crusts, scones and Classic Lemon Bars (page 365), among many other uses. See Other Essentials (page 116).

Pesto

Pesto is traditionally made with fresh basil leaves, garlic, olive oil, Parmesan cheese and pine nuts. It's pureed into a sauce that can be used in a number of ways; it's especially popular in pasta dishes, swirled into soups or used in dips or spreads. Pistou is a similar mixture hailing from Provence. If you have lots of fresh basil growing in your garden at the end of the season, harvest it before cold weather kills it. Make fresh pesto, transfer it to single-use containers, pour a little olive oil on top and freeze it for later use. Prepared pesto is available in most supermarkets; I prefer the fresh type in the refrigerated section to the jarred version. See the recipe for Chicken Pesto Pasta Salad (page 342), for one use for prepared pesto.

Plating

Formal dinner party service sometimes includes preplated courses, as opposed to family-style service. You may want to hire a waiter for assistance serving such a meal, as it's more labor-intensive. In addition, it's important to designate an area for plating and a predetermined pattern for plating, so each portion is similarly sized and presented. See Plating and Serving (page 149).

Potatoes

Potatoes are a pantry staple that can be used in a variety of ways. New potatoes, which are the young version of nearly any variety, make a great two-bite appetizer when boiled whole, whether scooped out and filled with other ingredients or simply topped with a bit of sour cream and caviar. Fingerling potatoes, which are young like new potatoes but long and irregular in shape, make for an interesting side dish or appetizer as well. Russet potatoes are best for baking or making french fries, while boiling potatoes — those distinguished by thin, waxy skins — are superb for cooking on the stovetop to use in potato salads or mashed potatoes. The resurgence of **heirloom** varieties has brought purple-fleshed potatoes to the market.

Puff pastry

Frozen puff pastry is a useful convenience item for party cooking. While I have made puff pastry from scratch before, it's not something I care to do again. The version available in the frozen foods section of most supermarkets does a great job as the basis for a number of appetizers (one of my favorite magazine recipes suggests small rounds of puff pastry topped with goat cheese and sautéed mushrooms). Puff pastry can also be wrapped around a wheel of Brie cheese before baking; better yet, slice off the top portion of the rind, spoon chutney over it and drape the whole thing in puff pastry, tucking the ends of the pastry underneath, then bake it. Puff pastry can also be used to make a number of desserts, such as apple strudel.

Recipes

Cookbooks, magazines and entertaining books like this one are terrific resources for recipes. So are websites like Epicurious (www.epicurious.com), Cook's Illustrated (www.cooksillustrated.com) and the reader-driven All Recipes (www.allrecipes.com), where users rate recipes and provide suggested substitutions or changes. See Part 2 of this book, beginning on page 201, for hundreds of my favorite party recipes, already tested and perfected.

Reduce

In this technique, you boil a mixture containing water, wine or broth until a portion of the liquid evaporates, thickening the remaining mixture, which is then called a reduction. This classic technique is used to make flavorful sauces, glazes and more. For examples, see the recipes for Oranges with Red Wine (page 397) and Spicy Garlic Shrimp (page 308).

Restaurant supply stores

Restaurant supply stores offer cooking and baking equipment, small appliances, serving equipment such as **chafing dishes** and sometimes even chefs' clothing, furniture and tabletop items intended for restaurateurs and caterers. Many of the offerings can also be put to good use by the avid home cook. Among my favorite restaurant supply shops are Ace Mart (www.acemart.com), Surfas (www.surfasonline.com) and Big Tray (www.bigtray.com).

Rice

Rice is a staple grain that shows up in appetizers, main courses, sides and even desserts in a number of cuisines. Long-grain rices include India's basmati and Thailand's jasmine; rounder short-grain rices include Italy's Arborio (used for risotto), Japanese rice (used for sushi rolls) and China's sticky rice. Medium-grain rices are somewhere between the two extremes; Italy's carnaroli, also used to make risotto, falls into this category. Brown rice is any rice that doesn't have the bran removed, meaning it's chewier, takes longer to cook and is more healthful; like whole-grain pasta, it was once on the fringes but is now gaining popularity for its health benefits. Brown rice is also used to make pasta for those on **gluten-free diets**. One of the most flexible ingredients there is, rice makes a great choice for a side dish to go with any number of menus: see the recipes for Spanish Rice (page 389); the

Greek-inspired Rice with Tomatoes and Peppers (page 412); and the Hawaiian-style Pineapple and Golden Raisin Rice Salad (page 385). Wild rice, which is not actually a rice at all but a marsh grass, is nutty and very chewy; see the recipe for Wild Rice Pilaf (page 378).

Roux

A roux is a mixture of flour and butter, pan drippings or another fat, which is cooked over low heat to various depths of color and flavor, then used to thicken soups, stews such as gumbo, gravies and sauces.

RSVP

RSVP stands for *répondez s'il vous plait* ("please respond"). This acronym is used on **invitations** when the host of an upcoming event would like an approximate head count for planning purposes. In today's world, it seems increasingly difficult to get potential guests to respond to an invitation in a timely manner, if at all. (Those of us who host parties frequently know better, so we always respond to an invitation.) You'll increase your chances of hearing back if you include an email address as well as a phone number on the invitation. Don't feel bad about calling or emailing to follow up before you do your grocery shopping for the party — you can always pretend you were worried that the invitation was lost in the mail. See RSVP (page 94).

Salsa

While this word simply means "sauce," it refers specifically to Mexican sauces and condiments, usually tomato- and chile-based, which range from cooked mixtures that can be served warm or cold to raw versions, also known as pico de gallo or salsa cruda.

Raw salsas are easy to make at home with summer garden staples such as tomatoes and peppers. Green salsa, or salsa verde, is made with tomatillos. Salsas can also include black beans, corn, chopped avocados and even fruit. Freshly prepared salsas are sold in the refrigerated section of supermarkets, and some upscale markets, particularly in the southwestern United States, sell house-made versions with varying levels of heat. Use salsas as a condiment with Mexican and Southwestern foods; as a dip, especially for corn chips; and on egg dishes. See the recipes for Salsa Fresca (page 391), Peach Salsa (page 361) and Mango Salsa (page 381).

Seasonal produce

Using in-season fruits and vegetables in your party menus isn't only fashionable, it's smart. You'll be using produce at the peak of its freshness and flavor, and you'll pay a lot less for it because it'll be abundant and not shipped from halfway around the world. Visit nearby farmers' markets, well-stocked produce departments that list origin on item descriptions, roadside farm stands and pick-your-own orchards for the season's best locally grown fruits and vegetables. See the Crop Calendar (page 22).

Seating arrangements

Use place cards to indicate where guests should sit for dinner parties that number six or more, and carefully consider the dynamics as you determine the best arrangement. The classic alternating male–female seating pattern makes as much sense today as it did back when etiquette pioneers first suggested it. Mix up shy and gregarious guests to inspire conversation, and separate any potential problem guests. See Seating Arrangements (page 97).

Security

Do you live in an urban or edgy area? Is your party likely to draw unwanted interest? There are times when it makes sense to hire a security professional (other than the resident dog) to keep an eye on the door and property perimeter. See When You Need Security at a Private Party (page 54).

Spices

These dried fruit and vegetable parts (they can be seeds, fruit, bark or roots), which are often ground to a powdered form for use, lend their aromatic characteristics to both sweet and savory dishes. For maximum flavor, toast whole spices before grinding. Cinnamon may be the most common spice used in North America, and is favored mostly in sweets like apple pie, pumpkin pie, carrot cake and many other classic American desserts. As with using **herbs**, using spices in your cooking and baking can elevate your dishes from the ordinary to the sublime. Prepared spice mixes, such as curry powder or pumpkin pie spice, are especially useful for cooks, as the combination lends a balanced depth of flavor and interest. Look for spices in local markets that have brisk business, as you want the freshest ones possible; World Market (www.worldmarket. com) carries its own line. Some online spice and herb sources include MySpicer. com (www.myspicer.com); Penzeys Spices (www.penzeys.com); Vanns Spices (www. vannsspices.com); and Adriana's Caravan (www.adrianascaravan.com), which also carries hard-to-find ingredients in other categories. Mulling spices, a combination of whole spices that lend holiday flavor to apple cider or wine, make a great gift. See Mulling Spices (page 76), Seasoning with Herbs and Spices (page 144) and Spice Mixtures (page 145).

Springform pan

An essential pan for bakers of cheesecakes, flourless chocolate cakes and other delicate desserts, the identifying characteristic of a typical two-piece springform pan is its tightly fitting removable sides. With the flip of the pan's latch, the sides expand to make removing cakes easier (cakes are often served with the bottom of the pan left in place); close the latch and the pan tightens back around the bottom. While some of these pans might be relatively water-tight the day you purchase them, they tend to loosen with use; as a result, recipes often call for wrapping the springform pan in two to three layers of foil when the dessert will be baked in a **water bath**. For one use of a springform pan, see the Pear Kuchen recipe (page 408).

Sugar

Sugar is a staple for those of us with a sweet tooth. The majority of bakers most often use granulated white refined sugar, which also comes in an organic version. Other types of refined sugar include a superfine variety that dissolves easily; confectioner's (icing) sugar (sometimes called powdered sugar), which is ideal for cake frostings and glazes, or can be sifted decoratively over baked goods; coarse sugar, which comes in a variety of colors and is sprinkled on top of sugar cookies and other baked goods for extra crunch and sparkle; brown sugar, which has molasses added; and sugar cubes or rock candy (sometimes coating a stir stick), which can be served with **coffee** or **tea** for a stylish presentation. Raw sugar is crystallized evaporated cane juice that's much less processed. Varieties include Demerara sugar, a coarse-textured golden sugar with a caramel flavor that can be used for baking; turbinado sugar, which has a similar texture, color and flavor (Sugar in the

Raw is a well-known example); and sticky, rich Muscavado sugars, which can in most cases be used in place of brown sugar. Look for raw sugars in specialty markets and well-stocked supermarkets.

Table linens

An integral part of your party decor, linens include your tablecloth or table runner and dinner or luncheon napkins. They soften the table, adding color and texture, as well as performing their more obvious duties. The feel of cloth napkins conveys a much more sumptuous, special-occasion ambiance than paper ones; that said, most people use paper cocktail napkins. In the southern United States, a set of fine white linen dinner napkins and a tablecloth, often monogrammed with an initial, is seen as an indispensable. The rest of us can take instruction from that and keep on hand a set of neutral, machine-washable, 100% cotton linens that can serve as the basic backdrop for a number of parties. Round out a neutral collection with colorful accents that can be pulled out for particular holidays. For the best presentation, iron linens well — and ahead of time. See Linens (page 62).

Tea

Afternoon tea is an appealing spread of dainty savories and sweets served with hot, freshly brewed tea. While North Americans like to call this "high tea," because it sounds fancy, in England that is technically a late-afternoon/early-evening meal with meat and fish dishes. An afternoon tea is a great choice for a baby or wedding shower. To brew a proper pot of black tea, first warm the teapot by swirling it with hot or boiling water. Add 1 teaspoon (5 mL) loose tea to the pot for each cup, plus one additional teaspoon for the pot (alternatively, you can put the loose tea in a large tea ball and add that to the pot), then add boiling water. Let the tea steep for 3 to 5 minutes, then strain and serve. You can strain the tea by pouring it through a fine-mesh sieve into a second warmed teapot for serving or strain it directly into cups. Some green and herbal teas require lower temperatures and shorter steeping times; check the label or ask where you purchase it. Teabags are a popular convenience option that allow hosts to offer a variety of teas so that each guest may select his or her favorite, though tea aficionados consider these to be a second-rate substitute to loose teas. When entertaining, it's a good idea to keep some herbal teabags on hand for guests who are limiting their caffeine intake; such herbal teas may be offered as an alternative to either black tea or **coffee**. See the Afternoon Tea menu (page 320).

Thank-you notes

Even when you're the one hosting the party, some post-celebration thank-you notes might be necessary. You're off the hook when you're able to verbally acknowledge a small contribution to the party, such as a plate of cookies, a bunch of flowers or a bottle of wine. For any gifts that you were unable to personally acknowledge, such as a small wrapped hostess gift that you didn't open until after the party, a thank-you note is definitely in order. You should also express written thanks for any party loans (such as linens or flatware) or above-and-beyond help (a friend who prepared the main course). See When Is a Thank-You Note Necessary? (page 96).

Theme

Every party should have a theme, but themes don't need to be, well, theme-y. Often, a theme is as simple as your reason for initiating the gathering: your husband's 40th birthday, a plethora of fresh tomatoes in the garden or your turn to host the book club — none of which necessarily includes costumes or crepe paper. Your theme will guide all related party choices — location, decor, guest list, food, beverages and entertainment — so establishing your theme is the first step in entertaining. Turn to the chapter on theme, beginning on page 16, for dozens of party ideas, and check out Part 2 for party menus, each built around a specific theme that can be adapted to a number of related occasions.

Thermometer

Thermometers are important kitchen tools. Oven thermometers can help calibrate your oven for successful baking and roasting; candy or deep-fry thermometers can help you establish when the proper temperature has been reached in any number of stovetop mixtures; and meat thermometers let you know when a safe internal temperature has been reached, which is critical for food safety. To ensure that your thermometers are providing accurate readings, test them in boiling water to make sure they register 212°F (100°C). Do not immerse instant-read or candy thermometers; use the wand to take the reading. See Thermometers (page 118). For examples of how thermometers are used in cooking, see the recipes for Garlic-Roasted Leg of Lamb (page 411) and Pear Kuchen (page 408).

Torch

Small hand-held kitchen torches, once a tool only the pros used, are now widely available to consumers for as little as $20. A kitchen torch's most popular use is for caramelizing sugar atop crème brûlée for the dessert's famous crunchy sugar topping. (While crème brûlée can be caramelized under the broiler, the hand-held torch does a better job of quickly caramelizing the sugar without heating up the chilled custard beneath it.) But people who own a torch often begin using it to melt cheese atop French onion soup or for any other task where a focused point of fire is handy. Look for kitchen torches at kitchenware retailers.

Vegetarians and vegans

Hosting someone on a special diet? Vegetarians typically consume no meat, fish or fowl, but do eat eggs and dairy products. Be sure to ask your guest ahead of time to clarify, as this is a muddy area. Some people who call themselves vegetarians are loose about it and will eat fish on occasion, while others are so strict that they'll avoid gelatin in packaged foods like marshmallows. Vegans are stricter, eschewing animal products of every sort and sticking to a diet based on nuts, grains, fruits and vegetables. See Accommodating Special Diets (page 109).

Vinaigrette

Vinaigrettes can be used to dress green salads, potato salads, corn salads and pasta salads. They're also sometimes used as dips and to dress cold meats and fish. Vinaigrette is traditionally made with one part vinegar to three parts oil; the mixture can then be dressed up with chopped herbs, minced garlic or mustard, if desired, and seasoned to taste with salt and pepper. Vinaigrette can be whisked together, though some cooks prefer to prepare it in a food processor, which makes sense for larger batches. See the recipes for Basic Vinaigrette (page 218), Stone-Ground Mustard Vinaigrette (page 219), Blue Cheese Vinaigrette (page 299) and Creamy Vinaigrette (page 311).

Vinegars

When making **vinaigrettes**, marinades or other vinegar-rich preparations, don't just stick to the same old red wine vinegar or cider vinegar — there are many more to choose from these days. Asian seasoned rice wine vinegar, for instance, can lend its mild, sprightly character to a number of dishes, Asian and otherwise. I like to use it in potato salads and tomato salads. Fans of balsamic vinegar might want to try white balsamic vinegar. And don't overlook such specialties as sherry or champagne vinegars, with their sophisticated tastes, or fruit-flavored vinegars such as pomegranate or raspberry, which give a slightly sweet tang to vinaigrettes.

Water bath

Also called a bain-marie, this method of cooking delicate items begins with a large pan of water, such as a roasting pan, into which you place a pan, bowl or dish of food. This technique is used to gently cook items that might otherwise break or curdle at high temperatures, such as baked custards like crème brûlée and some cheesecakes. The stovetop double boiler uses some of the same principles, only the bowl containing the delicate mixture (often melting chocolate or a sauce like hollandaise) doesn't touch the boiling or simmering water beneath it; instead, the upper container is heated only by steam.

Weather

Try as we might, there's no controlling (or even always accurately predicting) the weather. If you're planning to host an outdoor event and your locale doesn't boast a months' long dry season, as my corner of California does, it makes a lot of sense to have a plan B in mind. See Weather and Other Acts of God (page 53).

Wine

For many of us, wine is an essential element for entertaining: it pairs well with food, and it's easier to serve than cocktails, which is a bonus for the busy party host. And because wine is such a complicated category, with various grape varieties, vintages and points of origin, not to mention flavors that range from sweet to dry and everywhere in between, there's always something new to try and something new to learn. For party planning purposes, a 750-mL bottle of wine will yield five 5-ounce (150 mL) servings. White wine should be served between 50°F and 55°F (10°C and 13°C), and red wine between 55°F and 65°F (13°C and 18°C). This means that room temperature is usually too warm for red wine, especially in the summer months, and the refrigerator is too cold for white wine. Wine aficionados combat this by storing bottles in a designated wine refrigerator — such home "cellars" are now widely available in small versions. Others just remember to chill and set the bottle out far enough in advance for it to reach the right temperature. See **alcohol**; **wineglasses**; the Beverages section, beginning on page 167, which includes a wine glossary and bar charts; Cheese, Wine and Fruit Pairings (page 159); and the Wine and Cheese Tasting menu (page 332).

Wineglasses

While an all-purpose wineglass is perfectly acceptable, if you have the means to stock your bar with three sets of glasses (or more), you'll enjoy each type of wine in a vessel designed to make the most of its characteristics. Champagne and other sparkling wines are best served in tall, narrow flutes; red wines are often served in balloon-style glasses; and white wine glasses have a shape that falls between the two. See the glassware illustrations on pages 171–172.

Library and Archives Canada Cataloguing in Publication

Vivaldo, Denise
The entertaining encyclopedia : essential tips and recipes for perfect parties / Denise Vivaldo.

ISBN 978-0-7788-0219-8

1. Entertaining. 2. Parties. 3. Cookery. I. Title.

TX731.V59 2009   642'.4   C2009-902208-7

Index

More Great Books
from Robert Rose

Appliance Cooking

- The Mixer Bible
  Second Edition
  *by Meredith Deeds and
  Carla Snyder*

- The Dehydrator Bible
  *by Jennifer MacKenzie,
  Jay Nutt & Don Mercer*

- The Juicing Bible
  Second Edition
  by Pat Crocker

- 200 Best Panini Recipes
  by Tiffany Collins

- 200 Best Pressure
  Cooker Recipes
  by Cinda Chavich

- 300 Slow Cooker
  Favorites
  by Donna-Marie Pye

- The 150 Best Slow
  Cooker Recipes
  by Judith Finlayson

- Delicious & Dependable
  Slow Cooker Recipes
  by Judith Finlayson

- 125 Best Vegetarian
  Slow Cooker Recipes
  by Judith Finlayson

- The Healthy Slow Cooker
  by Judith Finlayson

- Slow Cooker
  Comfort Food
  by Judith Finlayson

- 250 Best American Bread
  Machine Baking Recipes
  *by Donna Washburn
  and Heather Butt*

- 250 Best Canadian Bread
  Machine Baking Recipes
  *by Donna Washburn
  and Heather Butt*

Baking

- The Cheesecake Bible
  by George Geary

- 1500 Best Bars, Cookies,
  Muffins, Cakes & More
  by Esther Brody

- The Complete Book
  of Baking
  by George Geary

- The Complete Book
  of Bars & Squares
  by Jill Snider

- The Complete Book
  of Pies
  by Julie Hasson

- 125 Best Chocolate
  Recipes
  by Julie Hasson

- 125 Best Cupcake
  Recipes
  by Julie Hasson

- Complete Cake
  Mix Magic
  by Jill Snider

Healthy Cooking

- The Vegetarian Cook's
  Bible
  by Pat Crocker

- The Vegan Cook's Bible
  by Pat Crocker

- 125 Best Vegetarian
  Recipes
  *by Byron Ayanoglu
  with contributions from
  Algis Kemezys*

- The Smoothies Bible
  by Pat Crocker

- 125 Best Vegan Recipes
  *by Maxine Effenson Chuck
  and Beth Gurney*